Beyond My Wildest Dreams

From Local Ministry to Worldwide Mission

A Memoir

D1417698

Thomas A. Kleissler

Cover design by Ruth Markworth
Text design by Kathrine Kuo

The poem by Irma Chávez (Lanzas) on page 190 is published in *Absolute Amazement: Mystical Poetry of the 21st Century*, p. 137, © 2012 by Irma Lanzas. Published by RENEW International. All rights reserved.

World map image on cover: Made with Natural Earth. Free vector and raster map data @ naturalearthdata.com.

RENEW International
1232 George Street
Plainfield, N.J. 07062
www.renewintl.org

Publisher's Cataloging-in-Publication data
Kleissler, Thomas A., 1931-
    Beyond my wildest dreams : from local mission to worldwide ministry / Thomas A. Kleissler.
    p. cm.
    ISBN 978-1-62063-123-2
    Includes index.
1. Kleissler, Thomas A. 2. Missions. 3. Missionaries--Biography. 4. Catholic church --Clergy --Biography. 5. RENEW International. I. Title.

BX4651.2 .K55 2014
262/.142 --dc23   2013920755

To my parents, Elizabeth and Edwin Kleissler,
who taught me about God's love

CONTENTS

FOREWORD

Some thirty years ago I was presented with a fine idea for pastoral renewal throughout the whole archdiocese. The work of the Holy Spirit was experienced early in that Fathers Thomas Ivory and Thomas Kleissler had each come up with almost identical plans for such an undertaking. The plan would foresee small groups gathering in homes or in other convenient places to reflect on the Gospels and to seek the guidance of the Holy Spirit in applying the gospel message to their own lives and the lives of their parishes and wider communities.

I saw their idea as a strong possibility and urged them to continue fleshing it out. The project would be called RENEW. In a short time, I announced its implementation.

Under the coordinated leadership of the two co-founders, RENEW bore spiritual fruit in tens of thousands of souls. Since then, RENEW has spread far and wide, not only in this country but also in many dioceses around the globe. The multitude of people touched in its first years in Newark has grown to six million participants. RENEW has given the lie to that old pessimist Qoheleth in the book of Ecclesiastes who many years before Christ said, "Nothing is new under the sun." Our Lord came and proclaimed, "I make all things new," and for many years the RENEW International team has spread that good news of renewal all over the world. Today, as RENEW International, the seed planted more than three decades ago is changing lives in small Christian communities meeting from Johannesburg, South Africa, to Manitoba, Canada.

Now, in his book, Msgr. Kleissler looks back not only on the beginnings and on his thirty years as director of RENEW but also to the beginnings of his own priestly vocation. He recalls the circumstances in which first his call to priesthood and then the focus of his ministry took form, and he recounts the steps in the establishment and growth of RENEW International, remembering all the women and men who contributed to what became an important response to the call of the Second Vatican Council for an infusion of new vigor in the people of God, the Church.

I still believe firmly that the RENEW approach to evangelization, building on small groups, is the most effective way of all to spread the gospel message far and wide. The impact RENEW International has had and will continue to have makes this memoir an important contribution to the history of the Church in the twentieth and twenty-first centuries. As it looks back to the challenges and achievements of the past, it helps to light our way into the future.

Most Reverend Peter L. Gerety
Archbishop Emeritus of Newark

INTRODUCTION

By God's grace, Father Tom Ivory and I cofounded and initiated RENEW along with a dedicated group of people from the faith community of Newark. It was my privilege to direct both the process of RENEW and the work of RENEW International for more than thirty years. Recently, I have been encouraged to tell its story—to set forth personal recollections of what contributed to its birth and its success. In recalling many events, I have been privileged to see more clearly how God's providence has been present throughout RENEW and even in those particular personal life events that led me to my role in RENEW.

Beyond My Wildest Dreams in no way proposes to be a full history of RENEW. A complete history would be a monumental task. Much research would be required, which would be difficult because we kept far from perfect records in much of the timeframe covered here. RENEW grew exponentially and was pastored by a relatively small team of people totally absorbed in serving dioceses and parishes.

I hope these thoughts give you, the reader, a feeling for the original spirit, energy, joys, troubled times, challenges, and low points, as well as the efforts that went into RENEW. Included are some of the principles we brought to it and some insights we obtained over the years. Hopefully, the work of RENEW International will be seen as God's work, because it truly is beyond any of us who have actually had the privilege of working with RENEW.

Beyond My Wildest Dreams certainly presents much actual fact of RENEW's history. But because it is written from the perspective of one person who has been with RENEW throughout its history, it is a memoir about events that led to my involvement in the initiation and work of RENEW in the decades that followed.

Countless people have been involved in RENEW from its earliest days to the present. Any project like RENEW is only as good as the team creating, developing, and serving the process. In that regard RENEW has been magnificently blessed with incredibly dedicated and spiritual people on its core staff and in dioceses and parishes who have brought wonderful gifts, creativity, energy, and time to the process.

Beyond My Wildest Dreams is written with heartfelt gratitude to all who have lived and contributed to the RENEW mission. Above all, we thank God.

In the early days of RENEW, Fr. Cassian Yuhaus said, "RENEW is truly a gift of the Holy Spirit." How accurate. All our efforts amount to nothing if God does not bless and will it. By God's grace this truth will continue to be the guiding awareness as RENEW International moves into the future.

Thomas A. Kleissler
President Emeritus, RENEW International

PART I

CHAPTER 1

Early Blessings

It happened in a tiny village in India. In a moment of frenzied fury occasioned by a family feud, Arul killed the wife of his elder brother Vincent and was sentenced to prison. Vincent vowed to seek out Arul on his release and kill him in revenge. He carried the knife he intended to use.

Meanwhile, a RENEW faith-sharing community sought out Vincent to help him deal with his loss. He eventually joined the community.

On the day of Arul's release from prison, members of the community decided to meet him and bring him to the RENEW meeting at which forgiveness was the chosen theme and his brother would be present.

The brothers ignored each other at the start, but in the midst of the meeting Arul fell on his knees, asked for forgiveness, and cried out, "Oh God, my sin is too great to be forgiven, please take my life in reparation for my sin."

On hearing this, Vincent leaped toward his brother, throwing off those who tried to restrain him. Everybody felt that at this moment he was about to kill Arul. Remarkably, as he thrust himself upon Arul, the two embraced and wept copiously for fifteen minutes.

Members of the faith-sharing community, overwhelmed by the reconciliation, wept with them and joined in praising God. Today the brothers are ardent members of the RENEW small community and live in peace and harmony.

Miracles often bring to mind thoughts of Lourdes or Medjugorje. The truth is many miracles occur in the daily lives of ordinary people. Our RENEW staff and I have witnessed thousands of these miracles in RENEW small communities all over the world where people come together to pray, reflect on Scripture, and open themselves to God's grace in their lives. The story of Arul and Vincent is truly astonishing. But it is only a sign of what magnificent changes take place when people open their lives to the Spirit.

What is a RENEW faith-sharing community in which such remarkable things happen? How did these groups come to be? Where did they originate and, by God's grace, how did they spread throughout the world? I will try to speak to these questions as I share my personal perspective in *Beyond My Wildest Dreams: From Local Ministry to Worldwide Mission*.

We start with the year 1931 when I first appeared on earth. The United States was experiencing the Great Depression. With banks failing and deposits lost, money was in short supply. Unemployment rose to 15.9 percent. President Herbert Hoover issued the Hoover Moratorium which proposed a one-year international postponement "of all intergovernmental debts, reparations, and relief debts" to promote a worldwide restoration of economic stability.

Many were desperate, and survival was key. Parents couldn't afford clothes or supplies to send their children to school. Radio programs and parlor games were entertainment for most families. Movies flourished to entertain the Depression audiences who could afford them. And Dick Tracy made his debut in the *Detroit Mirror*.

On the West Coast, California received approval to build the San Francisco Bay-Oakland Bridge, while on the East Coast, construction of the Empire State Building was completed and the George Washington Bridge was opened to traffic. The United States adopted "The Star Spangled Banner" as its national anthem.

Family Life

Born in the midst of the Great Depression, I was blessed to grow up in a family with great love and security. This was highlighted not only by my parents' love and devotion for each other but also by their total self-giving to their four boys. Family was everything in "Ireland" — that is, the Vailsburg section of Newark, New Jersey. Vailsburg and its focal point, Sacred Heart Parish, was a very tight-knit family community.

If I were to name particular gifts that would be helpful in my life as a priest and in my work with RENEW International, they would be gifts that came from my family. From my mother, Elizabeth, I received much love and a tremendous work ethic. She had perseverance and a great sense of responsibility. You stayed with the task until it was completed. When it was completed, if there was more that could be done, why not do that too? With her there was no giving up or resting on your laurels. Mom would say, "Self-praise stinks." (How would she ever handle this book?) The idea of responsibility that I received from my mom played out after the original RENEW had been established in Newark. It would have been so easy then, when I had experienced exhaustion and a heart attack, to forgo any attempt to take RENEW beyond Newark.

My Dad, Edwin, spent most of his free time with his boys. We did a lot of fishing together and took many walks. He gave us a strong sense of fairness and social justice. My father was also devoted to peace; war made no sense to him. I would hear stories about him paying workers during the Depression but not taking home a salary for himself. He also encouraged his workers to unionize their small sheet-metal fabricating plant. Later in my adult life, a business competitor would tell me that my father was the fairest and most honest person he knew in industrial Newark. These aspects of my father's life greatly influenced me.

My three brothers and I have a lot in common, including sports. My older brother, Ed, always encouraged me and took great pride in whatever I did. He has been a mentor in many ways, especially in the early years of RENEW before we had an official board of trustees. He has always been there to take an interest in RENEW and help me think things through. Bob and Dick, the twins, have been great companions on my journey. They have been deeply involved in ministries such as counseling, racial concerns, religious education, and Right to Life. Both are daily communicants. Our care for each other is profound. Not a week goes by when each of us is not in touch with the other three.

Youthful Years

In the fifth grade, Sr. Catherine Patricia, S.C., had a tremendous influence on my life. She planted in my mind the idea of being a missionary priest, presenting it in such a beautiful and meaningful way that it really caught hold of me. As the years passed, I was always thankful for her enthusiasm and love for missionary priests, particularly those working in China.

Years later, when I became a sub-deacon and could wear my collar and black suit and had a real commitment to becoming a priest, I said, "I'm going to go and thank Sr. Catherine Patricia." I visited her at Our Lady of Sorrows in South Orange, where she was teaching grade six.

When her classroom door opened, the words tumbled out: "Sister, I'm Tom Kleissler. You taught me many years ago, and I've come to thank you because I'm going to be ordained a priest soon. You're the one who planted this thought about priesthood many years ago. Little did you know that I took it in and felt convinced that priesthood is what the Lord wanted me to do with my life." You cannot imagine her response of joy. She brought me in to speak with her class. It was a very emotional meeting for Sr. Catherine Patricia and me. She came to my first Mass, and we became good friends.

Deciding about Becoming a Priest

After Sr. Catherine Patricia had planted that thought about being a missionary in China, a classmate, Tom Confroy, and I confided in each other what was still our secret idea of becoming priests. I remember asking when we were in the eighth grade, "Tom, are you still thinking of being a priest?" "No," he said, "I've discovered girls." But Tom Confroy became a Benedictine abbot at St. Mary's Abbey in Morristown, New Jersey, and you know where I wound up—ordained a parish priest for Newark and beyond.

While I was in the eighth grade, an interesting thing happened that set me on the course to priesthood without my having to make any declaration. I was very leery about what the guys would say if I told them I wanted to become a priest. Our parish sent all the graduating eighth-grade guys to Seton Hall Prep and the girls to St. Vincent Academy in Newark, free of charge. So a priest from Seton Hall came to our class. Each of us had to say which course we wanted to take at Seton Hall. One course was classical, for the guys heading for the priesthood; another was scientific, and another was general. The sister who taught our eighth-grade class stood at the desk as each of us came forward. For any boy who had an average of ninety or above she would say to the priest, "classical," which meant we were going to be priests.

There it was, "classical." I didn't have to say anything. I was on the way to the priesthood. The other guys were all furious when they got out into the playground, but here I was on the way to the priesthood because sister said so, and I didn't have to reveal my secret desire to be a priest.

One day in 1945, while I was walking to Seton Hall Prep as a freshman, it occurred to me that a business would never operate the way a parish does. How could a business be productive if everyone in the shop, as it were, wasn't concerned about productivity? The key would be to have everybody pulling together for a successful operation. If that were true, could not the same be said about the Church? At that time all a young teenager could see in the parish was priests and sisters pastoring and tending to souls and caring for people. I saw little opportunity for lay people to have a fully active role in the Church. My priesthood would be dedicated to creating that opportunity.

A year later, on a rainy day that kept me from playing ball outside, I was in the library and picked up a pamphlet in what proved to be a turning point in my life. The pamphlet was about the Young Christian Workers and its founder, Fr. Joseph Leo Cardijn (1882-1967) in Belgium. Fr. Cardijn was a remarkable man and was later made a cardinal of the Church.

When Fr. Cardijn returned home from the seminary, he was troubled because he didn't see his friends and former classmates going to church anymore. They seemed lost, as it were, in the factories. He met them in bars or wherever people tended to gather and formed them into small communities which began to have great impact.

He gave worldwide popularity to the effective pastoral approach known as "Observe, Judge, and Act." In the Observe phase of this approach, members of the YCW, meeting in small groups, carefully and precisely noted troubling circumstances that existed in their daily lives. In the Judge phase, through the guidance of the Holy Spirit and based on the Scriptures and the teachings of the Church, members discerned the proper way of life for the circumstances they had observed. This step led members to the Act, a concrete and specific action they intended to take regarding an aspect of their lives that had surfaced through their observations and through their prayer and reflection during the Judge phase of the process.

The story of Fr. Cardijn introducing young Christian workers to this process captivated me. I realized this was what I would do as a priest. I was not interested so much in small communities per se but primarily in social justice and the needs of the poor, which I saw being addressed in small communities.

These young people in Belgium were addressing circumstances in their surroundings and trying to change them—whether in the workplace or in the family, whether related to dating or to drinking—whatever circumstances young adults had to deal with. They considered how they could create an environment that would enable them to be truly Catholic Christians. The "Observe, Judge, Act" methodology proved to be very effective.

I was deeply impressed and inspired as I learned about the experiences of the Young Christian Workers. The desire I formed a year before to help lay people be more involved and effective in the Church and carry out their faith in all areas of life was made concrete in the approach that Fr. Cardijn had taken. People met in small groups where they could share in a common way and come to conclusions about how to make the faith more relevant in their lives, in their families, in their local communities, and in the world beyond.

These two convictions, lay involvement in 1945 and small Christian communities in 1946, became the centerpiece of what I wanted to be about, along with my deep concern for justice and the poor. The foundations of RENEW, increased lay involvement and effective small communities, were being formed within me. Today it is hard to realize that these concepts were not common in parish life back then. Far from it.

That day in the library was one of the most important in my entire life. A concrete vision and conviction about my priesthood was being formed. It would last for a lifetime. Faith had to be connected to people's daily lives. My priesthood would be centered on promoting the role of lay people and working toward a Church that would be much more significant and meaningful. It would have great impact on the world because it was going to involve everybody—priests, religious, and laity. There was never the idea of lay people "taking over" as some feared. Rather, each person—lay, clergy, or religious—would respect the roles of the others, working together in harmony and collaboration. It seemed this would enable the Spirit to be much more powerful in the lives of people and in the health of the entire Church.

Young Adult Years at Seton Hall University

The classical program at Seton Hall University was designed to lead us to be priests. Actually, throughout my time at Seton Hall I had no great desire to be a diocesan priest. The idea of becoming a missionary was still there. It was my freshman year when a group of us took a trip to the headquarters of the Maryknoll missionary organization in Ossining, New York. When we stepped off the bus and heard the cheering and roaring at the football field where the seminarians were engaged in a game, I thought, "This is where I want to be. This place is great. These guys are the marines of the Church." It was fantastic. Why did I never become a missionary? The answer gradually unfolded for me.

At that time you had two years of college at Seton Hall, and then you went to Immaculate Conception Seminary at Darlington for six years. So you graduated from Seton Hall while at the seminary. In my sophomore year of college, I wrote to every religious community in the country. Vocation directors came to our house to interview this prospective young man for their communities. It was a bit much. But Maryknoll was still in the back of my mind. At one point my parents asked me to sit down to talk about this missionary idea. They were cautioning me about the difficulties of missionary life when I interrupted and said, "If this is what this conversation is about, it's over." If I were being called to be a missionary priest, that would be it.

My parents were incredibly supportive of me. Never did they push the idea of priesthood. In fact, priesthood was never spoken of in our family. There never had been a priest in our family. Yet when they learned that I wanted to be a priest, they thought it was good, but it was never something they were counting on. I had total freedom. In retrospect, I'm very grateful for this. My parents were faithful Catholics but were not showy about it. The only two nights they were ever out of the house were when Dad went to the Holy Name Society and Mom went to the Rosary Altar Society. That's the kind of family it was. That's the kind of neighborhood we lived in. It was very family oriented.

I can remember visiting my Grandma Fagan, who came from Dublin. My mother must have told her I was thinking of the priesthood. My grandmother, at ninety-three, said in her strong Irish brogue, "We're countin on ya." But that's the most anyone in the family spoke about my studying for the priesthood. Still, once I became a priest my father's buttons were popping off his jacket because he was so proud. He became a daily communicant.

I was involved in small-community Catholic Action at Seton Hall University and led a disparate group that prompted the moderator of the existing group, Fr. William J. Halliwell, to say, "You're starting awfully young to buck the clergy." Our group at Seton Hall dealt with an encyclical about lay involvement. It was really a study group and boring at that. We wanted to bring some action to Catholic Action.

The small-community approach took a strong hold on me as I became involved in Catholic Action in college and then, as a seminarian, became deeply interested in the Young Christian Workers and the Young Christian Students, an American version of the YCW that engaged many students in our country. The Christian Family Movement, the American adult version of the YCS, helped married couples use the Observe, Judge, Act methodology, not just for their families and their marriages but for what we call a holistic spirituality that took in every phase of their lives.

During my sophomore year, a classmate, Jack Riley, and I went over to the Maryknoll office in Manhattan, New York. The priest there challenged us. He came on pretty strong: "Can you picture yourself somewhere in Asia, say China? You have a bathroom need and you have to sit on a pot in the middle of the street next to a woman. How do you like that?" That was a bit of a shock, but I remained interested in Maryknoll.

However, at the same time, for whatever reason, I was not drawn to any of the religious communities but continued to take the steps that would lead me to our seminary at Darlington. It's not as if I was eager to go to Darlington and become a diocesan priest. I don't know how to explain it, but it seemed that was what God wanted me to do. Little did I realize that after becoming a diocesan priest I would get to work in more impoverished areas throughout the world than I could have ever dreamed of.

On the Way to Priesthood

After my two years at Seton Hall, I set out for Darlington. With every turn on Route 202 I was praying that the seminary gate would not be there. That's how eager I was to get to Darlington. The Yankee game was on the radio, and I was very interested. My mother told me years later that she never thought I'd stay because I wouldn't be able to hear the Yankee games. In fact I wasn't a daily communicant or any of the things a church student was supposed to be. When we were summoned for our yearly "chat" in the first two years of college, I wouldn't let the priest ask me if I was going to daily Mass. Before he could ask anything I'd ask the priest a question. Those priests never got too close to what I was really thinking.

But seminary life was good. I was very obedient, quiet, and rule abiding. However, I must admit I could have done a lot more studying. Most of my studying was done in the weeks before mid-term and final exams.

Jack McDermott was my "chateau" mate. There was a little chateau (bathroom) in between two seminarians' rooms. When you opened those two doors you could talk. Jack and I sometimes talked during study time while shooting baskets back and forth with a Ping-Pong ball. Many times I'd just sit and look at the wall all night. Jack would say, "Why are you looking at the wall?" I'd say, "I'm thinking." While I was doing well with my studies, I spent most of my seminary life thinking beyond formal courses about questions I thought were of utmost importance: Does God exist? Is there truly a God? Is Catholicism really the right religion? Solidifying my belief in God and the Catholic faith early in life proved to be beneficial during the turbulent decades to come.

During my second summer at the seminary the guys in the class ahead of us went out to teach in summer classes in the parishes throughout the Archdiocese of Newark. One day a priest walked down the hall looking for Tom O'Leary and me and told us to go to the rector's office. When we arrived we heard we were going to help out in a couple of parishes. At the time I thought, "This is neat. We're getting out while everybody else is going to be back at the seminary for those six summer weeks.

I went berserk in that parish, St. Francis Xavier, Newark, in terms of apostolic energy. It was an incredible experience. We would take the kids across the street to Newark Stadium, where I developed a great relationship sports-wise with the African-American boys. During Christmas break, I would come back and visit with them. This was my first opportunity to express my zeal.

The following summer, as we were sent out from the seminary, I can remember, once again, going "bananas" with great energy. I was sent to Queen of Angels, an African-American parish in Newark. There were more kids than the classroom could hold. Some were outside the door and listening through the open windows. We would march around the playground singing "Shazam, Shazam" and all the current rock-and-roll songs. I loved talking to them about Jesus. It was a lot of fun and another pastoral outlet.

Seminary years were basically good with happy and pleasant memories, even though there was a tough regimen. In class, I paid careful attention when historical and theological explanations helped to affirm my Catholic belief. In second theology, I was given a house job as head of the infirmary, which proved to be a valuable ministry and brought me into closer contact with many seminarians. Toward the end of my seminary years, I was offered a position as head of Catholic Action, which gave me an opportunity to share with other seminarians the things that were exciting: mobilizing and energizing lay people to assume their proper role by being fully active in the Church.

A very significant day in seminary formation came shortly before summer break when Joe Scherer, a zealous seminarian a year ahead of us, invited Jim Ferry and me to go to Notre Dame with him to attend a conference on CFM and YCW. It was an opportunity for me to actually meet the people involved in this Observe, Judge, Act process. It turned out to be an incredible experience, one that would strengthen my convictions about the great involvement of lay people within the Church and about the formation of our people. Lay people using this process could make a real impact on society, bringing our faith seven days a week into family life, neighborhoods, the places and communities where we lived, and in the world arena. Catholic lay men and women were to see every aspect of life in a spiritual way. Can you imagine the impact if every Catholic in the country were really living out his or her faith fully and completely? Our country would change; our world would change. It was exciting.

At that point, the Midwest was far ahead of the East in many aspects of pastoral life as well as in the involvement of lay people. Fortunately, the midwesterners recognized that we strangers from the East were to be well treated and brought along with care. The work they were involved with in Chicago, for example, would have made a perfect blueprint for what the Second Vatican Council would later say in the *Dogmatic Constitution on the Church* (*Lumen Gentium*), the *Pastoral Constitution on the Church in the Modern World* (*Gaudium et Spes*), and the *Decree on the Apostolate of the Laity* (*Apostolicum Actuositatem*).

Behind the tremendous activity in the Chicago Archdiocese was the famous Msgr. Reynold Hillenbrand, rector of Mundelein Seminary. Hillenbrand was a tremendous believer of many of the teachings of Pope Pius XI about Catholic action and promoting greater apostolic activity among lay people. In particular, he became a strong advocate and promoter of the fledgling YCW movement and what later developed as the CFM and, in time, the YCS modeled on the same pattern.

As rector of the seminary, Msgr. Hillenbrand was responsible for turning out a decade of priests with a different kind of formation—an openness a collaborative approach that had wonderful aspects of implementing the full role that the Spirit was calling us to, with lay people taking a more rightful place within the Church and living it out in their daily lives. Hillenbrand was one of many outstanding Chicago priests at that time, including Fr. Dan Cantwell, who was a great mind behind justice formation, and Fr. Jack Egan, who gained national recognition as a creative and innovative thinker, a model for many priests and lay people throughout the country.

On this visit to Notre Dame with Joe Scherer and Jim Ferry, I heard a presentation given by Msgr. Hillenbrand, who was then pastor of a parish in Wilmette, Illinois, but also chaplain to all the specialized movements—YCW, YCS, and CFM. I sat there expecting great things but was keenly disappointed as he began his presentation. He seemed to be dull and unexciting. By the end of the talk, however, I had been transformed. I was on the rafters with enthusiasm and ready to go out and take on the world for the Lord.

What a man Hillenbrand was. As the week transpired I followed Hillenbrand around. He must have sensed, after several days, that he had a shadow. At one point he turned around and, in effect, said something like this: "Kid, why are you following me? What are you looking for?" I stammered, "I've been made the head of Catholic Action in my seminary and I don't know how to approach it. I'm wondering if you could offer me some ideas." "I'm happy to help you," said Msgr. Hillenbrand. "Give me your address. I'll work out a plan for your seminary and I'll send it to you." The plan arrived and we followed it religiously. During the ensuing year, I managed to get some of the most popular guys in the seminary to take a different aspect of lay involvement and give presentations. The whole thing was also a personal growth experience for me and a stepping-stone in building confidence. It called forth my ability to take on responsibility.

As head of Catholic Action, I led the formation of one hundred seminarians that met in small groups in the auditorium. We shared our insights from one of the books authored by the famous British liturgist Fr. Clifford Howell, S.J. Things we thought we would never live to see were discussed—such as celebrating Mass facing the people and praying the Mass in the vernacular. Ten years later things we never believed would happen were reality.

There were many more trips to Notre Dame, extending into the early years of my priesthood. On one of these occasions I traveled with Fr. Jim Ferry. When we arrived at Notre Dame, Jim, who had a very outgoing personality, said, "I think we should each go our own way." I'm sure he didn't really need this shy guy hanging on him like a leech. It was a very wise move, forcing me to go out and make my own contacts and connections.

August was typically the free vacation month for seminarians. In two of the summers, Jim, Jack McDermott, and I became involved in an extremely interesting mission in South Carolina. The Dominican Fathers in Kingstree were going into rural areas where people had never heard about the Catholic faith. The Dominicans had set up a chapel in a van where people could see the altar and have the Mass explained to them. Part of the mission was to have evening outdoor movies about the life of Jesus. The problem for some of the locals was that all were invited— black and white together. On the way down we read a news clipping about how some of the "boys" in town had driven by one of these gatherings, shooting over the heads of folks. Wow! Maybe even a chance for martyrdom. We could show the black community that Catholics really cared.

Our task was to go out during the day and invite everyone to the free movies. Some were understandably afraid. One evening my job was to stand by the road in the dark and warn everyone if trouble was coming. Sure enough, a pickup truck with "boys" from town rumbled down this rural dirt road. As it came close they turned their headlights off. The thought came: "This might be it." But, fortunately, they just drove by us, and we lived to see another day.

These experiences were both exciting and very formative. Years later they would help influence a basic principle of RENEW: to reach out to the most remote and isolated areas. The last parish and last person were important.

Life was good on the way to the priesthood. I couldn't wait for ordination.

CHAPTER 2

Influence of Early Parish Experiences

A few weeks after ordination, our class gathered at the chancery to receive our assignments. There was much anticipation and anxiety since these first assignments would have a great impact on our priesthood. My chair was directly in front of Archbishop Thomas Boland, just a few feet away. He gave a short talk, quoting St. Paul: "Let no one despise your youth." His eyes seemed to bore right through me as he read that passage. At the time I could have passed as a teenager. It was impossible to be any greener.

Our Lady of Mercy Parish, Park Ridge

The archbishop read our assignments aloud. Anxious and hoping fervently that my assignment would be to a poor inner-city parish, I waited with bated breath. "Fr. Kleissler," the archbishop said, "you are assigned to Our Lady of Mercy, Park Ridge." Startled, I had never heard of this town or hamlet. Could it be in our archdiocese? Before giving out assignments, the archbishop had announced that if anyone didn't know where his parish was he should come up afterwards and ask. Quite devastated, I was the only one in my class who had to go up and ask, "Where is Park Ridge?"

Assignments were received on a Tuesday, and the custom was to go immediately that day to meet your new pastor and then report for duty on the following Saturday afternoon. The trek north to Park Ridge seemed to be endless. How was I to know that it would be the last parish in the archdiocese, on the border of suburban New York, with the closest parish to it being St. Margaret's in Pearl River, New York?

Coming to the end of a side street, right before the town dump, I saw a little wooden church surrounded and covered by large trees. Next to the church, also surrounded by trees and with a barn in the back yard, was the large, ancient, wooden rectory. Where was the excitement of the inner city? As I rang the front doorbell, the pastor, Fr. Charles Lillis, yelled out, "Come in!" He immediately announced that Yogi Berra was a parishioner and was waiting in the Yankee clubhouse. I was an ardent Yankee fan, but I was also so disappointed with my assignment that I startled both my new pastor and myself by blurting out, "I don't have to report until Saturday. I'll see you then." Back home I told my family and friends, "Two streets crossed, and they called it Park Ridge."

Things got off to a slow start. On the first Monday in the parish, I asked the associate, Fr. Ed Duffy, if I could do something such as filing things in his office. Could he introduce me to some people who might help me run the Catholic Youth Organization to which I was assigned? "Go out and find your own people," Ed said. It sounded harsh at the time, but what a blessing. I was being given the freedom to go out and meet people, to take initiative on my own, and to do God's work. Without restraint, the door was open for pastoral creativity.

Ed was one of the most zealous priests who ever lived. He had organized the parish, which included four towns in sixteen square miles, into a system that comprised three hundred block captains who would report to the rectory the moment a new young couple had moved in from the Bronx. The waterworks would call whenever the water was turned on for a new family. Whoever was not on duty would fly out to that house, frequently still on a dirt road, to meet the new family and engage them in one form or another of parish life before the bowling league or anyone else could approach them.

My particular responsibility was to take the parish census in all the homes of Woodcliff Lake and the region of Montvale, up on the ridge, where the farms were located. Going door-to-door and engaging people of all faiths was a wonderful and exciting venture. Ed had a system in which every home within the sixteen square miles was registered by the faith of husband and wife. The territory was well pastored. My area, which would one day be the home of international corporations, was still rural. Going down little dirt roads through the woods would lead me to hidden houses where people could be connected to a faith experience. What a life. It was pure fun.

The pastor, Fr. Lillis, was like a second father. He enjoyed encouraging Ed and me and helping us grow. As time moved on, he nurtured that growth experience by giving me more and more responsibility. Little did I know on that day in June 1957 that I was receiving the best parish assignment of anyone in our class.

It would be years later before I would discover that Fr. Lillis had asked for me to be assigned to Our Lady of Mercy. I would come to know how fortunate I was. In years beyond that, I would come to realize that God's divine providence was involved in the journey at every step. At Our Lady of Mercy, I was to fall in love with the people, mature as an adult, and come to a fuller realization of the beauty of priesthood. Building relationships with parishioners would be a formative process, pastorally and spiritually, that I would value more than my formation days at the seminary. Our Lady of Mercy, Park Ridge, was to be the birthplace of RENEW.

My experience in Park Ridge strengthened an earlier conviction. No parish was without potential. None was insignificant. RENEW would later reach out to all and conduct training in the most remote areas, especially those most neglected.

What follows are far more than a sampling of early priesthood experiences. These events combined into a formative process, enabling me with the initiative, skills, organizational ability, leadership opportunities, and even the courage that prepared me to take on the role I was to play in RENEW.

Youth Work

Back in 1957, every young priest's first assignment was to work with youth. This involved altar boys, CYO members, and children enrolled either in a Catholic school or in a religious education program.

Early experience showed that I was not cut out to be a teacher. In the first year, one of my assignments was to teach religious education to high school freshman boys on Monday evenings. I visited every home in four towns that had a baptized freshman. These visits proved to be successful in that almost all of those boys came to the class. Why not? It turned out to be a circus. This young teacher struggled as the disinterested group, some of whom had now found the location of the church, went wild. One kid sat in the back corner of the room laughing hysterically at all the goings on. But you never know how God's grace will touch someone. A few years later he came to me saying he wanted to study for the priesthood. In time I was privileged to give the homily at his first Mass.

The CYO experience was more successful. I chose a young man, considered to be rather surly, as leader of the CYO, which proved to be a good move. He was a natural leader and quickly gained the respect of every teenager. Our CYO dances, ice skating trips to Bear Mountain, and all other activities drew kids from all over Bergen County to this northernmost parish. The importance of choosing good leadership and engaging people in the life of the parish were early lessons for me.

Young Christian Students

My deepest interests were the specialized movements of the CFM and YCS and the "Observe, Judge, Act" method that I loved.

The Young Christian Students, a movement that I had been following closely through college and the seminary, was now to become a lived experience. A teenage girls' group met in my office early Thursday evenings, followed by a teenage boys' group. Realizing that the pastor was quite conservative, I named the girls' group Sodality and the boys' group Junior Holy Name.

The teenagers and I learned a lot together as they began to employ the "Observe, Judge, Act" method. I soon discovered that the Observe stage would be the most difficult. Problems that surrounded our young people were such a normal part of life, endemic to our society, that the boys and girls failed to see them as problems.

Centering on this challenge, I asked the girls to take the following week to observe all the problems they saw students experiencing in Park

Ridge High School. At the next week's meeting, we would look at how to deal with those problems. When the girls came back they had observed two problems: one, there weren't enough mirrors in the girls' room, and, two, the boys didn't pay enough attention to them. There were no observations about students who were shunned or ostracized, failing in their schoolwork, or experiencing behavioral problems. Teenagers with alcoholic parents or poor family situations were not even noticed—nothing but the mirrors and the boys' lack of attention. Would this really work? Was my hope of following the method too idealistic? In any event, the girls kept coming.

The boys' group more readily got into some very real problems. Their dating, relationships with their parents, shooting over the state line into New York for drinking: nothing was out of bounds. They made themselves comfortable, some on the floor with their feet up on the wall. However, after their last meeting, I offered this comment: "I don't know whether this really worked. We haven't changed Park Ridge High School very much." Their response was both quick and strong: "No, Father, this was great. Where else could we talk about all these things and try to work them through?"

Six months later, when most of these young men were freshmen in college, I offered them a challenge. The year before, college students from Yale had spent their summer doing lay missionary work. I had never heard of a program like this. Why couldn't Our Lady of Mercy do the same? At Christmas, I spotted Tim McGann getting into his car and called out to him. "Hey Tim, how would you like to go and help the poor in Mexico this summer?" "Count me in," Tim called back before he hopped in his car and drove off.

Seven calls to other young men from the group followed quickly. Each said yes. That July they boarded a bus, and off they went to dig a well in a poor village in Mexico. The experience deeply touched their lives. Fifty years later I still hear from some of them, and they talk about that trip. The Young Christian Students' involvement had moved and formed them much more than I realized. The dream of Young Christian Students had become a reality. It did indeed work.

In the following years, we saw wonderful things happening with the Young Christian Students in terms of their growth as persons and in the way they related to social conditions and problems around them. Two hundred high school boys and girls became involved in the parish weekly YCS meetings. It reached a point where it was even more popular than the dances and basketball games. An outstanding group of zealous adults worked with the YCS. Each small group had an adult advisor who would meet with the leader to help prepare for the group meeting. Advisors also assisted the groups in forming themselves into communities and employing the "Observe, Judge, Act" method in ways that would lead the members to life-changing action. Peggy and Art Gelnaw, Don Cotter, Kathy Powers, Florence Craffey, and a host of others devoted tremendous time and effort to working with the young people.

In many instances the relationships that developed between advisors and group members provided the teenagers with solid adult friends who guided them as their lives progressed. Many of those relationships have been maintained for decades after that high school experience. One of the teenagers, Mary Noel Kuhn Page, has become a member of the Board of Trustees of RENEW International. Another young leader, Bob Stagg, became pastor of Presentation Parish in Upper Saddle River, New Jersey, which has long been known for great numbers of active small Christian communities. It has been heartening to see how many of those young people have moved on not only to be strong in faith but also to live out their faith in significant ways in their homes, in their communities, and at work.

A gigantic project coming from the small communities took place in the mid 1960s in Newark, New Jersey. The Young Christian Students, with the adult leadership of Joe and Dolores Duggan and the Gelnaws, decided to replicate Msgr. Bob Fox's *Summer in the City* project, which took place in inner-city New York. We had sixty YCS teens spend the month of July working in Scudder Homes, the poorest housing project in the state. They were housed in a dilapidated old wooden home in the local parish of St. Bridget's. A number of CFM adults volunteered to accompany the teenagers and help supervise the project. The sacrifice involved was great indeed. Joe, for instance, traveled every day from inner-city Newark to his job in White Plains, New York, and returned every evening.

The response of Our Lady of Mercy parishioners was unbelievable. That families would allow their teenagers to go into the very poor and dangerous area of the city was incredible to begin with. In addition, every adult who was asked to volunteer to spend their July in Newark immediately said yes.

Each day teenagers would go to the Scudder Homes and, in effect, run a circus of activities for the poor and deprived children of that housing project. The residents, young and old, responded with enthusiasm. It was more than a hot, humid summer with the sun burning off the heated asphalt. Something beautiful was happening in the poorest and most devastated area in the state.

This project continued into the third summer when, on one July evening, an incident happened between a cab driver and two Newark policemen. I would later be stationed at St. Ann's Parish on the block where the incident occurred. News of the event spread like wildfire. It marked the beginning of the famous Newark riots of 1967, which took the lives of twenty-six people. Unrest reached the Scudder Homes within an hour. Not only did we have sixty teenagers working in the playground that evening but over a dozen adults had come from Our Lady of Mercy to help adult residents with such issues as how to save money and how to shop more wisely.

From one of these classes in an apartment on an upper floor, I noticed a group of police cars with lights flashing down on the street. I whispered to the adult from Our Lady of Mercy, "The class is now over. Riots are beginning on the street." All the students and adults gathered back at St. Bridget's to behold a sight that they could never have dreamed of. Fires were breaking out. Gunshots filled the air. People were running up and down the streets with stolen goods. There was a sense of great and imminent danger.

News broadcasts reached Park Ridge where worried and fearful parents hired a bus to bring back all the teenagers and adults from the riot-torn city early the next morning. When the bus arrived in the parking lot at Our Lady of Mercy, residents cheered wildly and hugged and kissed their daughters and sons as tears flowed. Many of those students' and adults' lives would never be the same in good and positive ways. The small-community experience created a greater sensitivity and concern for the poor and underprivileged that would bring about meaningful change for everyone involved. The value of the small-community experience that would so deeply influence RENEW in years to come had been burned more deeply in my own soul.

More was yet to happen. Reports from Newark were telling us the many residents of Scudder Homes were deprived of food and were hiding under their beds for fear of bullets that were ricocheting off the buildings and coming through their windows. During the homilies at every Mass at Our Lady of Mercy on Sunday morning, I made a passionate plea for parishioners to bring food to the parking lot within the next few hours for the people in Newark.

It seemed that every parishioner had been transformed by the parish experience. Even those who might have been considered racist or red necked came forth with huge amounts of food. At 2 p.m., we filled a large laundry van with four tons of food and we were off to Newark. The National Guard wasn't letting anyone into the city, but somehow we convinced them to let us through. Our Lady of Mercy CFM members distributed food to the most grateful people you would ever want to see. We had all learned that we could make a difference, and that knowledge eventually would lead to the bold step known as RENEW.

The teenage YCS groups continued to meet on a weekly basis and make observations in the world around them. A couple of actions flowing from these observations still stand out in my mind. In one case, five girls in one of our groups noticed that the girls at their school, Immaculate Heart Academy in Washington Township, had little realization of the plight of countless people in Latin America. The YCS girls went to the principal of their school with an idea of how to increase awareness among their fellow students through concrete actions.

Impressed by their zeal, the principal set aside the last period every day of a given week for all the students to gather in the auditorium to hear presentations from the YCS members. The girls brought in speakers, showed videos, and used every means possible to convey to their schoolmates the situation of many people who went without food, lacked decent housing, or received little education. From it all the YCS girls organized outreaches that included students becoming pen pals with others their age in developing nations. It was amazing how five young women had such an impact on the lives of so many others.

In another instance, five eighth-grade boys noted attitudes of prejudice in our area and a lack of understanding of the circumstances of people of color. This was largely because the boys lived in what was at that time a totally white neighborhood. From one meeting on this topic, they set out on a Saturday morning to visit the Catholic Interracial Office in New York City. They returned home flooded with materials to help educate kids of Our Lady of Mercy School.

The boys approached the sisters, asking them to incorporate these materials into their classroom work to sensitize the children to the need for racial equality. The sisters were impressed and welcomed the boys' initiative and put their plan into action. Not only that, but they allowed the boys to hold a gathering in the auditorium for all students in grades five through eight. The boys showed a movie on racial equality and facilitated a discussion. Beyond that, the boys held an essay contest in the school on the importance of good race relations. They offered a prize of $25 of their own money to the winner. All this came from one meeting.

It is no wonder that a year later the Xaverian Brothers at St. Joseph's High School in Montvale were startled to find these same boys asking for documents from Vatican II so they could prepare for the Judge section of their parish YCS meetings. Clearly the YCS approach was having a profound effect on the young people at Our Lady of Mercy and also on this young parish priest.

In 1962, in the midst of this parish activity, another event took place that would lead me to get involved beyond the parish. This widening scope would open a door that eventually led to RENEW.

Widening the Scope

On a spring day in 1962 my classmate and friend, Fr. Ed Cooke from Maywood, came to visit. He had been asked to be chaplain of a group of select YCS teens from across the nation for a two-week formation meeting at St. Joseph's Camp on Lake Michigan that August. Now circumstances were making it impossible for him to fulfill his commitment. Would I take his place?

I assured Ed that this would be impossible. My pastor, Fr. Lillis, expected us to be full time in the parish and would never give me permission to take on this responsibility. To impress Ed with the impossibility of his proposal, I told him I would go across the hall and present the idea. Fr. Lillis looked at me and obviously saw a wonderful opportunity for growth. He stunned me by immediately saying, "That's fine with me. And, by the way, why don't you stop calling those groups Sodality and Junior Holy Name? Why don't you call them what they really are, Young Christian Students?" So much for pastoral deception. He was a good and wise man in bringing along his young associate.

It all happened so fast; it hit me like a ton of bricks. I was confronted with the realization that for the first five years of my priesthood I had been playing a mild game with the potential of these specialized movements, YCS and CFM. With Fr. Lillis's full blessing, now was the time to let them grow to their full potential.

The meeting at Lake Michigan was incredible. The goodness and quality of those teenagers were remarkable. You could picture these teens changing the world. We all hit it off fantastically, and it was no doubt my finest moment in relating to people of that age. I came home with renewed fire and zeal.

A month later, I contacted one of these outstanding students, Joanne Martin, who had committed herself to volunteering for a full year at the YCS National Office in Chicago with a recompense of $10 a week spending money. The role of that office was to promote YCS throughout the country. I asked Joanne to come to New Jersey for a few weeks to tour the Archdiocese of Newark. What wild and wooly weeks they were. We had appointments with a good number of parish priests along with key religious women and men ministering in high schools. Joanne stayed at the home of Dottie Doctor, a parishioner, who accompanied us on the frenzied tour from one appointment to another throughout the archdiocese. The net result was a total of forty parishes and high schools committing themselves to taking on the YCS movement. Something big was about to happen.

This burst of excitement and activity among the young priests of the archdiocese was not unnoticed by Fr. John Kiley, the archdiocesan CYO director. Fr. Kiley could have seen YCS as being competitive with CYO, but John was a good and wise priest, another providential person in life's journey. He reached out and offered an invitation to the "Young Turks" to come under the tent of the archdiocesan CYO. He offered us recognition, approval, acceptance, and freedom.

We held a meeting of priests at Ed Cooke's rectory in Maywood to determine whether we would accept Fr. Kiley's invitation. We decided with quick unanimity to accept the offer, and I was nominated to coordinate YCS in the Archdiocese of Newark. In a meeting shortly after, we expanded the scope of our endeavor far beyond YCS itself. Fr. Jim O'Brien took on the responsibility for large YCS conventions we would hold each summer; Fr. Bob Ulesky promoted grammar school YCS; Fr. Charlie Reilly headed up an inner-city tutoring program. Fr. Tom O'Leary guided the summer outreach programs throughout Appalachia. Fr. Jack McDermott worked with the sisters in the archdiocese, helping them to integrate Catholic Action principles in their apostolate and classroom work. My role was to oversee the archdiocesan YCS teenage movement and to work closely with and coordinate the other activities.

One example of these activities was Jack's outreach to the religious sisters. He visited the major superior of each of the major women's religious communities. Each superior was asked to appoint two outstanding young sisters who would work with him in promoting the Catholic Action type of activity with their students. The response from the superiors was favorable in every instance. Some of the young sisters appointed went on to become major superiors themselves. A formative process was developed to help them in their ministries.

One event that stands out was a visit with Chet Huntley, the anchorman on the CBS nightly newcast from New York, and other personnel who understood media responsibilities in choosing and reporting news items. They shared with the sisters how moral decisions were made regarding what would be acceptable to air. They offered suggestions and advice to the sisters on how to make a good impact on the media. In still another instance, Jack brought in Fr. Bernard Häring, C.Ss.R., a world-renowned moral theologian, to give a presentation to one thousand of our sisters. These were mind-expanding experiences.

The YCS movement continued to grow in the archdiocese, helping thousands of young students live more full and active Catholic lives, making them symbols of great hope for young priests and sisters in the archdiocese. Once again, Fr. Lillis was helpful. He realized that all this activity was not preventing me from fulfilling my parish responsibilities, and he offered to help with the archdiocesan YCS work. One of our parishioners, Jim Rice, had shared with Fr. Lillis that his daughter, Grace, had left the Maryknoll community and was looking for apostolic activity. Fr. Lillis offered to hire her as my secretary to expand the YCS archdiocesan work. He would cover her salary.

Within a couple of years the YCS work grew beyond my parish office to an archdiocesan office I directed at the Mt. Carmel Guild building in Newark. This particular branch of Mt. Carmel was in a dilapidated building that served as a rehabilitation center for recovering alcoholic men who took the Mt. Carmel trucks out each day to collect clothing. Msgr. Kiley oversaw the operation and lived a humble life in this dark woe-begotten building that now housed our YCS movement. In time our YCS office expanded to four people coordinated by John McCue of Pearl River, New York.

Years before, John McCue, a zealous promoter of lay apostolate work, had decided to mentor me at Our Lady of Mercy. John was held in high national esteem. Pat and Pattie Crowley, when they were retiring from the international leadership of the Christian Family Movement, had invited John and Kay McCue to take their place in Chicago. As providence would have it, John chose instead to coordinate our YCS office in Newark. The difficulty for me was to come up with a salary that would support John, his wife, Kay, and their six daughters, along with the other three people in the office. Fr. Jack McDermott ran a golf tournament to help support the YCS movement. Somehow, the money came.

From the YCS activity sprang another initiative. Some of us priests decided to form our own group, the Young Christian Priests, which would also use the "Observe, Judge, Act" method for our own lives. We gathered on our day off, Tuesdays, in stimulating meetings that were extremely helpful for our ministries. Among our activities was an *Aggiornamento* week-long gathering of priests that we decided to hold at a campsite at New Jersey's Lake Hopatcong. Interesting authorities such as Michael Novak, a noted young theologian, were invited to speak about lay responsibility. One of my responsibilities was to invite a young, eminent theologian, Fr. Hans Küng. I remember calling the switchboard at Tübingen, Germany, and asking for Fr. Küng. The operator replied, "Father, he's in his room now." She then continued with something she no doubt should not have offered: "Would you like his private number?" "Yes," I said. I remember well his response: "This is Fr. Küng speaking." Surely with some nervousness, I invited this distinguished figure to join us at Lake Hopatcong. He would be giving a presentation in Canada the week before, and I proposed he could tie in a visit with us on that trip. Unfortunately, his schedule did not allow it, but there had been no harm in trying. No doubt, summoning the courage to make calls like that would one day be invaluable experience when I was making calls for RENEW to bishops and priests throughout the country. The Lake Hopatcong event proved to be very successful, binding us priests closer together in communal and ministerial interests.

On a lighter note, some priests in Rhode Island had heard about our YCS work. They invited us to help them launch YCS in the Diocese of Providence. I remember us boarding a low-fare flight in Newark, flying to Providence on a Tuesday, sharing with them about YCS, and working on a plan for launching the movement. We then proceeded to the basketball court where we enjoyed a great game and then went to dinner. We were a happy bunch getting back on the plane for Newark that evening. It was a great day off, and life continued to be good.

With all of the YCS activity related here, and the off-shoot activities, more was happening than we realized at the time. The response of people was so heartening and the experience so rich that our own lives were being formed and transformed. I was learning from the goodness and initiative of lay parishioners young and old that the dreams of my youth of a lay-involved Church had not been pipe dreams. They were more than possible. They were a reality. And in the process, I was becoming aware of an ability to organize, which would be critical for my role in RENEW. Being given the opportunity to assume initiative and responsibility was not common for a young priest at that time. All these instances came together as strong underpinnings for the subsequent launching of RENEW.

CHAPTER 3

Planting Seeds of RENEW

My ministry with young people paralleled with my ministry with adults, which deeply influenced my life and my thinking.

Christian Family Movement

The CFM at Our Lady of Mercy followed the same "Observe, Judge, and Act" format as YCS. The couples involved in our CFM dealt with family life, neighborhoods, the parish, the four townships in which our parishioners lived, race relations, the economy, world issues, and every other element that was part of people's lives. This was all going on during the same period as the YCS activities. Religion and spirituality were not confined to Sunday morning or daily prayer time. It was a seven-day-a-week process, every hour of every day.

The goal of these movements was to have every Catholic transform his or her faith into positive action in daily life. This would go a long way toward making our nation and our world a place of goodness, love, peace, and justice. Those participating in these movements could undertake special projects, but more fundamental was taking the daily opportunities for action that could transform local communities and the wider society. It would take a book in itself to share the small and large actions undertaken by the couples in CFM.

For example, CFM couples were assuming leadership roles in parish and archdiocesan activities and in the local community. At one point the mayors and many members of the governing bodies in all four towns comprising our parish were members of CFM small communities. I well remember a Friday evening when a man at a meeting said, "Our corporation is involved in an unjust practice. On Monday morning at our board meeting, I'm going to challenge our corporation to change its ways." There were so many ways in which the families and young executives in our parish were growing in Christian responsibility.

Monica and Gary Garofalo and Dolores and Joe Duggan were among the many couples and families involved in CFM at Our Lady of Mercy in the late 1950s and '60s. These couples are two examples of the CFM experience that was to expand into RENEW.

The Garofalos, a young couple from Philadelphia, were invited to join a small-community meeting one Saturday evening, shortly after they moved into the parish. Gary brought two weeks of Catholic education to that meeting. At the age of twelve, after two weeks of instruction in the catechism, he received his first Communion and confirmation. Nevertheless, at that very first meeting, it was obvious that Gary made more sense in talking about the Mystical Body of Christ than all the Catholic graduates there. A star was being born. Monica and Gary became the leaders of a new group of CFM couples.

Gary was like a sponge, absorbing information from bishops' statements, papal encyclicals, and the documents of Vatican II. The Garofalos hosted frequent meetings in their kitchen to prepare for their biweekly CFM sessions. At these kitchen meetings, I worked with them in discerning how to deepen the spirituality of the CFM community, form stronger communal bonds, and refine the "Observe, Judge, Act" process. We and the whole CFM community were undergoing continuous formation. In fact, unknown to Gary and Monica, their six children would get out of their beds to listen to the CFM meetings from the top of the stairs. It showed later in their lives as the children grew to be responsible faith-filled people who took on leadership roles in places as far-flung as Peru, Bosnia, Malawi, Cuba, and the Middle East.

Gary was elected the first parish council president at Our Lady of Mercy. He was the first lay chairperson working with Archbishop Boland in the Archdiocesan Pastoral Council, the first elected lay leader for Region III of the U.S. Bishops National Advisory Council:

Pennsylvania, New York, and New Jersey. He was later elected chair of the national council. He assisted the bishops in writing their *Pastoral Letter on Catholic Social Teaching and the United States Economy*, which called for responses from select corporations. Johnson & Johnson hired Gary to write the company's response to the bishops' letter. Gary's involvement started at a meeting of a small community in a living room in Park Ridge. Monica brought her zeal and strong spirituality to a life-long involvement from the original RENEW to the many ministries of RENEW International.

The inner-city Newark project outlined earlier was the kind of involvement that the Duggans took from the CFM experience. Their home became a house of formation for any number of people who came to live for a period of time with them and later moved on to further apostolic involvement. Many foreign students found a home away from home with the Duggans. Dolores and Joe took particular interest in furthering projects in developing countries. They held prayer meetings in their homes and initiated all-night visitations to the Blessed Sacrament at Our Lady of Mercy. The Duggans and Garofalos truly symbolized the whole of the CFM community and helped demonstrate what church experience could be.

Working with the Christian Family Movement at Our Lady of Mercy, more than any other experience, became for me a process of matura-tion as a Catholic Christian and as a human being. It was in the small Christian communities that I learned what it was to be a priest in rela-tionship and in service to the community. More than the seminary or anything else, lay people in CFM formed my priesthood. From the CFM groups, people came forward seeking spiritual direction and evenings of reflection and helping me in so many ways to understand what it meant to be a priest in a servant-leader role within the Church. That experience of community, not only with small groups but with all the parishioners of Our Lady of Mercy, would last a lifetime and be the basis for a vision of RENEW in my future priestly ministry.

The communal experience of CFM also became integrated into our parish liturgical planning committee. We shared faith with one another; prayer was an essential part of the meetings. All liturgical ideas and planning arose from rich and prayerful experience. It was truly a liturgical planning community, not a committee. It was to be the seed of an idea that would later grow in RENEW: "An end of parish committees and the beginning of communities." That all parish ministry should grow from the richness of prayerful communities would become one of the great spiritual goals of RENEW International.

One of the main reasons for any success that RENEW experienced was the fact that, as a process geared for parishes, it had actually come from vital parish experience. Some other ventures at that time took a national approach that was based largely on theory, with little background of pastoral experience. RENEW's growth was gradual and real, based on success stories. Even more important was the rich parish experience from which it sprang. RENEW did not take off on a wing and a prayer, with hope that its components would work. In particular, the small-group experience from parishes like Our Lady of Mercy would lead to a conviction that parishes would respond well to RENEW. The practice of having staff people who have solid parish experience has been essential to the success of RENEW International's pastoral initiatives.

International Experience

My international interests, especially in developing countries, started long before inquiries about RENEW came from abroad—specifically, with a visit to Brazil and Peru while I was still a young priest in 1963.

In the early 1960s articles started to circulate about the plight of the poor in Latin America and about the Church's efforts to serve the needs of the poorest. Gary McGloin, a popular author on church and social issues, wrote an article declaring it was the eleventh hour for Brazil, which appeared to be on the verge of going communist. At that time, communism seemed to be the worst evil one could think of, and certainly a disaster for the Church. That realization, along with the fact that Brazil was the largest Catholic country in the world and bordered on so many other South American countries, was cause for great alarm. The situation called for action.

An article appeared in *Newsweek* about Franciscans working in the favelas (slums) of Rio de Janeiro. That was it! I would take my vacation in August 1963 in those favelas and get to understand the needs of those who were desperately poor. I would take the trip alone, since no one was free to go with me. Not knowing anyone in Brazil and not knowing Portuguese, I took off for Rio de Janeiro with considerable fear and trepidation.

I took a cab from Rio to the Franciscan friars in the favelas. The friars were surprised to find a visitor at their door but gave me a gracious welcome and offered me a room to stay in and an invitation to lunch.

Clueless in Rio, I set out with the address of the YCW office. Arriving there by some miracle, I found a young group of workers and we communicated as best we could. When I offered them financial help from an electrical union in New Jersey in order to fight communism, there was an immediate rejection: "We don't want any money from the United States." It awoke me to how many people outside the United States viewed us.

After I had returned to the Franciscan residence, a guided tour of the favelas opened my eyes and deeply touched my heart. How could anyone ever be the same after experiencing the terrible anguish and desperation of people fighting for an existence? I knew then that somehow my priestly ministry would have to help the poorest. Seeing this interest, the Franciscans steered me to take a trip to the most remote northeast corner of Brazil, Natal.

The bishop there, Dom Eugênio Sales, had gained worldwide attention for his work with the poor. He had stopped the building of a cathedral and had turned the shell of that edifice into a center for wide-ranging services to the poor. Little stations were set up throughout the diocese where people were taught to read and write and where women were taught to make their own clothes with the use of community sewing machines. The small Christian communities in the diocese were so effective that a living and vital Church became the center and the hope in people's lives. Communism had no chance in this famine-stricken, barren area. Dom Eugênio offered a good amount of time for sharing, since only one other American priest had ever made his way to Natal. That priest was Fr. Peter Gerety from Hartford, Connecticut, who would later become my archbishop and the "Father of RENEW."

A few months after I returned to the United States, Dom Eugênio accepted an invitation to come to New Jersey and give talks to the CFM couples and YCS teens in our archdiocese. He did a great job of raising our sensitivity to the needs of our poor brothers and sisters, which also resulted in communication and follow-through actions on the part of our people with our new friends in Brazil.

At that point Dom Eugênio had just been made apostolic administrator of Natal. He invited me to work full time with him taking a year to study the landscape and then setting up whatever lay organization I chose. After much thought and prayer I felt more called to work with our parish-based New York executives and business people who, very likely through their business decisions, were having more impact on life in Brazil than I could on location. It was somewhat like the Maryknoll decision, neither of which I could completely understand, but the Lord was making me wait for a greater opportunity to serve internationally, one that would come in time through RENEW.

From Brazil, I traveled to Lima, Peru, where Maryknoll priests took me to see Ciudad de Dios, which was another shocking and emotional experience. Over 100,000 people had come in from outlying regions of Peru to try to make a living in the big city. They wound up in this shantytown with shelters made of cardboard and flattened tin cans and existed on the barest of human essentials. Returning ten years later, I found the same people, now with poor but stable homes, giving great witness to the resilience of human nature. Unfortunately, there were another one hundred thousand people living in the same circumstances as the original settlers. Life for me could never be the same again. How could anyone experience such poverty without having a deep commitment to somehow respond and be of assistance?

Years later, when inquiries came in from Cameroon, Nigeria, and India, they would not be ignored—even with all that was happening with the RENEW explosion in the United States. That would be impossible. As we will see, our RENEW team was eager to set forth, especially to developing countries, and do all we could without any concern for cost or inconvenience.

The Civil Rights Movement

A few days after my return from South America, Fr. Joe Scherer entered the picture again. He called and asked, "Next week there's going to be a march on Washington, D.C. Are you going?" Though I had just returned from a trip, how could I not go? The Rev. Dr. Martin Luther King Jr. led the march. It was one of the peak moments of the civil rights movement.

The following Saturday, there was a gathering for the trip at Queen of Angels, an African-American parish, in Newark. On the bus heading for Washington, a young girl from that parish sat next to me, but she didn't say a word the whole way down. I didn't even know if she was able to talk. It was a tremendous experience driving into Washington. All the African-American people were on their doorsteps as the buses rolled down the street, waving and cheering as if the liberation troops had just arrived. Obviously with at least two hundred thousand people there that day it was an unforgettable and moving experience. On the way back, to my shock, that young girl could not stop talking. She was so enthusiastic. It was then that she revealed to me that her parents had told her not to go. They were convinced that they would never see her alive again. What incredible courage this young girl had. She inspired me with her example of courageously standing up for what she believed.

Racial equality was very much a part of parish ministry at Our Lady of Mercy. Through CFM groups, YCS, Sunday homilies, and many other means, people were being called to work toward a new social order. The encouraging response from parishioners was seen in the outpouring of food for the people in Scudder Homes during the Newark riots.

Very shortly after the riots quieted down, members of the parish undertook a beautiful venture. Under the leadership of a parish CFM member, Dave Foley, and with the backing of many other parishioners, the parish forged a union with Joe Cheneyfield, an African-American Catholic lay leader in Newark. A plan was quickly designed to have a huge outpouring of both blacks and whites, from inner city and suburban areas, to join in a mammoth Walk for Peace through the streets of Newark that had been ravaged by the rioting. The media were immediately attracted to the idea and called attention to the march. An overwhelming number of people, who truly desired to seek common ground where people could live peacefully together, came forth to witness. Once again the power of a few people in a parish small community, who took on action, was demonstrated.

During those turbulent times, someone came to me expressing a deep hatred for Martin Luther King. Only a few days later, on a Thursday evening, while I was hearing confessions for a first Friday, a man came to me in the confessional saying, "Father, Martin Luther King was just killed." This was on the heels of the assassinations of Jack and Bobby Kennedy. I wondered what was happening to respect, dignity, and civility? Our society was going crazy.

Dr. King's funeral was to be held on a Tuesday, which happened to be my day off. I could fly to Atlanta and back the same day without causing any ripple at Our Lady of Mercy. Fr. Lillis came to me and said, "I'm sure you'd like to go to Martin Luther King's funeral. I want to pay your airfare." The funeral was a memorable experience, although there was no way to get inside the church. A mass of people filled the surrounding area for blocks around. What a unique experience it was to be one of the very few whites among so many thousands of black sisters and brothers. Perhaps for the first time I realized the level of discomfort that blacks must feel in so many situations in our society. My experience in Atlanta would eventually resonate in Season III of RENEW, which would try to help put people in other people's shoes to feel how they felt.

Conversion Experience

There were a few more experiences that would contribute to the role I would eventually play in RENEW. One was a personal conversion—a call to a more personal relationship with God and a richer spirituality.

As the years went on at Our Lady of Mercy, along with working with the liturgy and small communities I spent a great amount of time absorbed in counseling. It became obvious that to better help those coming to counseling, I needed greater skills. I participated in the excellent pastoral counseling program at Iona College from 1969 to 1971. However, that occurred at a time of great turmoil in the Church when many priests and sisters in the program and among my friends were working through decisions that would lead them to leave religious life and marry.

One professor encouraged me to enter a follow-up program at St. John's that would lead to a doctorate in education/counseling within a year. Although being a licensed counselor and opening a counseling office in the neighboring town of Pearl River, New York, as a sideline to the regular parish work was an appealing idea, something else very important happened at this time. My classmate and good friend, Fr. Jim Ferry, had a remarkable, dramatic conversion experience. He had left us on a ski trip in Vermont to attend a weekend retreat given by Ralph Martin of the Charismatic Renewal. Jim was on fire with love for the Lord and making no secret of it. Some people thought he was off the wall. His pastor called asking me to straighten Jim out and get him to a psychiatrist because he had "flipped out" with his spirituality. Nevertheless, I was very impressed with Jim's new desire and attempt to totally surrender to God's will and be open to God's Spirit and direction.

Shortly after, Fr. Jim and I were on retreat in Darlington. At this point, I had been ordained some fifteen years and realized I was much better at counseling than at talking with someone about Jesus. The Holy Spirit was raising questions in me. What was my priesthood about? How much and how easily did we Catholics talk about Jesus?

I asked Jim if we could go for a walk. On our way, I said, "Jim, talk to me about Jesus and what he means to you." Jim taught me a beautiful process that I used then and have used many times since. It was a three-fold step to a personal kind of conversion experience. The first was to honestly admit your faults and sins and to be truly repentant for them. The second, the critical one, and the one that I found extremely difficult and challenging, was to surrender totally to God in every aspect of my life. To say, "Yes, I want to do the Lord's will in the most difficult areas of my life. What are my favorite faults and sins? Am I willing to let go of them?" That was a very challenging thing.

The third step Jim proposed was this: "You've got to call on the power of the Holy Spirit. When there are blockages in your life, the Holy Spirit can't really work powerfully." One had to have an undivided heart. Only when there was a total opening to the Lord could the full power of the Spirit be experienced. As a Church, it's as if we're going along on four cylinders when we were created to be an eight-cylinder vehicle.

That conversation led me to a new commitment to the Lord. It wasn't that my spiritual life would now be perfect. But I had a clear goal regarding the kind of relationship that would be important to be fully alive in Jesus.

The next week, in two instances of counseling, I interrupted my session and asked my subjects' permission to talk directly about Jesus. The transformations that occurred in those people were incredible. Panic and tears quickly turned to peace, calm, and prayerfulness—transformations that lasted beyond those counseling sessions. The Lord had certainly touched the lives of those two people but, perhaps even more so, my own life. While maintaining the greatest respect for traditional counseling approaches, I knew my own ministry was being called in a new direction.

The Lord's action and these experiences were certainly not accidental, nor peripheral. They would resonate as an important aspect of RENEW, along with small-community faith sharing and enriched parish liturgy. A profound and direct call to relate to the Lord in a deep and personal way would be central. Being immersed in the Word of God would make all actions for personal spiritual growth and social change far more powerful and effective.

This concept of conversion of heart would become critical for RENEW. It is God, not we, who changes hearts. "Unless the Lord builds the house, those who build it labor in vain" (Psalm 127:1).

Council of Priests

In the late 1960s the priests of the archdiocese elected their first Council of Priests. As a member of that council, in 1970, I was nominated to form a committee of council members who would develop a pastoral plan for the future of the Archdiocese of Newark. As a committee, we researched far and wide but ultimately came up with a plan that was based on our own priestly ministry. That plan was never formally presented to Archbishop Boland. Apparently someone judged it to be ahead of its time. However, the interesting thing is that the plan could

have served as a blueprint for RENEW and what would be accepted by
our new archbishop a few years later. Formulation of that plan proved to
be very helpful. It forced me to crystallize ideas that were arising from
parish experience, along with a number of thoughts of how the work of
Vatican II could more effectively become a living reality in the pastoral
life of the Church.

A Startling Invitation—St. Ann's

Memorial Day 1973 stands out clearly in my mind. The parade was
passing in front of Our Lady of Mercy while I was meeting in my office
with a member of our Liturgical Planning Community. A phone call
came with a startling invitation. Fr. Jim Finnerty from the Archdiocesan
Personnel Board was asking if I would leave Our Lady of Mercy and go
to St. Ann's, the most desperately poor parish in Newark, at a time when
Newark was the poorest city in the country. Only two weeks prior I had
rejected overtures from the priests from a neighboring parish in Newark
to become administrator of their parish. I asked Jim if I could have a
week to think and pray about the St. Ann's proposal. Before I even hung
up, I knew in my heart what the answer should be.

The picture at St. Ann's was bleak. The parish was situated in the midst
of the battleground area of the Newark riots. Many of the homes were
in horrific shape. It reminded one of a bombed-out city. The church
wasn't in much better condition. Plaster was falling from the ceil-
ings and walls; there were over two hundred holes in the stained-glass
windows; the parish basement hall was flooded with water and floating
garbage; a moat alongside the church was filled with sewage; the rectory
was frequently vandalized; parish collections hovered around $100 from
a very small church-going population. (One person attended our first
Sunday parish Mass.) There were three school buildings on the parish
property; one was rented to the Newark public school system for grades
one through six. A full-time Newark policeman was required to patrol
that school in order to keep things under control.

It is no wonder that the previous pastor had written to the chancery
saying that he was about to mail in the keys with the proposal that St.
Ann's be closed because there was no parish left. The bright spot was

our school with its dynamic principal, Sr. Pat Hogan, O.P. Best of all, Fr. Jack Martin, a tremendous priest from Our Lady of the Lake, Verona, was already committed to going to St. Ann's. Jack's work was always characterized by a fantastic love and passion for the poor. Working with Jack and Pat, and building up a strong and zealous team there, would prove to be a joyful experience.

Not everyone offered encouragement when we arrived at St. Ann's. Some in Newark cautioned me not to bring ideas that had worked in the suburbs. They particularly pointed out small communities as experienced in Our Lady of Mercy. Nevertheless, Jack and I forged ahead, starting with the one plan we brought to the parish: we would begin each day together in thirty minutes of prayer.

Many remarkable things happened. Within a year, the church was totally renewed and sparkling. The Hispanic Mass sometimes attracted six hundred Latinos, filling the church. The church-going African-American community increased several times over. Discipline and order were strengthened in the school. A strong parent-teacher association was formed with mutual agreement that the Catholic faith be taught at the parish school. Through visits to homes, religious education in the parish grew from eight to three hundred twenty children. The parish continued to grow as a center of hope and offered the neighborhood many social services.

Most striking of all was the fact that small communities were formed and cherished by the people. The communities were very prayerful, and lives were visibly being changed. This progress would continue for years to come under the pastoral guidance of Fr. Jack Martin and Sr. Pat Hogan and others who would join them on the core team.

A Turn of Events

While I was stationed at St. Ann's, Archbishop Gerety tapped me to form an archdiocesan volunteer committee to think through the implementation of parish councils throughout the archdiocese. My calls at 10 p.m. on Christmas Eve, at a time when people would surely be home and in good form, quickly resulted in the formation of our committee. In the course of the committee's work, a large one-day workshop on parish councils was held at Felician College in Lodi. The turnout was tremendous and at the request of Archbishop Gerety, Fr. Richard P. McBrien, professor of theology at the University of Notre Dame, gave the keynote address. Fr. McBrien's strong and concrete recommendation was to set up an archdiocesan office that would oversee the implementation of parish councils in each of the two hundred fifty parishes. I happened to be sitting next to the archbishop and wished I had some potion that would make me invisible. I had a vision of the office coming in my direction like a train racing down the tracks.

Shortly after, I was giving a report from the Archdiocesan Volunteer Committee to the Archdiocesan Pastoral Council. In it I expressed my belief that parish councils could surely work in inner-city parishes like St. Ann's, as well as in suburban parishes. There was no excuse for any pastor in the archdiocese to say a parish council wasn't suitable for his parish. Situations and cultures may differ but human nature is basically the same in our one human family. The same amount of goodness, talent, and capacity for leadership existed as much in the poorest parishes as those in privileged wealthier parishes. Later, the basic components of RENEW that appealed to human nature made it possible to go to widely varying cultures throughout the world and promise with assurance "RENEW will work."

The presentation at the pastoral council had apparently struck a note with Archbishop Gerety. He invited me to come to lunch at the cathedral the next day. The archbishop was to make an offer that I truly wanted to reject. However, I would eventually come to see that this was an offer I should not and could not refuse.

As indicated earlier, the parish experiences related here were not isolated and unconnected in meaning or significance. They were forming a pattern that would lead to the essential components of the RENEW experience. They also enhanced my personal growth and development that would make the task of leadership in RENEW less daunting and, by God's grace, even possible.

CHAPTER 4

RENEW Seeds Take Root

Lunch with Archbishop Gerety at the cathedral in early 1975 was a unique and interesting experience that I approached with some anxiety.

Landing in the Chancery

During lunch, the archbishop expressed his belief that the archdiocese should develop parish councils in order to promote shared responsibility throughout the archdiocese. The key question was, of course, would I be willing to take on this responsibility and start an office for parish council development?

"Archbishop," I told him, "I love my parish at St. Ann's and would really hate to leave it. We have a good parish team, but there is so much more left to be done. I'd really like to stay in the parish." The archbishop was wise enough to leave it an open question as I returned home to St. Ann's. At our second meeting that spring Archbishop Gerety again presented the question. Once more I demurred and felt I had gotten off the hook, but more was still to happen.

As planned, that summer I headed to Cochabamba, high in the mountains in Bolivia. It was reported to be the best place in the world for learning Spanish. It would have to be, because learning a language well seemed to me next to impossible.

Cochabamba was a city seven thousand feet in altitude with beautiful flowers and crisp, clean cirrus clouds in the summertime. The teachers are indigenous to the land and speak a very pure Spanish. To my amazement, I was making progress. However, one day the Maryknoll director of the language institute came to the door with a chilling message: my father had died of a heart attack. I was on my way, scrambling from airport to airport, finally getting back for the funeral, which was delayed fifteen minutes awaiting my arrival. It was devastating—the first personal loss I had ever experienced. Mastering Spanish would have to wait, and it still remains a dream of mine.

While in Cochabamba I would laughingly share with the other students how my archbishop was proposing an archdiocesan position for me to undertake. The joke would be on him since I had escaped all the way to South America. Guess what? A month later I discovered the joke was on me. The archbishop asked me to meet with him, and once again he proposed the office of parish councils.

It was in this third meeting that, as politely as possible, I tried to say, "Please forget me for this role." I then said, "This is what I think you should do." For ten minutes I went on proposing an archdiocese-wide plan of formation that would enable lay people to take on the ministries and responsibilities that Vatican II had called for. This process would be carried out over three years. It would be centered on spiritual renewal and would set a new climate in the archdiocese. Lay involvement could then flourish in a much wider process of lay formation. When I finally finished, the archbishop simply said, "That's what I want." What to do? "Archbishop, please let me think about it."

When I look back at that meeting, I am still amazed by Archbishop Gerety's unhesitatingly positive response. All kinds of statistics show that new ideas are almost always initially rejected or treated with skepticism. Not with Archbishop Gerety. He is a brilliant pastoral man who immediately embraced the vision of an archdiocese-wide spiritual renewal. His leadership and constant support would lead him to be rightly acclaimed as "the Father of RENEW."

Following my meeting with Archbishop Gerety, friends were not bashful about offering me advice such as, "Don't go to the chancery. You'll lose your soul there." But in my heart I know that Archbishop

Gerety was offering, on a silver platter, an archdiocese-wide opportunity to work toward the formation of lay responsibility. This is what I had dreamed of for so many years.

Early Beginnings

Establishing parish councils in two hundred fifty parishes and initiating the renewal process would be no small task, certainly not one to be taken on alone. Who would be the right person to start with?

The first person who came to mind was dynamic Sr. Suzanne Golas, C.S.J.P., who was serving at St. Therese Parish in Cresskill, New Jersey. This was a leading-light parish guided by Fr. Paul Kirchner, O.Carm., and Suzanne.

Suzanne was certainly surprised when I called inviting her to dinner on a Sunday afternoon at Sullivan's Restaurant in Tappan, Rockland County, New York, just over the Jersey border. After some amiable chatting I said, "Suzanne, you've achieved so much at St. Therese, don't you think it's time to move onto something new and exciting?" And then I proposed the idea of a team ministry to set up this office. Suzanne talked to some of her sisters who advised her, "Do not get involved with the archdiocesan network. It would be death." Having ignored such sound advice, Suzanne and I took steps to form our office.

Suzanne's involvement was providential and a great grace. Suzanne is an energetic and very smart worker in God's ministry. Her talent and great enthusiasm won countless friends among the clergy and laypeople for the initial efforts of the Office of Pastoral Renewal. As we will see when we come to Season III of RENEW in the Archdiocese of Newark, her work with justice and social concerns could set a matrix for diocesan offices and agencies.

Forming a Team

We established the tone for the Office of Pastoral Renewal right from the beginning with the only other person who would be on board with me when we formally opened the office in January 1976. (Suzanne was not free to begin work until July.) In hiring that person as a secretary, we set three criteria: a prayerful person who would call us to prayer on a daily basis; a community builder, who could foster a sense of spiritual community in the chancery; and someone who could type. By God's grace, all three surfaced in grand fashion in Liz Mullen. Liz would take the train from Brooklyn each day and call us to a half-hour of prayer. No matter how late Suzanne or I might be out doing workshops the night before, Liz's task was to see that we would be there for prayer at 8:30 a.m. Since there were only partitions surrounding our corner of a larger office space, our prayer time would prove to be interesting. The sound of hymns wafting above a partition definitely caused curiosity around us. The core of our efforts was to be praying and setting a spiritual tone for our ministry.

That spiritual tone was carried out diligently throughout the daily schedule: prayer in the morning and Mass at noon with sharing at homily time were essential. Every meeting started with a time of prayer and faith sharing.

Our work with parish councils would also be centered on the spiritual. More important than by-laws and Robert's Rules of Order would be time spent in prayer to discern what God's will was for the parish. Consensus, arrived at in prayerful reflection and a process of discernment, was encouraged for each parish in its decision-making. With this emphasis we hoped to avoid dealing with superficial items that were not germane to the parish mission and also to avoid bickering over the ideologies of right and left. Other dioceses started to take note of these attempts to put spirituality at the heart of council deliberations.

Liz was soon to be joined by a dynamic laywoman from St. Luke's Parish in Ho-Ho-Kus. Jeanne Schrempf was an expert in the area of religious education. Being part-time, Jeanne came in after initial prayer time one day. In my usual intense working style, I started right in with work discussion. "Tom," Jeanne said, "don't you think it's good to say 'Hello' or 'Good morning' before you start talking about work?" With that we laughed and absorbed a good lesson. Actually we all enjoyed working together and had a lot of fun in the process.

When Cathy Dambach Martin joined our team in 1977 it meant there was a full-time person besides me working on RENEW. Suzanne was fully engaged in parish council work. Cathy's goodness and zeal were augmented by her very high intelligence and wonderful relational ability. She was invaluable in planning, visiting parishes, working out logistical details, and overseeing evaluation processes as RENEW developed. There was little she couldn't do. She put her whole heart into her effort as an extremely valuable asset in the launching of RENEW.

In the very early days, Fr. Frank McNulty introduced us to a wonderful woman, Dolly Donahue. The first of our volunteers, Dolly helped us hammer out some important aspects of RENEW.

In 1979, Suzanne moved out of parish council work to start preparing for the justice theme in Season III of RENEW. That move began a Human Concerns Department within the Office of Pastoral Renewal. Sr. Mary McGuinness, O.P., came to work with parish and deanery councils, the Archdiocesan Pastoral Council, and the whole collegial process. Mary would play an extremely significant role in RENEW for the next thirty years.

Before the office had actually opened in January of 1976, in a meeting at Friendly's in Demarest, Suzanne and I decided that we had to be clear that the scope of this office would be more than just establishing parish councils. If we were to be truly about spiritual renewal and call people to a full sense of responsibility, and if the councils were to be effective, we needed to undertake that great formation effort I had discussed with the archbishop. We wanted to be clear from the beginning that we had a mandate and the freedom to do what was pastorally needed. The title Office of Pastoral Renewal was decided upon.

In a following meeting with the archbishop, while holding a folder that had a picture of a football team on it, I explained that this would be a team ministry. The archbishop quickly announced this would not be a team ministry—"You're responsible." In any event, Suzanne and I worked as best as possible to be a true team and to develop the project with parish councils, with much more to come.

A very strong sense of community, along with prayerfulness, characterized our staff. Our meetings were not always held in the office. Having experienced too many church meetings that emulated the environment of the business world, I preferred meetings in pleasant surroundings such as the park at the edge of Bayonne looking over into Staten Island, or Branch Brook Park in Newark during its nationally renowned cherry blossom time. Our sense of community was strengthened by meetings such as the one held at Liberty State Park in Jersey City. It was a magical setting with the Statue of Liberty just yards away. In our meeting on the lawn we had a fantastic prayer sharing followed by our business meeting.

Late in the afternoon, we boarded a Staten Island ferry and took a ride into downtown New York where we enjoyed Little Italy, dining on pesto pasta and other good Italian food. As a staff, we enjoyed having fun together, doing impromptu things like going to a movie. There was an *esprit de corps* that was great.

Besides the prayer that was an essential element for our communal gatherings, I was finding spiritual strength and guidance at the Bethlehem Hermitage in Chester, New Jersey.

In the first months, I took on the responsibility of going out and meeting with pastors, promoting the idea of shared responsibility in the formation of parish councils. This would prove to be providential. The visits would establish relationships and prepare the way for contacts regarding RENEW.

During the first three months, I visited one hundred thirty pastors throughout the archdiocese, including some who didn't know the arch-diocese remembered them. Some could not believe that someone from the chancery was calling on them. I visited the most remote and easily forgotten parishes, starting with breakfast meetings and continuing throughout the day, even, in one instance, beginning at 10 p.m. Some pastors responded by inviting me back to speak at all their Sunday Masses. It was obvious that under Archbishop Gerety's leadership some-thing new and important was starting and was to be taken seriously.

One of the first things Suzanne and I did was to help councils go through a planning process. It soon became evident that almost all the ideas that surfaced came from people's experience of Church ten or twenty years earlier. Very few new or creative ideas were surfacing. As social psychologists would say, something had to be done to break the ice and open minds and hearts if there was to be a stronger spiritual basis for parish activity and a new evangelization.

These planning workshops only confirmed the strong conviction of the need for the process that was to be RENEW. A new vision was needed for parish pastoral approaches and also for an archdiocese-wide pastoral climate.

A Shared Idea

In the spring of 1976 our Office of Pastoral Renewal was separated from its affiliation with the Planning Office in the chancery and moved to 300 Broadway in Newark. Our new home had once been a large insurance building and now housed a Catholic high school and a number of diocesan offices. By chance, our new office was next door to the archdiocesan Office of Religious Education directed by Fr. Tom Ivory. On a spring afternoon, Tom and I sat down to get better acquainted with the missions of each other's offices and to share reflections about Church and some of our hopes. To our amazement, we both had the same general idea of a massive diocesan effort for the formation of lay people and renewal of the Church, undergirded with a strong effort toward a spiritual awakening. It would be good to trace the steps that led each of us to this idea.

Fr. Tom Ivory, ordained in 1964, was a well-respected priest of the archdiocese. He was a theologian who had been a spiritual director at the American College of the Immaculate Conception in Louvain, Belgium where he had studied as a seminarian. Tom had been greatly influenced by his time in Louvain where he had become a good friend of Christiane Brusselmans who was resurrecting the centuries-old process that was to be called the Rite of Christian Initiation of Adults. Rather than having people learn about the Church, and possibly enter the Church, through individual instruction, RCIA was to be a communal experience. Tom was one of the forerunners of this exciting project that was to have incredible influence on the Church for decades to come, not only in the United States and Europe, but throughout the world.

From his experience working with religious education and promoting RCIA, Tom had come to believe that the problem was not simply how to initiate new members into the community. The larger parish community itself needed some kind of RCIA experience. The aim would be a renewal of faith that would enable parishioners to be more welcoming and more outreaching, invite others to learn about the faith, and, in a sense, to accompany people who are making the journey through RCIA. All parishioners would have a fuller experience of the beauty of our faith and would welcome neophytes into a larger community that had been truly renewed. Otherwise, it would be like putting a new patch on an old garment that would surely end with the new patch tearing away and never taking hold.

Tom had previously visited Archbishop Gerety and shared with him the idea of having a diocese-wide renewal program, the kind of experience for the whole community that the RCIA was providing. Such a program would strengthen the whole parish while creating a stronger body to incorporate the newly baptized. Archbishop Gerety favored and encouraged this idea.

I have already shared the background experiences that led me to this point in the story of RENEW. Obviously it was more than fortunate that Tom Ivory and I had come to be in adjoining offices and could share our hopes and dreams. The Holy Spirit was at work here and would continue to be the moving force in the formation of RENEW.

RENEW: A Coordinated Effort

High priority was placed on making RENEW a coordinated effort involving leaders from throughout the diocese. We decided to assemble a broad-based representative group that might respond to our idea.

We invited ninety people to attend a meeting on October 5, 1976. They included the most liberal, the most conservative, and every shade of ideology in between. Office and agency people, parish priests, laymen and laywomen from parishes, sisters, brothers, and bishops were all included. Sr. Mary George O'Reilly, S.H.C.J., from the Office of Research and Planning, was selected to facilitate the meeting.

The basic theology and spirituality presented at the meeting was attractive to all. We proposed major spiritual themes for five six-week periods over two and a half years. The meeting had an electric atmosphere and resulted in extremely positive and excited unanimity.

Tom suggested during the meeting that this project come under the Office of Pastoral Renewal since ours was the newest office and had an agenda that would allow us to follow through. It was put before the group, and there was agreement. Because the management was now in our office, I became the de facto director. At the same time, collaboration with others was to be a major goal. Along with his catechetical responsibilities and the initiation of RCIA in the archdiocese, Tom continued to be deeply involved in RENEW through the development of all stages of the five seasons.

I was to coordinate a group of twenty volunteers, including Tom, to work out more detail. We met every Friday from 9 a.m. to noon, spending quality time in prayer, faith sharing, and community building. In that spiritual climate the form and shape of RENEW came together.

All the offices and agencies of the archdiocese would be visited and brought on board as well as our major spiritual movements and organizations. A large archdiocese-wide prayer network would be organized. Prayer would be the power behind the whole process.

The fact that something new was coming to parishes in the area would be publicized in *The Catholic Advocate* (the archdiocesan newspaper) and in the secular press. Trainers would need to be enlisted and an extensive training process would have to be put together to prepare parish leadership.

A mammoth effort would be needed to engage and sign up the vast majority of parishes in the archdiocese. In the time between Friday morning meetings, it was the mission of the Office of Pastoral Renewal, namely Cathy and me, to accomplish these tasks. We approached these tasks with great energy and enthusiasm. The responses were beautiful.

Three main goals were articulated for the RENEW process:

1. to teach and witness to the Word of God
2. to develop and build small faith-sharing communities
3. to establish justice formation and action.

In terms of these goals, RENEW has been an incredibly successful experience.

Benefits from a Coordinated Approach

We made a real strong effort from the very beginning that we—meaning everyone involved—have common ownership, that it be *our* effort, not just the province of one office or the people who are actually directing it. It had to be seen as benefiting all offices and agencies. No one would therefore see it as a threat to his or her particular ministry. All would have input into RENEW and would be able to connect their particular ministries to it. In time their ministries would reap benefits from the great number of newly-involved people RENEW would bring forth. The key in this coordinated approach was to create a marriage of interests.

We presented concrete examples to each office and agency of how its original support would bring great returns. One example could be taken from the work of parish councils. At Our Lady of Mercy one hundred forty-five people ran for parish council because of an experience we had that was similar to what RENEW became. Each of the archdiocesan ministries could expect this kind of return. Later, when the RENEW process spread beyond Newark, we held workshops for all agencies and personnel in each new diocese.

The RENEW experience in Newark brought about much stronger communication among offices and agencies. In time, other diocesan personnel would report that they had never been in a mutual meeting until our workshop brought them together. From those experiences many dioceses created RENEW small communities that mixed together people from various ministries right within the diocesan center.

I personally undertook contacting and engaging many of the leaders of the spiritual movements. From years of parish experience and involvement in spiritual movements, I could speak with conviction about the benefits for each. Each movement could engage its members to pray for the spiritual enrichment that could come from this renewal effort. In turn, many new members would be flocking to them. The emphasis was that we were relying on God's power for the entire RENEW effort: Their involvement would raise awareness and anticipation of the introduction of RENEW. A strong spiritual atmosphere was growing and permeating the archdiocese.

The Prayer Network

I loved the archdiocesan Prayer Network and the work of helping it become a reality. Prayer would be at the heart of the RENEW experience.

The purpose of the Prayer Network was to encourage individual parishioners and all parish organizations and societies to begin to pray for the spiritual renewal of their parish, the archdiocese, and our Church. This was facilitated by a beautiful prayer composed by Bishop John J. Dougherty, auxiliary bishop of Newark. The prayer drew upon his rich scriptural background and became popular across the country. After RENEW was initiated, publishers asked for permission to print it in their missalettes.

The Prayer Network encouraged and challenged each parishioner to make a commitment of daily prayer for the success of our RENEW process. Some committed themselves to daily prayerful reading of the Scriptures; some to time in reflection or meditation; some to recitation of formal prayers; some to a simple, daily "Hail Mary" or the RENEW Prayer; some to spiritual reading, holy hours, or nights of adoration before the Blessed Sacrament. By the time Season II of RENEW came, a formal Prayer Commitment Sunday would be held to encourage these pledges. I'll never forget a woman in Montclair saying that she had started a few months before praying fifteen minutes a day for RENEW and was now up to two hours a day. "It isn't difficult at all," she said.

Early in the process, communities of women religious were committing themselves to strong efforts in preparation for the archdiocesan spiritual renewal. We visited the Carmelite and Dominican cloistered sisters and engaged them to participate in the Prayer Network. Visits to the various convents and motherhouses were inspiring and helped me to keep the focus on the fact that this would be the Lord's work.

For me, working on the Prayer Network was the most fulfilling of all the RENEW efforts.

A Unique Retreat

Shortly after we opened our office, Fr. Jim Ferry's creative mind came into play once again. At the time, Jim was leading a charismatic group of laypersons, sisters, and priests, some of whom lived with Jim in community at St. Antoninus in inner-city Newark. Jim called me and asked, "Why don't you come up from the office some day and brainstorm a plan for spiritual vitality?" I accepted the invitation. In the morning, we sat around and chatted with his community members for some time. I began to think, "When are we really going to get down to doing some work?" By then it was noon and time for Mass. Mass was a very prayerful and beautiful communal experience that went on and on, followed by a leisurely lunch. I couldn't help but think, "We're wasting a lot of time here. I've got to get back to the office." Finally, around 2 p.m., Jim said, "Let's talk."

In just forty-five minutes it was as if an excellent plan had fallen out of the sky and landed right in our laps. Jim may have had some of this formed in his mind, but, frankly, I was impressed. We could have sat down all day, busy with the work of "planning," but this leisurely time in prayer with a reflective community had done more to open our minds and hearts to the Lord's will than any brain working alone might have conjured. Once again, there was a confirmation of the power of prayer and the need for our whole RENEW effort to be built on a strong, prayerful community.

What emerged? A retreat for representatives of every deanery in the archdiocese that would serve as a preparation for the introduction of RENEW. To prepare myself, I went first to St. Joseph's Shrine in Stirling, New Jersey, for a three-day mini-retreat. This time proved to be extremely meaningful and resulted in my return to St. Joseph's for spiritual refreshment many times over the years.

We held the archdiocesan retreat—centered on the dynamic of God, the Father, the Son, and the Holy Spirit—at the seminary in Darlington in the spring of 1976. Each of the twenty-five deaneries in the diocese was invited to send the dean, a parish priest, a sister, a layman, and a laywoman. Archbishop Gerety headed the retreat team. Frank, a former member of a Trappist monastery, and Doris Hudson, a very gifted and active parishioner from Verona, represented the laity. Suzanne and I would complete the team.

When all one hundred thirty of us arrived at the seminary that first Friday night, I was anxious. Many of the deans that came were veterans, and some were not too open to the new ways of Vatican II nor necessarily open to a lot of lay activity. Surely a lot of credibility would be riding on this. The Lord would have to take care of it.

If these feelings came to me, I could only imagine what thoughts might have come to Archbishop Gerety's mind. He had been our archbishop for only a couple of years and was really going to be sticking out his neck. Perhaps he thought, "What have I gotten myself into?" He had placed a lot of trust in our new office.

Archbishop Gerety gave an overview in his opening talk on Friday evening. On Saturday morning Frank spoke on God the Father, and then there were small-group discussions on our spiritual relationship with the Father. The afternoon centered on Doris's talk on Jesus, which was followed by similar group discussions. On Sunday morning Suzanne gave a presentation on the Holy Spirit, and I concluded by speaking on the necessity of all our efforts being focused on God and strong spirituality. The retreat concluded with Mass.

God's grace was certainly with us. People opened up beautifully in the small communities and the sharing was rich. A comment from one of the participants moved me deeply. A woman in her sixties said, "In all my years in the Church, I don't remember us ever talking about Jesus like this." Wow, this struck right to the heart. We didn't know Jesus well enough, and we certainly were too inhibited to talk freely about Jesus. Yes, we were in a state of grace and were doing all the things that would assure us of salvation, but were we a community marked by a loving and personal relationship with the Lord?

After my talk, two interesting things happened. On a personal note, a dean who had been critical of what he felt was an upstart young priest too involved with lay initiative commented, "I had you all wrong. I didn't know you loved Jesus the way you do."

But something much more significant happened. Archbishop Gerety pulled me over and said, "Tom, let's get out of here. Come to my room. I want to talk." When we sat down he said, "Tom, this retreat has been fantastic. What's the next thing?" All the preparation work for the proposed three-year plan came tumbling out. "Archbishop, it's that three-year plan our committee has been developing." "Good," said the archbishop, "go and talk to the chancellor. We've got to move on this." The Lord's work in this weekend retreat had moved us all deeply and had confirmed Archbishop Gerety in his enthusiastic leadership role in RENEW.

The Multiplication of Retreats

From our weekend experience we developed a plan. Each dean and his deanery team were to go home and be the presenters in replicating that retreat for parishes in their deanery. Each parish was to send a similar delegation to those deanery retreats. In turn, parishes picked it up and held this retreat repeatedly for their members. A rippling effect went through the archdiocese. There was a spiritual stirring based on our relationship with the three persons of the Blessed Trinity. A spiritual openness was paving the way for RENEW.

This wonderful experience was repeated in still another way. Our Office of Pastoral Renewal formed a team to hold a similar retreat for all personnel in the chancery. The presenting team was to be headed by Fr. Mort Smith, an outstanding parish priest from St. Joseph's Parish in Oradell, who would eventually become Bishop John Mortimer Smith, head of the Trenton Diocese.

Chancery workers were given the option of taking off for two days and going to the seminary for the retreat or going to the office for their normal routine. I visited the various offices and agencies of the archdiocese to encourage people to attend the retreat.

On visiting one office that dealt with financial matters, I asked a question that better judgment may not have raised. "Would any of you know if you're working for the Church or for IBM here?" "No," they all shouted, "there's no difference." Whether that was true or not, the retreat was a resounding success and helped us all to sharpen our focus on the love of our triune God and the primacy of our spiritual mission. God certainly was preparing the way for something even more wonderful to happen in our archdiocese. The seeds of RENEW were planted and taking root.

CHAPTER 5

Cultivating RENEW Seedlings

By fall 1977, the basic outline of RENEW was complete. Parishes would initiate the two-and-a-half year process in October 1978. There would be five themes, based upon a cycle of conversion, spread over five six-week periods. Seasons I, III, and V would take place in the fall, and Seasons II and IV during Lent. The five seasons would have the following themes:

Season I	The Lord's Call
Season II	Our Response
Season III	Empowerment by the Spirit to Act Justly
Season IV	Discipleship
Season V	Evangelization

Challenging Tasks

In order to be prepared for Season I, we at the Office of Pastoral Renewal faced the tasks of signing up the parishes in the archdiocese, developing materials for the session, training parish leadership, and continuing work on coordination and publicity. It was time to move RENEW from an idea to a reality.

All the good ideas and planning in the world would be of small account if few parishes became involved. Was RENEW to be just one more program coming out of the chancery? Would it involve only the usual number of very active parishes and, even then, the usual small percentage of parishioners who take part in parish life beyond Sunday morning? Not if it was to live up to the dream of a gigantic archdiocese-wide spiritual renewal.

Signing up parishes would prove to be a huge task. The sign-up strategy, agreed upon by the group of twenty, was that each of us would take a deanery and be responsible for signing up its parishes. Five additional people were chosen so that all twenty-five deaneries would be covered.

This approach proved to be a disaster but provided a good learning experience. Apart from Cathy, Tom Ivory, and me, no one had fully reached out to and signed up their assigned parishes in their deaneries.

We learned that no matter how talented people may be, not everyone is comfortable getting on the phone to make contacts, and most are even more uneasy about visiting people in person. Many people are repelled by what seems to them the task of selling. In terms of evangelization, it is tragic. How are we ever to be about the agenda of evangelization? Personal concern, or perhaps fear of failure, overwhelms many.

While being extremely involved in the development of materials and planning for training, over the next few months Cathy and I needed to be engaged in an intensive, time-consuming effort to enlist parishes. We would have to personally try to sign up over two hundred parishes.

Cathy and I set up information sessions throughout the archdiocese to provide an opportunity for priests, staff, and lay parishioners to learn about the RENEW process and be motivated to participate. We called and visited many parishes to encourage a turnout for these sessions. Reactions varied greatly. While the information sessions went well, with a good number of parishes attending, commitments and sign-ups were considerably slower. After all, pastors were being asked to take a leap in faith by committing their parishes for the next three years to an untried process. These information sessions led to commitments from around fifty of the two hundred fifty parishes in the archdiocese.

We moved ahead largely through phone contacts and personal visits. I learned that the best time to connect with priests was between 9 and 10:30 a.m. and between 4 p.m. and suppertime. We made calls with relentless regularity, always gentle but persistent. We were tenacious to the point at which a pastor definitely said "No." Until then, out of concern for the parishioners, we gently and repeatedly made contact.

The Spirit Intervenes

An example might paint the picture. I remember Fr. Bob, who had a huge parish with three thousand families. He didn't arrive at the evening information session he had promised to attend. The next morning, I called: "Fr. Bob, how are you doing?" "Oh, good, Tom," he replied. "Gee, I missed you last night. You weren't there with your people to hear about RENEW." "Oh, that was last night?" "Bob, don't worry we have another one a week from now, not too far from you. We have these all over the archdiocese. So you can get to that one with your people." "Okay, Tom."

This went on for about seven calls. He never said, "No, we're not going to be involved." The matter still remained open ended.

After months of information sessions, we came to the last day. A man from Fr. Bob's parish called me, not realizing what had been happening. He asked, "Father, could I come to the information session this evening?" "Well, it is located quite far from you. Do you think you can do that?" "I'll be there tonight." I replied, "Only if you go to Fr. Bob, and he tells you that you can represent the parish."

When I arrived, my phone friend said, "I'm the man who called you. Fr. Bob said I could represent our parish." The man became so enthused about RENEW, he went home, talked to Fr. Bob, and signed up the parish. This resulted in three hundred people sharing faith and growing spiritually in RENEW small communities. That night at the information session, he had told me, "Father, I'm dying, and I won't live to see RENEW actually happen." But three hundred people became involved because of that one man. That's the kind of stories we heard. So many beautiful things were going on. Word was spreading. Momentum was building. Eventually, two hundred out of two hundred fifty parishes signed up. The archdiocese had never seen anything like it.

Later, as RENEW started to spread across the country, I'd explain the dynamic of parish sign-up to a bishop in this manner. "Bishop, the first twenty percent of your pastors are zealous go-getters. They'll quickly move forward and become involved. The next fifty percent are good priests, but they lack confidence in taking on a substantial project. They don't know what to do or how to go about it. When give them all kinds of help—training, good materials, and pastoral assistance—they begin to believe that it can't go wrong. How could they do anything but say yes? We are up to seventy percent now. The next twenty percent are hearing about it on golf courses, or wherever. Other pastors are all talking about RENEW. As the momentum builds, more pastors jump on board. This leaves the last ten percent who won't get on board because they are always contrary. Whatever the diocese wants, they go the other way." The bishop would then laugh and say, "You just described my diocese."

RENEW Parish Outreaches

To accomplish total involvement of parishioners, we chose four methods of outreach to saturate parishes with the weekly themes of RENEW:

- Sunday liturgy
- large-group activities
- meditation booklets for personal reflection, and
- small faith-sharing groups.

All four methods had considerable impact in the Newark RENEW experience. The spiritual theme emphasized at Sunday liturgy would be carried on throughout each week in personal meditative reflections, in large group prayer services and activities, and in the many small faith-sharing groups meeting throughout the parish. Other normal activities would continue, but organizers would try to connect them with the RENEW themes as best as possible. We encouraged parishes to give a priority to RENEW since all ministries and parish activities would benefit from the basic RENEW experience.

The small-group faith sharing had a strong appeal to people and sometimes overshadowed the benefits that RENEW provided in its other outreaches. It was providential that the faith-sharing small groups were part of this larger overall parish effort. For some, at that point in time, an isolated promotion of small groups might have produced a negative reaction because of its unfamiliarity and newness. Being part of the larger and accepted parish project gave the small groups an opportunity to prove their value and enable them, in many instances, to develop into strong small communities.

Materials

One can only imagine what it was like to develop these four outreaches. Creating meditation booklets, worship aids, and materials for small-group meetings, large-group activities, for each of six weeks over five seasons meant thirty sets of materials for each outreach.

The immediate task was the development of materials in sufficient time for Season I. This had to take place in the year preceding Season I, along with the sign-up of parishes, the many training sessions, publicity, and all the other required preparation steps. The two full-time persons working on RENEW was expanded to include Sue Elsessor, who was recommended by Fr. Phil Murnion, who then served on a bishops' committee on pastoral life. Sue's focus would be the development of materials. In all, it turned out that two hundred volunteer writers would be involved in the project.

Sue suggested the name RENEW for our three-year process. I was in favor of *Kairos*, a Greek word that meant, "Now is the appropriate time." When I mentioned this to Archbishop Gerety he immediately said, "Give it an English name." I had thought RENEW sounded like a laundry detergent. But after a few weeks I gave in to the providential choice of RENEW. The choice of that name—always in caps—proved to be more helpful than we would ever have imagined.

We were fortunate to have two expert liturgists, Fr. Charles Guzmer and Fr. Richard Groncki, assisting us throughout the whole liturgical process of RENEW. Fr. Pat Donohue, an archdiocesan parish priest, wrote simple and very popular small-community faith-sharing materials over several seasons. All three of these priests were invaluable.

Piloting of Materials

In every aspect, RENEW was to be pastorally grounded. We would not use materials if we weren't confident they would fly well with people in the parishes. We chose three particular parishes to officially pilot the small-group materials: St. Andrew in Westwood as the suburban parish, Our Lady of the Valley in Orange as a parish situated between the inner city and the suburbs St. Bridget in Newark as the inner-city parish. St. Bridget's had a good number of Filipino people in addition to Hispanics and African-Americans. Other parishes took the initiative to pilot RENEW and share their findings.

The results of the piloting threatened our printing timelines. Piloting showed that some writers had included personal agendas. On the other hand, the responses revealed that the sessions that focused on Scripture were most popular—but not every session included Scripture. That would be changed, and a scriptural emphasis would be one of the main reasons for RENEW's success in Newark and continued growth beyond. From our piloting it was obvious that a major overhaul was needed in the one week before we went to print.

I began the week by locking myself in my rectory room and spending the day hammering out a small-community option for Season I. It was simple and direct, down to earth, and, from a pastoral perspective, spoke to where people were. That night I raced up to see Fr. Ed Ciuba, a scripture scholar and the rector of Immaculate Conception Seminary, asking him to check out the scriptural content. "Is it sound? Are the Scriptures being used properly?" Fortunately that option met the need, and, in fact, became very popular.

This process continued for the rest of the week, and the material got to the printer on time.

Keeping materials rather simple and easily understood was particularly important. Adult faith formation had not nearly reached the point where it is today. Once again, a tremendous strength of RENEW is that it was created and developed by people well-grounded in successful parish experience.

One of the first dioceses outside Newark to become involved with RENEW at first recoiled at the simplicity of the materials. We were told that adult faith formation in that diocese had already progressed beyond what RENEW was offering. Our response was that adult educational programs were usually drawing a comparatively small percentage of parishioners. The RENEW approaches and materials would extend that number of involved people greatly. We were confident we could easily triple, or more, the number of people who were involved. With some persuasion, the diocese went along with what we proposed. Two years later, I ran into a leader from that diocese who was gushing about the large numbers of people who had become involved in RENEW. After a moment's reflection, the woman stated, "Your materials are very simple, aren't they?" Materials were on target for the needs of the time.

Inclusivity called for the full involvement of our large Hispanic community from the beginning. This was not to be a hand-me-down—simply translated from English with no regard for cultural differences—as were so many other things produced at that time for Hispanics. Fr. Tom Ivory volunteered Dr. Maria Garcia from his staff. She did a tremendous job with both the materials and all Spanish training. From its onset, RENEW was both Spanish and English.

Special efforts were also made to provide RENEW materials in the language of each of our ethnic communities. Our local African-American leaders asked for and helped to prepare materials for our African-American community. We provided Braille materials for the visually impaired and offered assistance for the hearing impaired. Over the years, RENEW was to be adapted to many different cultures and provide materials in forty-five languages.

A man teaching religious education at Our Lady of the Valley in Orange, New Jersey, reported, "I'm using the RENEW materials for my sophomore class, and they've been the best classes I've ever had." From Season II on, materials for youth would be essential parts of RENEW.

RENEW's Three-Prong Approach

Parish experience contributed to the realization that training and formation would have to be conducted for parishioners who would be implementing the RENEW process. It would not be enough to produce and provide materials, no matter how fine they were. Pastoral and theologically sound materials, excellent training, and continued pastoral contact with parish leaders would come together in what we've called RENEW's three-prong approach. This approach was vital for Newark's success and would also distinguish RENEW in years to come from many other efforts that solely, or almost totally, relied on providing materials.

Parish Training

A core community composed of lay parishioners—people who "knew how to get things done"—was needed within each parish. A good coordinator, who kept things moving, would be critical.

I firmly believed this kind of natural talent existed in every one of our parishes. Finding this talent called for looking beyond those who might readily volunteer or who were already involved. This is something that we were preaching and proclaiming widely. Talent is there. We need to look for and unearth gifted people in our parishes.

While the pastor was the leader of the project, he did not have to be involved in all the required tasks. The pastor's strong support and enthusiastic leadership would speak clearly to the entire parish. The core community would take on great responsibility and free the pastor for his rightful role as spiritual leader of the parish community.

In planning the training, one of the first steps I took was to visit Fr. Jack McDermott of Presentation Parish in Upper Saddle River. Jack made an immediate contribution. He said, "Something special happens when you take people away for an overnight experience. A bonding occurs and creative juices are released that are invaluable." I was grateful for the reminder. We both knew how true that experience was. Proposing an overnight for the pastor and key parishioners for every parish in the archdiocese proved to be magic.

That contribution was only one of many that Jack would make throughout the course of RENEW. Not only was he my best friend and golfing companion, he was also a very insightful and pastoral person. Jack had more ideas on how to run a good parish than you could imagine. His rich pastoral experience made him a valuable advisor over the course of time. As someone to bounce ideas off and someone to evaluate whether something would fly with parishioners, none better could be found than Jack.

As we signed up parishes, pastors were aware that their commitment would involve going away with their parishioners for this initial training. In light of that, it is remarkable that two hundred pastors made the commitment while still not completely understanding all that was to come about with RENEW. A beautiful bonding occurred between priests and parishioners during the course of this training.

The involvement of priests in that initial core community training continued throughout the follow-up training and also through the following seasons. I can remember being at a training session on a Sunday afternoon midway through the three years of RENEW in a large jam-packed auditorium, when a visiting priest from outside the diocese remarked how unbelievable it was to him that so many priests were deeply involved.

We believed it was advisable to have a trainer come in from outside the archdiocese. For this role, Tom Ivory, our RENEW co-founder, made a major contribution in suggesting Fr. Cassian Yuhaus, a very talented Passionist priest, who worked with the Center for Applied Research in the Apostolate. Tom and I interviewed Cassian—or, I should say, he interviewed us. He wanted to make sure that RENEW was well thought through. We all came to a point of agreement, and Fr. Yuhaus proved to be an ideal choice.

Fourteen parish training sessions were held, running each weekend January through March. As luck would have it, on the day of our first training, Friday, January 13, 1978, it snowed heavily. To our delight and amazement, people came trudging in with boots and covered with snow. Some had traveled by train from Hoboken to the station at the edge of the campus of the College of St. Elizabeth in Convent Station. Every parish was present and accounted for.

Best of all, Cassian was brilliant. He mesmerized everyone, painting a broad picture of all that was happening in the world at our point in history. Changes of a kind that usually took hundreds of years to evolve were happening in a decade or two. This had never occurred before. The Catholic Church, more than any other major institution, was taking leadership in this through Vatican II, and through RENEW, this magnificent process would bring all the Church's progress to flourish within the parishes of the Archdiocese of Newark. People were ready to rush out and change the world.

Two interesting things happened on the concluding Saturday of that first overnight. One was feedback given to me by a man who set up

Barnes & Noble stores throughout the country. He said, "Father, you've got to cut out some of the theological jargon in explaining RENEW. Talk in simple, straightforward language that all parishioners can readily understand." That night I went home and rewrote our RENEW brochures and information pieces. What a gift that man had been to us.

Another immediate follow-through was with a pastor whom I'll call Fr. John. Seen by some as somewhat "crusty," Fr. John could at times put people off with a sarcastic remark. At heart he was truly a great and zealous priest. During the overnight experience, Fr. John was deeply moved and convinced that RENEW would transform him and his parish.

The first parish step was to form the parish's core community. Fr. John couldn't wait. He invited all those who had gone to the training to return immediately to the rectory. They had to start working right away. Even though the core community was to be of such importance, and potential members should be visited personally, he felt that contact had to be made that night. He and the group reviewed the entire list of parishioners and singled out eight additional people. John got on the phone and personally called each one. Every person was flabbergasted. The pastor was so excited. Everyone said yes. His core community was formed, and people could go home.

John then sent out a letter to every parishioner. He told them RENEW was what he had been waiting for. It would be the greatest thing in the history of the parish. With enthusiastic leadership like that, RENEW was sure to be a magnificent experience for the parish. Fr. John and I became good friends. I admired him immensely.

Cathy and I would carefully observe participants at the training sessions and evaluate the reactions of all the parishes attending. The response of parishioners was always very positive. In some instances, we noted pastors being less involved. We gave those parishes particular attention through continued contact.

We took very seriously the need to pastor the RENEW effort. Wherever help was needed, we were ready to be out on location in the parish. An example of our pastoring occurred during a blizzard. What would happen to those dozen or more parishes coming to that training?

Would they be lost? Would they drop out? How could we respond to this emergency?

Shoveling snow outside St. Antoninus Rectory, I spotted a bus coming along. Remembering that all of my RENEW materials were at the office, I hopped on the bus as a lone rider to downtown Newark. Another bus appeared in the swirling snow and it got me to our office at 300 Broadway to obtain the names and telephone numbers of all the people who were supposed to be at that training.

Back at the parish, I placed a call to each of the snowbound pastors who was trapped in his rectory and arranged a new date for training. Snow time provided a good opportunity for connecting through phone calls. This kind of pastoring was being carried out while sign-up of parishes and training were simultaneously going on.

The Wheel of Responsibilities

During the course of the overnight training, Cassian made still another valuable contribution. We had been talking about the various responsibilities that would have to be undertaken by the core community and the many volunteers that they would need to engage to prepare for RENEW. Cassian suggested the following visual: the Wheel of Responsibilities that would prepare parishes and launch them for success.

Materials were developed spelling out the responsibility of each of the committees on the wheel. For me personally (as an ENFP on the Myers-Briggs grid), spelling things out in detail was a maddening experience. Such clear and precise direction left little room for failure.

Our spring training sessions also helped parishes in meeting their different ministerial responsibilities. Parishioners appreciated the amount of assistance they were receiving.

The development of small groups was new to many and required special attention. Participants were invited to report "good news" stories coming from their ministerial work. People would share beautiful stories that were happening in their parish RENEW work. The excitement was infectious. There was a growing sense of anticipation for the fall.

Involvement of Parishioners

A major challenge was how to involve large numbers of parishioners in RENEW small groups.

Encouraging small-group participation was not to be left to a parish bulletin notice or to an announcement at Sunday Mass. If we were to set a climate throughout the archdiocese and have a truly major spiritual renewal occur, we would have to involve massive numbers of people, far greater than the usual level of participation. Some say, "You shouldn't worry about numbers. Quality is what counts." Of course quality is necessary, but we were convinced the quality of faith sharing would be outstanding and provide a true growth experience for people involved. If this was to be so, then what would be wrong in wanting to involve great numbers of people in that quality experience? It doesn't have to be "either/or," quality or numbers. Axioms like that stifle parish vitality. Quality and great numbers together are ideal.

Three main avenues of signing up people were Sign-Up Sunday, the telephone campaign, and home visits. To do that we went back to my experience in Our Lady of Mercy, where we had worked with all three outreaches to engage people in small groups. I remember how those efforts brought three hundred people into small groups. When reporting this to our community coordinator, Gary Garofalo, he responded to those of us involved in recruitment, "That's not nearly good enough.

Why don't you go out and get more?" We wound up with six hundred. The effort of priests and parishioners working together was the ticket.

Sign-Up Sunday

The approach, originally used at Our Lady of Mercy, and now being applied to RENEW, called for RENEW small-group registration at all Sunday Masses shortly before Season I. A critical aspect of Sign-Up Sunday would be the selection of the best possible speaker. Ideally the speaker would be credible to a wide range of parishioners and have outstanding motivational ability.

To strengthen our input on how to best motivate people to make commitments, I went to Washington, D.C., and visited a woman named Sarah Lee Farmer. Sarah Lee headed an organization that promoted volunteerism. She had been working at this for thirty-five years and explained the three main reasons why people stepped forward to become involved.

- They want to meet new people.
- They want to better themselves.
- They want to change the world.

The benefits of each made sense, but we chose a fourth motivational factor and moved it to number one: "People want to know and love God better." As we expected, the greatest number of people participating came from Sign-Up Sunday. When it came to other dioceses taking up RENEW, parishes that followed our more complete instructions for Sign-Up Sunday did extremely well.

Telephone Campaign

Dolly Donahue and I developed a telephone campaign for committing people to RENEW small groups. Parishes were encouraged to place motivating calls to both active and inactive parishioners.

One of these calls was made by Sr. Eileen Dumshaw, S.S.J., of Our Lady of the Valley in Orange. She was understandably a bit nervous about the first call and decided to choose a good prospect, one that would be easy. She called a woman whose children always came to religious education class. Fortunately, the woman said she would join a

RENEW small group. She went on to say, "How did you choose to call me? How did you know? I haven't been to church in years. Thank you for this call. It's time for me to get back."

Home Visits

A third approach for small-group sign ups was to conduct home visits. Home visits would register a smaller number of participants but would bring the highest percentage of positive responses per contact. The more personal the appeal, the better the response.

There was an electrician in Westwood who didn't have any experience with "door-to-door selling." He'd never done anything like that, but he did manage to sign up one hundred twenty people for RENEW small communities in his parish. When asked "How do you approach it?" he responded: "When I'm walking toward the house, I pray that God will give me the right words to say, and while ringing the bell I pray they'll respond 'yes.'" Each person had his or her own beautiful spiritual approach. Everything had that spiritual tone to it.

A few years later, when I was giving a presentation at my home parish at St. Elizabeth in Avon, there was a retired man who sat in silence. I was surprised to hear that this gentleman had signed up one hundred seventeen people by going door-to-door, inviting them to join a small group. Feedback from parishioners always provided such exciting news, and we saw the Spirit of God working in them.

A Million-Dollar Idea

Years of parish experience had led me to the realization that, by and large, appeals made for parish involvement were done very poorly. Whether it was timidity or following "the same old, same old" ways, parishes usually did not make strong enough efforts to involve people, rarely trying anything other than Sunday morning announcements and bulletins.

At our training sessions, we presented the following scenario, which would make all the difference. We came to call it "a million-dollar idea" that would change parish life. It would result in large numbers of people being involved in RENEW.

1. The parish bulletin is the weakest way to elicit a volunteer response. I would explain: "If there are any parish secretaries here who work on the parish bulletin, please don't take offense. One vicar-general told me, 'I'm going to get married, announce it in the bulletin, and no one will know.'" Everybody would laugh, because it's true.

2. A better approach, still not good enough, is an announcement made at Mass.

3. Still better is to send a letter out to every parishioner. Particularly if the letter comes from the pastor, it will get attention. It may not draw any immediate response, but it will create a good climate for other contacts.

4. Making telephone calls is better yet. A parish telephone campaign brought good results. The contents of a call made to recruit members of the core committee should be limited. Instead of trying to make a direct appeal over the phone, use the call to set up a personal meeting. "If you have some time Sunday afternoon, I'd love to stop by for a brief chat. I want to share an idea with you." If that call comes from the pastor when we are looking for someone for a key position, it will be particularly effective.

5. The most favorable approach is always a personal contact. A person-to-person meeting always affords the best opportunity to read the person to get a sense of how you might want to approach your appeal and to provide motivation.

In the case of RENEW, it meant conveying an event was about to occur that might be the most significant thing in the parish's history. RENEW would be totally spiritual and exciting. It would not be another appeal for funds. It would be a good experience for them, and they would be doing something very valuable. If presented well, the personal approach will flatter the person, rather than make him or her feel put upon.

This training took place before the digital age, but the principle of "the more personal the appeal, the greater the rate of success" still applies.

Paying careful attention to this schema greatly benefited RENEW. People were spiritually motivated to overcome their fears. Using the best of these approaches would change parish life and help make vital evangelization come about.

Priest Involvement

In preparation for Season I, we held large gatherings of priests in the archdiocese to help them realize how they could best become involved so the parish could have a successful RENEW experience.

A variety of speakers and approaches were used that would appeal to priests of varying pastoral convictions so that across the board all could see that this RENEW process would be helpful to them. We made a special appeal to invite priests to join a RENEW small group in their parishes.

Between the seasons of RENEW in Newark, priest meetings continued. Priests had the opportunity to share their experiences from the previous seasons and prepare for the upcoming season. It is no wonder that years later when a priest from a southern diocese was asked to be diocesan coordinator of RENEW, he decided to test the waters of original RENEW in Newark. He randomly chose the names of six Newark priests from the *Official Catholic Directory* and called them. He asked, "Was RENEW really as good as I'm being told?" Each priest told him it was the best thing that had ever happened in Newark.

Momentum Building

Through the spring, summer, and fall of 1978, momentum continued to build. The archdiocesan paper, *The Catholic Advocate*, continued reporting major stories of RENEW's progress. One week, for example, *The Catholic Advocate* reported on a training session, the next week on an upcoming event, the next week an interview—all keeping RENEW in the public eye. Secular daily papers published stories; local shopping newspapers also were used to bring the message home.

Fr. John E. O'Brien, a respected historian at Seton Hall University and a successful pastor, became a full-time staff person with RENEW. His task was to keep a strong parish focus on the spiritual nature of RENEW. He went about giving talks and evening retreats for parishes and for parish core communities.

In the spring, preparation began for the small-group leader training that would be held in September. Parishes were instructed to approach people no later than June and ask them to be small-group leaders. This early commitment assured a good response from prospective leaders. Asking someone to accept a responsibility several months ahead is far better than approaching him or her shortly before the activity involved.

Pastoring on our part continued. In one instance, a call came from Fr. Ed Oehling from St. James in Springfield who indicated his team had been hoping to get three hundred people in small communities. Accordingly, they had sent out thirty letters to some of the best people in their parish. Not one indicated a willingness to be a RENEW small-community leader. I assured Ed that things would be all right. I recalled our training session and reviewed with him the various approaches, starting with the weakest, the parish bulletin. His letter had been a midlevel approach. I reminded him that in enlisting small group leaders a very personal contact would be the best approach. Fr. Ed called back two weeks later. "Tom, don't worry about us. We have our thirty leaders."

The Home Stretch

In the meantime, our office was being flooded with orders for RENEW materials, including liturgy materials, large-group activities, meditation booklets, and small-group options. We had urged the parishes to order twice as many faith-sharing books as they thought would be necessary for the parish. Nevertheless, a good number of parishes had to come back to us for many more.

In September, small-group leader training was held almost nightly in a couple dozen locations throughout the archdiocese. At those meetings, we shared the needed skills for one to be a good facilitator in encouraging faith sharing. Basic group-dynamic skills were shared and practiced. Above all, the meetings were to be centered on faith sharing. RENEW leaders were to facilitate good sharing that would lead to concrete actions, actions that would not only help participants' personal spiritual lives but also stress service to others. We knew from experience that the small-group meetings would be extremely positive.

To our delight, many continued meeting after each season. Some still continue thirty years later. Some groups held family picnics and other gatherings as the members bonded. They were truly growing from small groups to small communities, something that we would emphasize more and more as the seasons continued.

Final Alert

No imaginable stone was left unturned. The week before Season I, I went to a park in South Orange and sat on a bench to reflect. What more should still be done? Was there anything to be strengthened? I decided to send out a fax to the parishioners involved with coordinating the small-group leaders. With all that had been said in our training, they were asked to keep two cardinal rules: 1. They were to foster and encourage faith sharing, not be teachers. 2. They were to keep the group focused, not allowing it to stray from the topic.

Obviously much preparation had taken place, but more important than all human effort was the fact that God wanted to touch human hearts. After all was said and done, RENEW was God's work.

CHAPTER 6

Season I

RENEW Blossoms

How could we best provide an initial spark that would ignite the kind of excitement we expected in Season I? Even in our wildest dreams we could hardly have imagined the magnificent flame that would engulf the diocese.

Cathedral Kickoff

To launch Season I, "The Lord's Call," we held a large celebratory service at Sacred Heart Cathedral on a Sunday afternoon in late September 1978, one week before the startup. Archbishop Gerety presided and every parish was invited to bring its RENEW core community and other parishioners. Each parish created a banner and marched into the cathedral in procession. Drawing on my football interest, we called the service the RENEW Kickoff.

The city of Newark was still considered a dangerous place to visit or drive through. How would parishes react? Would suburban parishes come? Fortunately, the day was flooded with sunshine and a lively spirit of jubilation. The cathedral was packed with one thousand six hundred people. Seldom had it been so crowded. A wonderful spirit prevailed and people went home spreading a buzz of excitement throughout the archdiocese.

Perhaps I was the only distracted person in the cathedral. The Giants were playing, and I had resisted wearing an earplug with a transistor.

But who was winning the game? Speaking of winning, one thing was certain. RENEW was already a colossal success.

The next day Archbishop Gerety called me in for a visit. Like everyone, he was thoroughly enthused. Looking for ideas, he wondered aloud how we could build upon it. "Let's start thinking about a renewal for priests," I responded. Along with the input of many other voices, the archdiocese explored the possibilities of the *Emmaus Program for Priests* and the *Ministry to Priests Program*. Eventually, the archdiocese had a very successful *Ministry to Priests* program.

RENEW Themes Resonate

The RENEW themes of Season I struck home immediately and had a stirring impact. The first week of Season I presented to many participants a different approach to spirituality. Reflecting on the gospel account of God sustaining the lilies of the field and the birds of the air, and numbering the hairs on our heads, helped people realize how deep and intimate was God's love for us. It counteracted the experience of many who had been raised with a great fear of God. Seeing themselves as God's wonderful creation, they began to take greater ownership of their own goodness and value. The word of God was offering badly needed personal affirmation. It brought home that God created all of us with equal dignity, a point that had meaningful impact as the RENEW process spread to varying cultures throughout the world.

The positive themes and tone of Season I proved to be very uplifting. People realized and appreciated that they were part of a purely spiritual experience with no secondary strings attached. Archdiocesan morale was at an all-time high.

Surprised Priests

Around the second week of Season I, an archdiocesan gathering of priests was held in the auditorium at St. Philomena Parish in Livingston. I don't remember what the topic of the day was, but priests were coming up to me from all directions, bubbling with enthusiasm about what was going on with RENEW. They couldn't believe the number of people who had signed up and were participating in the RENEW small-group meetings. They had never seen numbers like this before, and the excitement of their people was infectious. I was thrilled to hear their reactions but was somewhat taken back by their surprise. I thought, "Wow, didn't you know this was going to work?" Some priests had apparently gone into RENEW with hesitation. But now they were clearly seeing the bonanza they had.

If there had been any doubts before, the vast majority of priests were now solidly on board and remained so throughout the entire RENEW process. These priests included men of all ages and pastoral ideologies. They were reaping the benefits of RENEW in many ways. Priests reported increased attendance at Sunday and daily Mass along with more people volunteering for a variety of parish ministries. Many priests shared that a number of people who had been away from the Church for twenty or thirty years had come back through the sacrament of reconciliation. When asked what had brought them back, they shared that it was their involvement in RENEW. This touched me the most.

About a year into RENEW a priest, who I thought would be one of the least enthused about RENEW, came running up to me at the cathedral. "Tom," he said, "I'm so pleased with RENEW. For one thing, our collections have really gone up." It was something I had been preaching strongly from the beginning. If we feed people spiritually, finances will take care of themselves.

A good barometer of the enduring impact of RENEW was that the same number of priests who attended the original RENEW Kickoff also attended a closing ceremony at the cathedral at the conclusion of Season V. Many other positive results were being reported.

Small Groups

RENEW small groups literally burst onto the scene. The fact that over forty thousand people were involved in RENEW small groups drew attention from everyone in the archdiocese. News started filtering out to people in other dioceses.

Small-group meetings were new to people at that time, but they liked the friendly and informal atmosphere. Most groups met in homes, which made people immediately comfortable. Inviting everybody in the group to participate was important. Many people were tired of being "talked at." Small-group participation was providing a breath of fresh air. Every participant was taken seriously and encouraged to share.

The small groups usually consisted of ten to twelve people, and the format of the meeting was simple. It began with opening prayer. A scripture passage was then proclaimed, followed by a reflection connecting that passage with the weekly theme. Questions provided in the RENEW booklets encouraged faith sharing and helped people decide on what concrete actions they could take to apply their faith to their daily lives.

It was amazing how quickly people opened up in sharing their faith experiences. The witnessing of personal, spiritual experiences deeply touched their lives. People were moved and motivated by the faith of other members, while at the same time they reflected on how God had been working in their own lives. A synergistic effect took place that raised the spiritual sights of everyone.

The Scriptures took on exciting new meaning for small-group participants. Catholic men and women who had not been familiar with Scripture were making a wonderful discovery, much like the early Christians. Going beyond following rules and carrying out required religious practices, they were developing a personal relationship with the Lord that invigorated their whole spiritual lives.

The ability to speak openly about Jesus, and to realize a more personal relationship with him, was expressed well by a RENEW small group in Jersey City. This particular group consisted of hardworking and rather rugged men who were unaccustomed to open displays of spirituality. One man recounted his experience in this way: "It was into the fourth meetin' before one of the guys in our group mentioned the name Jesus. Once that happened, you couldn't stop the guys from talking about Jesus." What a breakthrough it was for thousands of people to have a format that allowed them to take ownership of their faith and openly express their love for their Lord and Savior.

Hearing the witness of this man reminded me of an experience from my days in Park Ridge. Kathy, a high school girl, obtained permission from her principal to invite me to speak to her class at an all-girls Catholic school. The session quickly became an open forum with all kinds of questions that were surfacing in the 1960s. "Why shouldn't we live with our boyfriends before marriage?" was the hottest topic. I went on for some time with all kinds of psychological reasons why this might not best prepare them for choosing a suitable partner and getting into a good and lasting marriage. That approach was going nowhere fast.

Suddenly, I stopped and said, "I'd like to talk to you about Jesus for a few minutes." The girls listened with rapt attention. At the end of class the girls volunteered that no one had ever spoken to them like that about Jesus in their four years at the school. If true, how sad that seemed. Were we trying to help people lead good lives, keep the laws, and strive for perfection without sufficient motivation? How could we rise above other alluring and competitive voices in society without deeply experiencing God's love for us and responding with a very personal love for our Lord? We need the power of God's Spirit. How could we otherwise have a faith that so trusted in him that we would do things his way rather than being pulled in other directions?

Most RENEW participants had never owned easy-to-read translations of the Scriptures. But that was quickly remedied. People wanted their own copies of the New Testament so that they could reflect and pray over the course of the week and then bring the Scriptures to their small-group meetings. There was a boom in the purchase of Bibles throughout the archdiocese. One parish bought six hundred New Testaments and sold them all within a week. Opening the treasure of the Scriptures had infused new life and vitality into the spiritual lives of many people.

The basic needs of volunteers that Sarah Lee Farmer had expressed to us were certainly being met. People wanted to meet new friends, better themselves, and change the world. But, above all, people's hunger to get to know and love Jesus in a deeper way was being satisfied.

Getting to know Jesus personally was opening people to an appreciation and wonder at God's love for us, expressed in the Incarnation, and, through Jesus, they were discovering the fullness of God's love and the magnificent communal love of the Trinity.

For personal feedback, I needed to go no further than my weekend assignment in Presentation Parish, Upper Saddle River, New Jersey. I had learned much from the effectiveness of their pastoral outreaches.

These included the manner in which they welcomed newcomers, the way they involved people in lay ministries, and in the great number of weekend retreats they held. Now, with extraordinary effort, they had expanded their outreach to engage one thousand five hundred people in RENEW small groups. Their excitement was palpable.

People of all ages and backgrounds were attracted to the RENEW small groups. Becoming a member of a mixed group based on a mutually convenient time and place for meetings proved to be more popular than joining a neighborhood group. In one instance, a woman was shocked to arrive at her first meeting and find that her estranged neighbor whose back yard adjoined her own was in her group. Within two weeks, those women experienced a wonderful healing and began a new flourishing friendship. Broken relationships, families, and even parishes were reporting healing during Season I. When people were able to share their common love for Jesus and see the love of God in each other, their hearts were opened, and all kinds of tensions and strains began to disappear.

Not only were small-group participants benefiting, but they were also bringing their fervor to Sunday liturgy where they were building up the parish community through their outreach and hospitality toward others.

Cathy oversaw a thorough evaluation of Season I, and parishes overwhelmingly expressed extreme satisfaction with the RENEW small groups. It was interesting to see that small groups, once considered somewhat far out, were not only in the mainstream of parish life but were the "hottest item in town."

Liturgy

All across the archdiocese the weekly RENEW themes were being integrated into the Sunday liturgy. Parishes received rich materials that provided an introduction for each Sunday Mass, suggested penitential rites, homiletic materials, and prayers of the faithful, along with suggested music selections. Great care was taken to honor the *Lectionary* readings of the day.

Materials were helpful not only to the main celebrants and homilists but also to the liturgy planning committee, the liturgical ministers, and the whole participating community in whom Christ is present in the liturgy. In the first season of RENEW, the number of parishes having active liturgy planning committees more than doubled.

From the Sunday liturgy there emanated a spiritual atmosphere that would carry the weekly themes throughout the week in meditation booklets, bulletin inserts, and small groups. Even parishioners who had no involvement beyond Sunday Mass were being called to a special time of spiritual reflection and growth. RENEW was like a spiritual retreat for the entire parish.

As Season I progressed, we saw a weekly spiritual-life cycle being lived out in parishes. It is a cycle that our team had long promoted. The cycle flows as follows:

1. Parishioners were striving to live by Christian principles and values throughout the whole week, not just on Sundays.

2. The RENEW small groups were breaking open and reflecting on the word of God and connecting the word with life. They came to new insights that influenced their daily lives. Growth in appreciation of the Scriptures, in those small communities during the week, prepared them to be more attentive and receptive to the word as it was proclaimed and reflected upon in the Sunday liturgy.

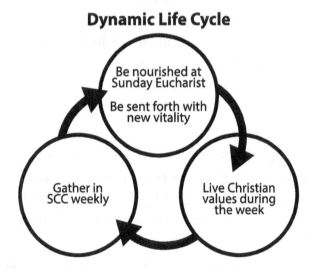

Dynamic Life Cycle

Be nourished at Sunday Eucharist

Be sent forth with new vitality

Gather in SCC weekly

Live Christian values during the week

3. Those participants then took all the aspects of life that had been reflected on in their small groups and brought them to the parish

eucharistic celebration. As they offered their lives at the sacrifice of the Mass, they entered into union with the Lord present in the eucharistic banquet. Strengthened by the Eucharist, they were sent forth to live Christ's mission wherever they were called—in their families, their community, the larger church, the workplace, and the social arena.

The third part of the cycle, the eucharistic celebration, is essential because "The liturgy is the summit toward which the activity of the Church is directed; at the same time it is the fountain from which all its power flows" *Constitution on the Sacred Liturgy*, 10 (*Sacrosanctum Concilium*).

RENEW was helping parishioners to experience the vitality of this dynamic life cycle in more conscious and helpful ways.

Meditation Booklets

Daily meditation books weren't as common in 1978 as they are today. Many parishes purchased a RENEW meditation booklet for every parishioner attending Sunday Mass. These booklets contained a daily meditation for the six-week period of the season. Immediately they were extremely popular. Parishioners were experiencing a specific call to daily prayer through the booklets. They also inspired further prayer efforts. One parish, for example, created a parish hotline that parishioners could call each morning to hear a spiritual thought to reflect on and carry out throughout the day.

A favorite story about the meditation booklets came from my former parish, St. Ann's. Sadie lived in a half-burned-out tenement house on South Sixth Street, the same street on which the Newark riots had broken out ten years earlier. That area was even more devastated in 1978.

Sadie, a single mom raising thirteen children, wasn't Catholic, but the sisters invited her to join a RENEW small group that met in the convent. In the first week, each member was given one of the RENEW daily meditation books. With all that was on her plate, how could Sadie possibly have time for meditation?

Two weeks later, Sadie came to the small-group meeting. Looking around at each member, she said, "I have to get up at 5:30 every morning to get in my meditation. How are you all doing with your meditation?" The sisters and other members started to blush with embarrassment.

When the sisters told me of the incident, I was pierced to the heart. Sadie lived on the poorest street, in the poorest neighborhood, in what was then the poorest city in the United States. Most people would pay little if any attention to her. But Sadie was getting up at 5:30 every morning for her meditation. Wow! Men don't cry, but I could feel tears welling up. How was I doing with meditation in my life? I went straight to church and made a holy hour before the Blessed Sacrament.

I was the beneficiary of many such moving stories about the faith and goodness of lay people. My brother priests could say the same. The impact of RENEW upon the lives of lay parishioners was challenging us to greater spiritual growth in our own lives.

Meditation booklets were showing up everywhere. They appeared in hospitals, nursing homes, in prisons, and on commuter buses and trains. Returning home from her work at Covenant House, a good friend, Sr. Cecilia King, C.S.J.P., reported seeing someone praying with the meditation book at midnight on a New York subway. RENEW was becoming part of everyday conversation.

Large Group

The large-group activity in Season I, and throughout the process, was the least talked about of RENEW's four main outreaches. People were accustomed to large-group parish activity as compared to the RENEW small groups that were creating so much excitement.

Nevertheless, many parishes put talented and creative people to work on developing the large-group aspect of RENEW. Large-group activities included talks given by special speakers, services held in church, activities in parish halls, and elaborate parish celebrations. One even involved a RENEW procession through the city of Hoboken with banners and displays. Many activities were done extremely well.

Because of the great amount of work that went into the large-group activities, they were usually limited to one or two a season. Many parishes worked closely with the RENEW small-group committee to have large-group activities that drew upon small-group participants to celebrate the seasonal theme of RENEW. Some of the most effective ones high-lighted the importance of family life and brought out whole families to participate. Others held large gatherings at the end of each season for small-group participants to celebrate and witness to the wonderful spiritual and supportive blessings that were happening in people's lives.

During Season I of RENEW, Hank Traverso, a parishioner at St. Philomena's in Livingston, joined a small group. Hank had not been able to find work as a design engineer for two years. During the sharing one evening, Hank revealed his predicament. He and his wife, Laura, had raised seven children, one of whom had been severely injured by a bicycle accident when she was a little girl. They were having diffi-cult times due to his unemployment. The others in the group listened sympathetically and prayed for Hank, but it wasn't until the large-group celebration that the answer to Hank's prayers came. That evening Hank recognized Paul Wasdyke, another parishioner, from a newspaper photo he had seen. Paul's company had worked on a new light bulb and Hank went up to Paul asking, "How is the light bulb coming along?"

The next week Hank received a phone call from Paul's company. Hank was hired as chief engineer to design the equipment to produce the new light bulbs. Such is the grace of God.

Coming Home

Starting with Season I, and going through the entire RENEW process, we estimated that at least three thousand people returned to Church and to the sacraments. One instance I remember fondly. After a small group I was visiting had finished their meeting, people moved into the dining room for a simple repast and conversation. Two people, who individually wanted to talk with me, hung back in the living room. Each had been away from the Church and sacraments for over thirty years. They wanted to come home. Both were extremely grateful to have their confessions heard and to receive the sacrament of reconciliation. The next morning I called their pastor and alerted him that two newly active parishioners would soon be approaching him. The priest was a good and zealous man and was encouraged to welcome these two new friends with open arms.

Instances such as this were happening frequently.

Growing While Pastoring

Our own RENEW team, while busy serving parishes throughout the archdiocese, took time for our own spiritual and communal growth. We could not call others to what we were not striving for ourselves.

Every Monday we took the entire morning to meet at the convent of our editor, Sr. Carol Heller, S.C., in Fair Lawn, gathering in a big, wonderful, and homey room. We started by sharing about how things had gone for us over the weekend. Cathy would share stories about her visits and observations of RENEW's connection to Sunday morning liturgies. Fr. John O'Brien filled us in on his nights of reflection. We shared stories about how the small communities were progressing. We would then take a good bit of time in reflection on a scripture passage and follow with prayer. Finally we would get to the business of the following week. No matter how frantic our work schedule was, it was imperative that prime time be given to the Lord. The spiritual tone and fervor that emanated from these meetings enriched us and influenced and impacted our contacts with parishes.

Pastoring RENEW parishes continued relentlessly. After a full day of RENEW activity at the office, every night we would head out, each visiting one or two small groups. While affording the opportunity to offer good pastoral ideas and assistance to the groups, these visits proved invaluable to us.

One such evening, while visiting a group in Paramus, I was taken aback by hearing the leader start by saying, "I haven't done any preparation for this meeting. I was just given the materials and told to lead the group tonight. What do you want to talk about?" You can imagine what happened in that meeting. It went in ten different directions at once. The parish had underestimated the number of people who would sign up for small groups and had sent an inadequate number of people for leader training.

This was in sharp contrast to a small group I visited later that evening whose leader was well prepared. From that point on, we doubled our efforts to have parishes send more people to training than they judged were needed. It was better to have fallback leaders than to be caught short. There was a constant process of planning, training, evaluation, and modification as needs arose. Pastoring continued to be as important as good materials and sound training.

In the midst of Season I activity, our team was busy preparing for Season II. We needed to prepare materials for Season II, training sessions for core communities and small-group leaders, and special sessions that would be held for priests. We were like the teacher trying to stay ahead of the class.

Looking Ahead to Season III

As a RENEW team we tended to live and breathe RENEW seven days a week while having fun in the process.

One Sunday evening, I visited Suzanne at her convent. We were engaged in a lively discussion about upcoming events when I said, "Suzanne, you have been working very hard with parish councils. Don't you think it might be time to focus on something new? Suppose you start centering on preparation for Season III? We both care strongly about the issue of justice, and you have a passion for justice work. What if we were able to move you into a position that has us really well prepared for Season III on justice?" Suzanne responded immediately to the idea. How would we go about this? How could we create a department on peace and justice under the Office of Pastoral Renewal?

It happened that shortly before, for various reasons, the archdiocese had closed its Justice Office. There was a vacancy that needed to be filled. We went to our administrative superior, Sr. Anastasia Hearne, S.S.J., and proposed that Suzanne fill that role and focus on preparing for Season III of RENEW. Anastasia and, in turn, Archbishop Gerety, were very agreeable to the idea, and we were off and running.

Suzanne did an amazing job. She spent the next year training forty-five lay volunteers who would be prepared to assist and be of service to an enormous number of new social concerns committees that would emerge from Season III. Suzanne developed a diocesan approach for a specific ministry that would serve our archdiocese extraordinarily well. It could still be held up as a ministerial model for all other ministries in dioceses across the country (Cf. chapter 8, "The Network of Forty-Five").

A St. Joseph, Oradell, Story

Previously, I mentioned that Fr. Mort Smith had witnessed at a priest gathering, urging his brothers to become involved in RENEW. Initially, however, Mort did not have that kind of fervor for this new process.

Back when we were signing up parishes for RENEW, I had decided that St. Joseph's in Oradell should be one of the first parishes to visit. They had a team ministry composed of Fr. Lew Papera, Fr. Richie Iaquinto, and Fr. Mort Smith. Mort was a personal friend, and I thought this would surely be an easy sign-up. However, what I presumed would be a piece of cake wasn't progressing well. After forty-five frustrating minutes, I said, "Mort, what is the resistance?" He replied, "So much is going on in this parish. We've already got everybody involved. We're just overloaded." I responded, "Mort, do you have any people who don't go to Mass on Sunday?" "Yes, of course we do, probably hundreds of people." I then said, "Why don't you just do RENEW for the uninvolved?"

Now that is a question we would ask and a proposal we would make as we visited dioceses across the country. "Do you have people who are not now involved?" Even for the parish where everything is going well, we would say, "Why not choose people who are not so involved and give them to us for your core community. Let us work with them." Fr. Mort and his team agreed to follow that advice. They tapped an uninvolved, fantastic coordinator and got six hundred largely uninvolved people into RENEW small communities—a huge success.

During Season I, Mort noticed the interest people were taking in Scripture. After the season, he announced he would hold a scripture class on a Tuesday afternoon at 1:30 p.m. in the parish hall. He optimistically set up twenty-five chairs. Over one hundred twenty-five people turned out. A hunger for the Scriptures had been created.

After Season I, the parish decided to invite all the small-community participants who might be free on a particular evening to meet in the parish hall. Of the six hundred participants in their small groups, four hundred ninety came out that evening. Nearly one hundred of them were young people. One after another, they got on their feet and witnessed to what wonderful things God was doing in their lives and about the value of the RENEW experience.

Ordinary people were being transformed. St. Joseph's was a parish where the priests knew their parishioners far better than most. And yet, as the priests sat through this three-hour meeting, they literally did not know a great number of the people who were giving witness. RENEW certainly had involved the uninvolved.

Twenty years later, Bishop Smith, in introducing *RENEW 2000* to his Trenton Diocese, stood before three hundred priests and lay people and shared the story of his conversion to the original RENEW.

Sparks Are Flying

We had completed only Season I of RENEW and yet letters and calls of inquiry were already pouring in from around the country. It was such a wonderfully hectic time. We were completely unable to answer such mail for the next two years. In time we would find that interest kept increasing dramatically. There was no time for looking back. The journey ahead and all its possibilities were exploding before us.

CHAPTER 7

Season II

Our Response

Parishioners approached Season II, "Our Response to the Lord's Call," with great anticipation. This was evident in the high enthusiasm of people coming to training. Cathy and I conducted thirty-two training sessions for small-group leaders in January 1979. It would be difficult to describe the joy and excitement of the large numbers that turned out. Buoyed with the success of Season I, we were ready to charge forward.

Parish Participation Soars

Many, as never before, were playing a significant role in church participation. They had carried out their leadership roles successfully—evidenced by their high spirit. The feedback of their wonderful stories would make a book in itself.

The kind of coordination that had taken place on an archdiocesan level during planning and preparation was now being seen in the parish experience of RENEW. Parishioners, religious, priests, and deacons were working closely together. RENEW's emphasis on spirituality had created a harmony that had seldom been seen.

One of the highlights in preparation for Season II was a workshop we held in coordination with the archdiocesan Liturgical Office. Fr. Joe Cunningham, from Brooklyn, was invited to give a workshop to assist lectors in the proclamation of the Word. More than nine hundred people turned out for his extremely effective workshop. Had any archdiocesan office conducted a similar workshop prior to the RENEW experience, the numbers would have been significantly lower. Our coordinated effort was making a valuable contribution toward enhanced liturgies.

Many of those in attendance were readers themselves. They, in turn, went home and passed on what they had learned in the workshop to all the readers in their parish. The resulting upgrade in the proclamation of the Word at the Sunday liturgy was immediately noticeable. I happened to be on the archdiocesan Liturgical Commission at the time, and it was remarkable to hear how every member of the commission was so taken up with what was transpiring. Not only were they exuberant about the way the Word was being proclaimed, but they also noted that people from the small groups were listening to the Scriptures with greater attention. The dynamic life cycle that we spoke of earlier was being lived out.

Conversion

Season II was extremely powerful and popular. It called for conversion in our lives, *metanoia*, and the change of heart that Pope Paul VI so strongly urged in his document on evangelization, *Evangelization in the Modern World* (*Evangelii Nuntiandi*).

People saw this season, in particular, as purely "spiritual." Our process had not yet fully come to the more holistic understanding of spirituality that would be forthcoming in the seasons on justice, discipleship, and evangelization.

Journeying through Season II proved to be spiritually exhilarating. The weekly themes flowed beautifully. They were based on the work of Bernard Lonergan, S.J. (1904-1984), a preeminent Canadian philosopher and theologian. Msgr. Dick Liddy, professor of Catholic Thought and Culture and director of the Center for Catholic Studies at Seton Hall University, had studied under Lonergan and is a respected authority on him. Dick, as a member of our ongoing RENEW development committee, directed us toward an article by Lonergan. His main points of conversion in that article became the backbone of our weekly themes:

Risk taking. We are unable to move forward if we are not willing to change. Giving up our comfort level and facing up to greater challenges requires risk taking.

Repentance. Repentance for our past sins and faults clears our minds and helps open our hearts to God's love.

God's overwhelming love. God loves us totally just as we are. Even more than what God has done for us, God's very nature of goodness and love is compellingly attractive.

Responding to God's love. We are called to give ourselves wholeheartedly to God. Will we say Mary's fiat, "Yes! I want to give myself without reservation, holding nothing back"?

Openness to the Holy Spirit. With no blockage left in us, God's Holy Spirit can infuse our whole being and enable us to do our Lord's will. We now find new energy, joy, and enthusiasm.

Ongoing conversion. Being human, we are very prone to weakness but we will always want to come back to that wonderful realization of God's love and say our total "Yes" once again.

Experiencing the conversion cycle helps us realize that perhaps as individuals, and even as a church community, we may not have been living at full strength. You might say we have been created to operate on six cylinders and have been struggling on two or four. By God's grace we are enabled to be spiritually alive to the fullest.

Many people felt a profound desire to share their personal growth experiences. A good number of parishes held services where people could publicly express their wonderful change of heart in commitment to the Lord. Other parishes used other creative means for people to express their intention to live in a way that exemplified Mary's fiat. Great numbers of people had been deeply moved by the conversion journey of Season II.

So many agendas can cloud the good news of Jesus and the mission of the Church. God's grace working through the RENEW process had firmly established the archdiocese as centered on spirituality.

Publications

Good news was certainly traveling fast. As early as Season II, I received a call from a group of priests in Rhode Island asking if I could come up and share with them about RENEW. On the flight to Providence, I was pinching myself to see if this was real. Could it be that people as far away as Rhode Island might actually be thinking of doing RENEW? Little did I know there would be countless more RENEW trips to far more distant places.

As inquiries continued to pour in, it became obvious that we were ill equipped to respond. If this need to share were to be met, our publications from a local printer wouldn't be adequate. The question of putting everything in published form was being raised.

Bob Heyer, a personal friend, was chief editor at Paulist Press. While RENEW was still in the planning stages, he saw great value in our project and was urging that the materials be published.

This presented a great dilemma for me. We had already rejected ideas that tended toward commercialism. At the very first training for Season I, a man had proposed to undertake the production of RENEW hats, pins, Frisbees, boomerangs—you name it. In no way did we want to compromise the focus that RENEW was about spiritual renewal and not about money.

On the other side of the dilemma was the reality that we were not equipped, with our publication schedule, to respond to interested people across the country. And so it was that I found myself in the Paulist office in New York signing a contract. I'll never forget driving home on the New Jersey Turnpike with many conflicted feelings. "What did I just do? Was this a terrible mistake?" In truth, what other way could we go?

Talk about being overwhelmed. While still pastoring Season II, we were also preparing training and materials for Season III, trying to raise money for a film connected to Season V, and we were going to be editing Seasons I and II in preparation for publication. Somehow, with God's grace, it all came together.

Preparing for Season III

Staying one step ahead of the class meant that the weekly themes for Season III had to be determined and materials prepared. We decided on a trip to Washington to visit Fr. Peter Henriot, S.J., and Fr. John Haughey, S.J. Both had backgrounds of strong spirituality and deep concern for justice, which was to be the theme for Season III.

Our first visit was to the Center of Concern where Fr. Henriot made an extremely valuable suggestion: If you're going to change people's attitudes and actions to conform more to the Gospel, you have to reach them on a feeling level. "Help people," he suggested, "to recall a time in their life when they have been treated unfairly. Whether it was a large or a small matter isn't the point. The fact that they remember it indicates that it troubled them. From that, help them to reflect on people who are always being treated unfairly because of their race, social background, or other reasons. They will then be more easily moved to take concerned action." This approach fit nicely with our desire to engage people where they were. We weren't interested in providing a righteous, shock treatment.

John Haughey's comments built upon this previous suggestion. You don't want to stop with charitable outreach. To be about the work of justice you have to get to root causes and work for systemic change. Understanding how whole social systems can treat people unfairly would be a new awakening for many. They could then consider concrete actions in an attempt to change these systems. Sometimes opportunities for these actions exist right within the framework of our everyday lives.

On the way back from Washington, building on the advice we received, we wrote down specific themes for each of the six weeks. The themes of Season II and III flowed progressively in beautiful fashion.

Enthusiastic Reactions Continue

Two small examples reflect the incredible diocesan climate. One morning, as I was about to take a flight from Newark airport, a nineteen-year-old man spotted my clerical collar and approached me. "Father," he said, "do you know about RENEW?" I responded that I was aware of it. "Well," he continued with great enthusiasm, "I discovered Jesus in RENEW."

The fact that this young man had no realization that I'd had any connection with RENEW, and approached me in a crowd to share his excitement with me, was very meaningful. It reflected the widespread enthusiasm for RENEW.

That memorable morning continued. The man sitting next to me on the plane struck up a conversation. Again, he didn't know I had any connection with RENEW. He started telling me about the wonderful things that were happening with RENEW in his parish. He said, "Father, every parish in the country must be doing RENEW." He simply presumed this because all the parishes north, south, east, and west of his parish, Corpus Christi in Hasbrouck Heights, were doing RENEW. The atmosphere and climate of spiritual renewal throughout the archdiocese that we originally dreamed of was definitely occurring.

Beyond Newark

In 1979, shortly after Season II ended, I found myself sitting in the Milwaukee Pastoral Center on my birthday, June 12. Can you believe this? There I was sitting with the archbishop and diocesan leaders sharing about RENEW in a large Midwest diocese. It was a long way from my inner-city parish in Newark. The meeting concluded with a consensus that enabled Archbishop Rembert Weakland, O.S.B., to come to a decision: Milwaukee would initiate RENEW.

Upon leaving the building, I walked along Lake Michigan on that beautiful sunny afternoon. Scores of sailboats dotted the lake. The sky was clear but I was walking on clouds. I boarded the plane but probably could have flown home without a plane. A diocese outside of Newark was going to do RENEW. This called for a celebration, a glass of wine and two bags of honey-roasted peanuts.

CHAPTER 8

Season III

Empowerment by the Spirit

There was a span of nearly seven months between Seasons II and III. Would all sense of continuity and momentum be lost? There was no history that would allow us to assume people would automatically stay on board over the whole period of three years.

Maintaining Momentum

To address this concern, Season III, "Empowerment by the Spirit to Act Justly," and each season were treated as fresh and new. A large meeting of RENEW coordinators was held in June to help them lay out plans to utilize the summertime for a strong start in the fall. Trainings for parish RENEW teams and small-community leaders in September took on a new look each season, creating a specially designed ambiance in new locations. Re-sign-up cards had been provided for small-group members at the end of each season. Full-fledged parish sign-up methods were also used as they had been at the beginning of Season I. The process was not allowed to become stagnant. Amazingly, with these approaches the numbers of participants held up for all five seasons.

Approach to Justice

The first two seasons of RENEW had been a fantastic spiritual experience. Would the wheels come off this smoothly moving spiritual renewal process with the introduction of the topic of justice? Spiritual comfort zones might be rudely jolted when we came to areas where there are conflicting opinions and strongly held positions.

But there could be no turning back. Infinitely more important than orchestrating an uplifting archdiocesan experience was presenting a full and honest picture of spirituality. We made every effort to help people understand that acting to change unjust situations or systems is an integral part of Christian spirituality. Their accustomed notion of spirituality was being expanded. Previously, they may not have considered certain areas as being a part of their faith lives.

People deeply concerned about justice and social issues at the time frequently made extremely strong statements. Documents of that nature often took on a very self-righteous tone that, no doubt, gratified the producers but were very divisive. You might call it the shock treatment.

Diocesan offices for peace and justice were not immune to this approach. Unfortunately, neither had I been immune in the area of racial equality. A homily I gave at Our Lady of Mercy in Park Ridge would exemplify this. I spoke about how wonderful it was at the time that some people were climbing over the Berlin Wall, digging tunnels under it, and creating holes in the wall to break through to freedom. I then announced that there was one wall that no one ever got over, under, or through. It was the wall that surrounded Park Ridge and kept out black people. After Mass, some parishioners formed a line to congratulate me while others passed by loudly saying some pretty strong words not fit to print. The homily made me feel good and forthright, but it had been very divisive for the parish. The shock treatment would not be the approach for RENEW.

Fortunately, other practices at Our Lady of Mercy had proved far more fruitful. Through the Christian Family Movement and the Young Christian Students, people were accepted where they were and helped to grow in a natural way, integrating the gospel message for social matters in their attitudes and actions. Magnificent changes happened in people's lives and for the benefit of those in need. This gradual, but far more effective, means would be the way of RENEW. We would take people where they were and help them develop a fuller understanding of their faith and spirituality.

Special Preparation

Fr. Marvin Mottet proved to be the perfect person to engage for Season III preparation. I had known him from our Young Christian Student days in 1963 when he was a parish priest in Davenport, Iowa. He was deeply involved in the Cardijn method of "Observe, Judge, Act," with a passion for justice and social concerns. At the time of RENEW he was heading the national Campaign for Human Development out of Washington, D.C. He was, and is, a deeply spiritual man with strong love for the Lord and a great belief in the power of the Holy Spirit to change lives.

Marv brought a magnificent combination to us for Season III. He named three essential components of true spirituality: having concern for justice, addressing inequalities, and caring for those in need. He succeeded in opening the minds and hearts of those who would be leading the process to help others along the same journey. Huge crowds came out for his talks in September 1979.

Marv proposed a two-step process. The first step was to take direct action, either personally or as a group, in assisting people in need. The second step was addressing the root causes and systems that created injustice and harmed people in our society. These two steps distinguished between charity and justice and laid out an approach very much in accord with our themes and our RENEW team's shared convictions.

Naturally this didn't succeed in every instance. It would be unrealistic to expect that. For example, the topic of Season III was more than challenging for one of our best parish coordinators. As a successful executive, he was very pleased with the methodology of RENEW and its prayerfulness and was enthusiastic about the results in his parish. When he saw the small-group materials for Season III, however, he was taken aback by the pink cover the local printer had put on the book. "Ah, ha! Now I know what your agenda is," our coordinator said. "The pink cover shows your true colors. You're leading us to communism." Like the young man of the Gospel, he walked away sad.

Like those of Season II, the themes of Season III proved to have a fine flow and developmental process. The themes began by helping people start with their own life experiences. In order not to immediately turn some people off, we downplayed the word "justice." But by looking at unfair treatment in their own lives, they gained a greater feeling and affinity for those consistently being treated unfairly. Even the transition to work for institutional and systemic change went smoothly.

The proof was in the pudding. There was no outcry that this season was a break from spirituality. Instead, participants accepted a fuller understanding of spirituality. The groups took magnificent actions, similar to our experience in the Christian Family Movement during my time at Our Lady of Mercy (1957-1973). Participants provided care for the sick and elderly. People began taking greater notice of the poor and disadvantaged families in their area and were serving their needs. Communication developed between a good number of suburban parishes and inner-city communities that proved to be mutually beneficial. Some people were getting involved in interracial activities and others in advocating legislation to overturn injustices; some became more forthright in addressing issues in their businesses and places of work, and still others became involved in issues of local government. A wide variety of meaningful social actions was taking place among the forty thousand participants of RENEW.

The Network of Forty-Five

As with the issue of spiritual conversion in Season II, we recognized that this fuller spirituality embracing social concerns had to be much more than a one-shot experience. Toward this end, Sr. Suzanne Golas had been preparing, and was conducting, a well thought-out process that would have long-lasting effects.

In the year previous to Season III, Suzanne identified forty-five people from throughout the archdiocese who were formed into teams in each of our four counties. She chose people with that cherished combination of deep faith and spirituality along with great passion for justice. Suzanne devoted a lot of time and energy to a process of training and formation that prepared people for a strong follow-through to Season III. This preparation included careful study of the social teachings of the Catholic Church, which some call our best-kept secret. The Network of Forty-Five helped people appreciate and apply these teachings and become familiar with all the resources of agencies, research centers, and social programs that would help people continue to grow.

By week five of Season III, enthusiasm about social concerns had developed to the point where people could easily see that this momentum should not be lost. At the end of the fifth-week meetings, leaders distributed sign-up sheets to each of the small-group participants, offering them an opportunity to continue social action. They could make a commitment to become members of a new parish social concerns committee. In that one week, the number of parishes with social concerns committees in the Archdiocese of Newark grew from twenty to more than two hundred.

What would happen when these groups first came together to meet? How would they proceed? What approaches would they take? What guidelines and assistance would they have?

In one Bergen County parish, thirty-five people had signed up to be on their Social Concerns Committee. This parish was noted for its inactivity, and little or no assistance could be expected from parish leadership. That's where the Network of Forty-Five came into the picture. That parish was able to get direct assistance from our trained volunteers.

Members of the network immediately contacted each parish and made their services available. Their role was not to lead or direct the new committees but rather to be available as a valuable resource. These committees expanded their horizons through a process in which they discerned social needs, took action, and evaluated the results.

For example, a parish committee would recognize that poor people in the community needed food. The committee would collect and disburse food and determine that when that food was consumed, the need remained. Reflecting on this would lead them to look for longer-lasting solutions. Our volunteers would show the parish committee how to connect with Bread for the World, a network of millions of people around the world who try to reduce hunger and poverty. Based in Washington, D.C., Bread for the World provides in-depth information on legislation affecting both issues. The parish committee would become familiar with legislation that could address food and nutrition needs. Soon the parish committee members would be writing to their government representatives, urging them to enact needed legislation. Other parishioners would be urged to do likewise. Through this process action could take place that would bring about systemic change for the betterment of some of the most underprivileged and neglected people.

A number of the people involved in this process moved on to do truly remarkable things. John and Mary Bins are examples. They had always been involved with social concerns, but their involvement in RENEW Season III and their work with the Network of Forty-Five sparked them to even greater commitment. John was managing a sales firm of five hundred people but requested a part-time sabbatical so he could work in our RENEW office with Suzanne on developing parish social-concern efforts.

In time, Mary and John made the monumental decision to scale down their lifestyle and gave up their home in an affluent suburb of northern New Jersey to move into an integrated urban neighborhood. From there they started working full time helping parishes progress in the area of social concerns.

The unemployment rate among black residents of Newark at that time was fifteen percent, and it soared to twenty percent around 1983. John decided to open an employment agency in Newark to assist local job seekers. For eight years, John and Mary helped thousands of urban job seekers find employment. The RENEW experience had certainly impacted their lives and the lives of the countless people they served.

Coalition Six

Meanwhile, sparked by their RENEW experience in Season III, St. Ann's parishioners in inner-city Newark realized they had to take on greater personal responsibility for the plight of their neighborhood. They joined with people from Blessed Sacrament Parish and four other Christian congregations in the area to establish what was called Coalition Six. For years Coalition Six worked effectively on community-improvement issues. One of their first actions was to get abandoned tenement houses in the area boarded up. These homes had been serving as shooting galleries for drug addicts and also had been used to launch local thefts. Coalition Six also discovered that some funds were missing and had not been accounted for by city officials. The work of the coalition called attention to an area of the city never visited by local politicians.

The social concerns actions of literally thousands of people across our four counties gained the attention of people beyond the archdiocese.

Others Take Notice

With all of our involvement and commitments in the Newark process, Cathy and I were also being drawn to respond to inquiries from other dioceses. This included visits with bishops, chancery staff, and priests in Ohio, Iowa, New Hampshire, Kansas, Michigan, and Ontario, Canada.

Fr. Peter J. Henriot from the Center of Concern in Washington, D.C. wrote to Sr. Suzanne in 1981, complimenting her on the accomplishments of Season III in RENEW and the continuing work of the Network of Forty-Five.

> "As you will recall, one of the things that attracted me to the RENEW program several years ago was the creative way it moved toward treating the mission of justice as the proper outcome of personal conversion and community strengthening. The involvement of thousands of parish people in this process is, I believe, unique among diocesan programs in the United States…. The emphasis of prayer and Scripture, which characterizes your approach, is surely bearing fruit in the connection being made between faith and social responsibility. What strikes me as particularly significant in your approach is the stress on involving 'grass roots' and 'mainstream' Catholics."

Fr. Phil Murnion of New York, who headed a temporary bishops' committee for parish renewal called "The Parish Project," wrote to Suzanne in 1981.

> "No effort in the country passes your own in building social ministry on a firm base of parish development and spiritual renewal." With regard to the follow-up of the Network of Forty-Five, he said, "Your readiness to assist parishes and develop their ministry in the variety of ways

necessary to meet their diverse needs is a great service by a diocese. Far too many simply impose one way of acting."

The renowned Fr. Jack Egan of the University of Notre Dame and the Catholic Committee on Urban Ministry, as well as the Office of Urban Affairs for the Archdiocese of Chicago, congratulated Suzanne and the work of Season III.

> I have had the occasion of visiting with, and speaking with, some of the people from the Newark Archdiocese who are involved in the RENEW program, which has been established in the Archdiocese of Newark, but particularly those who have been touched by the efforts in bringing about a clearer understanding of the teaching of Church on justice and peace. This has enabled the people, both Catholic and non-Catholic, black and white, to understand some of the needs of society in which we are living today. I have been so inspired by the impact that your work has made in their lives…. I must say to you that I have not seen, up to this time, as well-developed a set of principles and a program of action as you folks have in the Newark area.

Immediately following Season III of RENEW, a full-day workshop entitled, "Empowerment by the Spirit to Act Justly," was held in two archdiocesan locations. Three national leaders in justice issues—Fr. Larry Gorman, Sr. Marjorie Tuite, O.P., and Mr. Harry Fagan—were featured speakers. Hundreds of people attended. After the workshop, Sr. Marge exclaimed, "I have never met a group of people who were more prepared for addressing social justice issues than the people of the Newark Archdiocese. RENEW has done its job well."

For me personally, perhaps the most heartening result of this season came with research I did fourteen years later. At the conclusion of Season III RENEW had remarkably increased from twenty parishes with social concerns committees to two hundred twenty-two parishes. Fourteen years later, there were still over two hundred of those parishes with active social concerns committees. That's certainly an enduring impact! It is something that surely would have warmed my heart if I had seen it when I was a young man.

CHAPTER 9

Season IV

Discipleship

The average person's understanding of discipleship in 1980 was far more limited than today. The term and its meaning were unfamiliar to most people. Discipleship was commonly understood as those who follow Christ and try to live accordingly.

That's fine as far as it goes, but we were looking to communicate a deeper insight about discipleship that would strongly motivate people. Fortunately, Sr. Agnes Mallner, O.S.U., the spiritual director of Immaculate Conception Seminary in the archdiocese, was an outstanding theologian on the topic. Sr. Agnes framed discipleship as the internalization of the attitudes and values of Jesus, in contrast to a concept that simply stressed the imitation of Jesus. Her recommendation was to emphasize the inner change that would naturally flow into the way we follow Jesus and live our lives.

Discipleship, understood in this manner, would lead to motivated commitments that would be more authentic and long-lasting. Sr. Agnes spelled out the approaches to take in developing discipleship. Her suggestions formed the content, themes, and preparation workshops for Season IV.

Discipleship Retreats

RENEW's central theme of developing spirituality was carried out in preparation for Season IV, as it had been in the previous seasons. At the same time, Cathy developed an excellent retreat on discipleship as part of the Season IV experience. She trained an archdiocesan retreat team, and together they held discipleship retreats in several locations, making them available for leaders in all parishes of the archdiocese. In turn, these parish retreat teams went on to replicate the retreats in their parishes one or more times. The archdiocese was being immersed in a strong experience of discipleship.

Spiritual Friends

Before Season IV, we engaged a priest who had developed a spiritual instrument along the lines of Myers-Briggs (a personality-type indicator). This instrument intended to help people evaluate their spiritual lives and more clearly see where they were in their prayer lives and in the way they lived out their spirituality. He used his spiritual analysis in workshops preparing RENEW participants for discipleship. People found it fascinating to gain clearer insights into what steps they needed to take for improvement. Our intent was to help them fulfill new aspirations for spiritual growth.

In the meantime, we had enlisted Sr. Judy Mertz, S.C., who was engaged in training spiritual directors in our archdiocese. She trained one hundred thirty people for us who were to be seen as "spiritual friends." We were careful not to call these people spiritual directors, which would have required considerable more training and development. People were, however, very much enabled to be spiritual friends for others on their journey.

A central telephone number was then set up in the archdiocese. Anyone involved in RENEW, or any parishioner in the archdiocese, could call this number to be connected with one of our prepared spiritual friends. Through these contacts, spiritual friendships were established and continued to flourish. Sr. Joan Jungerman, S.S.N.D., coordinated the connection of these spiritual friends and interested parishioners.

RENEW Extras

These Season IV developments coincided with the United States bishops' national "Year of the Family" listening campaign. In our archdiocese this was conducted primarily through questionnaires distributed to members of all RENEW small groups. We provided many "extras" like this for each season to enhance and increase the impact of the spiritual theme.

This season also produced a beautiful moment of grace for Cathy who, as you will see, bore the brunt of leadership during Season IV. At the beginning of RENEW, Cathy had given a talk at Sunday Masses in one of our parishes. After Mass, there were a few folks still scattered in the church. On an impulse she slid in next to an older woman and asked if she was considering joining a RENEW small group. The woman said she didn't think she would be able to do that. Cathy listened, encouraged her to give it a try, and then left.

A year later, at a training session held for RENEW parish team members, Cathy reconnected with that woman, who had become coordinator for all her parish small groups. It was a special moment for Cathy as she experienced joy and awe at God's wonderful grace—a well deserved reward for her untiring efforts.

A Personal Detour

Season IV passed in a blur for me—with good reason.

In the midst of Season IV, we were preparing for evangelization in Season V and wanted to present this topic on a prime-time TV show in the coming fall. A late afternoon in February 1980 found me caught up in traffic in New York on my way to see the president of Metromedia, which operated WNEW Channel 5, the largest independent TV station at the time. I was running late and could very possibly miss this important appointment. A bit of panic set in along with what I would later know as angina.

Our meeting went well. I explained that we wanted an hour of TV time on a Sunday night in October. Walking away with a guaranteed 8 p.m. prime-time slot, I also carried the responsibility of raising the funds to pay for it.

When I woke the next morning I experienced unusual indigestion. My chest was tight with trapped gas, and doing sit ups didn't help. I stopped by the hospital to get the results of a cholesterol test and mentioned I wasn't feeling too comfortable. The doctor told me I had to stay. "I can't stay," I told him. "We have workshops coming up." I knew I had to get out of the hospital. Fr. Ed Braxton and Sr. Toinette Eugene were coming in that weekend to do a workshop on African-American evangelization for Season V. The day following the workshop there would be a gathering of the Black Catholic Community. But the doctor said, "You're having a heart attack *now*. You've got to stay here."

Suddenly my fast-paced, frenetic life came to a screeching halt. I couldn't believe it. Up to this point, I had had tremendous energy. I knew that life on earth would end at some time but was now confronted as never before with the reality of mortality.

The heart incident had its lighter side. While I was experiencing the heart attack, one of the doctors shared a personal story. He was very concerned because his son's car had been stolen. The next morning, I was lying in an oxygen tent in the intensive care unit when this same doctor poked his head in through the curtain saying, "Just wanted to tell you my son's car has been found," and off he went. I was still quite frightened by this whole heart experience and didn't know how to respond to his good news. Fortunately the oxygen tent saved me. What could I have said, anyway?

Two months earlier in my room at St. Antoninus Rectory I had prayed, "Lord, I know I'm killing myself with the hours I'm putting in. I think something really good is going to come out of this RENEW process— worth giving my life for."

During the period of recuperation, Charles de Foucauld's "Prayer of Abandonment" largely sustained me.

> Father,
> I abandon myself into your hands;
> do with me what you will.
> Whatever you may do, I thank you;
> I am ready for all, I accept all.
> Let only your will be done in me,

and in all your creatures.
I wish no more than this, O Lord.

Into your hands I commend my soul;
I offer it to you
with all the love of my heart,
for I love you, Lord,
and so need to give myself,
to surrender myself into your hands,
without reserve,
and with boundless confidence,
for you are my Father.

It was more clear to me than ever that my life, RENEW, and everything had to be in God's hands. Meantime, our marvelous staff carried on in my absence. No one is indispensable. All was well.

Yes, much more was going to happen with RENEW, and the Lord was going to spare me to be part of it.

CHAPTER 10

Season V

Evangelization

Evangelization was a term that Catholics at that point were neither very familiar nor comfortable with. To most it had connotations connected with Protestant evangelists and tent crusades.

Evangelization: Central Mission of the Church

In 1971 Pope Paul VI issued his famous pastoral on evangelization, *Apostolic Exhortation on Evangelization in the Modern World*. In that document he reasserted evangelization as the essential mission of the Church. It was imperative that evangelization have an important place in the RENEW process. Evangelization had to be more than techniques, catch phrases, or programmed dialogues with which to send forth people sharing our faith. There had to be a more complete understanding and appreciation of evangelization, an enlightened view as to how to spread the good news.

RENEW's Approach

We were particularly drawn to the evangelization approach of Dolores Leckey, executive director of the Secretariat for Family, Laity, Women and Youth at the United States Conference of Catholic Bishops in Washington, D.C. She suggested a four-phased cycle of evangelization: Accepting the Word; Living It Out; Sharing My Story; and Welcoming.

Evangelization was much more than getting people into the pews of our churches. The attraction had to be the witness of a people who had a deep faith, a desire to be touched by the Scriptures, and a deep love for God. People needed to see that Catholics knew Jesus and were, in fact, in a personal relationship with him. The emphasis was not a technique but a beautiful, lived-faith witness that would attract people, namely the unbaptized and those who had abandoned our faith.

At that time we knew that the second largest religious demographic in the United States, beyond Catholicism, consisted of people who had left the Catholic Church. People were saying they had gotten to know Jesus and love the Scriptures in an experience they had elsewhere. When meeting a young person we might happen to comment that we hadn't seen him or her in church for quite a while. The response might be, "I've been attending a church down the street." We would ask, "How come?" and go on to explain the logic of Catholicism. The frequent response would be, "But I discovered Jesus down the street." Certainly the truth and logic of our Catholic faith is important to communicate. However, many times people were looking for an experience of faith that was lacking in their lives and they were searching for a faith community that would warmly welcome them and provide that experience.

In preparation for Season V, we were fortunate to have Dolores come and give a brilliant workshop on evangelization for our RENEW parish teams and small-group leaders. People responded very positively. We also brought in Fr. Alvin Illig, C.S.P., who was an extremely zealous national leader on evangelization. Fr. Illig shared various pastoral approaches to evangelization, and he highly energized people.

No stone was to be left unturned. We held days of reflection for priests. We developed and disseminated evangelization folders, "Cry Out the Good News," throughout the archdiocese. These pamphlets emphasized the four phases of evangelization that Dolores Leckey stressed, which had become essential pieces of the weekly themes in Season V.

RENEW: Prime-time TV

One of the main projects for our evangelization effort was to develop a feature film on RENEW and to have it appear on prime-time television. The film, simply entitled "RENEW," turned out to be of excellent quality thanks to Billy Budd Productions and Cathy, who coordinated the production. They filmed a wide range of people giving witness to how dramatically their faith had come alive through the RENEW experience. It depicted a Church very vital and alive, worth looking into or returning to.

A moving experience occurred even before the film was shown. The film crew was visiting a parish RENEW prayer service in one of our churches. The church was crowded and totally dark. Candles were lit and as the light spread throughout the darkened church the congregation sang an earnest "Be Not Afraid." One of the non-religious-minded cameramen was so touched by the experience that tears were streaming down his cheeks.

The film was featured on the Metromedia station WNEW Channel 5 in New York at prime-time on a Sunday evening. At the end of the film an invitation was extended for people to inquire into the faith and a telephone number appeared on the screen where people could call in. A bank of our selected responders were equipped and prepared to connect inquirers with a parish in their area that had a good catechumenate.

Funding: A Learning

There was a catch to the production of the film. It would cost $50,000. Considering our financial straits at the time, this seemed as great a hurdle as raising a million dollars would have been. We looked for a foundation that would subsidize the production. I visited Harry John at the DeRance Foundation in Milwaukee, which was an interesting experience. When I arrived he announced that everyone in the building was to come to the chapel where Father would celebrate Mass. After lunch, I made my presentation. As I did, someone in the kitchen was signaling thumbs up to me, "You're doing good."

Nevertheless nothing happened until a week later when Harry John called. He said that he was looking at our proposal and then went on to share his reservations. I hung up from that conversation a little discouraged, but after a few minutes a light bulb went on. In the middle of the conversation, Harry had wondered what was unique about what we were doing. I then realized that that was the key and immediately wrote to the foundation. The letter went along these lines: "Dear Mr. John,

In our conversation today you wondered what is unique in what we are doing. RENEW's project is unique in the following ways:" a number of bullets with comments flowed down the page. A week later a check for $50,000 came from the DeRance Foundation for our film project. It was something we always remembered in approaching foundations: "What is unique, different, and important about our appeal?"

Publicity

How to get a good number of people to tune into our RENEW evangelization film was another challenge. We wanted an audience far beyond RENEW participants, one that would extend throughout the tri-state area of Connecticut, New York, and New Jersey. To do this we developed a number of audiotapes that were used as radio commercials. People were startled to hear RENEW coming across their car radios. We also created and developed television commercials on evangelization that were aired throughout Season IV.

In addition, we wanted all the New York area newspapers to publicize the showing of this special TV program. Dolly Donahue and I worked on putting together ads that appeared in *The New York Times*, the *New York Daily News*, the *New York Post*, *The Star-Ledger*, *The Jersey Journal*, and *The Bergen Record*. Where would we get the money to pay for these ads? Fortunately, our good friend, Bishop Joseph Francis, S.V.D., an auxiliary bishop of Newark, came through for us. He connected us with still another foundation that covered the cost of all the radio and newspaper promotions.

The whole evangelization process of Season V progressed well. The number of people calling in by phone during our film fell short of our high goals. However, a great number of people, who had previously been inactive in this regard were now engaged in the work of evangelization. And many others in the New York metropolitan area had been alerted to good things that were happening in Catholic circles.

Come, Follow Me

An evangelization incident typifies so many others that occurred during the five seasons of RENEW.

Gail, a young woman, attended a RENEW small-group leader training on a Saturday morning. From there she went to a local diner to meet two friends for lunch. She was so filled with enthusiasm that she kept bubbling about her love for the Lord and all the beautiful things that were happening with RENEW. The waitress couldn't help but be intrigued and lingered close by, taking in as much of the conversation as she could.

Finally she approached Gail and said, "I can't remember hearing a conversation like this. Where is it that you talk about Jesus so openly and in such a loving way?" When the waitress indicated that she was about to get off duty, Gail said to her, "Come and follow me," and led the woman to her parish, Holy Family in Nutley, New Jersey.

Amazingly enough, the Gospel for the vigil Mass that afternoon and the following Sunday morning was about Jesus turning to Simon and his brother, Andrew, inviting them to come and follow him.

Throughout the experience of RENEW, countless people were reaching out to extend an invitation to others, "Come and follow me," to learn more about our Lord and to make him their best friend.

Preparing for Beyond RENEW in Newark

While the many-faceted aspects of evangelization were taking place in Season V, our agenda was also very full with helping to prepare parishes in the Archdiocese of Newark for the time beyond RENEW.

We decided resources were needed to assist many who wanted to continue meeting in their small groups. We first produced a separate book explaining the "Observe, Judge, Act" methodology. Then our team began to develop a number of books that would form the *Pilgrimage Series*, published by Paulist Press, and later the *IMPACT Series*, published by Sheed & Ward, Liguori Publications, and RENEW International. These series would serve small communities for years to come.

We invited Sr. Marie Schultejann, S.M.I.C., and Fr. Ken Lasch, both leaders in the Paterson Diocese, to give a workshop on planning and implementing small sharing groups, which was very well received.

At one point during Season V, I shared with Archbishop Gerety our strong conviction that great archdiocesan emphasis should be placed on the continuation of our small groups. We wanted to develop them even more effectively into small Christian communities. Archbishop Gerety invited me to go to Maine for the weekend where we would talk more about this. He definitely didn't need to be convinced of its importance. It was a good break from work and an enjoyable weekend.

Sr. Mary George O'Reilly convincingly said to me, "Tom, don't let those RENEW core communities disintegrate. You have set up something extremely valuable. You may not realize how difficult it would be to re-create that system." Our RENEW team moved ahead with many workshops aimed at convincing parishes of the importance of not only continuing their small groups but also maintaining their core communities. The RENEW process had brought forth many participants who would be more than happy to provide fresh blood for those core communities. We would be committed to helping and working with core communities beyond RENEW.

Archdiocesan Pastoral Vision: Conversion and Community

Fr. Tom Ivory and I gave a workshop entitled "Beyond RENEW" to a large audience. We projected the importance of continuing the major themes of conversion and community, highlighting the RCIA and small communities. This would become the launch pad for our effort to develop an archdiocesan pastoral vision.

Archbishop Gerety also wanted the impact of RENEW to carry on in a way that would give direction for future pastoral work in the archdiocese. He called upon Tom Ivory and me to coordinate an effort that would develop that vision into a plan.

It was a mammoth undertaking, part of which would be to get the coordination and consensus of our thirty-seven archdiocesan offices and agencies. The vision that evolved was one that all archdiocesan offices and agencies, and parishes, were intended to build their pastoral efforts upon.

The two strongest themes of RENEW, conversion and community, were the centerpiece of this vision statement, the Archdiocesan Pastoral Plan.

Growth of the Office of Pastoral Renewal

Moving beyond Season V, our archdiocesan Office of Pastoral Renewal was composed of four departments: Shared Responsibility, Social Concerns, Small Christian Communities, and RENEW.

Shared Responsibility was headed by Sr. Mary McGuinness and dealt with parish pastoral councils, deanery councils, finance councils, and the archdiocesan pastoral council.

Sr. Suzanne Golas headed Social Concerns, which serviced the great number of parishes and social concerns committees in the archdiocese.

The Small Christian Community Department, originally headed by Sr. Joan Jungerman, S.S.N.D., and Fr. Bob Cozzini and later by Sr. Catherine Nerney, S.S.J., developed small Christian community resources and assisted parishes throughout the archdiocese with the development of small communities. They stressed that all parish ministries should be based on leadership formed in ministerial small communities. They also outlined a vision of the parish working toward being a community of many small communities, a vision suited for Newark and beyond. The fact that this department consisted of eight full-time people indicates the importance of following through with RENEW's emphasis on small Christian communities in the archdiocese.

The RENEW component would in a short time outgrow the three other departments. It responded to inquiries from other dioceses, helped them initiate RENEW, and provided service and assistance throughout their entire process.

As director of the office, I coordinated the four areas and was most directly involved in small Christian communities and RENEW.

Concluding Celebration

At the conclusion of Season V, there was a strongly felt need to praise and thank God for how profoundly his graces had moved people throughout the archdiocese. We celebrated our Newark RENEW process with a Sunday afternoon prayer service at Sacred Heart Cathedral. Once again the cathedral was packed. Momentum and enthusiasm had certainly carried well through the whole process.

I was sitting in the cathedral in the midst of the large group of priests and a mass of people from participating parishes. In the sanctuary, along with Archbishop Gerety and our other bishops, were the chancery priests and officials. In the middle of the service, Archbishop Gerety stopped and said, "Where is Msgr. Kleissler?" The priests around me stood up and pointed to where I was sitting. With that all the people in the cathedral rose with a standing ovation. It was a beautiful recognition, and I truly appreciated the moment. There was, however, no time for patting oneself on the back. That was fine for the moment, but it was also time to move on. There was so much more to be done.

Interest in RENEW was exploding beyond Newark. It was time to forge ahead. In Part II, we will explore how we spread our wings both in the United States and internationally in the decade from 1980 to 1990.

PART II

CHAPTER 11

Spreading Our Wings

I n terms of the sheer number of participants, the 1980s can be seen as the golden age of RENEW. As we grew internationally during this decade, more than one hundred twenty-five dioceses inside and outside the United States initiated diocesan efforts of RENEW or started cluster efforts.

Early Inquiries

A diocesan effort meant RENEW was promoted and encouraged by the bishop and a diocesan director was appointed to oversee the process. Diocesan leadership did not mandate that parishes participate. However, with great effort, almost without exception, over seventy percent of parishes participated. Some dioceses even approached ninety percent. So you can begin to imagine how many people became involved between 1980 and 1989.

Beyond diocesan efforts, even more people became involved when a cluster of parishes got together and decided to initiate RENEW. These "cluster efforts" were always approved by the local bishop but did not get diocesan support. Our RENEW team served these clusters directly with training and pastoral support systems.

Word of Mouth

Absolutely no promotional effort was taken by RENEW International to get the word out. In fact, the biggest weakness in the first two decades of RENEW was its lack of public relations and promotion. RENEW was catching fire in a very genuine grass roots manner by word of mouth.

As early as the first training sessions in 1978, parishioners in the Archdiocese of Newark began writing and talking to relatives and friends about this exciting venture. Good numbers of letters of inquiry started to come into our office.

What was attracting these inquiries? Certainly RENEW's encouragement of lay people by engaging them in spiritual growth and development was the main factor. RENEW's varied modes of outreach were also attractive. It was not simply one more activity in the parish but an effort to bring all parishioners together for a period of spiritual renewal.

A Gallup poll at the time indicated that people who were leaving the Catholic Church left

- to learn more about the Word of God
- to seek a greater experience of community
- to satisfy their desire for a sincere sense of welcome and belonging.

RENEW provided an opportunity for all three. Interest in this opportunity was coming not only from lay parishioners but from parish priests and from bishops. It seemed to be the very kind of parish renewal that many had been looking for.

One of our own chancery officials wondered where all this was going; how large was RENEW going to grow? My only answer was that we didn't know. It was the work of the Holy Spirit.

The Heart of the Matter

Saying it was the work of the Holy Spirit was more than pious talk. The spread of RENEW was all about the Spirit's action in hearts that were hungering for God, frequently far more than people had realized. Without changing church structures or other superficial signs, RENEW was helping people get to the true heart of the church—spirituality connecting faith to life.

We realized and always tried to convey that RENEW as a program could not renew anyone. It simply brought people into a reflective atmosphere and process that helped them experience God in new and exciting ways.

The easiest thing in our society is to lead very unreflective lives. Sharing with others who want to stop, look, and listen allows God to speak gently and directly to our minds and hearts. Scripture passages that we've heard a thousand times before come alive to us as if we were hearing God's word for the first time. We are touched and moved as we hear others share simply of their search for God in life situations that are very similar to ours. We even surprise ourselves as we share our own faith in more profound ways than we've ever allowed ourselves to explore. We start to connect our faith to the realities of our everyday lives. Our faith becomes stronger as does our desire to know and love God more.

RENEW was growing because it was an instrument to help people satisfy their deepest human hunger—hunger for God.

Responding to Interest

We did not make first contact with any parish or diocese, but once a parish or diocese contacted us we gave it great attention. Some called already having made a decision to do RENEW. Others were simply inquiring or exploring possibilities. We kept a log of every such call and maintained tenacious contact with the callers. In most cases, staying in patient communication paid off to the point where an invitation was offered for us to visit and share more fully in person. Inevitably those visits resulted in a commitment to start RENEW.

Another early approach was to hold three-day inquiry forums for people from other dioceses. On the third day of one forum, a priest sat at the piano during breakfast and started playing "The Sting." Everybody got a good laugh at his reaction to the zealous selling job they were receiving. At the same time they were impressed with the pastoral realism of everything they were hearing. However, it soon became evident that if we met with leaders in their own dioceses it would involve more of their people in the inquiry and also be more effective.

In 1979, we were invited to attend the annual conference of bishops in Washington, D.C., and conduct an informal session for curious bishops. Forty bishops attended our meeting, which was held during happy hour. At that presentation someone from the back row, whether it was a bishop or priest from the conference I know not, shouted out, "If it could happen in Newark, it could happen anywhere." That humorous interlude helped provide a very jovial and responsive environment for the bishops.

Yes, if it could happen in Newark it could happen anywhere. Time would prove that point.

Valuable Friends

We invited Fr. Phil Murnion to attend one of our training sessions at Felician College in Lodi. A thousand people attended, and we offered twenty-eight different workshops involving a wide variety of aspects of RENEW. It was preparation for Season II.

When Phil arrived we decided not to give him a guided tour; instead we invited him to spend the day going to different workshops as he pleased and encouraged him to talk with whomever he wished. This would provide him a first-hand opportunity to experience the high enthusiasm that existed and to evaluate the actual impact RENEW was having in people's lives. Upon leaving at the end of the day, Phil offered little comment except to say, "Why don't you come and visit me at my office?"

That meeting proved to be a pivotal moment for RENEW. For a couple of hours Phil grilled Cathy and me in his very logical way about every aspect of RENEW. I began to think he must hate RENEW. He concluded by saying, "You're really onto something. You've broken new ground. This is not about individual spiritual renewal (which was popular at the time) but about parish renewal. You're calling the whole parish to a spiritual experience and to a pastoral way of thinking." Phil explained he had a very interesting group of bishops on his committee who were exploring means for parish renewal. He offered to contact some of these bishops, and he encouraged them to extend us an invitation to share about RENEW.

Cathy and I were stunned. What an incredible breakthrough this could be. People had been discovering us on their own, but Phil was offering to make a direct contact for us with bishops who might have an interest. On the way back, Cathy and I celebrated at a restaurant in Hoboken and had a fine Italian meal as only New Jersey could provide.

Sure enough, Phil came through with the names of several bishops who were open to a visit.

My first visit was to the Diocese of Rockville Centre on Long Island. In my order of things, this could possibly be the most valuable of all dioceses to work with because of the huge size of the parishes there. In addition, Bishop John McGann was a friend from the priests golf camp where we both had vacationed in New Hampshire. Unfortunately, too much was happening in the diocese at the time. Before he retired in 2000, however, Bishop McGann did initiate RENEW as his final gift to the diocese.

Speaking of Long Island reminds me of a surprising call from a parishioner in St. Mary's Parish, Manhasset, New York. That parishioner was Mrs. Margie Grace, and she was looking for information on RENEW. She invited me to come and have lunch with her. Cardinal Leo Suenens (1904-1996), archbishop of Mechelen-Brussel, Belgium, was visiting with the Graces and would like to hear about RENEW. Cardinal Suenens' leadership at the Second Vatican Council had made him an architect of twentieth century Catholicism and he was one of my heroes. Would I have time for lunch with Margie Grace and Cardinal Suenens? I couldn't believe my ears. We certainly could find time! This was to begin long friendships with Margie, her husband Peter, the whole Grace family, and with that great man, Cardinal Suenens.

The following week Cathy and I arrived at the Grace estate. Margie was the perfect friendly hostess and the cardinal was a strikingly holy and humble man. Could you believe a luncheon that extended for four hours? Fortunately, the cardinal didn't fall asleep but listened with great interest. A man whom I had long admired became a wonderful friend. This friendship included visits with him at his home in Belgium, which further deepened my respect for his great intellect and, above all, his deep and vibrant spirituality.

It was my privilege to have been included in some important Grace family gatherings and to have felt part of the family on those occasions. Margie is a woman of keen intellect and deep spirituality. She studied theology at our own Immaculate Conception Seminary and translated some fine spiritual works from French to English. What attracted her to RENEW was that it was down to earth and served the people at the parish level.

RENEW Team Expands

Inquiries we received in the late 1970s and very early 1980s clearly showed a need to expand our staff. For RENEW to spread properly it wasn't enough to say, "Here it is," and wish parishes and dioceses good luck. A good amount of time, pastoral assistance, and training would be needed. To provide this, we needed a core staff of dedicated people who would constantly criss-cross the country.

In 1980, Sr. Donna Ciangio, O.P., whom I had known from St. Ann's in Newark, was invited to join our fledgling national team. She had participated in a parish RENEW small group and had captured the spirit of RENEW. For the next thirteen years, Donna proved to be a tireless worker throughout the United States and overseas. Donna developed a good rapport with bishops and priests that made her an extremely effective RENEW presenter. Lay people, likewise, responded to her and appreciated her humorous and down-to-earth approach. Donna quickly become an extremely valuable contributor on RENEW's journey.

Having completed the RENEW experience in Newark, we decided in 1981 to do a study of some of the most successful parishes in the United States. We were particularly impressed with Msgr. Bob Fuller, pastor of St. Pius X in Tucson, Arizona. Bob had written a book about his parish that was drawing great attention across the country. Visiting Bob, Suzanne and I were fascinated by the tremendous lay involvement and pastoral energy of the fast-growing parish.

Upon our return, we invited Bob to join our RENEW team, and his bishop released him for five years to serve with RENEW. Bob made an immediate hit with everybody.

I suggested that Bob begin with visits to dioceses across the country that had inquired about RENEW in the previous two years and to whom we had been unable to respond. Bob took off on an exhausting three-week tour from coast-to-coast. It began one of the most interesting aspects of his five-year stint, seeing first-hand the Catholic Church throughout the United States. He felt that in no other position could he have gained such an insight into parish and church life.

During Bob's tenure, he and I were busy responding to inquiries, making initial visits to bishops; parish, office and agency people; and diocesan presbyterates as they pondered the possibilities of initiating RENEW. Within a year I appointed Bob as director of the newly established National Office of RENEW. I continued my oversight of RENEW while working with the three departments in Newark. Bob Fuller played an extremely important role in RENEW's journey as hands-on daily director during RENEW's greatest period of expansion. He always succeeded in getting new dioceses on board.

Bob assembled a strong team of trainers, including Sr. Eileen Dumshaw, S.S.J., Sr. Ellen Golden, O.S.F., and Sr. Pat McGinley, S.S.J. Good training workshops and rich RENEW experience helped to quickly spread word of RENEW across the country. That word-of-mouth accounted for all the dioceses that were getting involved with RENEW without any promotional effort on our part.

The intensity of my personal schedule drew the attention of Sr. Mary Fran Kyle, S.S.J., and the Sisters of St. Joseph of Chestnut Hill, who were concerned about my health in view of my recent open-heart surgery. To help me stay alive and well, they assigned Sr. Alice Yohe, S.S.J., to be an administrative assistant who became my alter-ego when I was traveling. Bishops or others who inquired by phone in my absence were quickly won over by Alice. It is a wonder that either one of us managed to stay alive, since Alice's commitment to RENEW was twenty-four/seven. Her ability to relate to others made her a major contributor to RENEW from 1983 to 2006. I will forever be grateful not only for her reliability but also for the strong personal friendship that endures until today.

RENEW Branches Out

The involvement of the Archdiocese of New York was particularly surprising at the time. When Fr. Benedict Groeschel, C.F.R., came to visit and learn more about RENEW, I couldn't help but reflect—the unimaginable is taking place. New York is crossing the river to find out what is happening in Newark. What followed was a strong cluster of New York parishes headed by two tremendously zealous priests, Fr. John Budwick and Fr. Bruce Nieli, C.S.P. They went on to sing the praises of RENEW far and wide.

As overwhelming as the next five years was to be, so also would be any effort to chronicle the many dioceses that became involved. Instead, in the next chapter, I will simply offer personal vignettes of various dioceses. It was a hectic time but always fun.

CHAPTER 12

RENEW Vignettes

1980-1985

The following vignettes are sketches and in no way convey an historical account or evaluation of the dioceses mentioned. Our small and overworked staff could keep only sparse records of the whirlwind events of this period.

These vignettes represent brief personal snapshots from twenty-five to thirty years ago. Obviously other staff members from that time would be able to add more. I should be clear that my personal involvement, along with that of Bob Fuller, centered largely on receiving initial inquiry calls and arranging personal visits to dioceses. These visits, with bishops and diocesan personnel, led to presentations to all the priests of the dioceses. There, a more formal decision to move ahead with the process would be made. I would continue to follow through to the point at which diocesan RENEW directors were appointed. Other RENEW staff personnel were kept exceedingly busy with full training schedules.

1980-1982

Steubenville, Ohio

Although the Archdiocese of Milwaukee had already decided that it would initiate RENEW in 1981, the Diocese of Steubenville jumped into the picture, deciding to start RENEW almost immediately in 1980. The decision came about when Bishop Albert Ottenweller made a weekend visit to Newark with several diocesan representatives and made a decision on the spot.

The fact that Bishop Ottenweller decided to do RENEW was particularly significant at that time. He was a national folk hero for parish priests. Bishop Ottenweller had given a well-publicized presentation at the U.S. Conference of Catholic Bishops national gathering, speaking on behalf of parish priests. He described how over-burdened they were and how so many things were coming at them from all directions. He likened it to a funnel, the contents of which were pouring down on the heads of parish priests. The funnel was filled with programs, new agendas, added responsibilities, and whatever the latest whim of the chancery might be. Their heads were spinning, he said. The priests related well to the reality of the picture he painted.

Given that background it was most striking that, of all people, Bishop Ottenweller would be the first bishop to undertake RENEW as a diocesan effort. He clearly saw the potential that RENEW offered. For one thing, Bishop Ottenweller realized that in the one process of RENEW he could promote and strengthen all the different ministries and agendas that were being individually promoted. He could see that enough training and help would be provided to strengthen and enable lay leadership. This process would not overburden priests and would bring very promising results. Priests and lay people working closely together would create a wonderful parish and diocesan spirit.

As a result of the Steubenville experience, I developed a great appreciation for Bishop Ottenweller and established a long-lasting friendship with him. He loved to brainstorm new ideas on how to energize parish life. He was a pastoral man *par excellence*. The people of Steubenville were very fortunate.

1981-1983

Dodge City, Kansas

Memories of Dodge City that flash into my mind include a sane lifestyle, quiet and pleasant residential streets, the immortalized hangman's tree on Main Street, and the vastness of the diocesan territory. The fact that thirty-five thousand people participated in RENEW jumps out at me. One half of all practicing adult Catholics were members of RENEW faith-sharing groups!

One of my most humbling experiences occurred at a training session in a rural town one evening during the latter stage of RENEW in Dodge City. Upon arriving early, I was surprised to see people already sitting in neatly-arranged rows. Fr. Bob Schremmer, the diocesan coordinator, encouraged me to mingle and meet the various people. It was only on the way home that I learned that the evening had been publicized as an opportunity to meet the founder of RENEW. Some had traveled hours to attend. That evening gave me the humbling privilege of meeting a wonderful group of solid citizens and deeply devout Catholics.

Bishop Eugene Gerber is a most memorable person. His strong spirituality and cheerfulness came through in his quick and ready smile. Donna spoke of how Bishop Gerber had walked back and forth in the rear of the room carrying a little baby over his shoulder so the mother could be fully attentive to the training. That's the kind of man he is.

Los Angeles, California

We learned early that many dioceses considering RENEW would call our archbishop to find out if this program was for real and what Archbishop Gerety thought about it. With respect to the Archdiocese of Los Angeles, I am told that Archbishop Gerety's response to Cardinal Timothy Manning was, "If you appoint the right leadership, things should go fine."

As always, Archbishop Gerety was offering a good insight. Leadership at the diocesan and parish levels would prove to be incredibly important. In the cases where bishops appointed positive, zealous directors who enjoyed good relationships with the parishes, we came to expect tremendous results. That fact was unfailing.

The next step was strong leadership at the parish level from the pastor and lay parishioners. We do everything possible to assure that good leadership be appointed at every stage of RENEW.

Milwaukee, Wisconsin

Auxiliary Bishop Richard Sklba, along with Mary Ann Plada, did an excellent job in leading the archdiocesan RENEW process. More than forty thousand people participated in Milwaukee's RENEW small groups. Bishop Sklba's rich scriptural background brought out a beautiful dimension to their experience.

At the time, Milwaukee was a national leader in adult faith formation. A first look at the simplicity of the RENEW materials could have led to the conclusion that they would be inadequate. We pointed out that even the best religious education and faith-formation programs at the time were drawing only six to eight percent of parishioners. The simplicity of RENEW was geared for the time and would involve two, three, or more times the anticipated number of people. A whole new audience would be reached. That new audience, in turn, would be well prepared and motivated to move on to deeper waters as time went on. I believe that the numbers of participants that became involved backed that up.

1982-1984

Covington, Kentucky

Bishop William Hughes was another wonderful bishop, pleasant and great to work with.

After giving a presentation to a group assembled to make a diocesan decision regarding RENEW, I waited outside for their conclusion. I wouldn't want to do injustice to the following memory. Someone who was leaving the meeting shared with me what was transpiring. I may be misrepresenting what he said, but it went something like this: "They're making a decision between the RENEW spiritual renewal process and computers." Fortunately, and to my relief, the decision was for RENEW.

Being a football fan, I was naturally happy to learn that the Cincinnati Bengals' quarterback, Ken Anderson, Super Bowl XVI, was a RENEW participant. Actually, I rooted for Cincinnati that year only to be crushed when they lost by two points in that bitterly cold contest.

Grand Rapids, Michigan

RENEW continued to be a learning experience for me. I discovered that Grand Rapids was the founding headquarters for Amway and also the "American Vatican" for the Dutch Reformed Church. One of my best experiences was being taken on a trip by Fr. Gus Ancona to the shores of Lake Michigan. Coming from the Jersey shore, I was startled to find the beautiful, large white sand dunes abounding along the coast. It seemed to me that this was one of America's best kept secrets.

New Ulm, Minnesota

It took a few years for RENEW to be invited to New Ulm after the diocese first expressed interest. The reported obstacle to an earlier invitation was that folks there didn't want a monsignor from the East coming and telling them what to do. What a relief it was after the first presentation to have a sister come up and give me a big hug, saying, "I was the one who didn't want a monsignor from the East to talk to us." She was totally sold and became a great leader for RENEW.

The unique community style of this diocese made it one of my favorites. Bishop Raymond Lucker was a remarkable man. The diocesan chancery sat at the edge of New Ulm and opened to a stretch of farmland. Bishop Lucker had established a form of governance in which some of the people on the diocesan staff worked and lived in common. Their quarters were located in a part of the building where they enjoyed a beautiful and friendly living style. They prayed in common, ate together, and shared deliberations. Each had certain responsibilities to enable this lifestyle. Bishop Lucker's responsibility was to tend to the garden and bring the vegetables to the table. In addition, he was a wise, kind, and compassionate leader.

Another memory involves Fr. John McRaith, the vicar general at that time, driving me to a presentation in Bird Island. All I could see was farmland on all sides. Fr. McRaith, a warm and zealous priest, expressed his deep love for his homeland. "Look at that rich, wonderful black soil," he said. I was very embarrassed. Being a city person from the East, I thought, "I'm missing something." All I could see was dirt. Fr. McRaith became the bishop of Owensboro, Kentucky. He would subsequently undertake RENEW endeavors two different times in his new diocese.

We were beginning to see that the most fertile territory for RENEW was in the northern Midwest. With the leadership of Bishop Lucker, Sr. Kathy Warren, O.S.F., diocesan coordinator, and representatives from all the diocesan departments who helped to make up the RENEW diocesan team, it was no surprise that RENEW flourished. Kathy eventually became a valued member of our national RENEW team.

St. Louis, Missouri

An extremely successful RENEW experience took place in St. Louis. This was due largely to the leadership of Msgr. John J. Hughes, Fr. Bill Sheid, and Sr. Mary Ann Klohr, C.S.J. St. Louis had fifty thousand participants in RENEW small groups. Amazing news like this spread quickly in the early 1980s.

Msgr. Hughes is a well-known and widely-respected Church historian. His strong belief in RENEW, theologically and pastorally, surely gained the respect of thoughtful people in his diocese and beyond. Fr. Sheid's popularity among priests also was a great factor in over ninety percent of the two hundred twenty-five parishes participating in RENEW.

Msgr. Hughes and the people of St. Louis were extremely hospitable and gracious from the first moment of their inquiry. In 1983 they hosted a convocation of leaders from the dioceses involved in RENEW. There was much to be celebrated. For years afterwards, Msgr. Hughes in his writings, talks, and retreats throughout the country continued to praise RENEW and cited its influence in our Church during that period.

Toledo, Ohio

Bishop Jim Hoffman inquired about RENEW and decided to fly out with Msgr. Bob Donnelly to spend a weekend with us to learn more. They breezed into Newark like a breath of fresh air. A dynamic and energetic man, Bishop Hoffman didn't waste any time and wanted to soak in all he could about RENEW. He liked everything he heard and over a pizza and beer at my rectory table, he decided to initiate RENEW.

After joking about Toledo years ago with Cathy, I couldn't have envisioned what a successful experience RENEW would be there and what a joy it was to work with their team. Bishop Hoffman was well-liked by his priests and gave great leadership for RENEW. He wisely appointed my good friend Msgr. Donnelly, who, in turn, enrolled Sr. Gemma Fendert, O.S.F., to work with him. After RENEW, Msgr. Donnelly was ordained auxiliary bishop of Toledo and remains a good friend.

In 1984 one of our most successful convocations of RENEW leadership for various dioceses was held in Toledo. Being the pastoral people that they were, Bishop Hoffman and Msgr. Donnelly were totally involved in every session and the joyful parties during the convocation.

1983-1985

Albany, New York

Years earlier, my good friend Msgr. Ed Ciuba, then rector of our seminary, told me about Bishop Howard J. Hubbard. He was so excited and happy at the news that Fr. Hubbard had been made a bishop. He described Bishop Hubbard as a street priest, a man with and of the people. In my experience with the bishop, I found him to be worthy of all the superlatives.

One summer day in 1982, Bishop Hubbard called to inquire about RENEW. When he asked if we could meet, I told him I'd be happy to drive to Albany, but he quickly insisted on meeting half way. So it was that we had a fine dinner and sharing on a pleasant summer evening in the Catskill Mountains.

Albany was the first diocesan RENEW effort in that part of the country, and it proved to be very successful. Over twenty thousand people participated in RENEW small groups.

Billings, Montana

In the summer of 1982, I took a trip with two priest friends to Glacier National Park and then on to the Canadian Rockies. The sights were spectacular and memorable.

Also memorable was the beginning of my trip, starting with a meeting with Bishop Thomas Murphy and a group of outstanding priests he had invited for an evening in one of their rectories. A lively meeting clearly indicated great interest on the part of Bishop Murphy and the other priests. It was a great kickoff to an enjoyable vacation break and also the beginning of a good RENEW experience.

Helena, Montana

Right from the beginning, Bishop Murphy said that he would try to enlist the involvement of his neighbor in Helena so that the entire state of Montana would be sharing the same spiritual journey. Bishop Elden Curtiss was agreeable to the idea and both Montana dioceses began together in 1983. Fr. Bob Beaulieu became the diocesan director of RENEW and was eventually granted a five-year leave of absence by Bishop Curtiss to work with our national RENEW team.

Other memories of Montana include wide-open spaces with an unobstructed view of the sky in all directions. I had never seen anything like it before. Travel between workshops in Montana was also quite amazing and thrilling. Since there were no speed laws in Montana, we flew along the roadways at incredible rates. Meanwhile, trying to live a low-cholesterol diet in cattle country with my heart history was quite challenging.

Joliet, Illinois

Bishop Joseph L. Imesch is a great down-to-earth man, ordained the same year as I was. We hit it off well.

Fr. Bob Fuller returned to RENEW from Joliet after several priests' presentations at which he stressed that RENEW is a process and not a program. He extolled the advantages of a process over a program. Afterward, the first thing the bishop said to Bob was, "If there's one thing I can't stand, it is a process." Nevertheless, Bob had done a great job of presenting to the priests, and RENEW made good pastoral sense to Bishop Imesch who went on to initiate the process.

Orlando, Florida

In 1982, in addition to RENEW, I was still working with three departments in Newark, one of which dealt with the collegial process in parish councils. I went to the convention of the Parish and Diocesan Council Network being held in Orlando. PADICON was a national organization of diocesan planners and parish council staff people. We made many fine contacts for RENEW at that conference, one of whom was a young layman, Bob Shearer, who was representing the Orlando Diocese.

Bob liked what he was hearing about RENEW and wanted us to make contact with the diocesan leadership. During one of the breaks at the conference, we visited the chancery and talked with diocesan staff about RENEW. This led to an appointment with Bishop Thomas J. Grady who also responded well to RENEW and decided to call a gathering of all the diocesan priests to hear about the RENEW process.

The day of that presentation proved to be quite interesting. Usually, I would try to mingle with the priests before any presentation to get a feel for the diocese, the mood of the priests, their hopes, and their concerns. I was well aware that a large contingency of the priests were Irish born. Someone pointed to Fr. Guy Sheedy, noting that he was the leader of the Irish contingent. As I engaged in conversation with him, I could immediately see that he was extremely friendly and an outstanding priest. That meeting went well and, at its conclusion, Bishop Grady asked for verbal feedback from the priests to see if they thought RENEW would be good for the diocese. Upon hearing an extremely favorable response, Bishop Grady announced that he would initiate RENEW.

Fr. Guy Sheedy, Fr. Guy Noonan, and Bob Shearer were appointed to leadership positions for RENEW. A year later Fr. Sheedy reported to me the number of people returning to confession after having been away for a great number of years. When he asked them why they were returning, they replied it was because of RENEW. No doubt it was also due to the leadership of Fr. Sheedy who did a tremendous job with RENEW in both his parish and the diocese.

St. Cloud, Minnesota

Being in St. Cloud helped me catch up with my geography. I was surprised to find that the Mississippi River runs alongside St. Cloud. My vision had always pictured the Mississippi River farther south, without giving thought to its origin.

On the other hand, my memory is clouded by the fact that I had the shingles during my stay. The temperature was two degrees above zero, with the wind chill factor considerably lower. Unfortunately, what I best remember is how painful it was getting in and out of the car. Fortunately the RENEW experience in St. Cloud was far from painful; in fact, it was most successful.

San Diego, California

I have friends in San Diego who helped make my work in that diocese especially enjoyable. The fact that San Diego has the best climate in the country was certainly an added benefit.

Fr. John Dickey and Sr. Mary Jo Nelson, O.L.V.M., saw to it that the RENEW process in that diocese enjoyed strong and effective leadership. Fr. Dickey had previously coordinated the California Bishops Conference. His position was extremely important there, since California could really be a country in itself. He brought the skills and talents he honed in that position to San Diego's successful RENEW experience.

1984-1986

New Orleans, Louisiana

My first meeting with Archbishop Philip Hannan occurred on the evening he had returned from a meeting of the U.S. Conference of Catholic Bishops in Chicago. He was a former military chaplain and was on the news that evening as part of a small minority of nine bishops who voted against a pastoral letter calling for nuclear disarmament. The resolution had passed with a vast majority of the other bishops. Frankly, I didn't know what to expect in meeting with him the next morning.

Archbishop Hannan proved to be a very impressive pastoral man. As I was explaining the process of RENEW to him, I mentioned how the archdiocese could use RENEW to its advantage by addressing local concerns between seasons. He immediately called the seminary rector, who happened to be a scripture scholar, and asked him to join us. He explained to the rector that RENEW would foster a great love for the Scriptures in the local people and would leave them ready to learn more about the Word of God. Speaking to the rector, Archbishop Hannan said, "As you know, we're in Bible-belt territory and Jimmy Swaggart is much larger than life in our region. In between seasons of RENEW, I want you to organize scripture courses throughout the archdiocese that will counter this fundamentalist approach with a more correct understanding of the Scriptures."

I realized that Archbishop Hannan, perhaps more than any other, had caught what we were really trying to do. We wanted the local diocese to take ownership of RENEW and build upon it. RENEW would create tremendous interest among the people and inspire them to be open to agendas that were critical to the needs of the local Church.

We moved from his office into the next room where a large group of archdiocesan personnel had gathered. They quickly expressed their liking for RENEW, and the next day the priests of the archdiocese voted overwhelmingly for the archdiocese to initiate the process.

Although I can't remember their names, the priest and sister coordinators were excellent diocesan leaders and very enjoyable to work with. What I am sure of is that working with New Orleans was the beginning of my conviction that the people of Louisiana were the friendliest people in our country.

Baton Rouge, Louisiana

I was scheduled to return home from New Orleans on Friday evening, but upon hearing that Baton Rouge was less than two hours away I decided to explore the possibility that Bishop Stanley Ott would be available on short notice on Saturday morning, and he was.

Bishop Ott was returning in a sweat suit from his daily jog when I arrived at his residence on Saturday morning. That was the beginning of a wonderful friendship with a man whom our whole staff deeply loved and respected. He was for empowering lay people. He was totally committed to spiritual renewal.

Bishop Ott was surely the only bishop in America who had a baseball and bat on his coat of arms. His cousin was the famous Mel Ott, a Hall of Fame right fielder who had played for the New York Giants. This humble, down-to-earth bishop immediately expressed his desire to initiate RENEW.

Not surprisingly, Bishop Ott appointed an excellent diocesan RENEW team. The director, Msgr. Bill Greene, was well liked and very effective. He ran a large, magnificent parish and brought the same pastoring skills to his diocesan work. Sr. Susan Monda, O.S.F., and Hermann Schluter ably assisted him.

Hermann had a very interesting background. As a young Catholic man he had gone to what he thought was a weekend seminar on a topic totally unrelated to faith. He was shocked to see that the first speaker was a priest and was told that he was sitting in the midst of a spiritual retreat. Hermann, who had little interest, wondered what he was doing there. During the weekend, he was to have a profound spiritual renewal experience that would last a lifetime.

At the time RENEW came to the diocese, Hermann held an executive position with Exxon. He surprised himself by agreeing to leave that lucrative position and work for the diocesan RENEW effort, which caused a drastic change in lifestyle. For many years afterwards, Hermann kept in touch with us and was a wonderful supporter and advocate proclaiming the virtues of RENEW. It is no wonder that this outstanding team, starting with Bishop Ott himself, would lead an extremely successful effort in Baton Rouge that involved the entire diocese, including a successful effort on the campus of Louisiana State.

Bishop Ott proudly proclaimed his belief in RENEW by having a prominent RENEW bumper sticker on his car. He said, "Originally, we had dreamed that ten thousand of the faithful would gather in small groups to pray, to read Scripture, and to share their journey in faith. To my surprise more than twenty thousand Catholics participated."

Cheyenne, Wyoming

My initial visit to talk to the priests of Cheyenne blew my mind. Being a city person from the East, I couldn't believe the wide-open spaces. Fortunately, the priests were very responsive, as were the parishioners. Margo LeBert was an outstanding Diocesan RENEW coordinator who would follow up by joining our national RENEW team.

Crookston, Minnesota

Because these days were so full and active, it is hard to recall many details. However, I do remember my initial visit with Bishop Victor Balke and a presentation to the priests. It was an upbeat day. Not only were the priests receptive, but Bishop Balke became extremely supportive and a long-time friend of RENEW. His encouragement helped participation rise to 99 percent of the parishes. Sr. Pat Murphy, C.S.J., coordinator, provided outstanding leadership and Fr. Mike Patnode, spiritual director of RENEW, provided the spiritual impetus. Both were ardent believers in RENEW. Thousands of people participated in Crookston's RENEW small groups including many couples in which one spouse was a member of another faith tradition.

Hartford, Connecticut

In 1983, Fred Perella, director of the Family Life Office, heard about RENEW and came to visit us. He immediately took interest in RENEW, which delighted us. Why not? Hartford was a large northeastern diocese that we could easily relate to, and it was also the first diocese in New England to show interest.

Fred went home and spoke with Archbishop John Whealon and the priests of the diocese. Little did I realize at the time that outside of our own archdiocesan experience in Newark, Hartford would have the most successful RENEW experience of all dioceses and that its impact would be long-lasting.

The leadership provided, not only by Archbishop Whealon but also by the diocesan RENEW team of Auxiliary Bishop Peter Rosazza, Mrs. Pat Linehan, and Sr. Joan Bernier, S.N.D., were incredible. We had regarded New England as the area least responsive to RENEW, but Hartford had one hundred ninety-nine out of two hundred twenty-two parishes participating with thirty-five thousand parishioners involved in RENEW small groups. An average of two hundred per parish signed up, with the top figure being a total of six hundred fifty in one parish. To this day they have followed through actively with small-community development. It is from this Small Christian Community Office created as a follow-up to RENEW that, under the direction of Br. Bob Moriarty, S.M., the highly successful *Quest* publication for small groups is published.

From Brookfield comes a story about individual change wrought by RENEW. It concerns a man who had been away from the Church for years but wanted to give God "one last chance."

Upon going to his local church, he found it was Sign-Up Sunday—the day on which parishioners were asked to make a commitment to RENEW. Not really knowing what RENEW was all about, he signed up for a small group as part of his "last chance" resolve.

God won the man over. Not only did he return to church permanently but he also became the head of the parish RENEW team's Sign-Up Sunday Committee.

Oklahoma City, Oklahoma

Fr. Bob Fuller and Sr. Donna Ciangio had much more involvement than I did with Oklahoma City. I remember some initial phone calls that opened the door for our visits there, but I especially remember years later eventually getting to Oklahoma. Finally I had visited all fifty states in the Union.

St. Augustine, Florida

I could easily talk the same language with Bishop Jack Snyder. He is a wonderfully pastoral man from Brooklyn. Understandably, when he heard about RENEW, he offered an invitation for me to come and speak to his priests. The priests were receptive, due in no small part, to the strong leadership given by Bishop Snyder.

On a subsequent trip, I had the opportunity to speak with all the diocesan offices and agencies, helping them to appreciate the value of RENEW and to get on board in support of a diocesan effort. I also made a suggestion that the office and agency personnel form small faith-sharing groups themselves.

On that occasion I became friendly with a layman who worked with Catholic Charities. To my delight, he wrote me a letter a few weeks later saying that he had been made the leader of a RENEW small group that met at the diocesan community center at 7 a.m. every Thursday. In the letter he wrote, "Oh, by the way, Bishop Snyder is in my group!"

Fr. Mike Larkin became the diocesan director and a good personal friend. He is still pastor of a large dynamic parish he had at that time, along with his RENEW duties. It is no wonder that RENEW was strong in St. Augustine.

Washington, District of Columbia

Another memorable RENEW experience was meeting Cardinal James Hickey who was gracious and welcoming for our successful initial presentation to the priests. He appointed an outstanding diocesan team that included Fr. Ray Kemp, S.J., a very outgoing and gregarious leader. Ray was simply great fun to work with. He was strongly involved locally and nationally in the adult catechumenate and currently works as professor at Georgetown University. He is also a senior research fellow at the Woodstock Theological Center.

John Butler, Ph.D., shared a key leadership position with Ray. John became a strong believer in RENEW and, fortunately for us, is now one of the most valued members of our Board of Trustees.

RENEW in Washington also connected me with Bill and Mary Noel Page whose marriage ceremony I had performed in Our Lady of Mercy, Park Ridge, New Jersey. Mary Noel's experience with small communities goes back to her early high school years as a leader in one of our parish Young Christian Student groups.

Along with Beaumont, Texas, Washington, D.C., had the largest participation from the African-American community.

Rockford, Illinois

My initial visit to Rockford provided me with still another geography lesson. I had never made a close association with Rockford and Chicago. On the way to the diocesan priests' meeting, Fr. Karl Ganss explained that a good number of people commuted from Rockford every day to work in Chicago. All kinds of lovely suburbs were blossoming in the area.

Bishop Arthur O'Neill was magnificent. A pleasant man, he became a long-time friend of RENEW. Karl became the diocesan RENEW director and, along with Sr. Regina Baker, O.P., associate director, oversaw a strong RENEW process that engaged ten thousand people in small communities. All pastors reported satisfaction with the vast majority expressing very high praise.

According to Karl, RENEW accomplished many things: "It reenergized the Catholic faithful with a larger image of Church; it created a groundswell for a deeper biblical understanding and increased a spirit of volunteerism. It gave participants more confidence in witnessing to their faith. People led prayer and openly shared their lives with one another."

Karl described another major benefit accrued from RENEW: it helped to establish a ministry-formation office to equip lay Catholics to realize their gifts in service to their parishes. The office developed courses and hired instructors "to energize the already-excited lay people of the Rockford Diocese."

1985-1987

Buffalo, New York

One day I stopped at a phone booth at a busy intersection in Elizabeth, New Jersey, and called the office asking, "Is anything new happening?" Alice shared that Bishop Edward Head called, and I was to return his call. When I did, he told me he had decided to start RENEW. I probably surprised him by saying I would make believe I hadn't heard him say that. It may sound risky not to immediately take him up on his word, but I preferred that there be a process by which the whole diocese buys in. When I did get to speak to the full presbyterate of the diocese, I was interested to learn that all but two priests in the diocese had encouraged the bishop to initiate RENEW. By this point, I could not help but be confident that the priests would respond very positively.

Bishop Head was wonderful to work with, as were his RENEW diocesan leaders, Fr. Tom Maloney and Sr. Louise Alff, O.S.F. Louise eventually came to work with RENEW for five years and wound up staying eight years. Words fall far short in trying to explain the virtues of Louise. She is truly one of the most humble, self-effacing, zealous, and genuine people you could ever hope to meet. With people like her, and with Fr. Tom at the helm, Buffalo could hardly fail but to touch the lives of many.

In an article written by Fr. Maloney, he quoted Msgr. John Gorman, then pastor of St. Michael's in Orland, Illinois, and later auxiliary bishop of Chicago. Referring to the RENEW process in his parish, Msgr. Gorman remarked, "In fifty percent of our many groups there were one, two, sometimes three people who were not churchgoers, but because of the style and the location in homes and the kind of discussion they felt comfortable in coming, and every one of them had a very fine experience. Some, in fact, came back to the formal practice of their faith."

Grande Island, Nebraska

Although I didn't work directly with Grande Island, I can say that one of the finest blessings that came out of that diocese's RENEW experience was that the director, Fr. Tom Dowd, came to work as part of our national RENEW team, giving excellent service for many years to both the English- and Spanish-speaking people.

Little Rock, Arkansas

Little Rock's participation in a diocesan RENEW effort was noteworthy. Little Rock was the origin of the very famous and popular *Little Rock Scripture Series*. For Bishop Andrew McDonald and his team to choose RENEW as a follow-up was a great compliment. Just as interesting was the fact that Fr. James Mancini, who played a leadership role in the *Little Rock Scripture Series*, became the diocesan RENEW Director.

Trenton, New Jersey

By 1985 my family had long been living in the Trenton Diocese, so for RENEW to come to Trenton would be very special for me.

Bishop John Reiss was extremely receptive to the idea of RENEW. The talk to the assembly of Trenton priests brought me a little bit more tension and excitement. Fortunately, the priests moved overwhelmingly for Bishop Reiss to start RENEW.

Fr. Michael Walsh was made the diocesan director; a finer director there never was. Mike is gifted with an exceptional ability to relate to others, and he did a superior job in rallying the support and involvement of priests and lay people alike.

The City of Trenton benefitted from the RENEW process in another way. A building contractor, Robert Nami, participated in the process in his parish—St. John's in Allentown, New Jersey—and was inspired during a small-group discussion to consider how he could use his special gifts to help others. Robert felt he could build low-cost homes if the opportunity presented itself. He discussed the idea with Trenton officials, met state requirements, and bid on a group of lots where he built sixteen three-bedroom houses selling for under $50,000. Nami remarked, "I don't want to just build houses; I want to build homes, places where people can raise their kids."

Things were going better for RENEW than one could have dared to dream. We were well on our way to eventually involving over five million U.S. parishioners in the RENEW small groups, and the process was about to be enriched even further.

CHAPTER 13

Enriching RENEW

The passing of time provides insight and can certainly heighten appreciation. It is amazing how God's providential care guided and responded to RENEW's needs at every step of the way. Certainly Bob Fuller's coming to minister with us is a case in point. He arrived just as RENEW's great expansion was beginning, and he brought so many personal talents to us in the early 1980s. Now a new specific set of needs was arising, and another unexpected gift was about to appear.

In early 1983, I participated in a small-group study day in Washington, D.C., where I conducted a morning workshop. The afternoon gave me time to attend a workshop given by Fr. Tom Caroluzza of Virginia Beach, Virginia. I had heard of Tom and of the magnificent job he was doing with small communities in his parish. As I listened, I found it almost unbelievable. It seemed that even in detail we approached and carried out the work of small communities in the same way. Since not everybody at the time shared similar enthusiasm for small communities, discovering someone with his view and passion was a great gift.

Tom and I talked, enjoying the fact that we had so much in common. I thought Tom might like to visit our New Jersey RENEW office. We could show him first-hand how our RENEW small groups were spreading and convey the value of our common convictions. On April 6, 1983, Tom visited and, in short time, received permission from his bishop to join our RENEW team. I could hardly have fully realized then the importance of this turn of events.

At that time, we were concerned that our liturgy materials were wanting. Original RENEW had centered on specific years of the liturgical cycle: the readings that ran between October 1978 and the fall of 1980. We had created an interim solution, but we needed to prepare for the future.

Tom called a two-day meeting with some of his outstanding, nationally regarded liturgical friends to seek a solution. The resolution we came to meant undertaking a huge task. In short, we needed to develop ninety weeks of new and improved materials. In a timely order, the task was addressed and accomplished.

RENEW and the RCIA

No sooner had our previous concern been addressed than a new and potentially more damaging one surfaced. Respected leaders throughout the country were beginning to see and speak of a tension they saw between the agenda of RENEW and the emerging Rite of Christian Initiation for Adults.

Christiane Brusselmans (1930-1991), a Belgian theologian, had, along with others, done a great deal of research in church history and felt that leaders in the early days of the Church had used a much finer way of introducing and initiating people into the Catholic faith. The approach involved several stages:

1. Inquiry
2. Catechumenate
3. Purification and Enlightenment
4. Mystagogy or Post-baptismal Catechesis.

As we know, this Rite of Christian Initiation for Adults involves a beautiful communal approach that introduces people to our faith in a manner vastly different from times past. Until that time, one-on-one instruction was usually given by the parish priest. In the RCIA, people were not only learning intellectually but they also were having a rich experience of Church that culminated in the celebration of the sacraments of Christian initiation at the Easter Vigil.

The introduction of the RCIA in parishes called for a lot of pastoral change and emphasis. To catch hold, RCIA needed to be vigorously promoted; that task was taken on largely by the North American Forum on the Catechumenate. Not only was the RCIA an outstanding approach to initiating people into the faith, but it also highlighted a way of church life that would be most healthy and renewing for the entire parish. In view of this, some saw RENEW as a competitor, distracting people from the Church's true renewal process and from emphasis on the newly-developed liturgical cycle. Some believed that following the Church's liturgical process and incorporating the RCIA would alone bring true renewal for parishioners. In this view, the great popularity of RENEW was providing a diversion from the Church's very sound pastoral approach.

Fortunately, Tom and I saw things differently. We felt that rather than competing, the processes could complement each other. RCIA and RENEW could help each other in advancing their important common goals.

I was also heartened at the time to attend and hear an address by the well-respected liturgist Fr. Aiden Kavenagh, O.S.B., at a conference for RCIA leaders. Recognizing the current tension, he made a point of saying that the work of church renewal should be looked at in a wider sense, with plenty of room for various approaches.

Tom was highly regarded by leaders of the RCIA movement. He was vice-president of the North American Forum on the Catechumenate and a very close friend of Fr. Jim Dunning, who was president and the nationally recognized leader of the RCIA. Tom thought it would be beneficial to call together a three-day session for liturgical and RCIA leaders. Christiane Brusselmans and many catechumenal leaders came to New Jersey for the meeting. It helped that Jim Dunning, Christiane, and many other participants knew that Tom would not be promoting and working for a cause that was detrimental to liturgical principles and the RCIA.

From RENEW's perspective, we believed that all four stages of the RCIA process would be enhanced with the use of small communities. RENEW would be an ally in bringing to the work of the RCIA many people who valued small Christian communities. In his parish, Tom himself had used small communities for all stages of the RCIA process, even conducting the inquiry stage in parishioners' homes.

I saw great value in leading people into the RCIA process from RENEW and also had strong interest in small communities for the mystagogy stage. I believed then, and believe even more strongly today, that after baptism too many neophytes could land in the larger parish community and become lost. Unfortunately, the style of parish life could be quite disappointing to many after their rich experience. Why not create a normal flow with the expectation that every newly baptized person join a small Christian community as an ongoing, strong component of his or her faith life? Since statistics have proven that too many people are, in fact, lost to the Church in a few short years after their baptism, this period of mystagogy must be seen as critically important.

Some dioceses we worked with in Nigeria, where huge numbers join the Church each year through the RCIA, quite readily picked up this principle. That practice could well be applied everywhere.

The results of our three-day session were extremely gratifying. The whole realization of complementarity, and even unified promotion of our collective agendas, was strongly affirmed.

Tom Groome and Shared Christian Praxis

From the earliest days, we wanted RENEW to be more than just another program. Programs come and go. We proposed that small communities become a part of regular parish life. Because RENEW engaged large numbers of people in small communities, and response to this involvement was so overwhelmingly positive, it became obvious that this momentum should not be lost.

In all our presentations and workshops, we continually promoted the idea of continuing and developing small groups into true small Christian communities that took on the full mission of the Church. We gave special attention in the last year of a parish RENEW effort to assure that essential pieces be kept in place long term to further that end.

As stated earlier, Sr. Mary George O'Reilly suggested that those core communities should become permanent in the parish after RENEW, taking on new blood and interest from people who had emerged in RENEW small groups. Our efforts worked strongly to augment that.

We also realized that establishing diocesan small-community departments would go a long way to fulfilling our goals. Tom suggested that toward this end it would be helpful for us to use Tom Groome's methodology, known as *Shared Christian Praxis*, for adult learning and formation. This approach consisted of five main components: present action, critical reflection, dialogue, the story, and the vision that arises from the story. We held two-day diocesan sessions that gathered parish and diocesan leadership, along with the diocesan bishop, to help them reflect on the meaning and value of the RENEW process and come to concrete decisions and actions about what was needed for follow-through.

We piloted the use of this approach with the Diocese of Orlando as it was nearing the end of its three-year process. Our entire RENEW team took part in this pilot experience so that any of us could carry out the process in our many involved dioceses. The pilot was not only successful but also a fun occasion for our staff. It brought us together at a time when we were frequently scattered across the country.

Use of this process in Buffalo stands out in my mind. The process went well, with many outstanding reflective comments being made about how meaningful the RENEW small-group experience had been. A clear consensus was emerging for a future direction. Toward the very end, Bishop Edward Head, whom I immensely enjoyed, engaged me in conversation. Ignoring the process, he asked me, "Tom, what do you think we should do?" "Well, Bishop, that's what the process is really about, leading you to a conclusion." "But Tom, what do you think we should do?" "Well, Bishop, I wouldn't want to be too direct in answering that." "Well, Tom, you're never too direct. Tell me." "Bishop, I think you should start a diocesan office for small Christian communities to develop and promote them on a permanent basis throughout the diocese!" Buffalo proceeded to start a diocesan small Christian community office and appointed an outstanding person to direct it.

Amazingly, at one point in the 1980s, through the workings of RENEW, over sixty dioceses had established small Christian community departments flowing out of their RENEW experience. Perhaps it was all too good to be true. When a time of national recession arrived, diocesan budgets were slashed dramatically. In many instances, the last office formed, the newest kid on the block, was the first to go.

Addressing Priestless Parishes

In 1985, RENEW International was asked to co-sponsor a conference on the future of the Church to address the worldwide problem of increased numbers of priestless parishes. Although we were cash-strapped, we readily agreed because the project was so worthwhile. That June, Christiane Brusselmans convened church leaders to reflect on this concern at the International Symposium on the Local Church near Bruges, Belgium. Many of the invitees were people with rich small-community experience.

Knowing many of the catechumenate leaders in Europe and the United States, Tom Caroluzza was deeply involved in the conference. It was an historic gathering, held in an old castle surrounded by a moat, now the Abbey of St. Trudo. Entrance to the castle was over a bridge. The exchange of ideas that took place was incredibly rich, with people from every continent and every region engaged.

On the last morning Cardinal Basil Hume from Westminster gave the final talk to the assembly. I was surprised that in addressing this problem of parishes without priests, he mentioned in a favorable light the ordination of married priests. The conference—including Cardinal Hume's comments—received good press coverage.

Meanwhile, Back in Newark

As RENEW was gaining national attention, our Small Christian Community Department in Newark, a direct outgrowth of RENEW, was developing insightful ideas regarding small communities that would become incorporated into the fiber of RENEW and eventually be promoted worldwide. Since I was still involved in overseeing the SCC Department, I became quite engaged in much of the brainstorming, which I enjoyed immensely.

One of our first undertakings was to look at what components made small communities successful and what made them fail. We arrived at five essential elements for authentic small communities.

1. Sharing: talking freely about God and about life experiences while reflecting on these in the light of Scripture and Tradition.

2. Learning: acquiring a greater knowledge and understanding of the Scriptures, the Catholic Church and its teachings, along with the application of those teachings to everyday life.

3. Mutual Support: encouraging one another in faith and in authentic living out of the Gospel. We emphasized this element not to counteract society's failing in this regard but, even more, to encourage members to develop friendships in faith.

4. Mission: going far beyond wonderful sharing to concrete, positive action. The community's actions were to affect participants' lives in the family, workplace, neighborhood, and the wider society.

5. Prayer: realizing the centrality of God's active presence in the lives of community members and in the community itself.

It is interesting to note how widely accepted these principles of small communities became in circles far beyond RENEW.

A Community of Many Small Communities

As early as 1981 our Newark Department of Small Christian Communities made an important decision that would capture a vision of parish life we would hold and propose for decades. The idea, simply put, was that the parish becomes a community made up of many small communities. Interestingly, Pope John Paul II in his millennium address to the Church of the Americas (2000) endorsed this vision for parishes.

In this vision, not every parishioner, but a large number of parishioners, would choose to be members of small Christian communities. This experience would help them transform their lives to live out their faith in every possible life situation. Imagine thousands of Catholics formed in a way that helps them act upon the ideals and of their faith in every area of life.

Catholics are the largest denomination in our country. If every Catholic in business, finance, politics—you name it—lived out his or her Catholic faith in these vital areas, our country and our world would truly be transformed for the good. This approach would move us beyond the practice of taking on laudable projects to the even more needed practice of living out our faith where we already are. Every one of us lives in situations of influence. Living our faith, not just on Sunday mornings, but seven days a week, would make all the difference. Small Christian communities have a potential to move us toward that end.

And so we continued to help people look at the dynamic life cycle introduced and diagrammed in Chapter 6. People gather in small communities weekly, bring that experience to Sunday Eucharist for further nourishment and strength, and then are sent forth to live their Christian values during the week and bring the fullness of their weekly faith life to their small community meeting. This model presents an exciting life cycle for enriching parish life.

RENEW continues to propose and encourage this pastoral direction.

From Committee to Community

"An end of committee in the Catholic Church, and the beginning of community" was a slogan we loved to proclaim. Parishioners were finding so many meetings boring and dull—another business meeting at the end of a long work day.

In our talks and training, we contrasted that experience with what parish life could be. Imagine every parish group, committee, and meeting starting with an unhurried and reflective time of prayer and shared faith. This prayerful faith experience could easily flow into the business of the meeting and influence it for good. Parish finance committees would find that financial considerations were balanced with a healthy awareness of parish mission. Parish pastoral councils would more easily avoid potentially contentious discussions and exchanges because of their common shared faith and their heightened awareness of Christ's presence.

The list of possibilities could go on, but the point is clear. Our parish meetings need not emulate the style experienced in our everyday world, but rather reflect the rich experience of communal shared faith life.

Continual insistence on and promotion of this idea has been one of RENEW's greatest contributions to the Church. RENEW has truly helped make unrushed prayer and faith sharing at the beginning of parish meetings much more accepted as a parish way of life today.

More Divine Providence

God's divine providence continued to be at play. In 1987 I received word that, for various internal reasons, Newark was seriously considering closing the Department of Small Christian Communities. Would we continue the work by incorporating that small community activity at our RENEW office in Plainfield? I happily agreed, and with the responsibility for small communities came one of RENEW's greatest gifts, Sr. Mary McGuinness.

Mary had been with our office in Newark as far back as 1979 and lived and breathed every aspect of RENEW and its pastoral approaches. Mary became the coordinator of all our publications and quickly raised the bar to a far more professional level. While excelling in that area, her gifts were used in every possible aspect of RENEW. That included writing, brainstorming, and giving road presentations, while maintaining a strong emphasis in all RENEW efforts on the centrality of Christ in spirituality.

Perhaps even more, Mary became our troubleshooter. Whenever a difficulty arose, we knew that the problem could be assigned with confidence to Mary, and that it would quietly and effectively be solved. Her keen intellect and theological background also proved invaluable when doctrinal challenges were presented later in *RENEW 2000*. In the role of publishing, she kept in constant contact with Msgr. James Cafone in Newark's doctrinal oversight committee to assure that all of RENEW's materials were sound and were approved by our archbishop. Other staff members really appreciated the troubleshooting assignments taken on by Mary.

Another exceedingly valuable person, Margo LeBert, came on board in early 1987. Margo had directed the successful RENEW effort in Cheyenne, Wyoming. Fr. Bob Fuller had worked with Cheyenne and encouraged her to join our RENEW staff.

Margo was truly brilliant. Given any possible assignment, she would have everything finished, typed up, and on my desk at the beginning of the next day. Margo developed our first set of materials on the *Catechism of the Catholic Church* that later developed into our *Why Catholic?* process. Her gifts extended to being a very popular and well-received presenter. She became the coordinator of our RENEW services to dioceses. Margo's move east was not only providential for us but also for her personally. It was here that she met and married her beloved husband, Bernie Lester.

Margo spent the next decade with RENEW, working doggedly for the development of *RENEW 2000* through extremely painful cancer until her death in October 1997.

Divine providence continued to bless us. At an event in the mother-house of the Sisters of St. Joseph of Peace in Englewood Cliffs, New Jersey, I had met and was very impressed with Sr. Cecilia King, C.S.J.P., retired provincial of her community. She was dynamite and ready to go from the first moment you met her.

Later, in talking with Bob Fuller about personnel, I told him Cecilia was a woman of great potential. He volunteered to visit her and sound out the possibilities of her coming to RENEW. Once again I was of little faith, saying I couldn't possibly imagine her becoming a RENEW team member. She should be heading a national organization. Bob returned and told me she had some interest. Not long after, Cecilia was studying theology at Harvard and the Weston School of Theology. Taking a chance, I called and asked if she would be willing to visit RENEW and explore possibilities. To my delight, she readily agreed.

Back in those days, the entire staff gathered whenever a prospective member visited. You might say it was a collegial hiring process. Upon listening to Cecilia, in the middle of the meeting, Tom Caroluzza called out, "You're hired." And that was it. Cecilia came to RENEW.

Some of my most wonderful and enjoyable RENEW experiences were on the road working with Cecilia in India and Nigeria. She was a wonder woman, as she very directly called bishops and priests to RENEW involvement. It was almost exhausting to watch her in action. Our days usually ended with prayer, followed by time spent sharing the day's progress over a bottle of Star beer. In the most trying living conditions, Cecilia would greet me at breakfast saying, "Isn't it a privilege for us to be here?" She is the most zealous and courageous person I've known. To this day Cecilia calls RENEW the finest experience of her long religious life.

While these three fortuitous gifts were arriving on the RENEW scene, other developments were taking place that would affect my personal life. A Newark official told me that chancery leaders were concerned that I was doing too much. Heading RENEW along with three departments in Newark was seen as overload. Actually, at the time, my heart was in excellent shape, and I was going at full steam with great enthusiasm. But I was given a choice. Give up RENEW and head up the three Newark departments, or give up the Newark departments and stay with RENEW. My response was that I would pray and deliberate and give my answer directly to Archbishop Gerety himself. The answer, in any event, would have been RENEW. But that was made all the more imperative by the fact that both Fr. Bob Fuller and Fr. Tom Caroluzza were being called back to their dioceses by their bishops.

The meeting with Archbishop Gerety was very profitable in that I came away from it with the full-time services for RENEW of one of Newark's priests, Fr. Dominic Fuccile. Dominic's presentations on the road were well received as he conveyed keen insights into human nature and spirituality.

I spent these years living and sleeping in an office in Plainfield where I worked and spent the early mornings on an exercise bicycle in the basement.

But life couldn't have been better. RENEW was booming, and life was wonderful. Little did I know that some dark clouds were on the horizon.

CHAPTER 14

Low Tide

As a Jersey Shore man, I would say that the waves were riding in high for RENEW—there was high enthusiasm and the tide was all flowing our way.

But the eventual low tide was about to occur, not in the RENEW experience itself or in its continued growth but in a distraction that was about to drain some of our time and energy.

As RENEW grew it was inevitable that it would start receiving closer scrutiny. One day in early 1986, Archbishop Gerety called me in. He had heard some complaints about our materials and wanted to clear up the issue. He felt confident in the soundness of the RENEW process but asked me to send our materials to Archbishop John R. Quinn in San Francisco, who was at that time the head of the Bishops' Doctrine Committee. He asked that the Bishops' Doctrine Committee review our materials for any needed clarification. A subcommittee consisting of Bishop William Levada, Bishop Elden Curtiss, and Bishop Donald Wuerl were to conduct the actual review.

In November 1986, Theodore McCarrick, the newly-appointed archbishop of Newark, received a response from Bishop James Lessard who, at that point, was chairman of the bishops' doctrine committee. The bishops' report started with a section entitled "General Commendation of the RENEW Process." They spoke of the significant success RENEW had in dioceses and commended RENEW for analyzing the spiritual needs of our people and developing a process that built more vigorous faith-enlivened communities. They then went on to say the following:

> Our review of the published materials which describe the RENEW process, and our dialog with some bishops who experienced it, confirmed the positive evaluation mentioned above. Since the accomplishments and promise of this process are so significant, we address the following concerns in an effort to improve it.

The bishops listed four areas of concern they wished us to address:

1. a tendency toward generic Christianity
2. greater balance and completeness
3. more emphasis on the cognitive dimensions of faith
4. a broader definition of Eucharist with an emphasis on sacrifice and worship.

We welcomed these critiques. In truth, we had seen RENEW as a simple spiritual exercise for our Catholic audience that was being built upon solid catechetical and faith formation in our archdiocese. (We had never envisioned that RENEW would become the major player in so many cities and towns.) Since RENEW had now become such a major influence in church life across the country, it was understandable that there be an expectation of it being more thorough and complete in faith formation. Expectations had gone beyond the simple spiritual exercise we had originally envisioned.

The critique was not so much about what was stated incorrectly in our materials as it was about elements we needed to add in order to provide a fuller understanding of our Catholic faith. Since our commitment from day one was to serve the mainstream institutional Church, we quickly went about making the necessary improvements.

In the conclusion of their report, the bishops wrote, "Even though we offer several suggestions for improving the process, we want to make it clear that we recognize the overall value of this renewal effort for our people."

When we had completed our revision of RENEW materials, we sent them to the Bishops' Doctrine Committee. On December 16, 1987, Bishop Lessard sent a letter to Archbishop McCarrick stating:

> The Committee on Doctrine commends the Archdiocese of Newark for its careful and comprehensive process for review of RENEW materials. Recognizing the basic soundness of the RENEW process, and strengthening of the RENEW materials as a result of the review and revision, the Committee on Doctrine is pleased that this effort has been completed in keeping with its recommendations and feels confident that the RENEW program will be richer and more helpful to dioceses and parishioners as a consequence of this collaborative effort.

Archbishop McCarrick, in turn, sent a letter to all bishops in the country in 1988, assuring them of the completion of the review and of its positive conclusion.

The process of modifying the materials had naturally taken a great amount of time and effort. In this we were greatly assisted by a theological review committee in our own archdiocese that Archbishop McCarrick had set up to work with our RENEW team. Over the years this theological team has been extremely valuable to our RENEW process. In particular, Msgr. James M. Cafone, S.T.D., assistant professor of religious studies at Seton Hall University, has generously given an extraordinary amount of his time and insight in helping us at RENEW.

Despite this very positive process, The *Wanderer*, a national Catholic weekly newspaper, and some other naysayers, continued to speak in very negative terms of RENEW and the review of our materials. We came to realize that regardless of the positive results of the review, nothing could be said that would satisfy their criticisms. We stood by the actual report and the facts of the matter, which were more than enough.

Perhaps the most fitting conclusion was that two of the three members of the Review Committee, Bishop (now Cardinal) Levada and Archbishop Curtiss, both initiated RENEW, not once but twice, repeating the process a second time in new dioceses they headed.

While a great amount of effort was put into working with the bishops' Doctrine Committee, it was time well spent and extremely valuable to us. That was not the case with some of the critiques received years later when *RENEW 2000* was initiated. Critiques, at that point, were coming not from ecclesial authority and not from bishops designated to assure the accuracy of doctrine but from individuals who worked the Internet.

Many of these criticisms came from people who obviously had little or no theological grounding. They often went on for pages and pages and even went to such extremes as to say how diabolical our content was. Some of it was as logical as accusing you of beating your wife although you didn't have a wife.

In one instance a website expert claimed to have spent six hundred hours studying the evils of RENEW. What was not mentioned was that this person was not allowed by the local bishop to appear and speak in her own chancery.

The problem for us was that people believing what they read on the Internet would send questions or complaints to their bishops about what was going on in their diocese. The bishop, in turn, would send these complaints to our own archbishop, who would in turn send them to me to deal with. I in turn, would send all these questions and complaints to her to work up a response. After reviewing each response, I would send the response to Archbishop McCarrick or to whomever he had designated.

One instance proved particularly interesting. A woman I had known for many years, knowing my home address, had sent me a letter. Upon seeing the return address, I was pleased, thinking it was a nice note from a friend. However, upon reading the letter I wasn't so pleased. It stated how I once had been such a wonderful priest and, in effect, it was so sad I had now become a heretic. We accepted each critique as having been made in good faith, and we politely responded to each one. My response in this instance was no different.

Two weeks later, Archbishop McCarrick sent me a stinging critique from the same person and asked me to personally respond in his name. In this instance I wrote another polite response, making clear that I was responding in the name of the archbishop. And so it went, on and on.

It is impossible to convey what a huge distraction these instances were and what a great amount of time and effort was spent in responding to Internet experts. So much positive energy was lost in the effort.

While this draining of energy speaks of times of low tide, there was another persistent and unending drain on our energy, one that constantly threatened our ability to serve—namely, our meager income level.

CHAPTER 15

Low Till

My sixteen years in Park Ridge had involved precious little time in fundraising. Msgr. Lillis had used me as a cheerleader for our one big financial drive. Other than that I was free to be about the work of parish ministry. Thanks be to God!

In moving to St. Ann's in Newark, I knew things would be different, and they were. Sunday Mass collections totaled $50 to $175. In view of that, running a parish and paying teacher salaries in our school every other week was a daunting task.

The Raskob Foundation

In 1973, after one month in the parish, my brother Ed introduced me to the idea of appealing to foundations. He mentioned the Raskob Foundation, and together we spent part of a day completing an application. I then called the foundation, and the director, Mr. Gerard Garey, told me we had just missed the cut-off date and would have to wait another six months. But, he added, if I was able to drive to Delaware by 4 p.m. that afternoon, he would accept the request part of our application. I was on my way.

Mr. Garey listened in rapt attention to my description of conditions in inner-city Newark, as I explained what we were attempting to do. It was 6:30 on a hot Friday afternoon in late July when I finally came up for air. Mr. Garey smiled, perhaps struck by the honesty of the proposal being made for $12,276.13. He suggested that I be in touch with one of Raskob's board members, Mrs. Sue Stanton, in Little Silver, New Jersey. I quickly responded, "That would be unfair to the foundation, because Mrs. Stanton's daughter plays with my niece, who is her neighbor in Little Silver. It gives me an unfair advantage." Mr. Garey must have felt he was dealing with an "innocent abroad."

In any event, in our successful quest for that grant, I was introduced to the world of development and would become a personal friend of Sue Stanton who deeply believed in our work, and, in turn, with all the wonderful members of the Raskob family.

Tell Me It Isn't So

While serving at St. Ann's was both exciting and meaningful, it did involve one decidedly low point. Working with Sunday afternoon bingo at the Falcon Hall was the pits. Leaving St. Ann's was heart wrenching, but a pleasant thought was that I was going to work in the chancery where there would be no more Falcon Hall. I would have a budget and wouldn't have to worry about money any more. How wrong I was. What a dreamer.

It took only two months for me to face some hard reality. I was being asked to start parish councils in two hundred fifty parishes in the archdiocese and was given a green light to pursue a spiritual renewal process that, as we know, turned out to be RENEW. But to do this, my meager budget of $20,000 covered only my salary plus part of my secretary's salary. In the meantime, I had already convinced Suzanne to leave her post to work in our new office in Newark. How clearly I remember attending her farewell party at St. Therese's in Cresskill. Everybody joyously celebrated her wonderful work there, sending her on to greater things in the archdiocese. I seemed to be the only distraught person in the audience, knowing I didn't have a penny to pay her.

In a call to Mr. Garey at the Raskob Foundation in 1976, I shared my new plight. "The foundation won't be meeting for many months," Mr. Garey responded. "However, we do have one provision in our bylaws whereby an emergency vote of all the trustees could be taken by phone.

But that would require a unanimous vote." Unfortunately the vote was not unanimous. One young woman in Maryland needed more information, and obviously some convincing. After work on Friday afternoon, a flight to the Baltimore/Washington International Airport enabled me to have a meeting with the all-important trustee. Fortunately the flight home was joyful. I could now tell Suzanne something that she was heretofore unaware of. There would be money to pay her salary.

So it was that we began the practice of always trying to make the right moves for the mission and for God's people, even if the funding wasn't in hand. Not realizing the till was empty, more and more unsuspecting people would be hired in the future. While a lot of hard work went into the challenging task of fundraising, by God's grace we stayed afloat.

The Raskob Foundation continued to support us over many years. Foundation members rightly took pride in the fact that they had believed in and supported RENEW from the beginning. Years later I was honored to celebrate Mass and give the homily at Mr. Garey's retirement celebration.

Other Supportive Foundations

In 1981, Mr. Anthony Brenninkmeyer and the Brenninkmeyer family founded the Brenconda Foundation in New York. Mr. Peter Robinson, a member of the Raskob family, was made the director, a position he held for many years. Peter, already a believer in RENEW, introduced me to Mr. Brenninkmeyer, a magnanimous man who also became a strong believer and supporter of our work. We received a generous grant in the first year of their foundation and further assistance over time. It's not that grants were automatically given based on strong friendship. Both men applied their extraordinarily keen and inquisitive minds to each application. Their knowledge of the Church was very extensive, and they were up to date on everything.

At one point, the Pew Foundation inquired about our work. The foundation was struck by the strong presence we held in the Catholic Church toward helping people discover the treasures of the Scriptures and how to share the Word of God. For several weeks I would receive an unexpected 4:30 Friday afternoon call from the foundation. Perhaps they were impressed that on late Friday afternoons we were still working hard. Contact with the Pew Foundation resulted in a very generous grant, the first Pew had ever given to a Catholic organization.

As mentioned previously the Graces became good friends and truly interested in all RENEW developments. After first getting to know Margie, and becoming a friend, I felt inhibited in asking for help. I remember walking in the garden at Darlington seminary with her secretary, Kay Thorton, and saying, "Kay, now that I'm a friend of Margie's I feel funny asking her for financial help." "Nonsense," she said, and encouraged me to ask for funds when we were in need. Margie came forth with assistance, but the big breakthrough came a few years later and I had nothing to do with it.

I was in New Zealand when Peter Grace called our office saying he would like to send one of his right-hand men, Tom Doyle, to do a study of RENEW. Sr. Alice received the call and gets all the credit for the result. She worked with Tom Doyle, who submitted a report to Peter that said every dollar given to RENEW would bring the greatest return of any philanthropic investment they could make. (Doyle also tried to hire Sr. Alice for the Grace Corporation.) So it was that they became our major supporters through the 1980s. On one occasion, when thanking Peter and Margie for the wonderful support of our work, Peter quickly responded. "No," he said, in the spirit of so many others. "We thank you for what you are doing for the Church."

Several attempts to make contact with the Lilly Foundation had failed. Eventually Sr. Jeanne Marie, a staff member at Lilly, was preparing to retire and encouraged us to apply for a sizable grant. She would give our application serious review. We applied for the granddaddy of all grants and spelled out in detail the huge undertakings ahead of us. I had long since become familiar with grant writing, but this foundation would require a very extensive proposal, backed up with great detail. John Landvater, our astute financial consultant, Mary, and I put together a really fine proposal. Time and time again more detailed information was called for. Mary, in particular, applied her patient and persistent efforts in follow-up reports. Finally the glorious day came when we had received our largest grant ever.

A contact was made for us with Bill Simon, who had been U.S. secretary of the treasury under President Reagan. My relationship with Bill Simon started when he granted me a fifteen-minute telephone interview. Fortunately, the interview went well, and Bill became a good friend. He not only gave grants from the Simon Foundation over several years, but he invited me to stop by his Morristown, New Jersey, office whenever convenient and update him on RENEW's mission.

My friend, Jack, knowing of the Link Foundation's generosity to St. Patrick School in Jersey City, New Jersey, where his sister, Sr. Maeve McDermott, S.C., was principal, made contact for us with Mike Catanzaro. Over the years the Link Foundation has been a steady and generous supporter of RENEW through Mike's extreme goodness.

One of my most pleasant days each year was spent visiting St. Mary's Foundation in northwest Pennsylvania. A flight to Pittsburgh was followed by a flight to Bradford which, at the time, was a small and pleasant airport. Dick Reischer, a prince of a man, would have a driver there to bring me through the beautiful countryside at St. Mary's.

St. Mary's is a town with an interesting history. In the early days of our country a group in Maryland was experiencing anti-Catholic prejudice and moved lock, stock, and barrel, to a rural area in Pennsylvania, naming their town St. Mary's. The Reischer family founded the Keystone Carbon Company, a mainstay of the town, and also established the St. Mary's Foundation. Keystone Carbon always closed for holy days. Safe to say, a different kind of atmosphere prevailed at St. Mary's.

My first meeting with the Reischer brothers—Dick, Bill, and Bob— and their father Ben, was very special. Ben was eighty years old, a humble man of beautiful faith. How could I forget Ben's conclusion after my sharing about our work: "All these many years I've believed in the importance of lay involvement and what a difference the Holy Spirit could make in our lives, and now you've come here to tell me that all this is truly happening!" His sincere and direct response left me humbled.

My approach to foundations over the years was not to make a great number of written proposals to numerous foundations. Rather, it was to keep steady and close contact with those who really knew and truly believed in our work. Life is all about relationships. The people we were keeping in contact with were very intelligent and exceptionally good people. They were the kind of people with whom we could share freely because they truly appreciated what we were doing at RENEW. They helped us very substantially, and my life was immeasurably enriched through these friendships.

Faithful Friends to the Rescue

The folks from Our Lady of Mercy were the "originals" of RENEW, long before it had a name, and they have remained life-long friends. I always thank God that I've had such wonderful companions on life's journey. We try to be there for each other in good and happy gatherings and also in times of sickness and need. These friendships have included their care for our RENEW ministry and their concern that the ministry faithfully flourishes.

Without exception, they've all been very supportive of RENEW's financial needs. Some have been able to be extraordinary in their assistance. Unfortunately, Gary Garofalo died a number of years ago, but his wife, Monica, has remained very faithful to the RENEW mission, making provision for RENEW to continue its service to people most in need. Their son Marty serves as a valuable member of our Board of Trustees. The Foley Family has stepped up in special ways. Dave served as our volunteer accountant for a number of years, while Pat and a good number of their adult children generously supported us each year at our golf outing. While Jim and Ginny Collins have moved away, their ongoing support helps to assure that what began years ago in Park Ridge continues.

In the very early years, RENEW faced some desperate situations. Dave and Hilda Dievler were always there to help me face the problems. One year, in late November, when we were still a part of the diocesan network, I was told our office would be closed if we could not come up with $75,000 by Christmas. That was tantamount to hearing that I had to find a million dollars somewhere out on the street. Dave and Hilda helped us meet the crisis and move forward.

I speak here of people who were in original small groups and who believed deeply in the value and importance of RENEW. We were close enough that they knew what a terrible strain our financial situation was on me personally. Those "originals" were soon joined by the Donahues. As recorded earlier, Dolly came as a volunteer helping to put together the process of RENEW before it began. She and her husband, Dr. Floyd Donahue, joined our original small group of supporters and have become good friends. Dolly's brother, Bob Dempsey, has not only been attorney adviser to RENEW but also has generously supported the mission.

More friends would soon join the RENEW family in incredibly generous ways.

The Big Breakthrough

No one cared more deeply about how RENEW fared than Msgr. Jack McDermott. While helping at Presentation Parish on weekends, I had the opportunity on a weekly basis to chat with Jack on Saturday evenings. Jack was more than a good pastoral sounding board. He took RENEW to heart as his mission to promote and grow.

Almost every other pastor would be so conscious of his own fiscal needs that he would be very cautious and leery about money leaving the parish. Jack was just the opposite. He encouraged his parishioners to give to RENEW according to and beyond their means.

One day Jack suggested that we visit Richard Santulli, a man who had by chance come to Mass on a holy day and was amazed with the vibrancy of Presentation Parish. When we arrived at Richard's office, Jack said, "I'm going to ask him to give RENEW $100,000." I almost dropped dead on the spot. I'd never heard of something like this. How could he get it out of his mouth? Where would I look when he asked? Jack presented Richard with an extraordinary need we had at that time, a need to raise $250,000, and then got those words out. Richard shocked me by explaining he would not be able to do what he would like to do, which was to give us the whole $250,000, but he would give us $100,000. I managed to maintain some kind of composure but was overwhelmed with gratitude.

An unsettling experience for Jack when he first arrived at the parish was to find that there was literally next to nothing in the parish bank account. Parishioners George and Pat Erdman came forward and asked what they could do to help him get out of the hole. Not only did they become mainstays of the parish but Jack quickly introduced them to

RENEW and to me, and they have been leading donors to RENEW for many years. More than that, I've been gifted with their very close and caring friendship.

Jack's mission never stopped. He visited Jack and Kathy Norris who shared that they wanted to support a cause they could put their whole heart and soul into. Before I knew it I was having dinner at their home. Shortly after, Jack Norris indicated he would like to see me after Sunday Mass. I felt he was going to give RENEW a generous gift. He more than surprised me with a gift ten times greater than my hopeful expectation.

A year later, Jack Norris dropped by at RENEW, and we had a wonderful hour-long chat. At the end, Jack reached into his shirt pocket and apologetically offered me a rolled up spit-ball looking piece of paper he had been carrying for months. The unraveled spitball was an extraordinarily generous gift. That's the way Jack and Kathy have been—again very close friends. When Jack walked away from the New York scene he came to work as a volunteer at RENEW for over a year. He also courageously went on a RENEW mission to a dangerous area in South Sudan. Jack joined the Board of Trustees in 1996, served as both treasurer and vice-president, and chaired the finance committee.

Jack McDermott decided to hold annual cocktail parties for the support of RENEW. The Erdmans, the Norrises, and Sean and Fiona Duffy organized these gatherings, which introduced many people to the RENEW mission and family.

Jack's best moves were about to come. From the things I've been sharing it might sound as if RENEW was well off and floating in money. Jack knew that was far from the truth. He realized that our service to developing countries alone represented a deficit of a few million dollars, as we never asked a penny from the people of developing nations or from parishes in the United States that could not afford our service. Jack also knew that the fees we did charge parishes in the United States were meager and far from meeting the expense incurred in serving each parish. He felt that the time and energy I devoted to financial concerns could be better directed to the tremendous opportunities that RENEW could be pursuing.

Jack came up with a brilliant idea. Once again I thought he had gone beyond the realm of reality. He wanted to shoot for the moon. Jack, as well as everyone across the country, had heard that Peter Lynch, the Babe Ruth of the financial world, was about to retire. Why not the two of us visit Peter in Boston? Through a parish contact, Jack arranged for me to call Peter Lynch at 6 a.m. as he arrived at his office on a specific day. For me, it was 3 a.m. since I was on the Pacific Coast. With more than a bit of tremble in my voice, I called Peter who readily set up an appointment for Jack and me.

What a visit! Jack wouldn't leave until Peter made a commitment. Peter agreed to have breakfast with us in New York the next month. That breakfast led to Peter traveling to India with us to experience our RENEW mission. He wound up jumping to his feet and giving impromptu pep talks at our training sessions. "This is the kind of Church we need to be," he would say. His wife, Carolyn, traveled to Nigeria with us on another RENEW mission and became a member of our Board of Trustees.

More was yet to come. Jack had come to work full time at RENEW and had the idea of running a banquet at Ellis Island. He set a goal of having the biggest fundraiser ever held in the state of New Jersey. Working a hundred hours a week, Jack set out to meet that goal.

Racing from one contact to another, Jack assembled an unbelievable group. Friends at Presentation would now be joined with a group of supporters who would each give $50,000 or more to support RENEW at this Ellis Island Gala.

From that group, Ray and Cathy Donovan have been extraordinary, with Ray a regular visitor to RENEW and member of the Board of Trustees. Jim and Nancy Moritz reached out to all their friends to rally fantastic support. Bill and Pat McLaughlin, who had gone to the very first RENEW training session in Newark, jumped into the cause, with Bill also becoming a trustee. Jim and Jackie Higgins, Jim and Jeanne Burke, Les and Ann Quick, Joe and Marlys Heintz, and Bobby and Carol Williams also rallied to RENEW's support. The Williamses are strong believers in small communities and Carol serves as a Board of Trustees member.

In the meantime, Jack made contact with Marylane Burry, who sponsored our *Healing the Body of Christ* program at the time of the sexual abuse scandal and remains a strong member of the RENEW family. Jack flew to Chicago when a contact led us to Pat Ryan who committed himself enthusiastically to the RENEW mission. In the meantime, Larry Walsh from Presentation came forward with a deep interest in our work in developing countries and has remained a faithful friend and supporter to our RENEW mission. Joe Franzetti and his wife, Patty, have been extremely generous to RENEW. Joe is currently president of the Board of Trustees, a member of the Development Committee, and an ex-officio member of the Executive Committee. His deep love of RENEW has led him to be involved in many aspects of our ministry.

Jack had still another idea. Why not have our Ellis Island Gala honor Peter and Carolyn Lynch for their outstanding work in support of poor parishes, their beautiful family, and their outstanding work and support of the Church? Their great respect and admiration for the work of RENEW, along with Jack's encouragement, led them to make a mind-boggling donation of $1,000,000 to RENEW for the occasion. And they have continued to open their hearts and homes to us. Yes, Jack saw to it that the RENEW gala set the state record for fundraising. His deep commitment and belief in RENEW came from the unique way he ran his parish.

The experience of faith sharing in small communities affects people's lives in many positive ways, including their philanthropic giving. This is certainly true of Florence Jacobson, a close friend. Florence's many years involved in parish small communities and her time working in our Small Community Department have convinced her of the importance of RENEW and motivated her to be a major financial supporter.

My good friend Tom Burns, a man beloved by everyone, had a dream in which he believed that he should give a substantial donation to RENEW, which he did. Dream on, Tom, dream on.

Our staff members John Dolan, Jose Hernandez, and Bill Reilly, in turn, kept good personal contact with donors and regularly sent out general appeals.

None of this meant that we didn't still have a financial challenge. Our service to every state in our country and our outreach to twenty-four other countries had become a mammoth undertaking. Some years we still landed in the red to an astronomical degree. But God's grace had touched the hearts of many fantastic people who have kept the ship afloat. Sr. Terry Rickard, O.P., our current president and director of RENEW, has continued to carry the banner of enlisting strong supporters like Frank and Mimi Walsh.

My heartfelt gratitude extends far beyond those who help in extraordinary ways. One anonymous donor of more limited means comes to mind; she gives to RENEW in magnanimous ways that are appreciated as much as a seven-figure donor.

At RENEW, we hold in our hearts and remember in our prayers all of our benefactors, including the hundreds of people who respond to our written appeals. I remember one woman who sent two crumpled dollar bills in an envelope, along with a plea for her special prayer intentions. Her note touched me so deeply—the widow's mite. Who knows but that the one who gives the least to our mission is the one who, in the eyes of God, has given the most? We are so blessed!

It's a funny thing how we can forget a problem once it has passed, even if the disappearance is temporary. A child runs outside with glee the day after being home deadly sick. And when a headache passes we feel free and wonderful. Although the never-ending financial crisis has been a heavy burden, it has been great to momentarily forget that burden while writing about the tremendous people who have responded to God's call and have become such treasured friends. Over and over again, we can only thank God.

CHAPTER 16

RENEW Vignettes

1986-1990

The following are some insights from my perspective into RENEW activity in the booming years of the 1980s.

1986-1988

St. Paul-Minneapolis, Minnesota

In the Archdiocese of St. Paul-Minneapolis an amazing fifty thousand joined small groups and participated in the RENEW process. Deacon Peter D'Heilly, diocesan director for RENEW, and associate director Bev Quintavalle attributed that response to the people's thirst for spirituality.

So striking was the RENEW effort there that Archbishop John R. Roach, when submitting his quinquennial report to the pope at the Vatican, listed it as the most significant event to take place in the archdiocese. The Holy Father was hearing similar reports from other American bishops who were making their five-year journeys to Rome.

In the area of justice, Sr. Mary Zirbes, O.S.F., quoted the testimony of a parishioner in one of their gatherings.

> In the first two weeks of Season III, I was angered and felt the local option was too strong on justice. Many of us are already active in the parish: we donate when asked and volunteer time to help the homebound. We felt we

shouldn't feel the guilt we were feeling. As we continued meeting, we began to see where the guilt was coming from. For me, the guilt was that I pre-judge the poor and those on welfare.

In the closing weeks, as we continued to share our feelings, life experiences, and our understanding of Scripture, I faced my prejudice against the poor. I, and others in my group, experienced a revelation. We saw Scripture in a new way.

With regard to the possibility of other dioceses picking up RENEW, Deacon Peter D'Heilly said, "To anyone who is considering adopting RENEW I say—take a deep breath, pray always, and go for it."

Seattle, Washington

Greg Kremer of our International Team, reported the following story that flowed from RENEW Season III on justice in Seattle.

At a small-group meeting one participant, Shawn, who worked at a Catholic Community Services family shelter in Tacoma, Washington, told of his pain in trying to help families find affordable housing. Too often he had to tell them, "Nothing is available."

Moved by Shawn's account, one member suggested that the group involve itself in the problem. "I think God wants us to stop talking and start doing," said another. For the next five months the group met weekly. They researched housing needs. They wrote grant applications. They prayed for guidance.

They formed a corporation called Mi Casa, requested and received non-profit status, and began to search for apartment units they could purchase. They applied for a $130,000 grant from the state and solicited contributions from friends and parishioners.

Eventually Mi Casa was able to purchase two six-unit apartment buildings. Mi Casa hired a religious sister to manage the buildings and to assist the residents with other needs and development work. All twelve units were quickly filled. Mi Casa was a success. And it started with RENEW.

Erie, Pennsylvania

RENEW in Erie was not only blessed with the leadership of Bishop Michael J. Murphy, but also with the very effective and zealous leadership of Sr. Nancy Fisher, S.S.J. Nancy is one of the "greats" in my book. She is one of the strongest believers and promoters of small Christian communities in our country. This showed up very clearly in the excellent RENEW experience of the Diocese of Erie.

Nancy had never been involved in small Christian communities before she was asked to become the diocesan director of RENEW. The friendly mandate given to her was "to run the best RENEW experience of any diocese in the country." If, in fact, that wasn't achieved, her efforts certainly came close: Through zealous work with small and large parishes, Nancy involved twenty thousand people in RENEW small groups. While the diocese had experienced other movements, RENEW kick-started a widespread interest and involvement in small communities at a new level.

Nancy believes that RENEW brought our Catholic faith out into the open from the dark, private place it frequently occupied in people's lives. For the first time, husbands and wives and all sorts of people were sharing their faith, expressing their love and belief in the Lord. She saw the Church becoming vital in the lives of people to whom it had been inaccessible.

In the small parish of Christ the King in Houtzdale, an elderly woman, who for years had not been able to go to church, experienced being part of the parish again when her daughter brought a RENEW group into her home.

For twenty-five years since the diocese completed RENEW, Nancy has continued to promote and develop small communities throughout the Diocese of Erie. She has also served on the board of North American Forum for Small Christian Communities and the National Alliance of Parishes Restructuring into Communities.

Community is the passion of Nancy's life. She says, "RENEW was the catalyst that made a difference for many people in our diocese. It gave them a whole new insight and brought great vitality to their spiritual lives." Nancy knows that RENEW made a great impact in her diocese and acknowledges, "I'm doing the job, but it is God who is changing hearts and lives."

Birmingham, Alabama

An incredible ninety-six percent of parishes in the Diocese of Birmingham participated in RENEW. Considering the very small percentage of Catholics in that southern diocese at that time, it is amazing that more than eight thousand people, one out of every three parishioners in the diocese, were in RENEW small groups. The credit for much of this goes to the director, Sr. Mary Ann Klohr, C.S.J., along with Fr. Ray Dunmyer and Msgr. Michael Sexton. Fr. Dunmyer was particularly active and helpful in getting the diocese on board.

Through RENEW, the diocese moved from three or four parishes involved in social concerns to forty-six parishes. Scripture, community, and new leadership were listed as the most significant areas of progress. The interest in Scripture and the importance of strong community were very understandable considering how overwhelmed Catholics were in their Bible-belt region.

One parishioner reported, "I've been in the parish twenty-six years and have never seen the likes of it before." Another said, "Our group has moved from being Sunday Catholics to being about Scripture reflection and sharing with others. The spiritual growth in our group has been fantastic."

Two thousand people attended the concluding RENEW celebratory Mass at which Bishop Raymond Boland said, "RENEW has provided new perspectives, new challenges, and new opportunities—one might say the possibility of a new spiritual adventure in which we no longer live for ourselves but for him."

Sioux City, Iowa

The RENEW results in Sioux City resulted from the tireless efforts of a strikingly effective diocesan leadership team composed of Sr. Mary Lechtenberg, O.S.F., Sr. Margaret Jungers, O.S.F., and Fr. Tim Schott.

Bishop Lawrence Soens introduced RENEW to his diocese to provide a practical method to revitalize parish life and strengthen the spiritual lives of parishioners. RENEW provided all he hoped for in these areas.

As always, the small Christian communities did exceptionally well, but liturgical celebration also made giant-step improvements. For many parishes it was their first experience of having a liturgy committee with well-planned liturgical celebrations. Good liturgical music was also advanced greatly.

These diocesan strides were largely due to the unique RENEW team. Margaret brought previous experience as a diocesan RENEW director. Mary brought rich parish RENEW experience, and Tim brought outstanding pastoral experience as a parish priest and diocesan liturgical director. His role was to help priests get on board with the process and to encourage them to take the huge step of giving moral support to the parishioners while, in many instances, allowing and enabling the parishioners to actively take responsibility for conducting RENEW.

The strength of their leadership came from the communal experience they enjoyed among themselves, not only during RENEW but since. For the last twenty-five years they have gotten together for two days every three months to share faith, pray together, strengthen each other in their calls to ministry, and enjoy each others' company. From a spiritual communal base such as this, one can understand why over seventy percent of the parishes in Sioux City had a wonderful RENEW experience.

For Tim, the RENEW experience was the work of the Holy Spirit, but much more so than in a general or cerebral way. RENEW was a "practical, palpable experience of what the Holy Spirit does in the lives of people."

Salina, Kansas

The impact of RENEW in Salina is clearly seen in a quote from Fr. Bob Schneider, the diocesan director. "RENEW has touched more people and made others more aware of the Catholic Church than anything else in our diocese. We see lay leadership growing and developing, especially in the small groups. What a wonderful legacy for RENEW to leave in our diocese…lay people in active spiritual roles on the parish level!"

1987-1989

Biloxi, Mississippi

Going back to the Deep South, we have another example of RENEW's attractiveness and effectiveness in areas that were sparsely Catholic. Under the zealous leadership of Fr. Michael Tracey, more than eight thousand people became involved in RENEW small groups. These numbers are particularly significant and indicate a desire of people to strengthen their Catholic identity when they are such a small minority.

Amarillo, Texas

On a late night flight, I was headed to Amarillo to give a decision-making presentation to the priests. Noticing another priest on the fairly empty flight, I decided to go over and chat with him. He turned out to be the famous Bishop Leroy T. Matthiesen.

One of the main industries in Amarillo was a plant that produced nuclear weapons of mass destruction. Bishop Matthiesen was a heroic figure, standing up in speaking out against the production of these weapons. Considering that the livelihoods of the people in his relatively small diocese depended on this industry, his sense of moral justice and leadership was remarkable indeed. His diocese was understandably divided over this issue.

Nevertheless, the next day, and for the next three years, I would find out how strongly supportive of RENEW he would be and how he would use RENEW as an effective means of unifying people in our commonly shared faith and spirituality. Thirty-five of Amarillo's forty-one parishes participated in a highly successful RENEW effort, in no small degree due to the efforts of the bishop who took very personal responsibility for promoting the RENEW process. Everything I had read about the bishop I found to be true. As I chatted with him that evening and over the course of our shared experience in the following years, I found him to be a truly remarkable person.

Bismarck, North Dakota

Bismarck profited from the strong leadership of Bishop John F. Kinney and Diocesan Director Jeanne Lindermann.

A striking aspect of RENEW in Bismarck was the thousands of people who coalesced into a strong prayer network. Wherever there is strong prayer backing, results are positive. Increased attendance at daily Mass and daily recitation of the rosary were among the highlights of RENEW in Bismarck. One parish reported that participation in weekday Masses, which had been ranging from thirty to thirty-five, increased to seventy-five to one hundred seventy-five daily. Another parish reported that its food pantry, which had served twenty people a week, increased its reach to one hundred forty. There were many reported conversions to the Catholic faith and an increase in people signing up for parish ministries.

More impressive than large numbers are simple incidents from two very small, rural parishes. In one instance, a priest reported a call from a couple who wanted their marriage validated and their three children baptized. In another extremely small parish, consisting of one small RENEW group, a young father had his two children baptized and another group member started to take instruction in the Catholic faith.

1988-1990

San Francisco, California

The popular Archbishop John R. Quinn introduced RENEW to San Francisco, with Betsy Lamb and Fr. Gerard O'Rourke providing RENEW leadership.

The RENEW experience in San Francisco may have been summed up best by parishioner Lillian Harkless who said, "Through RENEW, renewal is joy—pure, unadulterated joy—joy that makes you want to shout it from the housetops. Under all that jubilation is peace, the kind the world cannot give." Still another parishioner asked, "What's so special about a small-group meeting? It amazes me," she continued, "the beauty that the Holy Spirit brings out in ordinary conversation and reading of the Scriptures—that usually doesn't happen outside a special small-group situation."

In the first season alone fifty-nine thousand RENEW prayer cards were distributed in the ninety parishes of the diocese. They were printed in English, Spanish, and Chinese.

As for the need of great union between priests and parishioners, Fr. Patrick Michaels, associate pastor of St. Gregory, said, "RENEW has given me a new awareness of what parishioners want from their Church. The response has been so overwhelmingly positive that I am reassured we are moving in the right direction."

Fort Worth, Texas

Fort Worth stands out in my mind, starting with an exciting call I received one day from Bishop Joseph Delaney. He had just returned from Latin America and was eager to start small communities in his diocese. He saw RENEW as the best possible means to achieve this.

Under his leadership, along with the Diocesan Director Dan Luby, the bishop's hopes were realized. Over two-thirds of the people involved in RENEW small groups wanted to continue to make small groups part of their Catholic spiritual experience.

Scranton, Pennsylvania

I made initial presentations about RENEW to entire presbyterates in dioceses throughout the country, but I have a particular reason for remembering Scranton. Before the presentation I was told that one of the priests was coming "to shoot me down." As he entered the auditorium carrying several ominous-looking typed pages, someone pointed him out to me.

At the conclusion of my presentation, as always, I asked if there were any questions or comments from the priests. Naturally, that priest sprang to his feet and spoke a litany of the ills and dangers of RENEW. I immediately said, "Father, in all fairness, so that everyone might hear you well, why don't you come up on the stage and take the microphone, and I'll go and sit in your place. You've got something to say."

After about five minutes, one of the priests jumped up and yelled, "I can't stand this anymore. This is crazy." The whole auditorium went into turmoil as angry priests shouted at the nay-saying speaker. Bishop James Timlon turned to me and publicly asked, "Tom, what do you think we should do?" I responded to the bishop and all the priests, "I think it's very important for us all to hear everything this priest has to say." What a blessing. Obviously, the result was a unanimous vote for the priests to go ahead with RENEW. Our intended adversary had become our greatest ally. I thought, "From now on I want this priest to go with me and do this same thing everywhere I go across the country."

This was the beginning of a wonderful experience in Scranton.

1989-1991

Lubbock, Texas

The Diocese of Lubbock introduced us to Bishop Michael J. Sheehan who would become a strong friend of RENEW and eventually become a member of our Board of Trustees.

Bishop Sheehan was proud of the fact that all the parishes and missions in his diocese were involved in RENEW. The leadership team of Fr. David Cruz and Sr. Feliciana Majia, C.C.V.I., summed up the experience this way: "Perhaps if we look back through the annals of diocesan history we would soon discover that this is the first time every community has participated in the same spiritual renewal effort."

Some small parishes reported as many as three hundred people in small groups and other small parishes reported seventy-five percent of all parishioners were in small groups. This enabled Bishop Sheehan to boast that over fifty percent of the entire Lubbock Diocese was in RENEW small groups.

There will be more to say about Bishop Sheehan's role in the 1990s, when he moved to New Mexico, but RENEW certainly enjoyed remarkable success in the blooming 1980s. Praise be to God.

CHAPTER 17

Worldwide Explosion

The Americas

It always amazed me how word of RENEW continued to spread and stir up interest in some of the most unexpected places. I'd have to pinch myself and ask if this was truly happening. God's ways and wisdom are far beyond our meager imagination.

As you will see, RENEW's international growth brought me more and more to distant "mission" places, ones that, as a youth, I had envisioned working in. My wildest dreams were surpassed.

What follows might sound like a travelogue of exciting venues, but over the course of a great number of international trips, seventy of which were to developing countries, my busy schedule left almost no time for sightseeing. The conditions in many of the places we visited involved considerable physical discomfort. However, the most difficult trips are the ones I most fondly remember.

The Tablet of London

An article on RENEW by Fr. Edmund Flood appeared in *The Tablet*, a weekly Catholic newspaper, in 1979, just as we were concluding Season III of original RENEW in Newark. Given that *The Tablet* had worldwide circulation, news of RENEW was spreading quickly. Edmund Flood wrote a factual article describing the contents, workings, and pastoral approaches of RENEW from the point of view of his interest in small communities. He lauded the approach taken and the training provided and reflected that RENEW had well proven how small communities could work in the industrial West. It was not just a developing country phenomenon. Flood concluded that RENEW was a diocesan approach that was working where others had failed.

Canada

News of RENEW was certainly flying about. While we were still in Season IV of original RENEW in Newark in 1979, a call came announcing Mr. Gerald Woodman, the diocesan religious education director of the Diocese of Hamilton in Canada, and Fr. Tony Ciavarro were coming to visit us.

Both men proved to be delightfully zealous and readily believed in everything they were hearing about RENEW. After they returned to Hamilton, we were not surprised to receive an invitation from Bishop Paul Reding to speak to the priests of one hundred twenty parishes. By the time Cathy Dambach Martin and I got there, Fr. Ciavarro had jumped the gun and was starting RENEW in his parish. Favorable consensus was quickly formed, and the Diocese of Hamilton had moved ahead of ninety-nine percent of the U.S. parishes in starting RENEW.

Many glowing reports flowed in from Hamilton during the five seasons of RENEW. One story that particularly touched my heart involved a personal experience of Gerry Woodman. He recounted a breakfast conversation with his little daughter, Katie. Saturday morning was a special time for Gerry and Katie, which allowed Mom to get some extra rest.

Pointing to the crucifix on the wall, Katie said, "Daddy, that's Jesus on the cross. He died for us." "That's right, Katie," Gerry said. Katie went on to eat her breakfast. "But that's not the end of the story, Katie," continued Gerry. "Jesus rose up from the dead." Wow! That was great news to Katie. She jumped up immediately. In all her beautiful innocence she said, "Daddy, I've got to tell Mommy about this!" Such wisdom, from the mouth of a child, telling us the obvious: how we should be rushing out to share the Good News of Jesus.

Within a year, St. Catharines Diocese, a neighbor of Hamilton, had also initiated RENEW. Under the leadership of Bishop Thomas Fulton and a dynamic young priest, Fr. Richard Grecco, diocesan director, RENEW took off on one of its finest experiences.

One Friday afternoon an emergency developed in our service to St. Catharines. Our staff person, who was flying to Canada to conduct overnight training for parishes, was suddenly taken ill. Out of the blue, and totally unprepared, I was pressed into service. Grabbing a passport and little else, I tried to pull myself and my thoughts together. I had not been presenting that particular training and would certainly need both creativity and God's grace.

My panic would soon be relieved. Arriving at the training site, Fr. Grecco and Assistant Director Sr. Mary Kay Camp, I.B.V.M., said that the diocesan team would meet for an hour of shared prayer before the training began. That hour was one of the most wonderful experiences in all my time with RENEW. Everything was put in God's hands. A prayer was offered not only for RENEW in that diocese but also for each of the other dioceses that were either launching or considering RENEW. To their great advantage, the members of the St. Catharines team took the prayer aspect of RENEW seriously.

Having been launched with that prayerful spirit and right frame of mind, the weekend continued to be a true highlight experience. I can't say enough about the leadership for RENEW in St. Catharines. Bishop Fulton showed great wisdom in giving Fr. Grecco freedom to use his many gifts, which included creativity and an excellent vision for the future. RENEW in St. Catharines Diocese couldn't miss. Not surprisingly, years later Fr. Grecco was made auxiliary bishop in Toronto. Now, as bishop of Charlottetown, Prince Edward Island, he still holds high regard for RENEW.

However, Bishop Fulton was no slouch in providing leadership on his own. Upon hearing a report about the progress of RENEW in his diocese, it is said that he was "bouncing up and down in his chair with enthusiasm."

A sample of the RENEW experience after St. Catharines' Season III of RENEW included the following comments from participants:

- "It encouraged people to read the Bible."
- "It taught people not only meaningful prayer but also the power of prayer and fostered an increased warmth and friendship at Mass."
- "RENEW developed a deeper concern for others, the underprivileged, and our immediate neighbors."
- "Lay people are now claiming their full membership in the Church and are providing effective leadership."
- "Through RENEW there is more awareness of social justice and the remedies required."
- "All have become more aware of the Holy Spirit and how important the Spirit is in our lives."

Perhaps most important, four very concrete diocesan developments grew out of the successful RENEW experience in St. Catharines, results that Bishop Grecco still cherishes:

- formation of a Diocesan Liturgy Council
- formation of a Diocesan Family Life Council
- formation of a Bishop's Task Force on Youth
- publication of a diocesan newspaper four times a year—an expansion of the quarterly *ReNews* paper.

Back in Hamilton, an interesting development was taking place. Shortly into the RENEW process, Bishop Reding called his classmate and friend, Msgr. Bill O'Brien, a pastor who was thrilled with the spiritual outcomes of RENEW in his parish. One of the things that particularly struck Bill was how many people were coming to him for spiritual direction. Bishop Reding asked Bill if he would leave his parish and go to Newark for six months to study RENEW. The idea was that upon Bill's return, he would launch a Canadian office for RENEW. Another man of vision, Bishop Reding saw the potential for RENEW spreading nationwide.

At first Bill demurred, but in the summer of 1982 he arrived in Newark. Bill became a regular part of our RENEW team for the next year and a half and was an absolute delight. Fully prepared and imbued with the spirit of RENEW, he returned to his country in 1984 and launched a Canadian National Office for RENEW. Under his direction,

Clockwise from top left:
The Kleissler family
circa 1938; high school
graduation day, 1949;
the Kleisslers circa 1950;
Fr. Tom and his parents on
his diaconate ordination
day; Tom, as a seminarian,
working with children in
South Carolina.

Clockwise from top:
Fr. Kleissler in the
midst of Nigerian
villagers in 1991;
RENEW and Fr. Tom
receive a big welcome in
El Salvador in 1990;
Fr. Tom takes a
turn at the helm in
New Zealand; Fr. Tom
shares a RENEW video
with Pope John Paul II.

Top: Flowers and incense are part of the ambience as this RENEW small group meets in India. ***Above:*** Dancers add a touch of Indian culture to a RENEW gathering. ***Left:*** Sr. Cecilia King, C.S.J.P., saved this woman's life.

Top: RENEW leaders in India meet with Fr. Jerry McCrane, M.M., Peter Lynch, and Fr. Tom.
Left: Fr. Jack McDermott and Peter Lynch with RENEW leaders in India.
Below: Fr. Tom's grand-nephew, Jim McKeown, with some students he works with in the Diocese of Port Elizabeth, South Africa, September 2011.

Top: Fr. Tom at a typical hut in India. **Left:** Sr. Mary McGuinness, O.P., Fr. Tom, and Margo Le Bert show off copies of their award-winning book, *Small Christian Communities*, in 1991.

Top: The Kleissler family at the celebration of the 40th anniversary of Father Tom's ordination. From left, Ed, Gert, Tom, Bob, Dick, and Mary Jean. ***Bottom left:*** Fr. Tom talks with his friend Treva Young, a pastoral leader at St. Ann's parish in Newark and a RENEW staff person, during a RENEW event. ***Bottom Right:*** Fr. Tom shows off a football he received as a 40th anniversary gift from New York Giants General Manager George Young.

Top: The "four amigos" - Fathers Jack McDermott, Tom Burns, Jim Ferry, and Tom Kleissler. ***Above left:*** Archbishop Peter L. Gerity, seated, with Fr. Tom and former RENEW International director Michael Brough at the 2001 Gala. ***Bottom right:*** Fr. Tom with RENEW International's current president and executive director, Sr. Terry Rickard, O.P., at a RENEW golf outing.

Top: Fr. Tom chats with grandnieces in November 2005.
Below: Fr. Tom with some of the same grandnieces, plus others,
in May 2011, at the wedding of still another grandniece, Sara McKeown.

RENEW flourished, spreading to a dozen or more dioceses as far east as the Halifax-Yarmouth Archdiocese in Nova Scotia and as far west as the Archdiocese of Winnipeg and the Diocese of St. Boniface in Manitoba.

The Church in French Quebec reported that it was facing a critical situation. Sunday Mass attendance had fallen from a vast majority to somewhere between three to fifteen percent of the population. Anticlericalism was prevalent. Sr. ReJeanne Bourque, N.D., deserves great credit for opening many new doors to RENEW through her French translation and enculturation of resources. Through her outstanding efforts, RENEW was made available for all the French-speaking areas of Canada as well as for the English-speaking. Diocesan leadership in St.-Jean-Longueuil in Montreal had concluded that the development of small faith-sharing communities was the best approach to the French situation. RENEW was more than ready to serve that need.

I'm not exactly a fan of cold weather, which made some experiences stand out in my mind. Until that time, I had never seen houses equipped with battery chargers to start cars. Especially memorable was a drive from Hamilton to Thunder Bay to share with the people there about RENEW. The idea of going to Thunder Bay sounded exotic and had an "other-world" ring to it. How far different from my inner-city Newark. Little did I realize that upper Michigan was parallel to Thunder Bay.

Another chilling experience for me was in Sault Ste. Marie. Bishop Jean-Louis Plouffe was an absolute joy to work with. But the weather was like none I had ever experienced. It was forty degrees below zero as people arrived for our training. We parked as near as we could to the door and raced in with our overhead projector. Fortunately, despite the cold, there were many warm hearts awaiting us.

RENEW provided a beautiful example of across-the-border cooperation. Rainey River, Ontario, in the Diocese of Thunder Bay, is directly across the bay from Baudette, Minnesota, in the Diocese of Crookston. Fr. Larry Antus was the pastor of parishes in both places. His Rainey River parish of Good Counsel did RENEW with the Diocese of Crookston in Minnesota, giving them a one-year head start over all the other parishes in Thunder Bay.

In meeting together, people from both parishes learned about how much they had in common: their joys, sorrows, little and big successes, and failures. They also learned that God calls each of us just as we are.

At the RENEW kickoff in St.-Jean-Longueuil, Bishop Bernard Hubert read a letter he had received from Archbishop Gerety which stated in part:

> It is with genuine pleasure that I write to welcome the English-speaking parishes of your Diocese St.-Jean-Longueuil into RENEW. We in Newark are still reaping exceptional spiritual dividends from RENEW. Other dioceses across our country report the same kinds of things: committed Catholics making great strides in spiritual growth; witnessing to and familiarity with the Word of God in large numbers of people; many alienated Catholics returning to the faith; increasing concern for the problems of the poor, the disenfranchised, and the lonely; continuing development of small, vibrant faith-sharing communities. The list goes on and on.

Overall reports from Canada continued to strike common themes:
- great development in liturgical celebration
- strong belief and the flourishing of strong Christian communities
- a great love and thirst for the Scriptures
- wonderful lay enthusiasm and greatly increased lay involvement
- improved relationships between priests and lay people
- a hunger for more catechesis
- deeper involvement in helping the poor and in social action
- the beginning of greater networking among parishes.

The promoter of RENEW in Canada, Msgr. Bill O'Brien, remains very active as a priest of great dedication, energy, and spirituality. In reflecting on his RENEW experience, he had this to say:

> In my work as a parish priest I was always looking for something that would be a breakthrough in helping our people experience spiritual vitality. RENEW was just what we were looking for, God's instrument for spiritual

renewal. As I look back over my 61 years of priesthood RENEW has been a real blessing and highlight in my life, for which I thank God.

Belize

When a call came through from Fr. Bill Messmer, S.J., in Belize inquiring about RENEW, my first thought was, "Where in God's good world is Belize?" The wonderful beaches there (which I never did get to see) were not well publicized at that time. After doing some research, I learned that Belize is the former British Honduras and was enjoying its recent independence from the commonwealth in the mid 1980s. More than one hundred fifty thousand people live in this Central American country, which is the size of New Jersey. Being the only English-speaking country in Central America, it relates more closely with the African heritage in the Caribbean Islands.

Flying over Belize in January 1984, all I could see were forests. Arriving at the beautifully laid out capital, Belize City, I realized it was still recovering from a hurricane that had occurred some twenty years earlier and was marked by poverty. Bishop Osmond Peter Martin was most welcoming, a wonderful host, and liked everything he heard about RENEW. I was a guest at his residence, a wooden structure built on stilts, which communicated the feel of being in the Caribbean.

The first step was for Belize to send a small leadership contingent to one of our international training sessions. The director, John Cucul, was a wonderful young man who had literally grown up in the jungle and was not totally accustomed to the outside world. He was the only person I remember visiting us who looked up at the tall buildings in total amazement and awe. John was well-versed in his Catholic faith, intelligent, and thoroughly good.

We soon realized that the highly-organized American approach wasn't suitable for Belize. To best serve the people, we should have immediately taken into account a cultural disconnect and made more radical adaptations. This was in the mid-1980s, and we were still learning things that we would be able to implement in other cultures in the future.

We could have pared down the size and scope of the RENEW approach, making it more straightforward and less heavily organized. Having a deep understanding of the richness of local cultures in appropriating suitable methodologies would serve us well as RENEW continued to grow.

Leadership in Belizean parishes approached tasks in ways different from American leadership. This disconnect limited the number of participating parishes. In instances where parishes worked closely with our RENEW international team, RENEW did well.

Having tried to give an honest account from my cultural background, I must say that RENEW leaders in Belize saw results differently. They weren't caught up with percentages and numbers as we would be. They were pleased with God's action and the wonderful spiritual growth in the lives of the participants.

Our two RENEW staff people who served in RENEW formation in Belize, Kathleen O'Malley and Fr. Tom Dowd, both shared very positive and happy experiences. Kathleen had been an invaluable aide to Cathy Dambach Martin in the early years of RENEW. She went on to minister well in various RENEW capacities. Kathleen was now able to focus all her great zeal on international service in Belize. She loved every minute of it.

In particular, Kathleen noted how happy local people were that RENEW would extend itself to even the most remote of villages. Logistics meant that the villages sometimes were a bit neglected, especially one that was accessible only by a small plane. RENEW was getting into areas where world news seldom penetrated, including the fact that someone had walked on the moon.

Tom, a former RENEW director in Grand Island, Nebraska, made a point of visiting every parish in Belize. Of the many exciting things he heard, one small but significant incident stands out in his mind. During the open dialogue, a woman in the last row raised her hand several times, immediately retrieving it each time. Finally Tom invited her to share her thoughts. Viola shared that her RENEW small group had one particular meeting in which participants were faced with a difficult topic involving reconciliation.

Viola was deeply troubled. She realized that she and her neighbor were severely alienated and had not spoken for eighteen years. She knew that if she didn't move on her spiritual impulse quickly, her courage would be lost. Upon returning home she went straight to her neighbor, shocking her by apologizing profusely. The neighbor was totally taken aback and in turn apologized for all she had done to cause and continue this alienation. Both women cried in a warm embrace. Maybe it was a small incident, but it was hardly insignificant. Imagine if national diplomats, and all of us, approached life in this manner.

John's positive evaluation was reflected by grass-roots activity:

- RENEW small groups fed new life in the ministry to shut-ins along with hospital visitation and outreach to the poor.
- As RENEW progressed, the sharing in the small groups moved to a deeper and more significant level.
- People began to make commitments to concrete action.
- Sunday Mass attendance increased.
- More couples were celebrating their marriages sacramentally in the parish church.

Belize may be a small country, but John's report and stories like Viola's tell us that what happened in RENEW, by God's grace, was quite significant.

El Salvador

Dr. Irma Chávez, and how God has worked in and through her, is basically the story of RENEW in El Salvador.

Irma comes from a family of means in El Salvador, and that enabled her to study at some of the finest centers in Europe. She received a doctorate in philosophy at the University of Bologna, specializing in the work of Emmanuel Kant. Irma, along with a group of other very talented young adults, took on the best of learning and culture that Europe could offer. It was there that she met and married Waldo Chávez Velasco. Waldo became a well-known poet, writer, editor, and publisher in El Salvador.

Some years later, Irma had what she calls a "Paul-at-Damascus" experience, a spiritual awakening that brought her to feel a yearning for something more in her life. "I just fell in love with Jesus," Irma says. The full story of her conversion experience is incredibly moving. She went on to earn a master's degree in theology at St. John's University in New York.

Her quest to express her new zeal for Christ, and the richness of her theological formation, led Irma to inquire about a position at RENEW. The interview was so impressive that Irma immediately dove into working with the Hispanic apostolate of our Small Christian Community Department in Newark.

A few years later, Irma and Waldo visited me. The president of El Salvador had invited them to return home and help the country. Waldo was offered an important cabinet position. Irma was to receive a cabinet position in the area of cultural heritage. It was clear to see where the Lord was calling them. I was sad to realize that Irma would be leaving RENEW, but at the same time I was extremely happy for them.

A couple of years later, while Irma was visiting her daughter in the States, she called on us at RENEW. Irma shared how much she really missed a closer connection with Church work. We quickly concluded, "Why not have Irma launch RENEW in El Salvador?"

Irma returned to El Salvador and stirred up a whirlwind of RENEW activity. She had the faith, courage, and straightforward conviction to make appointments with a few bishops and meet with them personally. Bishop Marco René Revelo in Santa Ana and Bishop José Carmen Di Pietro in Sonsonate Diocese both showed interest.

I flew to El Salvador and joined Irma in further discussion with the bishops. She no doubt had them already convinced, but we both laugh at the moment when I had a sudden gift of tongues and immediately started speaking Spanish enthusiastically. There must have been something bouncing around in the back of my mind from failed experiences in learning Spanish that suddenly broke through.

I enjoyed Bishop Revelo, a jovial man who shared his belief that the priests of his diocese had been inoculated. When I asked him against what, he replied, "against spiritual renewal." We both laughed heartily. Despite this inoculation, Bishop Revelo and Irma did a great job in winning over the priests to RENEW. Great success followed. Both Santa Ana and Sonsonate launched RENEW—at that time known in Spanish as RENACER—in 1988 in the midst of a terrifying civil war.

Although El Salvador was wracked by civil war from 1980 through 1992, RENEW/RENACER continued to flourish in various forms, even to the present, with the support and direction of Irma Chávez.

After Season I of RENACER, Irma reported that pastors were very pleased with the results. She overheard three priests talking after Season I. One said with delight, "We have over forty RENEW small faith-sharing groups in our parish." Another reported, "We have fifty." Finally, the third spoke up, "We have four hundred small RENEW groups in our parish!" Any concerns that these priests may have had about their people's response to RENEW were quickly alleviated.

Over forty thousand people from two rather small dioceses met in RENEW small groups in El Salvador. It was a positive sign in the midst of the violence and turmoil, helping to create a more peaceful climate. The poorest campesinos, land owners, and members of the military gathered to reflect together on Jesus' way of love and peace, forming new bonds that provided hope for a very troubled land.

After Season III, I spent a week in El Salvador with Irma. The setting was unbelievably beautiful. Irma was fearless. She rushed headlong into the most dangerous war areas, traveling highways and back roads in her ever-ready truck. I remember giving my first presentation in a volcano. Fortunately, the volcano was inactive and was filled with water, forming a pleasant lake. A pier launched out onto the lake with a large wooden deck where the bishops and one hundred twenty-five priests from the dioceses of Santa Ana and Sonsonate had gathered for RENEW training and inspiration from Irma and me.

A mariachi band played to add to the atmosphere. All gathered were deeply involved in RENEW and had assembled to evaluate their progress in the first three seasons. All the reports indicated that many people had moved from being passive Catholics, solely because they were born into the faith, to taking strong and active ownership of their faith.

In 1992, three additional dioceses launched RENEW, bringing the total to five dioceses working under Irma's guidance. These dioceses reported eighty thousand adults, fourteen thousand youth, and two thousand children having been in RENEW small communities.

As if spearheading RENEW wasn't enough for Irma, she was at the same time professor and dean of humanities at the Salesian University of Don Bosco in San Salvador.

The success of RENEW in her homeland has been gratifying to Irma. "In a parish of twenty thousand or twenty-five thousand people, everyone is touched in some way. Up to eighty percent will participate in the program through prayer at home. The other twenty percent will be involved in the small groups that are a RENEW feature."

Once the people started to meet in small groups they could not stop. In the midst of the war one of them said, "Even if there are shootings, we will continue, because this is the work of the Lord."

RENEW Fervor Foils Raid on Catholicism

Pentecostals poured three million dollars into a media campaign and sent two hundred fifty ministers to make Santa Ana the first Pentecostal city in Latin America. Militant evangelists had targeted Bishop Marco René Revelo's Diocese of Santa Ana, determined to "save the people from their ignorance" and win them over to Jesus. Asked what he intended to do, the bishop thought for a moment and said, "Well nothing, really. In fact, this should be a real test of RENEW."

RENEW had taken root in Santa Ana. Through RENEW, the people developed deep personal relationships with Jesus and came to a great love for Scripture. They had been greatly strengthened in their faith.

The expected evangelists never arrived. One day the bishop asked the mayor of Santa Ana if he knew what happened. The mayor revealed that when the leaders had come to him to arrange permission to use the town square and public buildings he showed them five boxes full of notes, letters, and telegrams expressing displeasure at the "invasion."

Examining the letters, Bishop Revelo found that they all sounded a similar theme: "Dear Mayor: We are already involved in an evangelization process called RENEW. We don't need and don't want outsiders coming in to talk to us as if we were pagans. We're happy with RENEW. Please tell them 'thank you' but better they stay at home and convert their own people."

The bishop assumed that someone had organized a letter-writing campaign. He inquired about it at the next diocesan clergy meeting but learned that there had been no such campaign. People had acted on their own. It was wholly the work of the Holy Spirit, the priests concluded.

Says Bishop Revelo, "That is what I like to share about RENEW. When the Holy Spirit touches the hearts of the people, the bishop must be touched too."

The ministers moved on to evangelize elsewhere. The people of Santa Ana proceeded to plan for permanent small communities that would build on their RENEW experience.

Meanwhile, Irma continued developing and strengthening small communities and providing rich materials for small-community sharing. She also took on an enormous project for disadvantaged youth. During El Salvador's civil war, thousands of youth were trained to kill. They supported each other in dangerous gangs. As part of her RENEW activities, Irma worked with thousands of children and teens who were at risk, helping them to become re-acclimated to civil society and to reclaim the Catholic faith of their baptism.

Witness Brings Peace

Recounting Irma's RENEW exploits could go on forever, but perhaps one short story conveys the impact of her work. Irma was in a hospital waiting to have an endoscopy when the nurse asked her, "What do you do for a living?" When Irma explained that she worked with RENEW, the nurse grabbed her hand and cried, "I owe my life to you!"

The woman explained that her husband had left her for another woman and had abandoned their daughter and newborn son. The abandonment and postpartum depression had left her suicidal. A cousin told her about a small-community meeting in the house of a neighbor. At her cousin's insistence she grudgingly agreed to attend. She listened to others' sharing, unmoved until a middle-aged man related that his wife had left him for another man and abandoned their three children. He shared how he trusted in God, received comfort, overcame resentment, and was doing very well in his work.

The serenity of his witness came like a wave of peace washing over the woman. She came to grips with a God who was both powerful and personal. Abandoning all thoughts of suicide, she committed herself to joining the RENEW small group. She shared with Irma that she had been formed in faith and was raising her children with the support of the Holy Spirit and living peacefully, without rancor toward anyone.

Many thousands of people have been influenced and touched through Irma's RENEW leadership.

I conclude this El Salvador report with the following reflection from Irma.

> Being able to promote RENEW in El Salvador has been one of the greatest blessings I've received. I returned here during our civil war, and to people who were torn with fear and violence, but who were healed by the only way of hope, which was the Gospel offered in their own homes.
>
> This experience allowed me to be very close to the suffering of the most poor who have shown me God's face, a marvel that has made me grow in faith. Walking together with them in my mission I learned that
>
> We come into the world
> not to be admired,
> not to be understood,
> not to worry.
>
> We are here to have our soul kneeling
> and our eyes wide open
> in absolute amazement
> before God.

CHAPTER 18

Pacific Islands, Australia, and Asia

A s a parish priest for years I had nurtured a special idea. If only I could tour the world, identifying the best pastoral practices to be found anywhere. Wouldn't that be of great value to our diocese? That assignment never came, but in 1984 I met a man who had undertaken that exciting task.

New Zealand

Brother Richard Dunleavy, a Marist brother from New Zealand, was touring the world looking for those good pastoral ideas to bring home. After visiting countries in Europe and elsewhere, Richard set about exploring leads in the United States. Wherever he went, the name RENEW kept popping up.

I remember the day Richard called, asking if he could visit us at RENEW. Could it be that there might be interest in RENEW from the farthest place in the world? Yes, New Zealand was the southernmost country on the other side of the globe.

Richard's visit led him to be highly enthused about the possibility of RENEW for New Zealand. It seemed that in all his travels RENEW was the pastoral project he was looking for. He was returning to New Zealand shortly and would be giving a report to the Bishops Conference of New Zealand on his exploratory tour. He would ask the bishops to extend an invitation for us to give a presentation to them and all priests in each of their six dioceses. But first he asked me, "Would you be willing to travel to New Zealand and give presentations on RENEW?" "Would we be willing? How fast can we fly there?"

For years I had heard about how extraordinarily beautiful New Zealand was. I was not to be disappointed. This was the first extensive RENEW trip of many more, and in many ways it was very likely the most memorable and enjoyable.

It was easy to like the people of New Zealand and their beautiful country where the landscape included semi-tropics and lush green rolling fields that reminded me of Ireland. New Zealand also had a beautiful port in Wellington. At the time, seventy million sheep grazed peacefully in a country of three million inhabitants.

Someone wisecracked that the country had creatively named its two islands North Island and South Island. The South Island brings you totally into the culture of England in the city of Christchurch and into Scotland in Dunedin. One of its main attractions is the Southern Alps with beautiful Queenstown and the world famous Lake Milford. Unfortunately, no presentation was scheduled for this area in the mountains. Invercargill, located at the southern base of the island, is the southernmost city in the world and possibly the rainiest.

Sr. Ellen Golden, O.S.F., and I embarked on this trip of thirty-some hours, landing in Auckland, New Zealand's largest city, in a time zone sixteen hours ahead of ours back in New Jersey. When it is 8 a.m. for us, New Zealanders are already into the next day.

In Auckland, we had a pleasant and welcoming visit with Bishop Denis Browne followed by a presentation to the priests of the diocese. This would be a presentation long remembered. Anything coming from the United States—that faraway, domineering giant—was to be viewed with caution. Perhaps that also applied to the presenters. In any event, a presentation, including questions and answers, that would last one-and-a-half hours in the United States and lead to a very satisfactory conclusion, would last nearly four hours in Auckland.

The question-and-answer time was most interesting. A priest stood up with an article by a well-known American liturgist that soundly criticized RENEW. The Auckland priest quoted at some length from the article, which he read with great emphasis. It seemed obvious that he was nailing our coffin tightly shut. Who would even consider RENEW as he carried on?

I sat patiently through his monologue, giving him every sign of respect. When he had finished, I explained to the priests that we had held a large conference bringing together liturgical experts like Christiane Brusselmans and many others to explore how RENEW could best promote excellent liturgical practice. I explained that I had invited the author the priest was quoting from to be part of the conference. We would pay his airfare and all expenses. The author's response had been, "I don't know anything about RENEW, so I don't think I'm qualified to be part of your conference." With that, the Auckland audience started turning favorably toward RENEW. No more needed to be said.

Near the very end of this lengthy session, one priest stood up to make his case. "I tell you," he said, "you've given us a pretty slick presentation, but I still have some hard questions." That priest went on to become the national director of RENEW for New Zealand.

The next stop was Hamilton. There I was stopped cold with a call from the United States informing me that my mother had fallen, breaking her hip, and was in the hospital. The rest of the trip would be punctuated with calls to and from the States, as my mother was well up in years at the time. That fall was to be the beginning of her declining health.

The Hamilton presentation on a Sunday afternoon was open not only to all the priests of the diocese but also to laypersons. I was forewarned that a family would be coming that was gunning for us. Their constant focus was to find orthodoxy in all things. This new possibility of RENEW deeply concerned them. They would try to shoot it down.

Just before the presentation, a family walked in the side door, across the room in front of everyone, and made themselves comfortable, except for one young male member of the family, who went to the back, sitting on a table swinging his legs throughout the meeting. It was obvious this family was coming to challenge RENEW. At the end of the presentation, the young man sprang to his feet, denouncing the presentation because it did not include devotion to Mary.

Whether or not my response was an inspiration of the Spirit, others will have to judge. I do know I have great devotion to the Blessed Mother. I thanked him for that reminder and asked him and the group to pray a decade of the rosary for my mother.

This meeting, as in Auckland, ended in a very positive response. On the way out, the mother of the family, who had come to gun us down, stopped to speak with me. "Don't worry about my son," she said. "I'll take care of him when we get home." So much for opposition in Hamilton.

The trip continued to go well. In the southernmost part of the country there was particularly strong anti-American feeling that had to be overcome. The United States had a large submarine base there to protect our interests in the Antarctic. For many, that presence was not welcome.

A constant theme that Ellen and I would raise was that we were not there primarily as Americans. We continually stressed we were there as brother and sister Catholics in a universal church. We deeply shared a faith in common. The things that appealed to people in RENEW also held universal appeal.

Of course, I noticed cultural differences. For instance, the way New Zealanders pronounced "yes" sounded more like "yeese" to my ears. And it was really different to hear big, strapping men use the term "goodie." Also, I enjoyed consuming the wonderful dairy products. It seemed as if dessert was worth nothing if it wasn't piled high with whipped cream. Cholesterol was certainly not a concern at that point.

The result of the trip was most gratifying. All six dioceses in New Zealand were on board to initiate the RENEW process. Arriving home, I was also relieved and pleased to see my mom who, while still experiencing considerable pain, was peaceful and most happy to see me home.

Universal Appeal of RENEW

Each diocese followed through by forming a diocesan team and sending the members to the United States in the summer of 1984 for training as to how to conduct the RENEW process. Fr. Paul Shanahan, S.M., and Fr. Gerard Whiteford, S.M., were named national directors of New Zealand and were ably assisted by Sr. Paula Brettkelly, S.S.J. They enjoyed their stay at RENEW, and we were delighted to have them as very joyful and energetic companions on the journey.

While with us they were very much impressed with the pastoral background of Fr. Tom Caroluzza and his connection with the North American Forum on the Catechumenate. Tom was invited to go to New Zealand the following year and help them promote the very logical connection of RENEW with the RCIA. While parishes were still doing RENEW, this would prepare them to follow up with a strong push on implementing the RCIA.

The New Zealand National RENEW team took seriously the acculturation of all aspects of RENEW. Materials were acculturated into Samoan, Tongan, Tokelauan, Vietnamese, Italian, and Maori—the language of the native New Zealanders.

One beautiful undertaking for each country implementing RENEW was to choose their own RENEW logo. We enjoyed the various logos and how they would immediately cast RENEW as a local effort in the minds of parishioners. For their logo, New Zealand chose a picture of the mamaku, an indigenous New Zealand tree fern. One hundred thousand RENEW prayer cards with this logo were circulated throughout the country.

RENEW results in New Zealand were amazing. Ninety-five percent of all the parishes in the country participated in the RENEW process. More important was the highly enthusiastic reaction of participants.

- Participants experienced a new way of being church, a way of shared faith, hope, and love.
- People began to encounter the person of Jesus as discovered in the Word.
- The RENEW process strongly brought forth the leadership qualities of women and men.

A final RENEW report from the National Team summed up by saying, "There can be no shadow of a doubt the church in New Zealand will not be the same as a result of RENEW. All bishops are clear on that. It has released a force and a direction in church life that will keep going on." Cardinal Thomas Stafford Williams responded by saying that he intended to take a copy of the RENEW report to the pope on the upcoming *ad limina* visit to the Vatican by all seven New Zealand bishops. He indicated that he would be promoting RENEW while there.

The impact of RENEW in New Zealand was significant. Perhaps, for me, the most telling commentary happened by chance. My brother Ed and sister-in-law Gert, years later, were visiting New Zealand. As they were coming out of a Sunday morning Mass, a priest asked where they were from. "The United States," they said. "Where in the United States?" "New Jersey," they replied." "Do you know Fr. Tom Kleissler?" he asked. Their response was they surely did. The pastor went on gushing with them about the wonderful impact RENEW had made in his parish and in all New Zealand. From booming success in little New Jersey parishes like Pius X in Old Tappan and St. Ann's in Newark, RENEW was now flourishing in faraway New Zealand. Thanks be to God!

Guam

I was first introduced to the island of Guam as a boy closely following the course of World War II. In 1986, under much more peaceful circumstances, I traveled to Guam.

Arriving in the mild climate of Guam in the middle of our winter was pleasurable, but there was even more pleasure in store for me. It was very early Monday morning in Guam but still Sunday afternoon back home. I could hardly believe that Bishop Anthony Sablon Apuron had a shortwave radio that enabled him to keep in good contact with the States. Here we were at four in the morning listening to the Giants play the Washington Redskins in a critical game. Was it possible the Giants could beat a tough Skins team? Dare I imagine the Giants finally being the best in football? The Giants won the game. The next month they won their first Super Bowl. Joy and jubilation!

The hospitality in Guam was beyond that of any diocese back home. I returned from this successful visit with a beautiful wooden hand-carved nameplate for my desk. More significantly, I was flying back with an agreement from Bishop Apuron to send a leadership delegation in the coming summer to study and prepare for the launching of RENEW in Guam.

On the tenth anniversary of Newark's original kickoff, Sr. Donna Ciangio and I found ourselves sitting in a huge field house in Guam for the RENEW kickoff. It was spectacular. Surely not as spectacular, but daunting for me, was to be the homilist at that Mass before such a huge gathering. They outdid our original experience by having three thousand five people, twice as many as Newark had had.

Later in the Mass, Donna spoke about the growth and development of RENEW symbolized by the RENEW tree. Each pastor came forward to the applause and delight of their parish delegations and received three small coconut trees they would plant at their individual parishes. The growth of RENEW in Guam would be symbolized by the growth of these coconut trees planted outside their churches.

Guam was faced with a challenge at the time of RENEW. Prosperity had come to the island. High-rise luxury hotels were on the way, and they would take over the wonderful beaches. Japan was saturated with holiday locations. People were looking for new vacation venues in the Pacific, and Guam was seen as an ideal place.

The RENEW experience in Guam was also facing a challenge. It was one that we faced everywhere. A pastor can unilaterally terminate the whole RENEW process, as in the case of any other pastoral initiative. After the initial enthusiastic launch, a number of priests, much to the disappointment of Bishop Apuron, had backed off.

However, many magnificent graces came through the RENEW process in Guam. Any number of people expressed how RENEW had been a godsend in their lives. With priests' support many groups flourished and, in instances lacking such support, people continued to carry on by themselves. RENEW was once again witnessing that wherever people are gathered in God's name the Spirit is alive and active.

While my priestly experience in parish life was so exhilarating, I also realized that working in an individual parish involves inherent limitations. With my RENEW involvement in Guam, I was reminded of the blessing it was to be God's instrument for spiritual growth for so many people in this faraway, beautiful island.

Western Samoa

Cardinal Pio Taofinu'u of Samoa, with a nine-person delegation, blessed us in 1986 by coming to our summer RENEW training. At the end of the training the cardinal, along with each of his representatives, explained RENEW in their native manner of dance and song. The native dance performed by the Samoans was certainly a highlight of our training session.

The cardinal and the delegation left New Jersey both enthusiastic and excited about taking RENEW back to Samoa. While keeping close contact with the Samoan experience, logistics and other circumstances rendered ongoing visits impossible. However, Cardinal Pio continued to update us with positive progress reports. He shared that RENEW in Samoa had taken on the "flavor" of the culture with much of the process done in song and dance.

How fortunate for readers not to be able to see me conclude this report by doing the Samoan RENEW dance.

Australia (1987-1989)

While original RENEW was still taking place in Newark in 1980, inquiries from Australia began coming in. Over the next few years these inquiries came from Australians who were updating themselves with theology and pastoral courses in the United States. They were hearing the buzz about RENEW from enthused Americans. While we answered those inquiries with written information, we were not in a position at that point to conduct any real follow-through.

A very serious turn of events occurred in 1984. Fr. Rex Curry, a pastorally gifted priest from the Armidale Diocese, was spending a few months in Lincroft, New Jersey. He was assisting at St. Leo Parish in the Trenton Diocese. At the time, Trenton was preparing for Season I of RENEW and there was much excitement among the parishioners. Fr. Curry became interested. He contacted us and participated in our International Inquiry/Information Sessions in late February 1985.

Returning home to speak with the bishops in Australia, Rex enthusiastically shared news and information of RENEW. It quickly became evident that Fr. Rex really knew how to make things happen. He lined up six dioceses, including his own, where bishops were interested in having us make presentations to their priests. I had never heard of the dioceses of Maitland, Port Pirie, Sandhurst, Armidale, Townsville, and

Wagga Wagga, but it all sounded very interesting. Little did I realize that Townsville was three thousand miles northeast of the other dioceses. It was to be a very tiring but fruitful trip.

Via a stop-over to touch base with RENEW leadership in New Zealand, Sr. Eileen Dumshaw and I undertook our Australian tour in March 1985. In each diocese we personally visited with the bishop and then gave a presentation to him and all the priests. As you can imagine, the questions ranged widely, always expressing a certain amount of concern about how an American experience would apply to Australia. We would then step outside and leave the priests alone while they came to a resolution about undertaking RENEW. While Eileen and I waited for their decision we prayed the rosary for the priests' guidance.

When we arrived in Wagga Wagga, we were taken aback by the fact that Bishop William Brennan was not home. However, we were extremely impressed when we heard why. He had been in South Africa, rallying with people from around the world in support of Archbishop Denis Hurley who was being accused by the apartheid government of causing dissension in South Africa. His "dissension" involved speaking out in favor of justice for the black and other non-white populations. The worldwide response and fury against the South African govern-ment caused authorities to back down and free Archbishop Hurley of any charges. Bishop Brennan was en route to Wagga Wagga where he would immediately meet with us.

In one diocese, the priests listened in rapt attention to my presenta-tion. However, when Eileen's turn came to present there was a very sad and troubling occurrence. Two priests in the last row turned their chairs around so that their backs were turned toward Eileen and their faces only a foot or two from the wall. At the end of the presentation, all the priests, except for these two, voted to undertake RENEW. Walking back to the rectory, I noted that these two priests were seriously engaging the bishop in conversation. With good reason, I became concerned.

Arriving at the rectory, the bishop said he was having second thoughts about RENEW. He was changing his mind, despite the overwhelming favorable vote of his priests. These two men had created doubts and fear that left him feeling very vulnerable to further criticism. Fortunately, after we responded to his concerns and encouraged him, the mood changed. "After dinner," he offered, "I'd really like to take you and Eileen on a ride out to the outback." He was going to do RENEW.

All six dioceses had decided to do RENEW. Alleluia!

Our tour also included visits to Brisbane and Melbourne. Fr. Peter Nicholson, director of religious education for the Archdiocese of Melbourne, was keenly interested. After our departure from Australia, Fr. Nicholson, accompanied by Fr. Paul Dalton, went to speak to Archbishop Frank Little to strongly encourage him to endorse RENEW for Melbourne.

Archbishop Little decided to form an archdiocesan RENEW team that would join with the RENEW teams being assembled in the other six dioceses.

Fr. Nicholson undertook a leadership role for all the Australian dioceses that were coming to the United States for our international training in June/July 1985. That training also included people from Ireland, Wales, England, Scotland, and Bombay. Part of that training included the national delegates going with us to Liberty State Park in Jersey City, New Jersey, to watch the New York fireworks on July 4. A bit of Americana!

Two other incidents occurred earlier on the Fourth of July. One was an excessively long limousine displaying American affluence passing through our picnic site. How well I remember the embarrassment. That embarrassment was furthered when the Australian delegation soundly beat us in a softball game. There I was, striking out to an Australian pitcher in what I thought was our American game.

The Australian team returned home highly enthused and ready to conduct a thorough preparation over the next year. They enculturated and translated RENEW for every conceivable culture and dialect in Australia.

They also engaged the Diocese of Cairns in the outback, thousands of miles north. The Cairns Diocese involved a large number of aborigines and was marked by small outback centers, visited only periodically by a priest. Our goal of reaching out to even the most remote of God's people was certainly being served.

The Australian RENEW leadership team had extended the original group from six to eight dioceses that were prepared to begin RENEW in 1987. They proceeded to carry out the RENEW process very effectively, keeping us apprised of progress with detailed reports.

The reports from parishioners indicated high enthusiasm and significant growth. Over and over again, the highlights from different dioceses showed striking similarities: a great spirit of prayer, stronger and more dynamic Sunday liturgies, emergence of lay leadership, closer relationships between clergy and lay people, valuable networking between parishes, a renewed sense of mission and confidence, faith integrated into everyday life, a thirst for further faith education, and the joy of belonging to something so alive and life-giving.

The percentage of parishes participating in RENEW was remarkable. Over ninety percent of parishes in dioceses were engaged in our process. The number of parishes and participating parishioners was far beyond expectations. RENEW was providing spiritual nourishment for those hungry in spirit.

The RENEW process eventually spread to twenty-two dioceses in Australia. Not that numbers are the be-all of anything. But realizing the value of the rich spiritual experience people were having and multiplying that by the enormous number of participants, paints a picture that is truly significant.

A part of the world that we sometimes refer to as "down under" was looking like the top of the world.

Asian Tour

Fr. Neil Diaz Karunaratne, the assistant secretary general to the Catholic Bishops Conference in Sri Lanka, came into our RENEW lives in 1988. Because of the rebellion going on in Sri Lanka, the bishops had told him in 1982 to take a much-needed break. He worked for a half year in a parish in California, which he experienced as "completely dead." Before Neil left, a young priest was asked to pastor that parish, and he agreed on the condition that he would be able to start RENEW there.

At that point, Neil had to leave for Sri Lanka, but a year later he returned to the parish and was amazed. He found greater attendance at daily Mass. People stayed after Sunday liturgy and had a great communal spirit. People who traveled eighty miles each day into Los Angeles for professional jobs returned home to their small-group meetings in the evening. They not only participated but committed themselves with great enthusiasm at the meetings. Neil's inquiries into the transformation all came down to the fact that the RENEW experience had changed the parish.

In 1988, Neil was helping out in a summer assignment at St. Margaret's in Little Ferry, New Jersey. He was delighted to connect with us at our home base. So strong was his belief in RENEW that he was convinced it had much to offer the Church of Asia and graciously arranged for Donna and me to accompany him on a tour of Asian dioceses where we could speak with bishops and diocesan leaders. The tour included the cities of Tokyo, Taipei, and Bangkok, the city-state of Singapore, Malaysia, and the Philippines.

While the trip was most interesting, it proved what we had long believed: a short one-time explanation could hardly be expected to elicit any commitment or substantial follow-through. Still, it was great to visit the Franciscan parish in Tokyo, which was in the midst of its own wonderful RENEW experience. In Singapore, we were surprised to find a pastor who had learned about RENEW and had implemented it on his own with one thousand people in RENEW small groups.

Bangkok proved to be life-threatening. Our driver, on a six-hour round trip, raced on a two-lane road at one hundred miles an hour, weaving in and out of cars and trucks. Having survived that, we got the payoff of the whole tour at our last stop in Manila.

Philippines

A visit had been arranged for us with the famous Cardinal Jaime Sin in Manila. Cardinal Sin, world renowned as a spiritual leader, was instrumental in the Filipino people's struggle for political freedom. The visit was good and pleasant but also brief. We last saw the cardinal rushing off to a waiting car, surrounded by an entourage, taking notes. However, something much more promising was about to happen.

Neil made contact with Bishop Cirilo Almario of Malolos in Bulacan. Neil thought that Bishop Almario, who was the head of a biblical commission for the Philippines, might be interested. Bishop Almario went out of his way to join us to learn about our RENEW process.

Bishop Almario quickly realized the pastoral potential of RENEW and the opportunity to connect our process to his biblical work. He was sold and was a man of action, ready to go. Bishop Almario contacted other bishops, encouraging them to look into the RENEW process with him. He called Bishop Paciano Aniceto of San Fernando, Pampanga, and arranged for us to also speak to the priests of that diocese.

Our Asian tour had ended on a very high note with a great future for RENEW awaiting us in the Philippines. God had saved the best for last on this trip, and we returned home grateful for how the journey had been graced and for the great contribution Neil had made to RENEW.

Philippines on Board

As early as January 1989, Donna and I were back in the Philippines to make presentations to bishops and priests. The reception we received from priests in both dioceses was great. The result was that Bishop Almario in Malolos and Bishop Aniceto in San Fernando, Pampanga, made firm commitments to launch RENEW in 1991.

This called for a tight preparation schedule and kept Donna, in particular, extremely busy. We needed to develop materials, form diocesan teams, and conduct many training sessions.

The most pleasant aspect of our work in the Philippines was the wonderful, friendly, gentle, and humble nature of the Filipino people. What a joy they are. Moreover, the very familiar relationship between the Philippines and United States enhanced our work. In many ways an American can feel right at home in the Philippines. Our RENEW work there was fitting considering that in the original RENEW in Newark, one of the three pilot parishes was largely Filipino. Filipino people had already embraced RENEW long before we got to the Philippine Islands.

Local customs are always charming and one, in particular, struck me. A birthday celebration lasts for three days; at least it did for Bishop Almario. Every conceivable type of delicious food was spread over a large dining room table. Every person in the diocese was welcome to stop by and participate in the feast at any time during the course of the three days. People would bring contributions for the table and would consume as much, or more, before they left. It was the most delightful and friendly atmosphere. The bishop and his people all greeted each other in great friendship. What a wonderful human aspect of church I was experiencing. This was not "business as usual" or "maintenance." This was a loving community.

We would have the privilege of servicing five more dioceses in the Philippines in the coming decade. I would like to slip into that decade for one training that occurred in Malolos in January 1990.

I must admit to being distracted during this training. Finally, at one of the breaks, I asked someone how I could possibly find the score of an NFL playoff game that had occurred on Sunday, the day before. CNN was available as if I were really back home. On Monday morning we turned the TV on just in time to see a video of the last play of the game. To my dismay, we watched the Los Angeles Rams' Henry Ellard catching a pass and running through the Giants' end zone and straight on into the locker room with the winning touchdown.

My spirits sank into a dark tunnel of my own making. Fortunately, those football spirits were to re-emerge a year later. The Giants would win their second Super Bowl.

Of far greater significance was the fact that in the following years the RENEW experience would strongly impact the Filipino people with God's loving action.

CHAPTER 19

United Kingdom

Another gift from heaven dropped in on us in the form of David Barker of the Brenninkmeyer family in London. David directed the foundation and had become very impressed with all that he was hearing about RENEW.

He felt that the bishops of the Church in the United Kingdom should become versed in this RENEW process that was helping great numbers of people in so many parishes. He came up with a financing plan that would enable several bishops from the United Kingdom to come for a week to our RENEW office, bringing with them several key people for reflection and consultation.

In March 1985, six bishops from England, Wales, and Scotland, along with representatives from each of their dioceses, came to spend the better part of a week with us in at our offices in Plainfield, New Jersey. Of those bishops who reacted well to RENEW, two stood out by dint of their great energy: Archbishop Thomas Winning from Glasgow, Scotland, and Bishop Cormac Murphy-O'Connor from Arundel and Brighton. Both men would become cardinals.

It was a rather intensive and exhausting week with our visitors expressing much concern about whether RENEW could be adapted to the United Kingdom. Even with adaptations, how well would it be accepted, coming from the States? Would the small communities work as well as they did in the United States? Would cultural mores mean that the people in the

U.K. were more reserved and reluctant to open up and share? The tides of possibility seemed to swing widely back and forth over the course of those days.

Archbishop Winning and his team had a major concern. They were already engaged in a ten-year renewal program provided by the Better World Movement. While committed to their ten-year program, they were attracted to some aspects of RENEW that they felt they were not then experiencing.

In contrast to their ten-year program, RENEW not only presented an understanding of community but actually brought people into community so that the experience might speak for itself. The fact that people were so immediately brought into faith-sharing and sharing about the Scriptures was also very attractive to our visitors. It presented the strong spiritual, experiential tone they were looking for. It might also be more attractive to a good number of parishes that currently were not actively involved in the diocesan process. Perhaps it was the appropriate moment to inject RENEW into the parishes and then continue with the longer-term process.

We believed that Archbishop Winning was a man of action and was ready to proceed almost immediately. In addition, we were pleased that still another Scot, Bishop Maurice Taylor of Galloway, was showing signs of strong interest.

During the week I had the opportunity to spend a lot of time with Bishop Cormac Murphy-O'Connor and establish a good relationship with him. I had come to deeply appreciate what a truly outstanding man he is. With the support of Msgrs. Patrick Olivier and Tim Rice, along with Karen Goldsmith, all of whom accompanied him, I could see him warming up more and more about RENEW over the course of the week.

On the final day, we had an excellent conversation in which, in effect, Bishop Murphy-O'Connor expressed his belief in RENEW and his strong inclination to initiate the process. At the same time, he was cautious with understandable concern about how ready and receptive his priests would be. He would return home and approach the whole subject of RENEW in a gradual step-by-step manner.

Scotland

Glasgow

When Archbishop Winning and his team returned from Plainfield, they were raring to go. Communication continued and they gradually became more comfortable with the compatibility of RENEW and their program.

In short order, Donna and I were in Glasgow giving information presentations for the priests of the diocese. RENEW came through as extremely practical for these parish priests, and it seemed to give them new energy. While there, we also worked with Fr. Hugh McEwan and his archdiocesan RENEW team. Fr. McEwan had written to us a few years earlier inquiring about RENEW and was now the enthusiastic, designated RENEW director for his diocese.

The sign-up of parishes, which followed shortly, went over extremely well. Of the one hundred nine parishes in the archdiocese, a little over one hundred committed themselves to launching RENEW. Of these, the vast majority would stay deeply involved throughout the course of the three years.

The sign-up was followed by overnight training sessions for parish RENEW core teams. These also went very well. They were on their way.

Galloway

In the meantime, Archbishop Maurice Taylor of Galloway also had his diocese ready to start RENEW in the fall of 1986. He was a cousin of Sr. Mary George O'Reilly, who was so helpful in launching original RENEW in Newark. In addition to all the other encouragement he received, Bishop Taylor had been hearing wonderful things over the years from his cousin in Newark.

Donna and I spoke with the priests of the Galloway Diocese. Bishop Taylor appointed an excellent diocesan RENEW team headed by Fr. Archie Brown. Interestingly, one of his key team members was a man who had lived in St. Cecilia's parish in Kearny, New Jersey, for a number of years. Kearny is a town in our archdiocese which has a significant population with roots in Scotland. More important was the fact this man had wonderful memories of RENEW and its effectiveness, which helped him bring extra conviction and enthusiasm to his work in Galloway.

As with Glasgow, preparations for RENEW proceeded beautifully. From May 16 to May 20, 1986, Donna and I had a memorable visit with Bishop Taylor and his diocesan RENEW team. Once again, I was able to experience the tremendous warmth and hospitality of the Scottish people. The absence of any pretense and unassuming ways made me very comfortable.

During the visit, Bishop Taylor took Donna and me to the site by the sea where St. Ninian, the first to bring the faith to Scotland, had landed in 397. He must have been an amazing man considering that he made this voyage well before St. Patrick's first trip to Ireland. That outing made for a very special day.

Bishops Conference of Scotland

On Tuesday, May 26, at the invitation of Bishop Winning, Donna and I were at the Catholic Bishops Conference of Scotland in Edinburgh to give a presentation on RENEW. To be speaking to a bishops conference was another first. We felt that the presentation and question/answer period went well, although the bishops showed no immediate interest. The dioceses of Motherwell and Dunkeld came on board two years later.

Evaluations of Season I in Glasgow indicated a high degree of success. Twenty thousand people had participated in small communities. Many indicated they wanted to continue their RENEW small-group meetings beyond the end of the season. Even priests who had been suspicious at the beginning of RENEW were gratified by what was happening in their parishes. Liturgies had improved, there was a new community feeling, and new people had come forward as pastoral workers. Human nature doesn't vary all that much from place to place. All reports indicated the same positive experiences with regard to prayer, the Scriptures, and faith-sharing.

The experience of Glasgow was being replicated in Galloway, as would also be the case in Dunkeld and Motherwell within the next few years. These most common human reactions strengthened our conviction that RENEW had struck a chord of human needs and wants that had universal appeal.

Dioceses of Dunkeld and Motherwell

Outstanding bishops were being attracted to the RENEW experience. In 1988 the dioceses of Dunkeld and Motherwell also launched RENEW. We had very pleasant experiences working with the two dioceses. Bishop Vincent Logan in Dunkeld was a very impressive and dynamic young bishop. The fire of his enthusiasm assured good response from his priests and people and a successful RENEW process. The fact that Bishop Logan appointed Fr. Joe Creegan, one of our most capable diocesan coordinators, was an important component. In each diocese, Donna worked tirelessly with coordinators and their teams.

Dunkeld absorbed everything and, not surprisingly, had our RENEW team back for a Day of Listening and Planning in 1989 as they approached the end of their RENEW process. The listening and planning process was the one that had been built on Tom Groome's adult learning process, which we had used successfully throughout the United States. It helped dioceses clearly think through how they wanted to build on the momentum of RENEW. As might be expected, it always brought forth a strong cry for continuance of the small communities.

Dunkeld didn't stop there. In 1990 the diocese sent a delegation to the United States to study the RENEW follow-through in the dioceses of Newark, Hartford, Providence, and Orlando. Dunkeld had certainly latched onto the larger picture of RENEW and all its possibilities. It was not surprising that ten years later Bishop Logan was calling upon us for *RENEW 2000* to keep the fires burning.

As I indicated earlier, I have wonderful personal memories of the Scottish people. I hadn't heard much about Scottish cuisine and was pleasantly surprised by some outstanding meals and the hearty appetite of the Scots. Food is a universal love.

Visiting Fr. Joe Creegan's rectory was a different kind of experience. It was a very raw and cold day, which perhaps influenced my thoughts. However, I was impressed with the simplicity of Fr. Creegan's residence. Like so many priests I met in my travels, his life was about service to the people more than seeking his own comfort. Of course the beauty of

Edinburgh, built at the edge of cliff, was awesome. I managed to have time to buy a pair of shoes there that my brother Dick admired for many years. I thought I might lose them to him at any moment.

Another memory, on a lighter note, was that Bishop Joseph Devine in Motherwell was a very active man. Unknown to him I had given him the nickname of "Jumpin' Joe Devine." I wonder what he called me.

Would you believe that I never did get the time to play golf in the homeland of that wonderful sport? Nevertheless, I do cherish more important and wonderful memories.

England

While I've never been to Lourdes, I have been blessed over the years with strong devotion to the Blessed Mother. It gave me special joy to hear about Mary's inspirational role in England's launch of RENEW.

Diocese of Arundel-Brighton

The Diocese of Arundel-Brighton in southern England has the beautiful tradition of a diocesan pilgrimage to Lourdes each year. During the pilgrimage in 1986, three men, Msgrs. Tim Rice, Patrick Olivier, and John Hull (the vicar general), had a chat about a matter very near to their hearts. They had been among those most closely concerned with the search for a program of spiritual renewal for their diocese. In this prayerful atmosphere they came to a unanimous resolve to invite me to come and explain RENEW to their diocese. They later thanked Our Lady for the blessing of that chat.

At the time, they may not have been aware that this was not the first serious inquiry about RENEW from England. In 1981, one year after RENEW finished in Newark, Bishop David Constant had visited us, learning about RENEW with great interest. The following summer he had sent a team to spend time with us in our annual summer training. In the long run, they were still apprehensive about how good a fit RENEW would be for the desperately poor situation of their territory in Central London.

The resolve of the three monsignors from Arundel-Brighton was strong and would reach fulfillment. The year before, they had come to visit us with Bishop Cormac Murphy-O'Connor in that week-long meeting, which included five other bishops and their consultative teams from the United Kingdom. Bishop Murphy-O'Connor had followed up on the visit with a number of consultative meetings throughout the diocese. For Tim, John, and Pat, the conclusion had become extremely clear. RENEW was the answer to their search. Surely these three men, helped the bishop affirm his own strong belief in RENEW. They invited me to speak to all the priests of the diocese in November 1986.

I drove with Bishop Murphy-O'Connor to St. John's Seminary in Wonersh on the day of that priests' presentation. He seemed to be more nervous than I was. After all, he was sticking out his neck. He may have been even more taken aback when I took a twenty-minute nap just before the presentation.

By God's grace we survived. In fact I thought the presentation went well. Some of the priests' questions were really not questions but rather pointed and critical comments. I always enjoy responding to questions and answers. On this occasion I also welcomed strong local support from Karen Goldsmith, the well-respected youth minister of the diocese. She witnessed beautifully to how strongly she believed in RENEW and how it could be adapted and made suitable for the needs of their diocese. Msgrs. Patrick Olivier and Tim Rice were also strong in their support of RENEW.

On the way back from the seminary, Bishop Murphy-O'Connor said, "You obviously knew things would go well, didn't you?" While that wasn't quite true, I did know by this time, after so many other presbyteral presentations, that RENEW had a lot to offer that would resonate with priests' parish experiences.

Decision Day

Naturally, nothing comes quite so easily. In follow-up consultations with priests throughout the diocese, Bishop Murphy-O'Connor found that there was still a strong opposition from some of the men. The bishop's excellent relationship with his priests obviously was a major factor all through the consultation process. However, all speculation ended when he announced that the Diocese of Arundel-Brighton would initiate RENEW.

The Tablet reported on RENEW's kickoff, which took place in September 1988 in the football stadium at Goldstone. The title *kickoff* was appropriate considering that Bishop Murphy-O'Connor was a rugby player and a great fan of the game. Fifteen thousand people attended. At least five hundred instrumentalists and vocalists provided music. Musician Paul Inwood wrote a special Mass for the occasion, including an original RENEW hymn and the RENEW prayer set to music. Teams of young people came from far-flung deaneries with RENEW flames, Olympic style. Each parish's RENEW team was commissioned and presented with acorns—their diocesan RENEW logo was the oak tree—that were to be taken home and planted so that they might grow and develop as beautifully as RENEW would.

All of this, and what was to follow over the next three years, did not happen by accident. Msgr. Kevin McHugh was one of the finest diocesan directors we ever had. An affable, confident, and thorough priest, he provided critically important guidance that contributed to an excellent diocesan experience. All training was overseen with great care, and the special elements of prayer, Scripture, liturgy, justice, and small community formation were implemented with great effectiveness.

In Season I, twelve thousand five hundred people were in RENEW small groups, which was no small accomplishment. Remember, numbers of Catholics varied greatly from diocese to diocese and country to country. Numbers themselves never tell the full story. I was extremely impressed with the high percentage of RENEW participants in relationship to parish membership. The percentages were off the chart.

One of the main concerns in England was that people would be very reserved and possibly wouldn't open up in their small groups. This apprehension faded quickly early in Season I. A smattering of quotes gives us a feel for the three-year experience:

- "Husbands and wives felt a great sense of closeness, creating a better understanding in their lives together, enabling more discussion and sharing of everyday matters."
- "Once we starting talking, we couldn't stop!"
- "RENEW has brought back into my life a spirit of love and forgiveness."

- A young parishioner reported, "We now feel we are ready to take on the world!"

In St. Leonard's parish a regular RENEW small-group meeting took place in the local prison. Members of a parish in Haslemere received prayerful support from parishes they had contacted in the United States, Canada, and Australia. In Battle, it was recorded that someone was received into the Church as a direct result of the prayer network. In Eastborne, someone commented that numbers at daily Mass had become "like a Sunday."

As the end of the process approached, I was once again impressed with the thoroughness of the preparation for activity beyond RENEW. All diocesan ministries were involved with planning and preparing for how the follow-through might best take place. Donna had worked closely with Fr. McHugh over the RENEW process and they now worked together on the plan for post RENEW. Donna and I conducted the Day of Listening and Planning, used so successfully in the United States, for a large gathering of the bishop, priests, and parishioners of the diocese. The conclusion was unanimous: the participants wanted to continue the promotion of small Christian communities in their parishes.

I remember well a conversation with Msgr. Barry Wymes who, although being a friend of Bishop Murphy-O'Connor, was skeptical of RENEW when it arrived. He was very negative because he had seen how many other programs had floundered. Nevertheless, he proceeded in faith, imploring his whole parish to pray for success, and later witnessed how prayer was the key. Besides RENEW having been very successful in his parish, he himself was profoundly affected. He said it gave him a deeper personal awareness of the working of the Holy Spirit. He had seen a whole parish community transformed by the power of the Holy Spirit.

I had a chance to visit Brighton, a beach resort, and it gave me a warm feeling because its boardwalk reminded me of my own Jersey Shore. I also was deeply impressed by the beauty of the countryside in southern England. I had heard many positive things about it, but one day in particular impressed me deeply. Driving on a narrow road through the lush trees, foliage, and beautiful wildflowers, I was overwhelmed with a sense of beauty and God's presence.

Perhaps my fondest recollection is of informal and relaxed chats with Bishop Murphy-O'Connor about church matters and everything else. While he was a brilliant man and would become cardinal archbishop of Westminster, he had a wonderful manner that projected instant friendship. A conversation with him was like a fireside chat.

By God's grace that friendship would continue ten years later when Cardinal Cormac Murphy-O'Connor initiated *RENEW 2000* for the Archdiocese of Westminster.

CHAPTER 20

Close to My Heart

Africa and India

Time, *Newsweek*, and all other periodicals and newspapers were filled with a sad and most intriguing story in 1986. All the people living around Lake Nyos in a remote area of Cameroon in Central Africa had been found dead. It was determined that chemicals or poison gases were being emitted from the lake. It was something like science fiction. What could possibly have happened?

Cameroon

Around that time, a priest from Cameroon visited my office, and he was from the diocese where Lake Nyos was located. I wanted to hear more about what was going on in this mysterious land. He shared freely and images started to form in my mind of a nation and people as far removed from my life as someone in outer space. The priest wanted to learn about RENEW, and he left feeling strongly that it could help his people in Cameroon. Within a week, another inquiry came from Cameroon. What was going on here? No one else in Africa was inquiring about RENEW.

When within a month a third, totally independent inquiry came from Cameroon, I realized this couldn't be an accident. This must be the work of the Holy Spirit, and it should be taken seriously. The third inquiry was from Fr. Michael DeRooy, a Dutch priest, who was vicar general of the Diocese of Buéa. The tone of his request for information indicated an interest beyond curiosity or passing inquiry. Michael and I continued communication through the mail.

The background of Catholicism in Cameroon is very interesting. On November 9, 1912, six German Sacred Heart missionaries, led by Fr. Gerhard Lennartz, set out for the German colony of Cameroon. These were men of courage and zeal beyond our imagination. The story is that as the boat approached land one of the priests could not wait any longer to start bringing the message of Jesus to the people of Cameroon. The ship was moving too slowly. In his zeal, he dove off the boat and started swimming for shore. The rudder of the boat ripped open his shoulder and a thick trail of blood followed him all the way in. It was the first clue of the heroic work that would be done not only by the missioners but by the Cameroonian people.

Another example of outstanding faith was the building of what might have been the first Catholic church in Cameroon. Stones had to be brought in by boat to build the edifice, and the port of arrival was over one hundred miles away from the building site. Picture this: Women from the parish would trek down to the port. Each one would take a huge stone and secure it on her head as best she could. Then she would take the seven-day walk back to the church site. The men then did the construction work but, after seeing the church, the lasting image I kept was hundreds of women carrying those huge stones on their heads. Unbelievable!

Within a few months of contacting me, Michael invited me to visit the three bishops in the English-speaking part of Cameroon. I would also be making presentations on RENEW to the priests of each of these dioceses. I had never been to Africa and was filled with wonder at what the experience might be like.

Most Cameroonians spoke French, the result of French control that went back to World War I. Air France brought me to De Gaulle Airport, Paris, where I got a motel room overlooking a meadow on the edge of the airport runway. It was a cold, raw, totally uninspiring day, and I had to wait until my flight took off for Cameroon that evening.

Rather than sitting in my room all day, I decided to take a bus into Paris. Having never been to Paris before, I certainly was not seeing it at its best. I left Paris sadly unimpressed. Our trips never built in time for sightseeing. I'm still waiting for that special visit to Paris.

Michael was at the airport to welcome me and he took me to a local parish and a rectory that was well-staffed by the Mill Hill Fathers. A warm, welcoming greeting by the community of priests was highlighted by a wonderful meal. I was told to be up early. Life started very early in Cameroon.

It was sometime before 5 a.m. when the shuffling of feet on the dirt road woke me. What a beautiful sight to see the throngs of people in their bright-colored best heading for Sunday Mass. I would learn that the early weekday Mass wasn't much different in terms of attendance and devotion.

That Sunday Mass was a spectacular experience. The church was truly alive. Priests in Cameroon need not worry about running overtime in their homilies. People there as in Nigeria and other African countries felt cheated if the homily went on for less than a half hour. The music was very lively and non-stop. The offertory procession included people sashaying up the middle aisle carrying animals and other local, meaningful gifts. At collection time, each person came up to drop his or her donation in a metal container. I'm sure that even a not too-well-trained ear could sense the amount of the gift.

My experience that afternoon was totally different. Much as they would be in a parish in the United States, all the priests were off to other places. I was sitting alone in the rectory with little to do except reach out the window and pick a fresh mango off the tree. Suddenly an idea struck me. Why not walk over to the church and make a visit?

Sitting in the empty, totally quiet church that afternoon proved to be a remarkable experience. There was a huge crucifix on the wall behind the altar, and I soon drifted into one of the finest reflections I can remember. I was alone, far away from family, friends, and everything that made me comfortable. Perhaps I even felt a bit abandoned here in a distant land. I had been stripped of everything. There was nothing left but God and the real and unvarnished me. My reflection then moved to a point of even greater nothingness. There was nothing but God. God was all and was everything. God was all that was. I certainly wasn't alone. Reflecting for a long period, I experienced that God was with me in a way I shall never forget.

Within a couple of days, Michael and I were in a jeep and on our way to begin a journey that would continue to head north for well over one thousand miles. The roads were incredibly poor as the jeep bounced around wildly. It was the dry season, and dust and sand from the distant Sahara had blown all over, covering everything and everyone. Michael insisted on sitting in the back seat of the jeep and giving me the seat of honor in the front. He was by far getting the worst of it all and was covered with layers of dust. How much I admired this man, approaching his 80s with the zeal of the newly ordained. He epitomized to me the best of everything a missionary could be. He was faith-filled and coura- geous, and he generously gave of himself.

Michael's faith and goodness prevailed. Each of the three bishops and their priests responded to RENEW beautifully. Bishop Paul Verdzekov of Bamenda, Bishop Pius Suh Awa of Buéa, and Bishop Cornelius Fonpem Esua of Kumbo all committed themselves to having the RENEW process launched in 1990. Much work would be done in advance.

In June 1988, Donna, Cecilia, and I were in Mutengene for a three- week training session for the excellent teams of priests, sisters, and laypeople that each diocese had provided. It was hot, humid, and a chal- lenging environment that found the never-complaining Cecilia covered with huge bug bites. However, no one's spirit could be diminished, espe- cially that of the Cameroonian RENEW diocesan teams. They absorbed and internalized everything about RENEW. Timelines fascinated them. What an interesting concept—different tasks would be completed by specific times.

This first African training session made it clear to us that all three of us from the international team would not be required in the future. Donna could shepherd the RENEW process in Cameroon. Cecilia's energy could be used in other new venues that were opening up. In fact, over the next decade Cecilia and I would work extensively in Nigeria and India.

As always, the RENEW experience went very well. In the Diocese of Kumbo alone there were nearly eight hundred small groups. In all three dioceses, hundreds of lapsed Catholics came back to church. Many marriages were validated and many potential converts were now receiving instruction.

Wedding Bells

In Buéa, Cameroon, Cyprian and Mary happily posed for pictures under a RENEW banner after their wedding. They had been living together for fifteen years. During that time, they attended Mass only at Christmas and knew very little about their Catholic faith.

When RENEW came to Cameroon they became part of the process. In the fifth season of RENEW, they decided they had to do something about their future and undertook the required pre-marriage course. The parish priest observed, "I had eight weddings last month—all from RENEW faith-sharing groups."

RENEW witnessed to the gospel promise that wherever two or three gathered in his name, Jesus would be present. People always loved sharing faith and having a new experience of the Scriptures. RENEW carried on in Cameroon for the first three years of the 1990s. RENEW was now well established in Africa.

Nigeria

Creighton University in Nebraska has long been noted for an excellent summer program on spirituality. So well-known was the program that news of it reached Nigeria where a young and zealous priest, Peter Otubusin, heard of it. In the summer of 1987, Peter participated in the program and thoroughly enjoyed it.

Over and over, Peter heard others at Creighton talking about their RENEW experience. "What is this RENEW?" he wanted to know, and they told him about all the exciting things they had experienced. One person, in particular, was from the St. Paul-Minneapolis Archdiocese and invited him to go to the RENEW office in St. Paul. The people there were helpful but said, "If you really want to get a good grasp of this, you should go to the National Office located in the Newark Archdiocese."

And so it was that on a hot and lazy August day our phone rang with a call from Peter Otubusin. After listening to him I responded, "Could you possibly come by to visit us on your way back to Nigeria?" I didn't know Peter well yet but found out that nothing could stop him.

We had a wonderful visit in our Plainfield office, as Peter totally understood and bought into the value of the RENEW process for his Diocese of Ibadan. He suggested I contact his bishop and try to arrange for a visit. Why not? After all, I would soon be making my first trip to Africa, traveling to Cameroon. Fortunately, Cameroon was next door to Nigeria.

After giving Peter enough time to get home and share with Archbishop Felix Job, it was time to make contact. After praying a Hail Mary, I picked up the phone to make my first of what could possibly be many attempts to contact Bishop Job. To my amazement, that first call went through immediately, and Bishop Job picked up the phone. Would you believe he was sitting at his desk talking with Peter? I arranged to visit with them in Ibadan on my way from Cameroon.

It was a short flight over the mountain to Lagos Airport (named Murtala Mohammed during construction) in Nigeria. It was my good fortune that when I arrived, the airport was quiet and deserted, free of the usual hassles of attempted bribes. What did concern me was that Peter was not waiting to greet me. I stood outside the airport, once again alone, this time in Nigeria, wondering what might happen next. Finally, a tall man in a flowing white cassock appeared. It was Peter Otubusin.

The journey to Ibadan, in February 1988, was quite interesting. I watched Peter handle the soldiers at the checkpoints, who were obviously looking for the usual bribe. What was even more interesting and joyful was the meeting with Bishop Job. He could not have been friendlier and took well to RENEW. Bishop Job immediately sent word out, and within a couple of hours all the heads of diocesan societies had assembled at his residence.

Here was a group that might be excited about the prospect but might also question how RENEW would work in their own societies. However,

God's presence was keenly felt and all agreed that RENEW would be helpful for Ibadan.

Bishop Job then made a proposal: "Would you be willing to return and speak to the bishops and priests in all the dioceses of their province?" Once again, I thought, "Could this really be happening?" "Certainly we would be more than happy to do that," I answered. "This is more than we could have ever imagined."

Shortly after, Cecilia, Dominic, and I were back for the tour of the province. This started with a favorably received presentation to the priests in Ibadan and continued on a bumpy, adventurous journey of the entire region.

Our first stop was scheduled to be with a bishop who was expected to be quite receptive to RENEW. However, we never got to see him. A flat tire and many other delays made us late, and then he had to leave for another appointment.

Instead of visiting with the bishop, we were asked if we'd like to visit the prison. We agreed. Upon arriving at the prison we were taken aback by an invitation to visit Death Row. Walking through an open courtyard among the many prisoners, I couldn't help but wonder what it would be like. We took a couple of steps down to a submerged door that led into Death Row. It was a damp and dreary atmosphere lined on both sides with cells, divided by a narrow corridor. Each cell contained ten men waiting to be hanged. The conditions within those cells were beyond description.

Yet it was the scene of the greatest joy I had ever experienced. All the men were dancing, singing for joy, and praising God. And why not? They had just been baptized into our Catholic faith at Easter and were ready and eager to go to heaven. These were so much more than men waiting to be hanged. They were joyful men with the greatest anticipation, waiting to be united with God in the glory of heaven.

I stepped outside Death Row a humbled man. We had come with the mission of RENEW. Now I was experiencing God already present here. I was beginning to understand the deeply spiritual nature of Nigerians and African people as a whole. God's presence was always alive and vibrant.

That deeply profound and humbling experience surely helped us as we made our way to the other dioceses. The result was that we would start a training process with Ibadan and three other dioceses that would launch RENEW in 1992. RENEW was coming home to the ancestral land of people I had worked with while I was in inner-city Newark.

Over the next decade, twelve other dioceses would also become engaged in RENEW. Some were located in the northernmost parts of Nigeria, in areas controlled by some radical Muslims. For Cecilia, other RENEW staff members, and me, this next decade would provide quite an adventure.

The mainstay of it all was Fr. Peter Otubusin who, to this day remains a close friend, carries the RENEW mission in his heart, and continues the work of RENEW throughout his ministry.

South Africa

As a very young priest in Park Ridge, New Jersey, I greatly admired a priest of South Africa. He was born in the lighthouse at the southern tip of Africa and was to become a shining light for all of South Africa and the whole world. Ordained a bishop at the tender age of thirty-two, he always stood up for justice and courageously fought apartheid early on.

I was receiving mission appeals from this great man, Bishop Denis Hurley. Can you imagine eagerly looking forward to an appeal? I loved to receive his letters and became excited about everything he was doing. What a man!

How could I ever have imagined that many years later, my hero, by then Archbishop Hurley, would walk through the front door of RENEW International. He had been at a conference in New York where a standing international committee was working on an ecumenical translation of the Bible. While there, he heard about RENEW.

Here he was, coming to listen to Donna and me. Could this really be happening? Archbishop Hurley listened intently and with obvious great interest. After forty-five minutes, he told us that the bishops of South Africa (under his leadership) had put together a pastoral plan that spoke strongly about justice. It was a plan to fight apartheid. Archbishop

Hurley had been a national leader fighting against apartheid long before others became involved in the cause.

He explained that the problem the bishops faced was how to implement their plan. That was understandable. It was probably like mission statements that hang on the walls of church vestibules, or like many other documents that are labored over and then stashed in a drawer.

The archbishop said that from what he had learned he had come to the conviction that RENEW would be the best means of implementing this plan.

Winter School of Theology

A year later I was invited by Archbishop Hurley to be the speaker at South Africa's annual Winter School of Theology. It was the yearly theological input and development opportunity for priests from around the country. How could I be the presenter at this great theological event? In the two preceding years, the speakers had been Sr. Elizabeth Johnson, C.S.J., and Fr. Ed Braxton, both brilliant theologians.

I could spell "theology" but obviously was a pastoral person. I was hardly a notable theologian but rather a parish priest who fell into something big. But that's what they wanted—a pastoral person. I was invited to go to South Africa in their winter, our summer, of 1989, and spend a week each in Pretoria, Durban, East London in Port Elizabeth Diocese, and Cape Town. Each week, three presentations a day were given to all the priests of these dioceses.

Pretoria

I spent the first week in Pretoria. I took daily walks in a beautiful suburban section adjoining the seminary where I was staying and presenting. Men who worked in the area, cutting lawns and the like, all wore full-length, blue uniforms. They could be spotted a mile away.

A vivid picture remains with me: a young white blonde mother leaving her house and getting into her car with two beautiful, little towheaded children. They were no doubt Afrikaners of Dutch descent. A terrible thought came to my mind. How could she and her husband live here raising these beautiful children? Ultimately, wouldn't they all be slaughtered when the vast majority of people rose up? But the impossible did happen. Through God's grace working in Nelson Mandela, Archbishop Hurley, Archbishop Desmond Tutu, and others, a true miracle would happen. A previously unimaginable peaceful transfer of power would take place.

Durban

I spent the next week in Archbishop Hurley's Diocese of Durban. Durban is a place a visitor has to love. This remarkable city goes right up to the west coast of the Indian Ocean. Beautiful and sanitized, it was in the "first-world" part of South Africa. Pulling into a gas station I could not help but notice that the cement floor had been painted and was washed down daily. It looked as if no one even walked there, no less driven through. Beautiful residential areas rose up over the hill that overlooked the ocean. Obviously, this was the home of the Afrikaners.

However, just a few miles inland were the townships where black people lived in terrible poverty. My hope was that RENEW would be particularly effective in these townships.

As expected, Archbishop Hurley's leadership was very influential in eliciting a positive response from the priests of Durban. The presentations were an interesting experience for me: they were totally pastoral, with some supporting ecclesiological input. It resonated with their lives and their ministry.

Port Elizabeth

It was winter in South Africa. East London was far to the south where it was very windy and chilly. Fortunately the reactions of the priests were much warmer, creating the feeling of being near the equator. Little did I realize that the Port Elizabeth Diocese would come back into the lives of my family twenty years later, when my great nephew would go to work with the church there, serving the poor. I'll write more about Jim in Chapter 27.

Cape Town

Cape Town was the scene of the last of the week-long presentations. The priests of Cape Town presented the greatest challenge. They seemed unresponsive and quite uninterested throughout most of the week.

One priest in particular was from an extremely conservative, cult-like community. I tried to befriend him throughout the week, and in fact thought we had become good friends.

On the last day my "friend" stood up and strongly challenged me in an accusatory tone for not having mentioned Jesus' suffering on the cross once throughout the week. It was quite a confrontation. Now all the priests were suddenly wide awake. One by one they stood up to denounce this man as unfair and unrepresentative of their feelings. My "friend" had done the unexpected. He had turned the priests around to be strongly in favor of RENEW.

Durban launched RENEW within a year. Cape Town, Pretoria, and Johannesburg along with four other dioceses would follow shortly in the early 1990s.

The last leg of the trip was to return to Durban and share the whole experience with Archbishop Hurley. He was excited to hear about the response to RENEW from the other dioceses. Of course, he was raring to go with RENEW in Durban and was already quite a way down the road with it.

Arriving back at the Newark airport was festive. Members of the RENEW team had gathered at the airport, waving and welcoming me. They were ready to party. Unfortunately, I had received an extremely sad phone call at Archbishop Hurley's residence. Dolores Duggan, one of the true founders of RENEW, had been diagnosed with cancer and was quite ill. I wasn't able to party. I was off immediately to visit Joe and Dolores Duggan in River Vale, New Jersey.

India

Underneath India's RENEW story lies another: the story of how I came to love India and its wonderful people. That relationship started with some apprehension and considerable discomfort, but it gradually grew into a true love affair. Some of my very fondest memories over the years of RENEW are those of India.

It all began with a phone call. A Jesuit priest, Fr. D'Souza, a professor at Xavier College in Bombay, was visiting the United States. He had heard about RENEW and wanted to learn more. He wanted to meet with me but was free only on Memorial Day 1983, when he would be at St. Peter's College in Jersey City, New Jersey.

My immediate thought was, "No, please don't tell me that. I'll be celebrating Memorial Day with my family in the wonderful hometown resort of Avon at the Jersey Shore." I was very cautious driving during an extremely heavy rainstorm amid holiday traffic. This might be the ultimate test. What could come from this meeting anyway? East is east and west is west. How could RENEW possibly fit in India?

It certainly was an interesting meeting. During the first hour, I shared about RENEW but seriously questioned whether it could be helpful for the Church in India. Fr. D'Souza, in turn, insisted that RENEW was precisely what was needed back home. He made a concrete suggestion: "Please call Fr. Bosco Penha. He is the rector of the seminary in Bombay. Here's his number. Talk to Bosco, and see what he thinks."

Placing a call to India in 1983 wasn't easy. Over the coming weeks I called again and again, but the calls did not go through. On my twenty-seventh try, a voice answered at the seminary switchboard. "May I please speak with Fr. Bosco Penha," I asked. Immediately Bosco was on the line. I was hearing the voice of an amiable and most welcoming priest. He didn't need to hear too much about RENEW before asking, "How would you like to come and visit? We'll talk about this, and I'll also arrange for you to give a presentation to the priests of Bombay." Without hesitating I said, "Happy to come. When is the best time to visit?"

The flight to India was a bit of a story in itself. To be honest, not every person on our staff was thrilled about seeing me go off to India at a time when we had so many other things on our plate. At the same time, many were excited and came to the airport to see me off.

At the airport, we met a doctor and his friendly family. Just as I was about to board, the doctor said, "I'm so loaded down. Would you please take this on board for me?" It was a heavy cassette player, and I happily agreed. As you can see, I was still quite naïve in January of 1984. But once I got on the plane I wondered, "What is inside this player? What am I doing here?" I quickly returned it, and very relieved, went back to my seat trying to get some sleep on our long flight.

Bombay (Mumbai)

Landing at Bombay International Airport at 3 a.m. was also an experience. I always find it a bit stressful going through all the passport checks. And the baggage conveyor belt had broken. All the bags were in one big pile considerably taller than me. Poor lighting didn't help the dull atmosphere. Climbing over bags, I eventually managed to find my own.

Finally, I stepped out of the airport into pitch black air. Here I was in Bombay in the middle of the night. "What happens next?" There were people holding up signs for travelers they were greeting. After a while I spotted a small sign reading "Fr. Kleissler." Thanks be to God, I'm not alone in Bombay. A seminarian had come to pick me up.

On the ride into the city I noticed little campfires in the midst of the meadow. "What could that be?" I asked the young seminarian. "People live there in the meadows," he replied. It was my introduction to severe poverty. I was in shock. "How could people be living there in that meadow?" In short time I would get up close to such poverty and realize that those unpurified meadow waters would be the common source for every conceivable human need.

Bosco Penha turned out to be a fantastic man. He was extremely bright and friendly, a man of great heart and pastoral concern, a believer in small communities, and a man who could have also been a successful executive in any career. One of the first things Bosco did for me was arrange an evening bus tour of Bombay with a seminarian. Sitting in the upper deck, I could see into St. Thomas Church and look through to the altar with amazement. The large church was entirely filled for weekday evening Mass. I thought there weren't many Catholics in India, but what I quickly learned was that Catholics are a minority in a highly populated country. However, they were a minority strong in their faith. Bosco said there were twenty million Catholics in India, six hundred thousand of them in Bombay alone.

Bosco and I really enjoyed spending time together. We had many things in common and realized we shared the same convictions. We both felt strongly about the value of small communities as a key to the Church's pastoral approaches. It was as if the Lord had brought us together, and we were truly brothers in his Spirit.

The one questionable part of that experience for me was the presentation I gave to the priests. I had made far too little adaptation to the cultural and pastoral needs of India. I realized immediately it would not evoke a resounding response to RENEW. At the same time, I was pleasantly surprised and happy to hear afterwards that some priests had left the presentation moved with a passion for small communities that would affect their priesthood and ministry.

I invited Bosco to a six-week international inquiry and training program that would be held in the summer of 1984. Bosco arrived in late June with the auxiliary bishop of Bombay and a couple of other key pastoral people.

Everybody enjoyed Bosco's delightful presence that summer. He devoured everything about small communities and was even more convinced of their value. He was already working with small communities throughout Bombay, setting up model parishes to provide witness to others. Shortly after his return, Bosco was made auxiliary bishop in the archdiocese and was launched into a wonderfully successful career of spreading small communities throughout Bombay and all through India.

Although Bombay had not picked up the whole RENEW program and process, I trust Bosco's visit had done its part in spreading a pastoral approach that would affect many people. It was a privilege to keep in contact with and share ideas with this great man, in a friendship that would last for years.

Madurai

A couple of years later another surprise came in the form a letter from Bishop Marianus Arokiasamy from Kotar, at the very southern tip of India, the place where Mahatma Gandhi had ended his long salt march.

A priest in Kotar who had read about RENEW in *The Tablet*, took it upon himself to compose a letter to us on behalf of the bishop seeking information. If I was surprised by the letter, the bishop was in turn about to receive his own surprise. He was about to receive a phone call from New Jersey.

By the time I received the letter, Bishop Arokiasamy had been moved and was the archbishop of Madurai. He may have already forgotten about the letter and was probably taken aback when a call came from our office. I explained that the best way to share about RENEW was to meet him in person. He suggested that he was going to be at the bishops conference in New Delhi, which might be a good place to meet. Donna and I were off to New Delhi where we had a fine meeting with the archbishop. That meeting set the stage for further communication and development.

A year later, 1989, Cecilia and I were in Madurai at the invitation of Archbishop Arokiasamy. Our first visit with the archbishop was a test. He quizzed us about our credentials. How Catholic was this RENEW? What was it all about? The archbishop liked everything he heard and immediately went into action. He said, "All the priests of the archdiocese will be here tomorrow to hear you present about RENEW." How he got that message out I'll never know but, sure enough, the word had been sent out, and every priest of the archdiocese was there the next morning.

Interesting presentation. We met a much-divided clergy. The older priests were all for renewal and prayer and for a more traditional approach to spirituality. The younger priests were all for social justice. It appeared that never the twain would meet. Talk about a challenge. Certainly, it was by the grace of God, we were able to satisfy both contingents that RENEW would provide what they were looking for. What a common blessing this could be, a shared process that could bring everybody together. The spirits of the priests picked up. The archbishop was delighted with their positive response. The Archdiocese of Madurai was now committed to RENEW.

The Province of Tamil Nadu

At that time Archbishop Casimir Gnanadickam, S.J., was visiting Archbishop Arokiasamy. Naturally, Archbishop Arokiasamy spilled out all his enthusiasm about his priests' reaction to RENEW. Archbishop Casimir now wanted to meet with Cecilia and me. One of those "wow moments" was about to occur. Madras was the largest city in the entire southeast region of Tamil Nadu. Tamil Nadu had a long history and a strong culture. Tamil was, in fact, one of the very first languages for our human family.

Archbishop Casimir listened to us and had only one question, "Will you still be in Tamil Nadu next Thursday afternoon?" A second wow moment was about to occur. "Would you be willing to come that afternoon and make a presentation on RENEW to our bishops conference, which comprises all fourteen dioceses of the whole southeast area of India?" This was incredible. We were scheduled to fly out of Madras late that Thursday night. The timing would be perfect. We would be happy to be there.

On the night before the presentation, Cecilia and I were preparing for the meeting when I received a message from our office that my good friend, Fr. Jim Ferry, who had long been suffering from cancer, had died. The funeral Mass would be the next day, the day of our biggest presentation ever.

Our immediate thought was to offer a Mass for Jim and also ask him to put in a word for us that God's special blessings would be with us and the bishops the following day. Somehow we got some wine, and a little bread, and began our Mass. The first reading, 2 Timothy 1:6-7, pierced our minds and hearts with its relevancy: "For this reason, I remind you to keep alive the gift that God gave you when I laid my hands on you. For the spirit that God has given us does not make us timid, instead his Spirit fills us with power, love, and self-control."

This was the mindset that God was calling us to for the next day, not to approach the bishops of Tamil Nadu with a spirit of timidity but rather open ourselves to be filled with God's Holy Spirit and to proclaim God's Word with great power and love. This was the approach that Jim himself had so often taken in proclaiming God's message. We were filled with a new sense of confidence and trust in the Lord.

At luncheon in the bishop's house the next day we were offered a special preparation of fruit cocktail for dessert. I had been so careful on the whole trip, but now on this last day got careless, forgetting that the fruit cup was made with frozen local water. This time I was overcome with a different "spirit," immediate and severe diarrhea. How could I ever be part of this presentation without disaster striking?

In the time before the presentation was to be given, we were each provided a separate room in which to rest. The room I was staying in was that which Pope John Paul II had stayed in on his visit to Madras. It was an atmosphere more than conducive to prayer.

Into the presentation we went. The fruit cup had left me physically weakened and certainly humbled. But Cecilia and I had both cast off fear and timidity. We were called to put aside any self-consciousness and to proclaim the message with power for the benefit of the many Catholics throughout the southeast of India, the entire Tamil Nadu Province.

Over the next forty-five minutes Cecilia and I gave an impassioned presentation. I remember describing the benefits of a diocese-wide coordinated effort. Priests and lay people across the diocese could come together in strong faith and share in common a beautiful spiritual renewal experience. The bishops were considering the possibility that a new and positive climate could be created within their dioceses.

Suddenly lightning struck or, to be more accurate, God's special inspiration came upon us. With strong confidence I presented a picture of what an incredible spirit and cohesion could come to all the Catholics of southeast India if they all embraced RENEW together and took on a coordinated effort. We had walked into the room hoping that a few of the bishops could see the possibility of RENEW for their dioceses. Now we were far exceeding that in envisioning all fourteen dioceses of Tamil Nadu, by God's power, experiencing new life and vitality. It was amazing. All the bishops were nodding their heads in agreement.

This was so much more than Cecilia or I could have ever dreamed. It was powerfully clear God was present and working in that room. After the presentation one of the bishops confided to us that it was the first time all the bishops had ever agreed on anything. Just a few months later, Cecilia and I would be back for the training of diocesan RENEW teams for all the dioceses. It was also the launching of my ever-growing love affair with India and growing number of faith-filled friends.

The next decade would involve twenty more trips to India. But that night in Madras was a night filled with a powerful sense of gratitude and a complete sense of joy. Our ebullient feeling had also embraced the reality that what had happened that day was totally the work of God. What a privilege to have been blessed in such a way. We could envision how powerfully God would work for years to come in our beloved India. Our plane took off at midnight, and my spirit rose with it above all the clouds and above anything that could dampen the human spirit.

PART III

CHAPTER 21

Life in the 1990s

The 1990s were marked by some devastating events in the United States. A major earthquake hit Los Angeles in 1994. The Alfred P. Murrah Federal Building in Oklahoma City was bombed in 1995. Two students opened fire and killed eleven people at Columbine High School in Colorado in 1999. Some unfortunate setbacks occurred overseas as well: U.S. embassies were bombed by terrorists in Kenya and Tanzania. Iraq invaded Kuwait, prompting a war with a coalition of forces led by the United States.

On the brighter side, East and West Germany were reunited and the first free elections in fifty-three years took place in Romania. Peace agreements were reached in Northern Ireland, ending over eighty years of terrorism and civil war, and the bitter war in El Salvador was over.

The Soviet Union collapsed and fifteen separate republics gained their independence. Nelson Mandela was freed from prison in South Africa. The Hubble Telescope was launched, and the "World Wide Web" became available for home use.

Within one week in 1997, the world mourned the deaths of Princess Diana and Mother Teresa.

Trends in the United States

Change was also happening within the Church. During the time Archbishop Jean Jadot was apostolic delegate to the United States (1973-1980), the priests chosen to be ordained as bishops had been largely those with extended pastoral experience. Their impact upon parish life had been significant. In the 1990s the trend was turning more toward appointing bishops with strong theological backgrounds who were noted for taking great care in preserving doctrinal purity.

As the shortage of priests developed, parish life was affected. Large eastern parishes that had two or three parochial vicars in the past were now reduced to one or none. In many instances the pastor was left alone to serve thousands of parishioners. Of even greater impact was the closing of parishes and the combining of two to four parishes into one. Large areas of the country were left without a priest.

The same trend was affecting Catholic schools. Because of financial difficulties and the declining numbers of religious sisters, schools were closing at an alarming rate. Frequently, regional Catholic elementary schools were formed.

Inner-city Catholic schools often suffered the most. Because the percentage of Catholic students was lower than that of other students, and because of dire financial difficulties in urban parishes, these schools were often the first to be closed. As a result, evangelization possibilities in the inner city were being lost. That trend continues today at a great loss to evangelization among our poorest people.

The greatly decreased number of priests and sisters resulted in a greater role for lay people in parishes and chancery offices. Changing needs also resulted in the greater utilization of talented women religious in parishes and in chanceries. It became more common to see women or men religious or laypersons carrying out the responsibilities of chancellors, heads of departments, and other significant roles.

RENEW International

By the 1990s, we were no longer the National Office of RENEW. We chose the name RENEW International, because our mission extended to other parts of the world. The following chapters deal with a great amount of international activity that occurred in this decade based on commitments made in the 1980s.

As the RENEW process continued to progress strongly in the United States, we changed gears in preparation for the Jubilee Year proclaimed by Pope John Paul II and for the new millennium: we developed *RENEW 2000*.

RENEW, never to be static, was constantly growing and maturing from experience. During the early 1990s, we continued the process of updating materials, training, and approaches. Much internal effort was involved in this, along with the work being done on the road in servicing dioceses.

Although the overall numbers of those becoming involved each year was not as large as it was in the boom years in the 1980s, numerous dioceses continued to embark on RENEW and had successful experiences. By the time *RENEW 2000* was launched in the late 1990s, RENEW International would have served approximately one hundred forty-five of the one hundred sixty-eight Latin Rite dioceses in the country. RENEW had become a household name.

While this was a great blessing, the strong association of RENEW International and the RENEW experience sometimes hindered us from drawing attention to other initiatives we were developing.

In the 1980s, RENEW was the first to develop parishioner-friendly materials that would help people navigate through, ingest, and share faith over the new *Catechism of the Catholic Church*.

Through the 1990s, and up to the present time, we have developed other programs and resources that have proved to be of great value to the Church and have served parishes extremely well. Among these are the following titles:

- *RENEW 2000*
- *RENEW: Spiritual Renewal for the 21st Century*
- *Healing the Body of Christ*
- *Why Catholic?*
- *RENEW Africa*
- *Campus RENEW*
- *RENEW Theology on Tap*

- *ARISE Together in Christ*
- *Longing for the Holy*
- *Sedientos de Dios*
- *Lifting Up Our Hearts*
- *Renewing the Priestly Heart.*

These new ventures were not a departure from our mission but rather a reaffirmation of our mission to serve the spiritual and pastoral needs of the Church, in particular the pastoral needs of parishioners and parishes. The original RENEW process was developed precisely to fulfill that mission. Despite its success, it was not intended to be our sole focus or to limit our mission.

Each of the new ventures was taken on because we kept our fingers on the pulse of the Church, sensing its current needs. Because people associated RENEW International only with original RENEW, it took time and renewed outreach for parishes and dioceses to connect our current pastoral services to their parish needs. That gap in recognition has now been closed as RENEW International is more and more associated with the concept of "connecting faith to life." We serve the practical purpose of helping parishioners see the value and impact of their faith in their daily lives and in their spiritual needs.

RENEW International's staff grew during the early 1990s and continued its high standards of service to dioceses with Fr. Dominic Fuccile; Sr. Carmen Olivera, O.P.; Sr. Maureen Colleary, F.S.P.; Msgr. Barry Wymes; Sr. Barbara Garland, S.C.; Julie Jones; Fr. Ken Davis, O.F.M.; Sr. Maria Iglesias, S.C.; Carolyn Newkirk; Fr. Jim Walsh; Fr. Jack Farley, S.V.D.; Sr. Cecilia King, C.S.J.P.; Sr. Louise Alff, O.S.F.; Sr. Stella Herrera, R.J.M.; and Greg Kremer.

One particularly significant change occurred in 1993. On an August day, Sr. Donna stopped by my office and shared the surprising news that she felt the time had come for her to move on. She had decided to join Fr. Phil Murnion and the National Pastoral Life Center at the beginning of the coming year.

Donna is a major figure in the history of RENEW. In original RENEW, as a parish staff person, she participated in a parish RENEW small group and carried with her the spirit of RENEW. As assistant director of RENEW under Bob Fuller, she continued to be a major player for the next thirteen years. Few gave more completely of themselves than Donna did in service both in the United States and internationally. She not only was an excellent presenter but established outstanding relationships that contributed to the betterment of RENEW. RENEW's work in the Philippines, England, Scotland, Cameroon, and South Africa was carried on largely through her personal pastoring efforts. She gave of herself untiringly and her departure was a significant loss to RENEW. In February 1994, Donna formally retired and moved on to the National Pastoral Life Center.

God's providence continued to guide RENEW International. In the previous spring Sr. Kathy Warren, O.S.F., had committed herself to join our RENEW International team in early 1994. Kathy had served as RENEW's director for the Diocese of New Ulm and had worked closely with Bishop Raymond Lucker. She was already seen as a star and would bring tremendous skills and dedication to her work at RENEW.

Women in RENEW

The concept of enlisting extremely talented women was an essential part of RENEW from the beginning. That is clear in the account of our journey so far, and readers can expect to read even more about the role of women in the 1990s and in the new millennium. In the 1970s, we began to see more and more sisters move from teaching in parish schools and become religious education coordinators, which gave them greater freedom to be creative and use their talents.

In the 1980s, RENEW was able to offer even greater opportunities for women religious to exercise their talents and to have extensive impact on whole dioceses. We were, in a manner of speaking, in a position to attract the cream of the crop.

This is not to downplay the role men played in RENEW. As we have seen, in the 1980s there were no greater stars than Fr. Bob Fuller and Fr. Tom Caroluzza. No one gave more diocesan parish training sessions and no one was in greater demand than these two. Both were called back to their dioceses by their bishops, and in the future fewer bishops would be willing to release their priests. Despite that, we managed with great effort and diligence to acquire valuable laymen, deacons, and priests.

Along with providing RENEW services throughout the United States and internationally, our priests were able to bring, through rich daily liturgies, a special spiritual presence to RENEW. Many, such as Fr. Abraham Orapankal, became spiritual directors for our large staff.

The principle from the beginning of Newark's RENEW experience was choosing people like Sr. Suzanne Golas, Cathy Dambach Martin, Jeanne Schrempf, Doris Hudson, Sue Elsessor, Sr. Carol Heller, Liz Mullen, and Sr. Mary McGuinness, always trying to bring on board the best-qualified person. The bottom line was not the gender of a person but the person's qualifications to best serve the needs of parishioners.

Service to our people was of utmost importance. Each person chosen to develop our faith-sharing resources or join our pastoral team was an ardent Catholic and strong in Catholic belief. At the same time, women were not singled out for a litmus test as to whether they would be "safe" and never say anything that would draw undue attention, particularly because it was coming from a woman. Such fearful approaches would not be most desirable for serving the Church.

As RENEW developed, a parish priest once asked me, "Why is it that you always appoint women to the most significant roles?" My response was simple: "I always try to choose the most qualified person." Choosing the most qualified people will not only continue to serve RENEW well in the future but will also benefit the Church as a whole.

China

A personal highlight of the 1990s for me, and one of my most enjoyable experiences, was going to China with a fine priest I had known since my early priesthood, Fr. Jerry McCrane, M.M. At the time, Jerry was working with us at RENEW International. As you might expect, missions were at the core of his being. Fr. Larry Murphy, M.M., led the trip. He knew the bishops and leaders of both the underground Catholic Church and of the National Catholic Church that operated under the auspices of the communist government. Meeting the wide variety of his friends and learning about the status and condition of the Church in China was truly energizing.

I will never forget being by myself on a newly renovated section of the Great Wall and experiencing one of the finest spiritually reflective moments of my life. I came home with the idea that we would have someone teaching a course on small Christian communities to Chinese seminarians, so that when things really opened up Chinese Catholics might enjoy an alternate model of the Church that was closer to the dynamic early days of Christian life. Unfortunately, that dream never materialized; nor did my dream of retiring in China and developing small Christian communities. However, as you will see in the next chapter, members of the San Jose Catholic Chinese Community have made an impact in this area.

CHAPTER 22

Original RENEW: Strong to the Finish

O riginal RENEW, which started in Newark and spread widely, continued to forge ahead. It was like the "Energizer Bunny" that never missed a beat. It continued that way through the 1990s until 1998 when we started to implement *RENEW 2000* in preparation for the new millennium.

A few brief snapshots from my personal experience stand out.

1990-1998

San Antonio, Texas

Archbishop Patrick Flores made a wise decision in choosing Fr. Bill Collins as diocesan director. Bill had extraordinary success in reaching out to brother priests and in convincing them of the value of participating in RENEW. He succeeded in getting one hundred twenty-two of the one hundred twenty-six parishes in the diocese to initiate the RENEW process.

When I asked Bill the reason for the success he responded with an old, familiar formula: "I'm very gentle in my approach with priests in parishes but also very persistent." It was the same formula that we had used in the original RENEW experience in Newark—always gentle and non-pushy in approaching priests but, at the same time, persistent in making contacts until we received a final answer, one way or the other.

In other words, the importance of the spirituality of the people that could be served was the highest priority. We made every effort to serve those people until we succeeded or were given a firm "no." Obviously, the result was that almost all priests gave a positive response.

RENEW also received strong support from wonderful Bishop Patrick Flores and the rest of the diocesan leadership. All these efforts paid off beautifully as twenty-five thousand participated in RENEW small groups. As with so many other dioceses, San Antonio experienced through RENEW a great deepening of faith, an increase of people assuming leadership roles, and overall greater love and awareness of the value of the Scriptures. The fact that there was high participation in the Hispanic community was also a plus for RENEW in San Antonio.

Superior, Wisconsin

My introduction to Superior was unusual. I had arrived to give the initial presentation to the priests of the diocese. The woman who drove me to the retreat location assured me my trip was futile. "I don't think there will be a lot of interest," she said.

The next day I was pleased to find out how wrong she was. The priests rallied in support of initiating RENEW in the diocese.

Bishop Raphael Fliss assigned Fr. Hugh Briody and Sr. Eileen Lang, F.S.P.A., to lead the effort, which clearly indicated that the interest from the priests was for real. Ninety-eight percent of the parishes in the diocese participated in RENEW.

A strong effort in Superior was helping people become more aware of their need for prayer and empowering them to go forth and spread the Good News. Parishioners were awakened to take on leadership roles in parishes and to see lay leadership as the enablement of others. The final summary from RENEW leaders in the diocese also highlighted how RENEW had challenged parishes to become more sensitive to the homebound, the alienated, and inactive parishioners.

The impact of RENEW on the diocese was heightened by the involvement of youth—not only teenagers but elementary school children for whom we provided special catechetical materials.

Baker, Oregon

Baker was a wonderful respite in a time of whirlwind activity that had taken me from India to several stops coast-to-coast in the United States and to South Africa, all within ten days. Bishop Thomas J. Connolly was a marvelous host, and my brief stay with him is a delightful memory. He lived on a small horse farm with a striking view of the mountains.

The gracious bishop and this beautiful setting made quite a combination. The priests of the diocese were receptive, and Baker went on to have a great RENEW experience.

Beaumont, Texas

Giving initial presentations to diocesan presbyterates had become customary for me. In time I would make nearly one hundred. But I wasn't sure how the vote was going to turn out with the priests in Beaumont.

Waiting outside the beautiful new Diocesan Community Center, I prayed the rosary. Naturally I prayed that God's will be done (which I'm sure I also wished would be my will). When the priests emerged with the news that they were going ahead with RENEW, I did not anticipate what a wonderful experience it was going to be.

The leadership trio, Diocesan Director Sr. Rita Norris, O.P., Fr. Bill Manger, Sue Mol, and our own staff member, Margo LeBert, who worked closely with them, made for an extraordinary team.

Bill is an outstanding priest with whom I kept in touch for years afterward. Sue Mol not only had extraordinary talent but had a calm and peaceful personality, which helped her relate to everyone and to all situations. After Beaumont's RENEW, Sue became part of our international team and worked closely with Margo in the '90s. Naturally, with a leadership team like that, RENEW was a dynamic experience in Beaumont and, in the longer term, RENEW International was greatly enriched with the addition of Sue Mol.

Mobile, Alabama

Archbishop Oscar Lipscomb was on the bishops' Doctrine Committee that reviewed our materials a few years earlier. It is interesting to note that he was another of the bishops on that committee to initiate

RENEW in his diocese. He is the picture of warm, southern hospitality, and we happened to have been ordained the same year, 1957. We hit it off well from the beginning.

Fr. Bill James and Sr. Maureen Kennedy, O.P., provided great leadership. James had an excellent reputation as a retreat master and was an outstanding proponent of renewal as proclaimed by Vatican II. The parishes of the diocese were open to renewal and RENEW experienced the same often-heard results: small Christian community participation; greater knowledge and love for the Scriptures; strengthened social justice convictions; improved parish liturgies; a great number of new parish leaders; greater hospitality; and increased visits to the sick and shut-ins.

The fact that seven thousand parishioners were involved in small Christian communities is a credit to the archdiocese in the Deep South where Catholics were a small minority.

Las Cruces, New Mexico

Leadership and parishioners worked hard at RENEW and enjoyed a rich experience in Las Cruces. But what stands out most in my memory is a silly event that took place on my way to give the initial decision-making presentation to the priests of the diocese.

I made the trip on a Sunday afternoon, with a stopover at the airport in Dallas and a continuing flight to El Paso from where I would travel by car to Las Cruces. It was the afternoon of the divisional championship game in the National Conference of the NFL. The contenders were the Dallas Cowboys and the New York Giants. The winner would go to the Super Bowl. The Cowboys were strong pregame favorites.

On my stopover at Dallas, the bars were bursting with activity and joyous crowds as Dallas had just taken the lead by scoring on an interception. My Giants' prospects were very bleak indeed.

The sleepy passengers on a late afternoon flight to El Paso were abruptly awakened with an announcement from the pilot. His words were straightforward and to the point: "The New York Giants are going to the Super Bowl." Forgetting that I was wearing my collar and losing all sense of decorum, I let out a joyous yelp. The woman seated next to me was quite displeased but couldn't dampen my spirits. That night in Las Cruces I stayed up late watching every television report I could find, but I managed to have enough steam the next day to encourage the priests to move ahead with RENEW.

Portland, Oregon

Knowing that Archbishop William Levada had worked in the Vatican, I pictured a man who might be rigid. I was delightfully surprised to find him warm, friendly, and very pastoral.

At my initial presentation to the priests, Bishop Levada made a comment in his conclusion that I will never forget. He said, "Through the efforts of the RCIA many people are coming into the Church through the front door." Then he added, "Is anyone watching the back door?" He was calling attention in a memorable way to a serious situation, losses of membership in the Church. An evangelization effort like RENEW that could stem that tide and bring vitality to parishioners and parish life was welcome.

Archbishop Levada, who would later be named a cardinal, served as prefect for the Congregation for the Doctrine of the Faith, was apparently pleased with RENEW in Portland as he went on to give strong leadership in introducing *RENEW 2000* in San Francisco.

I will always be grateful for the personal support and encouragement from Archbishop Levada. Great numbers of the bishops over the years have expressed their gratitude for what RENEW did in their dioceses. But Archbishop Levada stands out in my mind as he spontaneously sent letters of encouragement for the work we were doing. At a special breakfast in San Francisco that he had arranged for Michael Brough (who had joined our staff in 1998) and me, his parting words were, "Thanks, Tom, for what you're doing for the Church."

Baltimore, Maryland

The original inquiry from Baltimore came from Bill Johnson and Msgr. Richard Woy. We met in Maryland at one of those popular Route 95 stopover restaurants. As we shared about RENEW, they became enthused about its possibilities for Baltimore and decided to promote it and present the possibilities of RENEW to Cardinal William Keeler.

Their intervention led to my meeting with the cardinal, and he decided to set aside a day for the entire presbyterate to hear about RENEW.

That meeting was my first opportunity to experience what a truly outstanding, friendly, and pastoral man Cardinal Keeler is. The day with the priests went well, and with their support Cardinal Keeler decided to move forward with RENEW.

As we were leaving the Day of Reflection, Cardinal Keeler shared his feelings with great conviction: "Tom, I want RENEW to work. We want to go about this right. I'm prepared to do everything you suggest, and to follow your recommendation as to how to go about it. I'd like to see us choose one of our diocesan priests as coordinator for RENEW."

A few weeks later the cardinal called and shared that he felt the names being presented were not qualified for the position. He wanted someone outstanding who would be able to reach other priests and rally them behind the process. He explained that he had a man in mind that was a very good parish priest but didn't want to leave the parish to take on this project. My response was, "He sounds great. He doesn't want to leave the parish. His instincts are right on target, wanting to be with the people and not seeking the notoriety of a diocesan position." The priest was Fr. Joseph Luca.

Cardinal Keeler asked if I would call Fr. Luca and try to persuade him to take the position. That proved to be an interesting call. Everything Joe said presented a picture of an ideal director. He started by saying he was not a theologian but rather a man out among the people. His pastoral instincts and approaches led me to believe Cardinal Keeler had chosen the right man.

With every moment I became more excited about his possibilities. Finally, Joe said, "Yes." He turned out to be a great diocesan coordinator working along with Bill Johnson.

The cardinal's faith in his leadership team was well founded. Over thirty-two thousand parishioners participated in the RENEW small groups, and thousands of others who took part in other forms of RENEW.

RENEW's success was acknowledged by Pope John Paul II when he spoke in Baltimore in October 1995. The pope praised the priests for "your work in adult catechesis, as in the RENEW program."

Years later Fr. Joe, reflecting back on the RENEW experience, still had great enthusiasm and high praise. He said, "Over the five seasons of RENEW over thirty-two thousand people in the Archdiocese of Baltimore participated in small groups during *each* season. For most of them it was the first time they had ever prayed and interacted in small groups. I very frequently heard from parish leaders and parishioners alike how deeply touched they were to hear others speak so openly about their Catholic faith and how wonderfully they felt the presence of the Holy Spirit as they broke open the Word with each other and applied it to real life. It was a time of great blessing and renewal for our diocese." That blessing was more than the involvement of large numbers of people. Its impact can be more easily captured when brought down to the experience of an individual person.

There was a dentist in the Baltimore Archdiocese who was not at all pleased when his wife urged him to sign up for a faith-sharing group. Unexpectedly, the larger Church and the world opened up to him. This led him to enlist four other dentists who accompanied him to Ecuador for two weeks every year to offer dental services to the poor.

There is no way to calculate the number of lives that are touched when God is working in and through us.

Camden, New Jersey

Bishop Jim McHugh was a classmate of mine and a loyal friend. As auxiliary bishop in Newark he had gone out of his way to put in a good word for RENEW locally and also with the evangelization leaders in the Vatican.

As bishop of Camden he convened a diocesan synod in the 1990s. A question frequently asked in dioceses was, "How do we implement all these fine proposals?" On more than one occasion this presented us the opportunity to explain the value of RENEW. In Camden's instance, the synod had come forth with forty-five goals and objectives. Some were administrative goals that could be achieved only internally. Nevertheless, we proposed that RENEW would be of great value in implementing thirty-six of the forty-five diocesan objectives.

When asked to explain this in writing, we described, in detail, how each of these thirty-six goals would be addressed by RENEW. Too many times synod documents are left to collect dust. RENEW would implement the synod's objectives at the grass roots of parish life. This was the key to opening the door for RENEW in Camden.

Camden's RENEW director, Msgr. Roger McGrath, did an outstanding job that was reflected in the profound impact RENEW had in the diocese. His observations were that RENEW created a very healthy style of Christian living. People took on a sense of adult faith and ownership. They were willing to rely not only on the priests and sisters but also to recognize and take on responsibility for their own role.

Roger was impressed by how RENEW helped people overcome their fear of the Scriptures and experience them as a faith-nourishing reality. Through RENEW, people no longer saw spiritual life as something that occurred just in church but rather as something found in everyday life. His belief that the desire for this refreshing new experience of spirituality would remain long beyond RENEW came true.

This belief was confirmed in the story of a young woman who, in Season II of RENEW, read in her parish bulletin that the Glenmary Missions were looking for women aged eighteen to forty-five to volunteer in Appalachia. She was one of the fifty chosen from six hundred applicants. "Thanks to the growth I experienced in RENEW, I sought out the experience in Appalachia," she exclaimed. More growth ensued. "Now I continue to be active in pursuing areas where I can be of service."

Santa Fe, New Mexico

When Archbishop Michael Sheehan arrived in Santa Fe he was confronted with what was at that time the most desperate and scandalous situation in the American Church. The TV program *60 Minutes* had broadcast a damaging report on the situation there. Several women had made accusations against the previous bishop, and there were one hundred fifty-eight sexual-abuse cases waiting to be dealt with.

The diocese was the location of the most famous recovery place for troubled priests in the country. When many of the priests came to the point of being "cured," they understandably applied to work in the fine climate of the Santa Fe Diocese. However, troubled backgrounds caught up with many, resulting in numerous lawsuits.

As Archbishop Sheehan would later explain to all the bishops of the country, when faced with that situation, he turned to RENEW to change the atmosphere. He later made no bones about the fact that RENEW did exactly that—creating a much more positive outlook throughout his archdiocese.

I clearly remember my meeting with Archbishop Sheehan the day before giving the initial presentation to his priests. How impressed I was with his strong faith, his optimism, and his belief that RENEW was precisely what was needed. He knew this from his previous experience in Lubbock, Texas.

I must say that at the meeting the next day the priests were not the most enthusiastic group about taking on RENEW that I had encountered. Nevertheless, the archbishop's zeal and determination carried RENEW forward. He made a wise move in appointing a young man, Allan Sanchez, as director. The results were beyond imagination. Thirty-four thousand people became involved in RENEW small groups. Showing my eastern mentality, I would later joke on various occasions that I didn't even know there were thirty-four thousand people in Santa Fe to begin with. Yes, I was impressed. How could anyone not be with what had happened in Santa Fe?

I love the story of Lourdes and Russell Gonzales. Through RENEW, both grew stronger in their faith. Russell said, "I never read the Bible before. Because of RENEW, I started reading it during the day and prayed a lot more." Personal sharing in a RENEW group helped them resolve personal matters as they began sharing faith more deeply.

Russell explained that there was an issue that had been bothering him for twenty years. In 1973 his father died and, to Russell's dismay, his wife refused to attend the funeral because it was around Christmas. For twenty years he could not forgive her. During a RENEW session on forgiveness he realized it was wrong to hold a grudge. "I dwelt on it, I prayed about it, and finally I was able to let it go," Russell said.

Imagine how many beautiful stories, conversions, and wonderful changes of heart took place among those thirty-four thousand people.

A few years later a man in Brisbane, Australia, wrote to Archbishop Sheehan questioning whether it was wise for the archbishop to become involved in RENEW. In responding, Archbishop Sheehan reminded the gentleman that he was not only the archbishop of Santa Fe but had also just completed his term as chairman of the Evangelization Committee of the USCCB and that he was speaking out of his own experience with evangelization and RENEW. He then spoke of the great numbers and high percentage of people that were in RENEW small faith-sharing groups. "These faith-sharing groups are wonderfully gifted, and they reach many inactive and unchurched people. They also create an enthusiasm and excitement among Catholics, especially when RENEW is supported by the bishop and key priests. RENEW is unique in that it is an invitation for everybody in the parish to be involved in a worthwhile spiritual renewal process."

Allan Sanchez speaks of a college-age woman who invited another young woman to join one of the *RENEW 2000* groups. Each week, the second woman said that as her action response to the discussion, she would attend Mass. Some people didn't think that was much of a response—until the end of the season. Then the woman asked to be received into the Church. She hadn't been a Catholic.

The largest balloon festival in the world is held in Santa Fe. There, for thousands to behold, went a gigantic RENEW balloon floating into the sky. For RENEW it was up, up, and away!

By God's grace working through RENEW, the sun was shining brighter than ever in Santa Fe.

San Jose, California

RENEW got into the Diocese of San Jose through the efforts of one very good, zealous, and persistent woman.

A parishioner in San Jose, Margaret McCarthy, called me to express interest in RENEW. I suggested that she talk to her pastor, tell him how good she thinks RENEW is, and let me know if he's willing to have me call him. She called back saying the pastor was open to a call.

While I was talking to the pastor, he indicated that RENEW sounded interesting. I asked if he knew someone at the chancery he could speak with. As a matter of fact, he knew Fr. Al Larkin. The pastor followed through, talking up RENEW with Fr. Larkin, who, in turn, took enough interest to visit me at the Oakland Chancery on an occasion when I was speaking there.

Over the next couple of years, Fr. Larkin and I kept in communication about how to introduce RENEW to the diocese. But our efforts were pushed by the woman behind the scenes. Every few months Margaret would call me asking about what was happening with RENEW in her diocese. In turn, I would place a follow-up call to Fr. Larkin. Margaret was persistent, never giving up.

A few years later, Bishop Pierre DuMaine introduced me to a large audience of priests and lay people at the Diocesan Center in San Jose. As I stood up to speak, I looked out over the audience and asked, "Is Margaret McCarthy here? Margaret, will you please stand up? The reason we're all here is because of Margaret." The whole place burst into applause for her. One person had made all the difference in a RENEW process that was going to touch the lives of thousands of people. A wonderful RENEW experience followed in San Jose.

I would like to share a part of the San Jose story that started a few years earlier.

My childhood dream of being a missionary to China never came true. But in my older years, I dreamed that perhaps we might bring RENEW to China. To that end, I invited Fr. Ed Malatesta, S.J., to visit our office. Ed, founding director of the Ricci Institute for Chinese-Western Cultural History at the University of San Francisco Center for the Pacific Rim, shared with Mary McGuinness and me that if we ever hoped to fulfill that dream, we first needed to know the Chinese people in our own country. He suggested we contact the leaders of the San Jose Chinese Catholic Community and visit with them. The SJCCC is an established community of about 300 people recognized by the Diocese of San Jose.

I called Stanley Lai, the chairman of the group, and told him about the idea. We received an immediate welcome to speak with their community members. After flying to San Francisco and driving to San Jose, we conducted an information session. At the conclusion, the Leadership Team met and unanimously declared they wanted to do RENEW. We were happy to work with them and said in return that if they ever had the opportunity to take RENEW to China, we would be thrilled.

For the next three years, Mary continued to serve them while living with different Chinese families. Eventually, C.W. and Grace Chen adopted her as part of their family and she enjoyed their company, especially their two children, Yung-Yee and Yung-Jae.

Community members translated and printed our materials. Although the members were used to meeting in small groups for Bible study, the leaders were grateful and enthusiastic about both the content and the format of our materials, which helped them relate faith to their lives. Out of a community of about three hundred adults, between two hundred and two hundred fifty participated in RENEW small groups.

Joseph Ku, who served on the leadership team, declared, "After RENEW, our small basic communities really developed." Joseph wrote articles to introduce the community to each of the RENEW seasonal topics. These were published in the monthly magazine of the San Jose Chinese Catholic Mission, which was sent to over one thousand people, including small communities in Toronto, Atlanta, Los Angeles, and Seattle. Joseph, who "believes RENEW is a very important program for our Church," also guided the parish of St. Thomas Aquinas in Palo Alto through the five seasons of RENEW.

The SJCCC community members shared with others in the diocese their wonderful experience of RENEW, and when the diocese of San Jose decided to do RENEW, the SJCCC community enhanced their materials and went through the process a second time. Fr. Bernard Chu, a holy and learned Jesuit who served as friend and counselor to the community and became a good friend of ours, later brought our materials to Taiwan. Many other members with missionary hearts, in their own way, "became evangelizers to the people of China, but sadly their stories cannot now be told," said C.W. Chen.

Oakland, California

In the early 1980s, Paulist Press sent us to Oakland to give a promotional talk about RENEW. I've often joked that it took more than a dozen years of pondering before Oakland finally made a diocesan decision to do RENEW.

That actually presents an unfair picture as Fr. Dan Danielson and a number of other outstanding pastors started a cluster and worked with us in the '80s as a follow-through to the presentation we had made. Playing an important role in that cluster was Nora Peterson who was to become the diocesan RENEW director in the 1990s. This effort was a response to a diocesan strategic plan that had specifically mentioned RENEW.

To say that Nora Peterson did a good job as director of RENEW would be an understatement. She is, in fact, one of the finest people and effective leaders that I've had the pleasure of meeting and working with on our RENEW journey.

Nora believed that RENEW had a strong impact on the diocese and highlighted some of its contributions:

- It helped us to see ourselves as bigger than individual parishes and as part of the diocese and larger Church. People met people from other parishes and enjoyed the sharing with them.
- A lot of organizational skills were learned through RENEW. Many of these skills took root and continued years later to be strength for the parish.
- People in the RENEW small communities were close to one another and very caring for one another. This included strong prayer support.
- RENEW left an effective structure within which to organize the parish.
- RENEW provided a common theme and focus for the diocese. This brought various key elements like liturgy and faith formation to work closely together in a very enriching manner.
- Parishes gained a great deal from large-group experiences in RENEW. This influenced parish meetings, which began with stronger prayer and faith-sharing components.

- The momentum of RENEW brought out many more people than usual for liturgical workshops. These workshops could focus on individual aspects of liturgy, using some top liturgical expertise.
- Fifteen thousand people participated in RENEW small groups and there was an enthusiasm that was pervasive throughout the entire diocese.

Nora reported that at one of her RENEW training experiences, a woman stood up to speak about how RENEW was really helping people to open up the Bible and get to know the word of God. The woman said that when she was growing up there was a family Bible and her mother always hid money there because she knew no one would ever open it. What a difference RENEW had made.

Anchorage, Alaska

Flying into Anchorage was a beautiful experience. It was 3 p.m. on a December day in 1995, and the sun was already setting. It cast a beautiful shade of pink over the snow-filled mountains that were visible as far as the eye could see. This was the time of year when the days were short. At nine in the morning, people on their way to work were waiting in the dark for their buses.

The days may have been short, but there was no shortage of warmth in the welcome I received from Bishop Francis T. Hurley. He proved to be one of the finest bishops our team and I ever had the pleasure to work with. His diocese was unique.

Building community in a diocese where the Catholic population of twenty-seven thousand five hundred is spread over an area as wide as the distance between New York and the Mississippi River is quite a challenge.

About eighty-five percent of the Catholics in the diocese lived in the greater Anchorage area where nine of the twenty parishes were located. There were also eighteen missions. The means of communication for the bishops and priests serving this widespread area was by air. The priests were pilots who traveled by planes to parishes and missions. This included Bishop Hurley, who piloted his own plane.

The morning after my arrival, Bishop Hurley asked if I'd like to take a little spin with him in his airplane. When he called the airport the mechanic said the plane was experiencing mechanical trouble. I quickly assured the bishop that I was very willing to wait for another time.

I didn't realize until then that there was a high rate of tragic deaths, mostly of young people who were victims of land and air accidents in the rugged terrain. That, coupled with the fact that most of the people came from other areas of the United States, along with the Philippines, South Korea, and Russia, added to the need of a strong sense of community support in normal times and in times of tragedy.

Fortunately, the presentation to the priests went well, and Anchorage proceeded with RENEW, serviced by Kathy Warren. Bishop Hurley had been promoting stewardship for a number of years and found that RENEW brought a strong spirituality that was complementary and extremely helpful.

Bishop Hurley was pleased with the results of RENEW in his diocese. For many years afterwards at annual bishops' conferences he would go out of his way to extend his warmest regards and great gratitude for the gift of RENEW.

RENEW Empowers Hispanic Community

In all of our work, but especially in those dioceses in Texas and New Mexico, having someone present to do RENEW/RENACER training in Spanish with materials written in Spanish was very empowering to the Hispanic community. This was proof to the Spanish-speaking people that the Catholic Church was their Church too. RENEW's influence on Hispanics has been immeasurable.

While movements such as the Charismatic Renewal and Cursillo have had great outreach and done much good among Hispanics, much of what they do stays within the movement. The RENEW experience that Hispanics have had gives them the tools to start impacting the faith life of their parishes. The leadership skills they develop are something they have, and use, for the rest of their lives.

More to Come

Original RENEW was strong to the finish, but the Lord had much more in store for RENEW International as we prepared to enter a new millennium.

CHAPTER 23

RENEW 2000

For years people had been saying, "Please give us a renewed RENEW, a whole new renewal process." For various reasons we had held off on answering that request.

On November 10, 1994, Pope John Paul II issued his famous document *Tertio Millennio Adveniente* (*Toward the Third Millennium*). In it he outlined the themes he felt the Church should focus on in preparation for the Jubilee Year, and he issued a call for a new evangelization.

By 1996, conversations were under way around the world as to how to celebrate the coming of the third millennium. A celebration that comes once every thousand years stirred a lot of thought and creativity. The Church certainly was part of the planning, for the most obvious of reasons: it was the two thousandth anniversary of the coming of our Lord and Savior, Jesus.

On a summer day in 1996, I thought, "Now is the time." I called Margo LeBert and asked if she was free to visit. We needed to brainstorm a new RENEW experience that would focus on the coming of this millennium.

Margo and I walked the boardwalk in Avon brainstorming ideas for our new process, which was to be called *RENEW 2000*/RENACER 2000. We wanted to structure it in the same way as original RENEW with five seasons, each having themes for six weeks.

We chose basic themes from *Tertio Millennia Adveniente*, strongly emphasized the concepts of amnesty and forgiveness, and we gave special attention to the formation of priests. We also featured an updated look at issues of justice and human rights. As the process moved along, we decided to include reaching out to all Christian denominations and working with them for this celebration of the coming of Christ.

Returning to my apartment, we outlined basic themes for the five seasons of the process:

I. God: A Community of Love

II. Conversion

III. Outreach through Evangelization

IV. Reconciliation

V. Renewing the Church for the 21st Century.

We hammered out the details of the themes and many adjunct aspects of *RENEW 2000*. Later we brought the plan before our entire staff, which was excited about it and ready to move ahead.

An intense effort was required so that a good number of dioceses would be enabled to do *RENEW 2000* starting in the fall of 1998, concluding with the celebration of the millennium year 2000.

Margo LeBert

The most challenging and pressing need would be to develop solid materials in time for parish use. Margo would take that task on herself. A vast portion of the development of *RENEW 2000* rested on the slender shoulders but stout-hearted efforts of Margo. Margo was a brilliantly talented woman and an incredibly hard worker. But this task was to be more than Margo or any of us realized it would be.

In February 1993, Margo was diagnosed with ovarian cancer. Volumes could be written about the zeal and energy she poured into *RENEW 2000* and even more about the cross she carried in the process. By the grace of God, I believe she actually extended her life in stage-four cancer through sheer will power. She was determined to finish the project.

Probably no one in RENEW's history has ever produced such brilliant work at such a breathtaking pace. It seems that the greater Margo's pain and discomfort, the more beautiful and deeper were her insightful spiritual writings. Even in her final days, she gave the last of herself to *RENEW 2000*.

In response to an outpouring of prayer and good wishes for her health, Margo wrote a letter to thank our RENEW family. In part, she wrote

> These past weeks have been filled with physical pain, medical tests I didn't know existed, and the gentler care of doctors, my family, and friends. My promise for all of our RENEW family is offering my pain, my uncertainty, my gift of being carried in the hands of God for the renewal of each of us and of our Church, so together we can more deeply know that all our living and dying is to show the power and love of God.

She had the companionship and support of her loving husband, Bernie Lester, and she received great strength from her good friend, Kathy Warren, whom she had known for years in Minnesota. Margo and Kathy took on the task of designing in detail all the training that would be used by our RENEW team in the *RENEW 2000* process.

A Team Begins to Form

In 1996, Archbishop McCarrick designated three pilot parishes to test *RENEW 2000*. They were Blessed Sacrament in Elizabeth, St. Helen's in Westfield, and St. Mary's in Rahway. We formed a team to service these parishes. Fortunately, the reports we received from the pilot groups were highly enthusiastic. We were off to go and grow.

A chance visit before the Blessed Sacrament and an evening when we were giving a workshop in his parish led me to meet Bob Howlett. Bob became the first volunteer member of our planning team and then a RENEW team member, bringing his full gifts into play in the implementation of *RENEW 2000*.

Sr. Pat Crowley, O.P., a Dominican of Caldwell, joined our staff in 1991 after several invitations. She played an extensive role in the servicing of *RENEW 2000*. Pat is a gentle and reflective person, caring and conscientious. Her sense of justice shines through both in her insights and in how she preaches the Gospel through her actions. She was the perfect person to eventually succeed Kathy in coordination of the services. Pat remains a faithful member of the RENEW family. Pat also introduced her sister, Regina, who joined our staff to become our "copyologist" and a valuable member of our Publications and Resources Team. Gina became and remains a strong internal spirit for the RENEW team.

Sr. Louise Alff, a nationally recognized evangelist, brought her incredible talents to the planning and servicing of *RENEW 2000*. Because Louise is so humble and self-effacing, her zealous message was always received with open hearts. And no wonder. It's never about Louise but always about the Lord.

Another person who was always about the Lord was Mary Reddy. Mary, who previously served on the New York Archdiocesan Mission Team, was a gifted speaker. She attracted many people by her deep spirituality. Participants always gained new insights from her presentations.

Other team members included Dolly Bandura; Michael Brough; Sr. Margarita Castañeda, C.N.D.; Tim Castano; Sue Seltenright DeFerrari; Sr. Cheryl Erb, R.S.M.; Mike Fabian; Deacon Mike Hanly; Scott Leet; Fr. Francisco Molina; Joe Nuzzi; Sr. Beth Taylor, C.S.J.P.; Sr. Dot Urban, S.S.J.; Antony Visocchi; and Susan Winchell.

During this period Katherine Andrews joined our Resources and Publications team. She shared not only her superb editing skills and organizational expertise but also her beautiful spirituality, which helped to deepen us as a faith community.

Priests and *RENEW 2000*

The preparation of priests for *RENEW 2000* revolved around a four-day retreat that featured the pope's themes, which were also the themes of *RENEW 2000*. Each retreat team was composed of a priest retreat master whom we had engaged plus one member of our RENEW team. The themes were presented through talks, small-group sharing, and open forums. Our presenters included Msgr. Bob McDermott of the Diocese of Camden, Fr. Frank McNulty from Newark, and Fr. Shaun McCarty, S.T., from Stirling, New Jersey.

Diocesan priests responded positively to the retreat, feeling they were being positioned as leaders through their early involvement in the process. It was only near the end of the retreat that some of the nuts and bolts of RENEW were shared so the priests could go home not only spiritually prepared but also knowledgeable about what would be happening in their parishes.

As a result of the retreats, the priests were not only open to *RENEW 2000* but more inclined to be involved in leadership of the process in their parishes.

Ecumenism

Margo and I had planned a preparation and lead-in to Season IV on ecumenism, at which time people of mixed Christian denominations would meet in homes and share faith together. This would require early communication with local ministers, assuring them that they were not just buying into a Catholic program but rather a program that we had mutually prepared for well in advance.

We had two major disappointments with respect to Season IV. We had naïve hopes that the National Council of Churches in Riverside, New York, could work with us in facilitating this plan with Protestant ministers nationwide. However, we were told that the independence of mainline Protestant congregations made it impossible for the council to play a significant role. It seemed the initiative would have to come from individual ministers and congregations.

Even more disappointing was the apparent lack of readiness for a real grassroots ecumenical effort. It seemed that leadership at all levels, in our Church and in Protestant circles, was frightened that people were not ready for such an experience. Perhaps they feared that people in the small groups would be carried away by more persuasive members, lose the roots of their faith, and become members of another church. We don't believe that fear was well founded, but the idea of ecumenical faith-sharing was not embraced as we had hoped it would be.

Season V, with the theme of justice, also presented difficulties for some. This was particularly true in the section on the "Role and Importance of Women." Both ecumenism and justice were, of course, important themes in the pope's message for the new millennium.

Involving Dioceses and Parishes

While preparation of the many elements of *RENEW 2000* was under way, we confronted the question of how we would engage dioceses and parishes, in the short time available, to commit themselves to undertake the process. We were confident in *RENEW 2000*, but we needed to get the maximum number of people to benefit from it. This task was largely left to me.

The signing up of a diocese meant more than one simple visit. Even with dioceses that were most welcoming and looking for an instrument with which to celebrate the new millennium, many contacts were required. This included innumerable phone calls and letters to key diocesan people, eventually leading to a visit with the bishop, then the Council of Priests, and finally the entire presbyterate. In addition, the international aspect of RENEW was booming with continued training in India, Africa, and other countries.

By October 1998, thirty-four American dioceses (twenty-two diocesan efforts along with twelve good-sized cluster efforts) were ready to launch *RENEW 2000*.

RENEW 2000 Takes Off

RENEW 2000 took off in splendid fashion with a lot of energy nationwide. This time we thought it would be ideal to capture people's experience in a more verifiable manner. Our dire financial straits had never enabled us to take a formal sociological survey that would give scientific evidence of RENEW's impact on people's lives.

We were fortunate to have on our staff Greg Kremer, who had joined us from the Archdiocese of Seattle, Washington, where he headed a young-adult ministry. Greg, a very talented member of our team, had conducted a valuable survey on young adults and was well equipped to take on the task of evaluating *RENEW 2000*.

Despite our financial situation, Greg devoted a great deal of time and effort to providing us with our first thorough sociological survey. He engaged the Center for Applied Research in the Apostolate at Georgetown University in Washington, D.C., and CARA did a survey based on ten thousand RENEW participants throughout the country. As the results came in to CARA, they said, "We have never seen a volume of returns such as this. This means one of two things: either people are very enthused, or they are very disappointed and angry."

Fortunately, our personal experiences in serving dioceses and parishes proved to be valid. People were very excited about their *RENEW 2000* participation as the following charts indicate.

How much have the following increased as a result of your participation in RENEW 2000?

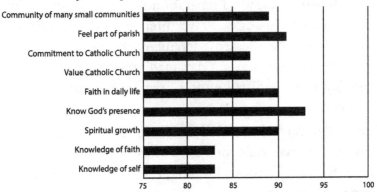

Percentage of persons responding "Very Much" or "Somewhat"

Chart data source: CARA

How much has RENEW 2000 encouraged you to:

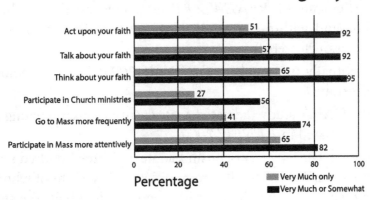

Percentage

The statistic I like best in addtion to these findings is that ninety-eight percent said they would be happy to recommend *RENEW 2000* to another person. The results of the survey and the impact *RENEW 2000* was having in people's lives were obviously remarkable.

Grass-Roots Experience

Good news stories poured in from all directions, such as people returning to the sacraments, participating in the liturgy, reconciling broken relationships, reaching out to those alienated from the Church or at the periphery of parish involvement. We also noted a much larger participation in the Hispanic community than we had anticipated.

Nearly one thousand five hundred *RENEW 2000* training sessions were conducted. This training communicated the need for all our renewal efforts to be based on prayer. Preparation for each season included the formation of prayer networks. Prayer preparation took various forms: Holy Hours before the Blessed Sacrament, the rosary, all-night vigils, commitment to a single prayer a day, meditation on the scripture readings of the day, and the distribution of prayer cards to the homebound and to prisoners.

RENEW 2000 carried on RENEW's long multicultural tradition. Small-community materials for *RENEW 2000* were made available in Vietnamese, Korean, Chinese, Hmong, Italian, Polish, Haitian French, and Portuguese.

A few facts and figures from Season I convey the feeling of building momentum.

- Participants of *RENEW 2000* numbered nearly five hundred thousand within the original twenty-two dioceses and twelve diocesan clusters.
- Eventually the number of *RENEW 2000* dioceses would reach fifty-nine.
- The CARA study indicated that seventy thousand young adults participated in *RENEW 2000*.
- The University of Wisconsin had nearly three hundred students in *RENEW 2000* small communities, eighty-eight of whom met in their dorms, involving nearly every resident hall. The students concluded one of their seasons with "an awesome Taco Bash."
- *RENEW 2000* took hold in one hundred ninety-four parishes in the Diocese of Green Bay, with over twenty thousand people in small communities.

- Nearly all the one hundred nineteen parishes in the Archdiocese of Kansas City joined in *RENEW 2000*, as some fifteen thousand parishioners shared in small groups.
- The relatively small Diocese of Birmingham attracted more than eight thousand participants to its eight hundred twenty-five *RENEW 2000* small communities.
- The Archdiocese of Louisville attracted over eleven thousand individuals in seventy-nine parishes.
- In the Archdiocese of Atlanta, eighty-five parishes yielded eighteen thousand *RENEW 2000* small-community members.
- *RENEW 2000* formed in one hundred nine parishes in the Diocese of Trenton, with more than eighteen thousand people gathering in over two thousand communities.
- In the Diocese of Albany, twenty thousand Catholics participated in *RENEW 2000* small communities.

"I now try harder to understand our religion and to live it, not just at church, but in everyday life," stated a RENEW small-community member from South Carolina. Another added, "We are now able to discuss the Bible and its messages more intelligently."

"People are now being encouraged to read the Bible at home," said Paula Andrade of St. John's Parish in the Archdiocese of Newark. "Think of how much more alive Scripture will be at Mass if people have discussed it in groups during the week."

Bishop George O. Wirz, who visited several RENEW small communities throughout the Diocese of Madison, remarked, "I am inspired by the spiritual renewal in so many parishes. The flood of prayers, the sacramental renewal, the testimonials of lay men and women, the numbers of people committed to participating in small Christian communities lifted my own spirit." The bishop continued, "The progress of *RENEW 2000* in our diocese assures that the Word of God can never be imprisoned in a cave."

In an article entitled "How *RENEW 2000* Affected Me," Bishop Howard J. Hubbard of Albany wrote, "For six weeks, I had the privilege of being part of a *RENEW 2000* small faith community. Each week, I gathered with my group for prayer, reflection, and faith-sharing.

Together, we explored the mystery of the Trinity and the wonder of God's creation. We spoke of ways we meet Jesus in our daily lives. We listened to each other and prayed together. During the week, between our meetings, we remembered each other in daily prayer. Each of us learned and grew; each of us contributed and shared.... The RENEW materials and discussion questions facilitated a dialogue, which was both stimulating and non-threatening. By the end of the first session, a rapport was established; and by the completion of the first season, there was a genuine bond of friendship and camaraderie.... My group was just one of three thousand other groups in our diocese—groups of young adults, youth groups, intergenerational groups, groups of men in prison, groups of religious women in motherhouses, groups of senior citizens, groups of school children."

As members of a faith-sharing community in St. Mary's, Closter, New Jersey, shared on the gifts of the Holy Spirit, one person remarked, "The greatest gift I have received is *RENEW 2000*."

Lucille Noll, *RENEW 2000* coordinator for three parishes in the Archdiocese of Kansas City, stated, "I felt that the RENEW process has drawn our three-parish community together with a better understanding of the needs of individual parishes. We still have our own parish identities, but we found out there are many parish activities that can be celebrated together."

A parishioner from St. John's Church in Madison, Alabama, remarked that *RENEW 2000* created a climate in which "individuals cannot only improve their own spiritual lives but are able to help their fellow Christians improve their spiritual lives as well."

"Our parish is diversity personified," said a participant from the Archdiocese of Atlanta. "*RENEW 2000* small Christian communities created an acceptance of these diversities of cultures, races, and ecclesiologies. We were amazed at the unity that resulted from praying in groups."

Bishop Joseph L. Imesch urged the members of the Diocese of Joliet to join in *RENEW 2000*: "Small communities are proven ways to help believers find God within themselves and their community. They have also attracted many inactive Catholics to 'take another look' at their faith and their Church."

RENEW 2000 Stories Reveal Growth

We were always looking for "good news" stories that lifted people's hearts. Here are a few.

Fifth Graders Love Rosary

At a parish school in the Diocese of Green Bay, Wisconsin, fifth-grade students volunteered to meet in a RENEW community. After the children discussed prayer one afternoon, the leader asked if they wished to learn how to pray the rosary. All of them thought it sounded great; by the next week they were praying the rosary on their own in their homes.

Sophomore Appreciates Mass

RENEW 2000 teen materials yielded encouraging results in the Diocese of Biloxi. One high school sophomore shared that Mass previously had bored her, but since she began *RENEW 2000* the Mass began to make sense. "Now, I listen to what the priest says during Mass," she recounted. "I started to look forward to Sunday morning."

Tripling the Numbers

The *RENEW 2000* mission that Holy Name Parish in Los Angeles held generated so much excitement that the number of small communities tripled.

Youth Want More

Lynn McDonald of St. Mary's Parish in Nassau, New York, described RENEW as "a great vehicle to get (youth) feeling comfortable asking questions." McDonald organized a youth small faith-sharing community at her church, which proved so successful the participants decided to continue to meet between the RENEW seasons. "They want more," Lynn said.

Hispanics Harvest Seeds of Evangelization

Fr. Isaac Calicchio of St Anthony's Church in Troy, New York, believed Hispanics grew in their ability and desire to share with one another due to *RENEW 2000*. "In addition, RENEW has already planted the seeds of evangelization, as parishioners have shown great hospitality to visitors. It will not be hard for Hispanics to share faith and pray," he asserts. "Hispanics will tell stories of faith and personal experiences."

Home-Grown Tomatoes Evangelize

In a parish in Evansville, Illinois, someone donated home-grown tomatoes to the food pantry, a few put in each bag. One hour after returning from the food pantry, a young woman called the parish office. She was crying. She had not tasted a home-grown tomato in three years, but now there were three fresh ones on her table. "I want to be part of any church that would reach out to me with a fresh tomato," she exclaimed. Ultimately, she moved to downtown Evansville and went through the RCIA at a local parish. How humbling! We sometimes plead ignorance about how to evangelize and, in this case, someone's kindness and a few tomatoes did it!

Vietnamese Enthusiasts

Fr. Joseph Tran ignited a blaze of enthusiasm for *RENEW 2000* among the Vietnamese community on both coasts. His success in The Bronx created such a stir that he received an invitation to help launch RENEW at St. Gabriel Parish, Los Angeles, California. Thanks to Fr. Tran's help, nineteen small communities, including three youth communities, were formed, all of them sharing in their native language.

Downpour of People

In the Archdiocese of Kansas City, *RENEW 2000* parish missions were greeted by terrible rain storms. Nevertheless, hundreds of people poured into the parishes despite the weather.

Food Pantries Grow

In the Diocese of Albany, New York, the RENEW small communities' commitment to putting their faith in action have strengthened several parishes' food pantry efforts.

Nine-Hour Travelers

At the end of *RENEW 2000* in Sault Ste. Marie, Ontario, Canada, I attended a diocesan meeting of parish leaders that was held to plan follow-through with Bishop Jean-Louis Plouffe. There was so much enthusiasm that some of the leaders traveled over nine hours to attend the session. It was one of the most inspiring meetings I've ever attended.

For me, the stunning results of the CARA study said it all. To my mind to have ninety-eight percent of thousands who responded to the survey say they would recommend RENEW to another person is off the charts and certainly the work of the Lord.

Upon the close of the second millennium and the end of *RENEW 2000*, interest in RENEW still remained very much alive. We modified and updated our materials under the title *RENEW: Spiritual Renewal for the 21st Century*. Ten dioceses and fifty-two clusters of parishes were involved until 2006. Some of my most memorable experiences came in this period with such dioceses as Scranton, Pennsylvania; Fall River, Massachusetts; Oklahoma City, Oklahoma; and Dallas, Texas.

CHAPTER 24

Along the Way

In this chapter you will discover more about our young-adult ministry, prison ministry, and outreach to the physically challenged, and you will get an update on Irma Chávez's work in El Salvador and Honduras and learn about additional priests who served on our RENEW journey.

Young Adult Ministry

Today is the biggest day in young Sara's life. She has unpacked all her belongings at the university where she hopes to spend the next four years and is now tearfully saying goodbye to her parents. Many emotions flood over her: separation, fear, and uncertainty for what the future holds, but mostly excitement over her new life. For the first time, she is stepping out on her own as a young adult, filled with wonderful hopes and dreams for the future.

It's also a traumatic day for her parents. As they ride home they wonder: Will she get enough to eat? Will she get along with her roommate? Will her social life distract from her studies? Will she be happy? Will she go to Mass and keep strong in her Catholic life?

Concerns for her faith are well-founded. Her parents, like all of us, look around on Sunday morning and don't see many young people at Mass. Sara was an exemplar at Holy Rosary Academy, and her faith has meant so much to her up to this point. What does the future hold?

One of the biggest things the future holds for Sara is challenge. Her roommate, Susie, has invited a boy to stay overnight the very first weekend. Susie and her boyfriend are very open in their affection and love-making. Sara has to wonder, "What's so wrong with all this? It seems so beautiful." Is everything she's been taught stuffy and outdated?

On Sunday morning Sara goes to the local church where she feels lost in an unfamiliar congregation. No one greets her upon arrival, the homily is ill prepared, and the music inspires little participation. Alone and away from home, she doesn't find her first Mass either uplifting or comforting.

In one of her classes the next day, it becomes immediately evident that the professor is an atheist and comes close to outright ridicule of anyone whose intellectual growth is so stunted as to still believe in a God or in anything more than what can be seen, touched, or tested.

What Could Change This Scene?

For a moment I would like to paint a more idealistic picture of Sara's new venture into campus life. How different it would be if small faith-sharing groups of students were there to welcome her—groups centered on sharing the very real things that will make up her life: intellectual pursuits, choice of vocation, sexuality, dating, alcohol, drugs, and, yes, faith. A real community where she could raise all the questions and doubts about her faith and share with other young adults. I feel confident this experience would strengthen Sara's faith. She would come to a point at which her Catholic faith was a new personal discovery—not a faith she had simply inherited, but one she had personally chosen.

Ideally, I would like to see upperclassmen from these small faith-sharing groups seek out Sara and help her not to be lost in a crowd but to be invited to a small community of young women and men who share a similar faith background, values, and ideals. I hope there would be a strong campus ministry at her university, but if she went to church off campus, I would like to see a minister of hospitality immediately recognize her as someone new and welcome her and engage her in conversation. That minister would call over a young adult from the parish who was engaged in a faith-sharing community and, once again, Sara would find immediate friendship and support.

Campus RENEW

These dreams on my part are, of course, based on the belief that small Christian communities should be a basic form of Catholic experience in parishes, campuses, and wherever people live out their lives. It is this belief that has led RENEW International to bring the RENEW experience to campus life.

In 1999, RENEW began to invest seriously in bringing small Christian communities to campuses with the hiring of Dolly Bandura, a dynamic young woman who came from the neighboring town to attend my Saturday evening Mass. An interview in the sacristy immediately convinced me this was the kind of young, faithful person we were looking for to reach out to other young adults.

In 2003, our *Campus RENEW* team was substantially expanded and started taking on a well-thought-out approach to working with students. A five-semester small-group faith-sharing process was specifically designed for the needs and topics of interest of college and university students. The process began with the development of a core community made up mostly of students, with the addition of a couple of faculty members.

Campus RENEW is launched at a university with an attractive retreat experience which moves students into RENEW small faith-sharing groups with relevant resources based on the realities of campus life.

Within a few years RENEW was working on nearly one hundred university and college campuses. These included well-known universities such as Rutgers, Texas A & M, Catholic University, Georgetown, Louisiana State, Wake Forest, University of North Carolina, Northwestern, Virginia Tech, DePaul, Marquette, Purdue, Indiana, as well as workshops for campus leaders at the University of Notre Dame.

Purdue University expanded from one small Christian community and, within a year, had spread to the involvement of four hundred students. A beautiful aspect of RENEW at Purdue was that it became almost entirely student-led. The students had taken ownership of the whole RENEW ministry.

Over two hundred students became involved in RENEW at Catholic University as we started to see RENEW become an endemic part of life on many campuses. It was not just an experience carried on for a four-year period but one that kept renewing itself as an ongoing opportunity for new students.

Covenant Commitments

Sometimes students decided on unique approaches. At Catholic University, members of many RENEW groups corporately decided to make a covenant commitment to the others in their small group. Composing the covenants was a truly moving experience. In their own words, each small community expressed a wide variety of commitments: making time to attend their weekly meetings, promising to be respectful of each other, praying for each other's needs, attending Mass as a group, encouraging others in their group to perform altruistic actions in daily life, confronting each other on moral issues, coming together to meditate and to pray the rosary, reading the word of God daily, and promising to be involved in a service project as a group at least once a month.

The unique way each community wrote their commitments displayed the reality of the deep faith experience they were enjoying and spoke volumes about the impact RENEW had had on them. So proud of their commitments, the groups shared them with the other small groups and together they assembled an attractive loose-leaf book. Sara's parents and all of us would be delighted to read them.

"To covenant with one another is to say that this is important. It's something that takes priority in my life," said a first-year varsity lacrosse player. When asked if it was difficult to make time to meet once a week, especially as a varsity athlete, she paused and said, "It's all in how you look at it. I have a ton of things going on, but RENEW is my chance to step back and refocus. It helps me to remember that God should be the center of my life." As one young man said, "It's been awesome. I never knew sharing about God could be this much fun."

The enthusiasm and zeal of young adults cannot be contained. One young woman in Florida felt the need for a spiritual boost during finals week but could find no members of her regular faith-sharing team available. She tried unsuccessfully to organize an impromptu session in the dorm lounge. Spotting three girls on the way to the swimming pool, she joined them and managed to initiate a RENEW faith-sharing session right there in the pool. Not only did the three young women enjoy the sharing of the day but they went on to become involved in RENEW faith-sharing communities over the next semesters.

Should we be surprised that some of the greatest enthusiasm for RENEW comes from campuses? RENEW believes that we should give our young men and women a realistic and appealing approach through which to embrace their faith.

Theology on Tap Comes to RENEW International

Theology on Tap had gained a reputation as the most effective outreach the Church was making to young adults. As we entered the new century, everybody was looking to Chicago and the dynamic duo of Fr. John Cusick and Kate DeVries who had initiated and kept developing this vibrant outreach.

The heart of their approach was going out to engage young adults in bars, restaurants, and places they regularly frequented. A gifted speaker would be invited to address a topic of interest to young people, such as personal relationships or becoming an everyday mystic. The talk would be followed by questions and then by an open discussion. Participants included those already involved in the Church along with those who just walked in off the street and may not have seen the inside of a church building since their first Communion or confirmation.

I was shocked one day to receive a call from Jack Cusick. He had an idea. The success of *Theology on Tap* in Chicago was overwhelming and more than enough to manage. Calls and inquiries were coming in from all over the country. In addition, programs using the *Theology on Tap* name elsewhere were being handled rather poorly. How could some kind of quality be maintained for *Theology on Tap* outside of Chicago?

Jack felt RENEW had contacts and involvement in every state of the union and had the best reputation for developing an outstanding spiritual project nationally. Chicago had been licensing parishes in other parts of the country that were committed to conducting good *Theology on Tap* sessions. Why not make a union with us whereby RENEW International would oversee and manage the spread of *Theology on Tap* beyond Chicago and assure that a high quality of performance was maintained? We were honored and eager to pursue the possibilities of working with *Theology on Tap*.

RENEW continues to play a very active role in initiating and engaging in *Theology on Tap* experiences. RENEW started within our own archdiocese with outstanding *Theology on Tap* sessions held in Jersey City and Hoboken under the direction of Fr. Jim MacNew and Margaret Rickard of RENEW International.

Over the years I have witnessed an incredible change in Hoboken, the town that was noted for the most bars of any square mile in the country. From an old and somewhat tired city, it has become a vibrant hub for young adults working in New York City. It is like "Young Adult Center USA." You can imagine my personal excitement at being involved in *Theology on Tap* in Hoboken and seeing inquiring young adults wander in off the sidewalks and become engaged with other people their age in the questioning, discovery, and revitalization of their faith.

We realized that we would be most effective in those dioceses that were undertaking a RENEW process as a diocesan effort, whether it be *ARISE Together in Christ*, *Why Catholic?*, or one of our other diocesan offerings. This approach continues and is proving to be effective, largely because it immediately gives us entrée to all diocesan leadership, including those ministries that involve young adults.

Symposia

Over the years we have conducted several symposia that brought together large groups of people to share about their involvement in RENEW's various young-adult ministries. Having venues on the West Coast, the Midwest, and the East Coast guaranteed our success. Young adults, in particular, appreciated the opportunity of meeting and getting to know each other. To be able to do this in a faith environment was a special gift.

There are two particular symposia I would like to mention: One was held in our own backyard at Convent Station, New Jersey, on January 5-7, 1997. This session brought together a good number of outstanding young adults, leading authorities on the attitudes and aspirations of young adults, and people with excellent pastoral experience in ministering to young adults. As Sr. Cheryl Erb said, its purpose was "to provide RENEW and the Church at large a comprehensive description of the values, pressures, dreams, struggles, and spiritual needs of young adults." The results of this symposium were collated in a book that became an essential part of the *RENEW 2000* project being developed at that time.

The other symposium I would like to note was one that was held, once again in New Jersey, in the summer of 2004. This symposium brought together over four hundred people from ten countries on five continents. It featured many outstanding presenters, including Scott Appleby, director of the Joan B. Kroc Institute for International Peace Studies, and professor of history at the University of Notre Dame, who was the keynote speaker and provided serious reflections on *Why Catholic?*

Of particular interest were the great delegations of young people that came from El Salvador, Honduras, and Slovakia. God had blessed us in a very special way as *Campus RENEW* had spread all the way to Slovakia and had involved all the colleges and universities of that country.

Much in the same manner as we experienced in Lithuania, the Slovakian young adults were finding religion, and their Catholic faith in particular, with all the excitement that comes with new discoveries. Living behind the Iron Curtain for more than fifty years, their parents had been raised as atheists. The process of creating the Church anew was under way. At the Catholic Student Center in the University of Vartislava, there were so many students involved in RENEW small Christian communities that they had to convert their recreation rooms for RENEW sessions.

The students from Slovakia, El Salvador, and Honduras were the hit of our 2004 symposium. They brought new life and energy not only to faith-sharing experiences but also to our recreational times when, dressed in traditional garb, they sang and danced with great verve. This session highlighted in a beautiful way the "international" in RENEW International. God's people from many parts of the world had gathered to share their common faith. It was the Lord who had them with a wholesome and wonderful spirit that can only come from God.

RENEW Behind Bars

Over the years we received a surprising number of reports of prison inmates meeting in RENEW groups. The hectic pace of the prime years made it impossible for us to record all this good news. However, here are a few examples.

First, to appreciate the value and impact that RENEW could have in a prison setting it is good to remember how prisoners often feel abandoned, discouraged, and fearful. What a gift for them to have support in a RENEW group where they break open the Scriptures and realize the tremendous love God has for them, helping them to know they are not alone in their confinement.

In Louisiana, one inmate, reflecting on Philippians 4:13, "I can do all things through Christ who strengthens me," shared his situation: "Things were so chaotic in my life that I was ready to give up. RENEW caught me when I was falling. I let down my guard and opened my heart. I'm ready to have a new start."

A woman inmate thanked the members of her RENEW faith-sharing group: "From the moment I met you guys your message was 'no matter what your circumstances are, don't lose hope.'" The sharing of faith by inmates in many instances had more meaning than any words a chaplain could offer. The participants, on their own, were discovering God's love.

In Spokane, Washington, Sr. Myrta Iturriaga, S.P., formed RENEW groups in two prisons where she served. She compared RENEW with Bible-study groups that she had previously conducted. "With RENEW I am more an observer. Leadership comes from among the inmates. They are learning to take responsibility and develop potential that will enable them to participate easily in parish life once they return to society."

Speaking of the seventy men and women prisoners she worked with in RENEW, she said, "They have learned to talk about and share their experiences and deepen their spiritual life. As a result of RENEW, through daily prayer, interior change is taking place."

One of my favorite persons in the RENEW journey is Deacon Sam Shippen from Mobile, Alabama. I well remember his enthusiastic call, looking to share and explore ideas about adapting RENEW for prison ministry. Based on his experience, he took it upon himself to develop a whole set of materials for RENEW in prison. Sam said, "For about thirty years now I have been working with the incarcerated. When I reflect on Scripture with prisoners, I used the process of relating what is read to real life and sharing the reflections in community. This I learned from RENEW."

In the Diocese of Columbus, Ohio, one parish located near three penal institutions purchased three thousand RENEW prayer cards to distribute to the inmates.

Change of Heart Forged by RENEW

For five months, a Hindu prisoner named Muraly attended twice-monthly RENEW faith-sharing sessions conducted in prison by the parish RENEW team in Pondicherry, India.

Muraly had assisted in the killing of seven people in Nepal, Bangladesh, and other areas targeted for political terror.

One day, after the regular RENEW Mass, he asked permission to speak to other prisoners, police, and prison officials. "I am a Hindu," he said. "You all know why I am here, what I have done (as a member) of an international group.

"I was brought here with heavy chains by policemen on each side. But today I am a changed person. Not changed by society, police, or anyone else but only by the word of God and prayers I have heard here. When I leave here I will go and meet my former companions and tell them about the word of God."

Again we are able to see how active God's hand was in many aspects of RENEW. From the millions of people involved in RENEW, we can only imagine how many took this experience into local prisons and immeasurably helped the incarcerated at a most difficult time in their lives. Jesus truly came to save, to heal, and to set the captives free.

Conversion of "The Scar"

Juan "The Scar" Martinez sat on a rock and listened as a handful of villagers in the rural parish sat under a tree and discussed their faith as part of a RENEW faith-sharing group.

Understandably, they were apprehensive. Juan had come by his nickname legitimately, the machete wound on his face giving testimony to his reputation not only as a fighter but also as a killer—"one who had sent a few to heaven," in the words of the parish priest—during El Salvador's twelve-year civil war.

Nevertheless, when Juan came a second time one of the men in the group invited him to join the meeting. He declined. He did not feel worthy, he explained. But he continued to sit on the rock and listen, his machete at his side.

"One day," reports Irma Chávez, "Juan suddenly started to tell his own story. He couldn't resist the feelings of faith and joy coming out of the group." Irma learned about the story from Fr. Vidal Rivas, the parish priest. She had asked Fr. Rivas if he was happy with the RENEW process. "I am more than happy," he replied. "A lot of people are coming back to the Church—people you wouldn't think of, people like Juan 'The Scar' Martinez."

After telling the story, Fr. Vidal noted that Juan had become "one of the main RENEW leaders in the parish. He has credibility. People have been touched by his conversion. When he tells them how good it is to read the Word of God and discuss it with others, they believe him."

Honduras

In 2003, Fr. Delio Diaz, O.F.M., pastor of St. Maximilian Kolbe Parish in Tegucigalpa, Honduras, asked Irma to help him to implement the RENEW process in his parish. Fr. Diaz had lived in El Salvador and knew how this process had succeeded in five dioceses. He had recently been appointed to the parish that, according to the last census at that time, had a population of around three hundred fifty thousand persons. There were only three friars to take care of the whole parish. How could so few priests properly serve an incredibly large number of abjectly-impoverished people? RENEW offered hopeful possibilities.

With Irma's help, dozens of people were trained as leaders for RENEW small groups and to care for the people in the area adjacent to their huts. A team of leaders that had worked with the process in El Salvador started to work with the leaders of Maximilian Kolbe Parish. After several years, the process was implemented and, despite the poverty of the area, the big political turmoil, and the violence in that country, the Central Committee is still working and there are small groups gathering around the Word of God.

The RENEW process provided a multiplying pastoral effect that was a great boon for the friars. RENEW had seldom worked so meaningfully in so poor a place.

Additional Priests Who Served

Part of the richness of the RENEW team was the diversity of people we worked with over the years. Lay people, religious women and men, deacons, and priests interacted in true communal fashion and brought from their life experiences valuable perspectives.

Freeing priests from their dioceses and religious communities was not easy. Nevertheless, we were able to gather for Mass as a team on an almost daily basis. These liturgical celebrations were the bond that truly brought us together as a spiritual community. Shared homilies enabled us to hear each other's rich insights and to appreciate the unique contributions that each was bringing to the RENEW mission.

Some of these priests have already been mentioned. Others included Fr. Tom McCloskey whom I had known and become friendly with at annual national parish council conventions. Tom had been pastor of a Spanish-speaking parish and had written a popular book on the faith, *Credo*, which we had used even before his joining us. Tom not only served well but was a life-giving spirit for our team, especially with his magnificent piano renditions.

Fr. Bob Beaulieu had been a diocesan RENEW director for the Helena Diocese in Montana. Bob served nationally and internationally and for a number of years coordinated RENEW's national services.

Tom, Bob, and I enjoyed living in community for several years.

Currently serving RENEW International is Fr. Alejandro Lopez-Cardinale, who leads our Hispanic RENEW ministry both here and in Latin America. Alejandro came to us in a most interesting manner. While working on his doctorate on small Christian communities, he discovered RENEW. His doctoral work could spring from his actual small-community experience with RENEW.

Alejandro's tireless efforts have not only extended across the United States but have also led him to incorporate RENEW in church life in his native Venezuela. He has set his sights high for the expansion of RENEW throughout Latin America.

Perhaps no priest has contributed more than Fr. Abraham Orapankal, who was a missionary priest in his native India. Abraham brought to RENEW the richness of strong parish experience along with a solid theological background from being a seminary professor. Best of all is his very vibrant spirituality and the ease with which he relates to people. Whenever Alejandro or Abraham celebrated noontime Mass at our RENEW chapel, the liturgies were extremely meaningful and always strengthened RENEW as a community.

CHAPTER 25

RENEW Opens
People to the Word

T he RENEW process was so successful in parishes in the
Archdiocese of Newark that people asked for resources
to continue meeting in their small communities after the
completion of the five RENEW seasons. As we were still developing
RENEW materials for Season V right up to the time RENEW small
communities were to meet, we were unprepared to provide this follow-
through. However, the Spirit was leading us, and we responded.

Small Christian Community Resources

We opened the Small Christian Community Department in 1980 as
part of the Office of Pastoral Renewal with two new staff members:
Sr. Joan Jungerman, S.S.N.D., and Fr. Bob Cozzini, an archdiocesan
priest. Together they worked throughout the diocese in developing core
communities that would encourage and support small Christian communities. They brought a lot of spirit to the team and kept us laughing for
two years. In addition, Joan, a skilled spiritual director, began to write
materials for small communities. In many ways, the story of RENEW
has been the story of so many extraordinary people who have served on
the RENEW team.

Eventually, the department had six road persons and two editors, Florence
Jacobson and Judy Andrews, who engaged authors and coordinated the

writing of small Christian community publications that became known as the *Pilgrimage Series*, published by Paulist Press. Other staff who wrote for the series were John Bins, Sr. Mary Elizabeth Clark, S.S.J., Tom DeVries, Sr. Lois Kikkert, O.P., and Sr. Catherine Nerney, S.S.J. Topics included the Gospels, community building, prayer, discovering our gifts, Advent and Lenten reflections, and prayer sessions for Social Concerns Committees.

The *IMPACT Series*

I embraced the idea that the Observe, Judge, Act methodology, used in Young Christian Students and Christian Family Movement small communities, was the most effective approach to helping people develop a holistic spirituality. This meant taking religion far beyond Sunday Mass observance and other special times set aside for prayer. Spirituality involved every aspect and every moment of our lives.

Because some areas of our lives present challenges and difficult decisions, some like to separate these difficulties from the realm of spirituality. Social responsibility is too easily characterized as political or totally secular and unrelated to the life of the spirit. The teachings of the Catholic Church, including the magnificent documents issued by our U.S. bishops, clearly contradict these false notions and present a beautiful understanding of full spirituality. In practice, this is usually the weakest part of parish life and people's understanding of their faith.

Sr. Mary McGuinness also deeply held these beliefs. We wanted to undertake a project that would move people beyond RENEW by providing small-community materials that would deal with specific areas such as media, interracial harmony, family concerns, ecology, and civic responsibility. We brainstormed a series of topics, the first of which would be called *Beginnings*, based on the idea of the "Green Book" —the introductory booklet used by Christian Family Movement in the 1950s.

We took a number of daily-life social issues, dedicating a single chapter to each of these areas. *Beginnings: Human and World Issues* treated eight social areas separately. Each issue would be spelled out in far greater detail in individual books in our *IMPACT Series*, along with a great number of other important life concerns and issues. This project was designed to help people realize that spirituality was not compartmentalized but included all life issues.

The *IMPACT Series* was intended to do precisely what its title said: impact individual people's lives and, in turn, help them have a greater impact on the world around them. The intent was not to take positions, to the right or to the left but rather to help people, by drawing upon the Scriptures and the teachings of the Church, to think through, in responsible ways, often complicated subjects. It was designed to help people ingest their Christian values and make good decisions accordingly.

Mary wholeheartedly took on the *IMPACT Series*. I have already mentioned the areas Mary was drawn into over the course of RENEW's history, but publications were her main everyday responsibility. She undertook it with great zeal. Mary and I would brainstorm various topics, but it was she who would engage writers, work consistently with them, edit materials, and see them through to publication. This project offered great potential in addressing a neglected but extremely important part of church life.

Along with Mary, Bob Heyer deserves much credit for this *IMPACT Series*. Bob was editor at Paulist Press when we published our RENEW materials and original small Christian community resources in the *Pilgrimage Series*. At this point he was editor-in-chief at Sheed & Ward. I've always admired Bob's true Christian integrity. In this instance he realized this series would not be a great moneymaker and could actually be a financial loss. But he, along with Mary and me, so deeply believed in the importance of this project to clarify and enunciate a full spirituality so vital to the Church that he readily embarked on the project with us.

The Archdiocese of St. Louis would be an example of a diocese that welcomed and made good use of the *IMPACT Series*. Having started RENEW in 1983 with close to one hundred percent participation, the diocese reorganized its education office with an emphasis on a growing need for materials for small groups. Ms. Pat Murphy, responsible for this area of continuing education, said, "The *IMPACT Series* is ideal because each unit is self-contained and usually runs for a period of six sessions. Parishes order their booklets through our office, and this facilitates programming."

St. Louis had dozens of parishes that began with *Beginnings: Human and World Issues* and carried on with many others in the *IMPACT Series*. Pat said, "Virtually all of those using the *IMPACT* titles report good to excellent responses."

Eventually, there were more than two dozen publications in the *IMPACT Series*.

Lenten Longings, with a separate faith-sharing book for each of the three years of the liturgical cycle, was and still is an extremely popular series written by Sr. Cathy Nerney as an *IMPACT* title and updated recently. Over the years *Lenten Longings* has enriched the spirituality of nearly fifty thousand people. Cathy is a very special person in the overall RENEW picture. Originally a member of Newark's Small Christian Community Department, she went on to earn a doctorate in theology, became associate professor of religious studies at Chestnut Hill College in Pennsylvania and now heads the Forgiveness and Reconciliation Institute at the college. Combined with her great intellect and writing ability, Cathy brings a deep spirituality to her efforts. She has been a special friend and contributor to RENEW over the years.

We wanted a book on the Blessed Mother so we invited Fr. John Phalen, C.S.C., president of Holy Cross Family Ministries in North Easton, Mass., to write *At Prayer with Mary*. He asked his community member, Br. James Posluszny to co-author the book. This best seller was a collaborative effort of RENEW International and Family Rosary, Inc., founded by Fr. Patrick Peyton, C.S.C. It is available in an updated edition through both ministries.

Through our RENEW work, we often met men who had been influenced by their RENEW small communities to enter the priesthood. We discovered this was true of Fr. Charles Pinyan. Charlie had been a professional writer before entering the seminary. It was a joy to work with him on our very popular *At Home in the Catholic Church*.

Mary delighted in meeting new people through phone contacts and engaging them to write for us. She had belonged to a Bread for the World group in her parish, so it was natural for her to call Art Simon, renowned founder and director for many years of Bread for the World, the nation's largest citizen lobby for combating hunger. Art Simon enthusiastically agreed to author *Hunger in God's World*.

Later she called Dave Beckman, president of Bread for the World, to inform him of the upcoming publication. This best seller received a rousing send-off with a pre-publication order of three thousand copies from Bread for the World. Upon receiving his order, Dave said, "Nobody can explain the problem of hunger and what we can do about it better than Arthur Simon. This booklet will change lives. It is clear, convincing, and spiritually profound."

While on retreat one year, Mary discovered a book on mysticism by Frank Tuoti. She contacted his publisher and asked that her letter be forwarded to him. Frank wrote *Awakening the Mystic Within*, which became one of our most popular books.

Mary's love of creation and the new scientific story of the emerging universe led her to collaborate with Sr. Miriam MacGillis, O.P., in writing *Our Origin Story: Continuing Foundations for Ecological Responsibility*. This book found its way to five continents.

Edmund Flood, a prolific English writer, had long been taken with the work of RENEW and was deeply concerned about social issues being seen as an integral part of spirituality. We were honored when this popular and well-respected writer undertook *The World of Work*. Renato Tagiuri, professor emeritus at Harvard University, was "deeply impressed by the organization and the appropriateness of *The World of Work*." This type of comment indicates the quality and professionalism with which the serious issues were treated in the *IMPACT Series*.

Sr. Mary Elizabeth Clark, S.S.J., who inherited justice genes from her parents, was a vibrant member of the human-concerns team. Naturally, we first thought of her to write *Discipleship of Nonviolence*. After the Columbine tragedy, one small community in Golden, Colorado, based a series of meetings on *Discipleship of Nonviolence*. They said they wanted to better understand the cause of violence and how to connect to the increase in youth violence. They invited teens to share with them. The teens challenged the parents: "What are you going to do about the violence in the world?" After the events of 9/11, we asked Mary

Elizabeth to write an additional chapter for the book, "Light and Love in the Hour of Tragedy."

I belong to a pot-luck small community with good friends including Mary Ann and Steve Jeselson, folks who daily live the Gospel. We turned to them to write *Civic Responsibility: What's It All About?* This book was published the year preceding presidential elections. As her action response one week, Maureen Flynn, a realtor who used the book, invited her realty company to insert voter registration forms in the packets they prepared for new home owners. She also got her colleagues to participate in building homes for Habitat for Humanity.

Through the years, Mary periodically spoke with Gregory Augustine Pierce, publisher of ACTA books in Chicago. After she read his book *Spirituality in the Workplace*, she asked if he would write an *IMPACT* book on the same topic. *Finding God @ Work: Practicing Spirituality in the Workplace* was the result.

Another example of how *IMPACT* materials were used can be seen in *Grieving the Death of a Loved One*. The horrific tragedy of 9/11 affected almost every parish in the New York Metropolitan Area. Great numbers of Wall Street people lived in Westchester County and Long Island, New York; and in the metro areas of New Jersey and Connecticut. Countless parishes in the area were in turmoil with the loss of treasured family members, neighbors, and parishioners.

To meet this crisis, RENEW International sent gratis twenty-five copies of *Grieving the Death of a Loved One* to every parish in the dioceses in those same metro areas along with parishes around the site of the Pennsylvania plane crash. The books were accompanied by the promise of providing more if needed. These books helped countless families and parishioners work through their grieving process. Since then, the same gratuitous process has been carried out for colleges and universities that have experienced tragic and violent deaths on campuses.

Mary's unbounded zeal led her to engage Sr. Helen Prejean, C.S.J., the author of *Dead Man Walking*, to write *Reflections on Dead Man Walking* for us. What a privilege it was to have Helen, together with co-author Lucille Sarat, see the importance of our *IMPACT* undertaking. You can only imagine how popular this book was. Whenever we went to talks given by Helen, she would hold up a copy of our book and encourage folks to purchase it.

When Sheed & Ward was sold to the Sacred Heart Fathers, we decided to publish through Liguori, a move initiated by Bob Heyer. After two years, however, we were selling more copies of our *IMPACT* books from our bookstore than Liguori was. It was then that RENEW International began in earnest to be our own publisher. Meanwhile, during the time with Liguori, Mary Ann Jeselson and Carole G. Rogers created two books for us that Liguori published, *Great Ideas from Great Parishes* and *The People's Prayer Book: Personal and Group Prayers*.

The *IMPACT Series* certainly made its own impact but, unfortunately, it was sadly overshadowed by RENEW itself and all the effort and time that was taken in meeting the demands on it from all over the country and beyond. As a result of poor publicity and weak marketing on our part, *IMPACT* never realized its full potential. It remains a project very dear to my own heart and those of us at RENEW International. Please God, the time will come when more of the titles can be updated and republished. Perhaps more than ever, our world, our nation, and our Church need to embrace the fullness of Christ's good news in a full and holistic spirituality.

Small Christian Communities: A Vision of Hope

In the 1980s, Mary and I realized the need to provide in one resource the whole picture of small Christian communities. We hoped to bring together the case for small Christian communities, practical pastoral ideas for implementing small Christian communities, and motivational pieces to help people undertake small-community projects.

Over several years, the project involved much brainstorming, research, spirited discussion, and a ton of just plain hard work. The result was *Small Christian Communities: A Vision of Hope* published by Paulist Press in 1991.

A Vision of Hope went through a couple of revisions, and in the 2003 edition Dr. William V. D'Antonio wrote the preface. D'Antonio was the principal researcher for the Small Christian Communities Project sponsored by Loyola University Institute for Ministry in New Orleans. In his preface he calls *A Vision of Hope* "A rich source of practical information about how to make the vision of the parish as 'a community of many small communities' come alive in today's parish."

D'Antonio pointed out how his committee's findings mirrored the experiences and ideas enunciated in *A Vision of Hope*: "Our research supports their models...about how to draw people, especially young people, into a small community."

A companion book, *Resources for Small Christian Communities: A Vision of Hope*, published simultaneously, offered six sessions for developing a core community, leadership skills for small-community leaders, and all the practical help needed to assist a parish in this endeavor.

While I contributed substantially with ideas and pastoral experience and Margo LeBert wrote a few chapters particularly pertaining to small Christian communities' relationship with RCIA and other aspects of parish life, Mary was the person mostly responsible for producing *Small Christian Communities: A Vision of Hope*. Mary did most of the writing, researching, and editing. In addition, she conducted the piloting and undertook the work of publishing. Her perseverance never faltered.

One day we were surprised to receive word that *Small Christian Communities: A Vision of Hope* won first place in a Catholic Press Association competition in the category of pastoral ministry. We had no idea that such awards were even given out and we were thrilled because in that category was a new publication by Evelyn and James Whitehead, experts in the pastoral publishing field. We were the newcomers.

Upon receiving word of this honor, the three of us stood outside our building and had a photo taken holding the books and then, naturally, went back inside to work on the next project.

Mary and I also wrote the script for a set of four videotapes to complement *Small Christian Communities: A Vision of Hope* and engaged Susan Garofalo to execute the project. This series, *Parish Core Communities: Renewing the Face of the Earth*, also received an award.

While many copies of *A Vision of Hope* were sold to individuals, the book is so basic to our convictions and mission that it was part of thousands of parish kits for *RENEW 2000*.

Sr. Joan Bernier, S.N.D., who worked on development of small Christian communities in the Archdiocese of Hartford before working with us, was one of the biggest fans of *A Vision of Hope*. We loved it when during her workshops she would hold up the book and say with great gusto, "This is the Bible for small Christian communities." She was one of many in the ministry of developing the parish as a community of many small communities who regarded *A Vision of Hope* as their main pastoral guideline.

The Hispanic Team, under the leadership of Sr. Maria Iglesias, S.C., had the materials translated and put in an Hispanic context. Paulist Press published the work in three books as planned by the team.

For me, *Small Christian Communities: A Vision of Hope* is a major source of gratification in my many years of priestly ministry. The same person who discovered small communities in 1946 in the library at Seton Hall Prep felt a sense of satisfaction in the compilation and publication of this book.

The *Catechism of the Catholic Church*

A dreamer particularly loves summertime. Perhaps it provides a little more time and freedom to let the imagination flow, to stop, to reflect, and to evaluate, and to conjure up new ideas and projects.

One summer day in 1994, much in the same manner as in the beginnings of *RENEW 2000*, I placed a call to Margo LeBert: "Margo, why don't you come to Avon for some brainstorming?" The *Catechism of the Catholic Church* had just been published. It was time for us to think through its implications for pastoral life. The very word "catechism" had frightened many who recalled memorizing and reciting by rote the content of the *Baltimore Catechism*. While filling young minds with much information, that approach didn't always manage to communicate the excitement of Jesus' presence and his sharing of the Good News.

Margo and I walked the boardwalk and talked about this new *Catechism*. It was very different from what most had expected. It was life-giving. The section on prayer was truly a source of rich spiritual reading.

We knew this voluminous *Catechism* would be read cover to cover by at best one in a million. How could we make it more available to people so they might have a better understanding and love of their Catholic faith and find it a source of spiritual growth? How could we help people discuss the content of the *Catechism*, integrate it in their daily lives, and actually open the *Catechism* and use it as their reference? We felt that our experience with RENEW gave us the know-how to get the new *Catechism* off the shelf and into people's hands. We needed to develop a small-community resource that would convey the content of the *Catechism*, help people become comfortable with it and share it so that it would enrich people's lives and encourage them to take actions helpful to themselves and others.

Returning to my apartment, we outlined a plan for a series that would first be known as *Breaking Open the Catechism of the Catholic Church*. The ball was tossed to Margo who produced the resource with her usual high quality and lightning speed.

Paulist published our series whose popularity was helped by its great timeliness. When Paulist ran out of several books in the series, we took the manuscripts and revised them. *Breaking Open the Catechism of the Catholic Church* took on a new life. As we will see in Part IV, this series was to become a complete process entitled *Why Catholic? Journey through the Catechism of the Catholic Church* and, in the Spanish version, *¿Por qué ser católico? El catecismo como camino.*

PRAYER TIME/OREMOS

Fr. John E. O'Brien, former RENEW spiritual director, wrote a series for the liturgical years A, B, and C entitled *Refreshed by the Word* to enable people to encounter spirituality in the concrete circumstances of their everyday lives, leading to a conversion of heart. This series, published by Paulist Press, enjoyed popularity for a number of years.

The positive reaction of millions of people had assured us of the impact of RENEW on peoples' lives. Even without sociological data to prove the point, we knew—from our own experience and from stories coming in from around the world—that one dynamic, lasting effect of RENEW was that parish meetings had become much more prayerful. Frequently, parish council and committee members would replicate the faith-sharing process engendered by RENEW. Strange as it may sound today, this was in sharp contrast to much previous experience. Even in great parishes such as my original assignment in Our Lady of Mercy, Park Ridge, a good number of people resisted anything more than a brief prayer to start meetings. "After all," they would retort, "this is a parish business meeting."

What was needed was a solid faith-sharing resource that would help people prayerfully begin every kind of parish meeting and that would provide an appropriate spiritual background and tone for conducting both parish ministries and practical business. This was the topic of conversation during a car ride in 1999.

Michael Brough, Bob Heyer, Mary McGuinness, and I were engaged in lively discussion on this matter. We quickly agreed on the need for a resource that would connect the weekly themes of the Church's liturgical cycle for Years A, B, and C with people's daily lives. For me, the most interesting part of this discussion was about what to name these three volumes. We kicked around possible titles until finally we spontaneously and unanimously agreed upon *PrayerTime*.

That was it, prayer time, *PrayerTime*! Naturally, every meeting should begin with prayer time, and *PrayerTime* would be the resource to enrich this time of prayer. Imagine an end of deadly boring meetings that wear people out after they have put in a hard day's work. Not still another business meeting. This kind of meeting would accomplish the parish's business but would also be what Church and parish should be about, enriching people's lives and bringing them closer to the Lord.

As editor of *PrayerTime*, Bob engaged well-known writers, including his wife, Jeanne Marie Heisberger.

Our Hispanic team translated and acculterated the materials for the Spanish-speaking community, and we published a version under the title *Oremos*. These resources, *PrayerTime* and *Oremos*, are included in our *Why Catholic?* and *ARISE Together in Christ* parish kits and have enriched the lives of thousands.

Heavenly Harmony Series

Jack Kreismer is an outgoing and enthusiastic person whom I have known since his boyhood days at Our Lady of Mercy. I was pleased to meet him in Upper Saddle River where he had a profound conversion experience, deepening his Catholic faith. Jack has his own warehouse and publishes books under the name Red Letter Press.

In his generous zeal, he offered to work with our staff in developing four books that would make up the *Heavenly Harmony* series: *Heavenly Humor, Heavenly Quotations, Heavenly Stories, Heavenly Humor for Children.* Jack would publish them, and he offered us as many copies as we wanted. We could sell these small gift books and return a very small percentage of the proceeds to him. In addition he also graciously offered to house our resources in his warehouse.

Music

Original RENEW resources were aided by appropriate music developed by Norma Catherine, a parish RENEW coordinator from Santa Clarita, California. These were the first tapes/CDs to accompany RENEW small-group resources. Since then, RENEW International has provided music with many of our resources.

RENEW's Resources Make a Difference

In the 1990s, the National Pastoral Life Center convened leaders from around the country representing different organizations working with small Christian communities. I found it fascinating that in almost every instance they traced their beginnings to the RENEW experience.

It is gratifying to know that RENEW, by God's grace, is at the root of much small-community vitality across the country and that our RENEW team has had the ability and the blessing to continue to serve small-community development in every state of the union. This has been largely accomplished through our small Christian community resources.

I'm particularly pleased RENEW has contributed to developing resources that address difficult areas of life usually avoided. Small Christian communities involve much more than bringing people together for a comfortable time of sharing. Without resources that challenge us to accept all the responsibilities of our faith and help us work through demanding issues, people could easily be left to stay in their comfort zones and fail to embrace the fullness of Christian spirituality. It is good here to recall the wisdom of Pope John Paul II: "True holiness does not mean a flight from the world; rather, it lies in the effort to incarnate the Gospel in life, in the family, at school and at work, and in social and political involvement."

CHAPTER 26

Europe

Ireland and Lithuania

I n May 1995, Sr. Cecilia King and I were preparing for one of our training trips to India. "Why not make a visit to Ireland on the way?" I suggested. Until then, our work had been limited to countries that first had made contact with us. But this would be different.

Ireland

There were reasons for making an exception for Ireland. After all, most of our staff was Irish: Cecilia is full-blown Irish, having been born and raised in Galway, and I was half Irish, coming from the Irish culture in the Vailsburg section of Newark, New Jersey. This was reason enough for us wanting to see RENEW come to Ireland.

Cecilia did some research on the bishops in Ireland, trying to determine which ones might be most open to something new, to something like RENEW. When we landed, I immediately got on the phone and, out of the blue, placed a call to each of these bishops: "We just happen to be here in Ireland and wondered if we could stop by and explain something very exciting that's making a big impact in the United States."

The bishops were caught off guard, but several were intrigued. Since we would be there only for four days, we had to make the appointments for the day of the call or as soon as possible. Six bishops agreed to have us visit.

The following days were absolutely wild. Visits were not arranged in an orderly geographic fashion. And so we dashed to the north, south, east, and west of Ireland at a frantic pace, dodging huge lorries on narrow country roads and managing to handle the roundabouts. The visits were most fruitful, with five of the six bishops agreeing to have us return and speak to the priests of their dioceses.

Clonfert

The visit to Bishop John Kirby from Clonfert was most interesting. He immediately gave a warm welcome and greeting to native-born Cecilia. I was rather nonexistent. When we suggested that we return and speak to his priests, he looked at me and said, "You can never speak to my priests." A bit startled I said, "Why not?" " 'Cause you're an American!" he said. I was put off, to say the least. I was tempted to reply that he could put one of his Irish priests on the stage and I could stand behind the curtain and whisper what the priest was to say. Fortunately, I kept my mouth shut, and the return visit was arranged.

When we got back in the car and were leaving town, I was furious. The issue of being an American had never been so directly addressed. What kind of man was this bishop? I was eventually to learn much about him. When we returned to Ireland, I actually did give the presentation with Cecilia, a presentation well received by the priests.

We also found out that Bishop Kirby had a deep interest in the people in the developing world and had just returned from Rwanda. There were many common interests we shared. He made a point of participating in every training session and became one of the strongest of all advocates for RENEW. Humbled once again, I realized how much I had to learn.

All five dioceses where the bishops had shown interest in RENEW were located in the west of Ireland, ranging from Sligo to the northern parts of Galway where many of our Irish-American people had come from. It was a very special week. I had the most magnificent salmon luncheon with Bishop Tom Flynn from Achonry. When I asked where this exquisite salmon came from, he pointed and said, "From the River Moy," which was flowing just across the street from us.

Roscommon

Celebrating Mass in Roscommon was also memorable. I had heard much about Roscommon over the years from Jack McDermott, who came to the United States from there as a child. We also managed one day to shoot down to the Limerick area and visit the "Hollywood House and Farm" of our good friends Peter and Carolyn Lynch for an overnight stay. The "farm" was beautiful beyond description, a bit of Irish heaven. It was a memorable week, with the only downside being the two tires that I destroyed, parking the car curbside on the wrong side of the street.

At our first orientation meeting, the Ballaghaderreen people shared two inhibitions as to whether RENEW would actually work in Ireland. The first was the fear of being overtly involved beyond the requirements of their faith and being labeled as "Holy Joes" or "Holy Marys." They felt unworthy of any leadership role and did not want to be seen as hypocrites. The second was their concern about how faith sharing would go over in light of the strong Irish religious tradition about privacy in one's relationship with God. These two concerns spelled out exactly what we would be dealing with in implementing RENEW. Would people open up in sharing about their lives and religious experiences?

It was a challenge and, to be sure, it started slowly. But the basic appeal to human nature prevailed. Gradually people warmed up to the sharing and started speaking more freely about their personal relationships and feelings about God. The universal love for the Scriptures, as always, appealed to them and helped them to see and love Jesus in a more personal way. For many the religious culture was changing because of faith sharing. Even priests' conferences started introducing faith sharing as a regular part of their meetings.

A Chastened Leader

One story that I particularly loved was about a woman who facilitated her small RENEW community. The topic was the most difficult one—forgiveness. To set a good example she shared about her relationship with her brother, with whom she had not spoken for many years. She promised that in the coming week she would contact him, break down the barriers that had separated them, and make amends. That would be her action step coming out of the meeting. No one else in the group made such a difficult promise.

At the following meeting, as always, the group shared what action they had undertaken from the previous meeting. To the leader's shock, three people volunteered how they had taken the most difficult step of contacting someone from whom they had been alienated and restored a relationship of friendship. The leader was shocked for more than one reason: she had done nothing about her big, bold promise at the previous meeting. Chastened by the actions of the others in her group she, once again, promised to contact her brother. This time she followed through and did as she said she would, restoring friendship with her brother.

Killala

Cecilia reported that there was a handsome man in Killala who said, "RENEW is the best thing that ever happened to me. It came at the right time. Due to downsizing, I lost my job and RENEW saved the day. My two sons, ten and twelve years old, are excited about the use of the Bible. They actually vie with one another in finding the scripture passage suggested in the RENEW take-home material and place it on the table for our morning reflection." Cecilia said, "Oh, I liked this man, not because he was handsome, even though that never hurts." I never met the man, but I also liked him and marveled at the way God had touched his life through RENEW.

RENEW Enhances Liturgies

We were so used to extremely positive feedback about small communities that it came as a bit of a surprise that the Irish were also excited by the suggestions that RENEW offered to enhance the Sunday liturgy. One of the highlights for RENEW in Ireland was the liturgical experience. The RENEW materials that helped parish liturgical committees who prepared the Sunday liturgy made a big hit. People were very pleased with how RENEW had opened the doors for many of the elements of Vatican II that provided for greater participation and a richer Sunday Mass experience.

Armagh

In September of 1997 Cecilia and I made a visit to the north of Ireland. As expected, we were stopped by the Northern Ireland police at the border separating the Republic of Ireland and Northern Ireland. We passed the test and were able to proceed on to Armagh and visit with then Archbishop Sean Brady, the primate of all Ireland. Armagh was the diocese that St. Patrick presided over, and it had a long and rich history.

Working over the years with Archbishop Brady, who was named a cardinal in 2007, was one of the more delightful experiences for our staff. He was very involved in meetings, working with leadership among Protestants and Catholics trying to restore peace. His renowned peace efforts had a positive effect on our whole RENEW experience there.

Archbishop Brady's rectory became the friendly and welcoming stop-over for all our staff when they were passing through Ireland. In 2003, we brought the archbishop to the United States to honor him for his peace efforts at our large annual RENEW Gala. Sr. Maureen Colleary, our zealous and extremely gifted staff member, became particularly friendly with the archbishop as a result of her outstanding work in the Archdiocese of Armagh. Her close relationship with him and his diocese continues to this day.

Literally hundreds, if not thousands, of positive comments came from RENEW participants in Ireland. There were two that I particularly enjoyed. One was from a man who said, "We could talk about our faith like we could talk about football." I knew how meaningful that comment would be, not only for my own love of football but especially from the extraordinary passion that the Irish bring to their football. To be sure, it is the main topic of conversation at any living room or pub. If RENEW helped people speak as freely about God as they did about their football, that was saying a lot.

The second comment that struck me was about how RENEW was filling the longing for God—that holy longing that is in each of us. Our human condition carries with it the weight of that emptiness that is part of our nature. Even in the best of times there is a certain amount of un-fulfillment. About life, Peggy Lee sang, "Is that all there is?" There must be more.

I can think of no finer kudo than that, by God's grace, RENEW in Ireland was helping fill that age-old longing for God.

Lithuania

Sometimes you wonder about the value of the time and energy spent in having information tables at major convocations of church leaders. Most times the value probably doesn't go beyond curious passers-by picking up brochures that are only going to get lost in their luggage.

One day, however, we struck gold at a large convocation in the Midwest. Sr. Igne Marijosius, M.V.S., who was of Lithuanian background, perused various exhibits, but RENEW was the one that caught her attention. She recognized it as a wonderful tool for post-Soviet Lithuania and immediately contacted our RENEW headquarters and asked, "Will you come to Lithuania and under what conditions?" She was thrilled to find out that we would travel there and speak with the bishops without any cost or obligation. In that fall of 1997, Cecilia and I were on our way to visit with bishops, priests, adult religious education leaders, and with anyone else who would lend us an ear.

Igne fully realized the daunting task that our Catholic faith in Lithuania faced at that time. She had spent her life divided between serving here in the United States and serving in her beloved Lithuania. She realized what more than fifty years of an atheistic, secular, Soviet society had done to the Church there.

For more than half a century children had been raised with no knowledge of God or exposure to faith. I was startled to hear that a church in the capital of Vilnius had been changed into an atheistic museum. On a systematic basis, children were brought from schools to visit the museum, which highlighted all the worst points in the history of the Church and ridiculed anyone who would be foolish enough to believe in a God.

RENEW would face the challenge of a Soviet psyche that was still quite prevalent. That meant you were to keep to yourself, look out for yourself, engage in no self-disclosure, sparingly trust anyone, and abhor making a commitment to any group. The Soviet system had relied on people reporting to the government any anti-Soviet sentiments held by people, even within one's own family. How would people open up and engage in RENEW groups given this background of zero trust?

Almost every family had a member who had been sent to Siberia. Igne's aunt, also a religious sister, shared about the eleven years she had spent in the most remote corner of Siberia where she worked as a slave crushing rocks. Her deportation from Lithuania was the result of her giving some medicine to a man whom the Soviets had labeled a dissident. The number of atrocities like that was immense.

But what appeared to be a problem situation was also a blessing. The Church had a chance to literally start over in a new and fresh way. We found the bishops of all seven dioceses to be very open and interested. Maureen and Cecilia followed up our visit with initial training and the launching of the RENEW process.

Continued oversight and involvement was maintained by two of the finest religious sisters to ever work with RENEW, Cheryl Erb and Maureen. Both are incredibly zealous and giving of themselves in their RENEW mission. Lithuanians were fortunate to have these outstanding women at their service. Maureen is in her sixteenth year with RENEW, showing no signs of let-up in traversing the world.

My personal most joyous Lithuanian experience was working with youth and young adults. While many young people in the United States were drifting from church, these young Lithuanians were excited about the faith they were discovering. Their parents never told them anything about God or faith. It was only natural for young people to take to something that was theirs, their own discovery. For many, the only way they knew about God and religion was from their grandparents, who told them of their religious experience many years ago. Now RENEW was giving young people the opportunity to play a leading role in the renewal of the Church. I can't exaggerate my own delight in working with Lithuanian college students who had incredible zeal and leadership qualities I had seldom seen.

Perhaps the greatest indication of RENEW's meaningfulness and success there is that a young woman, Vaida Spangeleviciute-Kneiziene, who worked with Sr. Igne in leading RENEW fifteen years ago, is still the coordinator of RENEW for Lithuania. God is blessing RENEW in our first East European experience.

CHAPTER 27

Africa

South Africa, Ghana, and Nigeria

T his priest of Newark found some of his greatest joys working in Africa. The three countries we will speak about are vastly different in many ways. We will start with South Africa, which could be a bit of a paradise and yet has been wracked with so much pain and poverty.

South Africa

The Republic of South Africa is the southernmost country on the continent. Until 1961, as part of the British Commonwealth, it was known as the Union of South Africa. Bounded on the east coast by the Atlantic Ocean and on the west by the Indian Ocean, it has incredibly beautiful terrain. During the 1980s and '90s, the people experienced great suffering under apartheid, the policy of strict racial segregation and political and economic discrimination against nonwhites. The RENEW processes have helped in the healing of people until the present day.

Durban

On a gorgeous sunny day in 1989, thirteen thousand Catholics in the Archdiocese of Durban packed themselves into an outdoor stadium to pray and celebrate a RENEW liturgy. How incredibly fortunate I was to be in Durban at that time. Not only was this the kickoff forRENEW in the Archdiocese of Durban, but it was also a celebration of Archbishop

Denis Hurley's fiftieth anniversary of ordination. It was a celebration quite unlike anything I had ever experienced. The Zulu people felt free at any given moment to run into the middle of the stadium, dance, and race back to their seats. A spirit of great freedom and joy prevailed.

And why not? The Zulu people, the Coloured community, and the more affluent whites all loved Archbishop Hurley, as few bishops have ever been loved. You can imagine how thrilled I was to be concelebrating on this occasion with the hero of my young priesthood and hear him proclaim to the entire stadium, "The high point of my forty-two years as bishop of Durban is RENEW." How could RENEW possibly miss the mark in Durban with leadership like that?

The impact of RENEW on the archdiocese can be exemplified by the Zulus in the Natal province. This province was very much in the news at that time, with great tension between two major political factions. Over and over it had been stated that devastating violence would have been much greater had it not been for RENEW. So great was the tension that initially people carried guns and bush knives when they were going to Mass. As RENEW progressed, the Kiss of Peace took on greater meaning as peace developed in the hearts of people.

We learned a lot in the Zulu community. Healing, not only among the Zulus but throughout Africa, was extremely important. Providing opportunities for healing experiences, RENEW would be critical, and Jesus' healing would be stressed in the eucharistic celebration, in the sacrament of reconciliation, and in many other creative ways.

We also learned that the strict timelines of western thinking did not always apply. If the topic was important, why not stay with it for a few weeks instead of marching on in some obligatory fashion to the next topic in the book?

It is no wonder that, on still another occasion, Archbishop Hurley called the time of RENEW "the honeymoon years of his priesthood." He was a man who early on fought against apartheid. RENEW brought together the black, Coloured, and white communities with respectful and uplifting spiritual sharing as nothing else had ever done. An example that stands in my mind would be Fr. Angelo, a robust Zulu priest who asked, "Can you imagine me, a proud Zulu man, sharing his deep concerns with two white women?"

Bishop Wilfred Fox Napier, O.S.F., who is now cardinal archbishop of Durban, shared a couple of interesting RENEW stories. By coincidence, he had an experience similar to that of Archbishop Gabriel G. Ganaka of the Diocese of Jos, which is described on page 311. While visiting a parish in Ireland, Bishop Napier was intrigued by the RENEW Prayer card and carried it with him, reflecting on it frequently. When he landed back home in South Africa the first two people he met at the airport were Sr. Donna Ciangio and me. Naturally, we were talking up RENEW with him, something he had known nothing about at that time. He found this meeting to be more than a coincidence.

On another occasion Bishop Napier was talking to a young Scottish woman who had just arrived in South Africa to serve as a nurse in a hospital that had great need. The bishop asked her what had prompted her to come to South Africa to give her life to this work. Her reply: "I was in a RENEW group in Scotland, which led me to reflect on the needs of people, and I decided to give of myself in this way to be of service to others."

Pretoria

RENEW thrived throughout South Africa in Johannesburg, Cape Town, Port Elizabeth, and many other dioceses. I particularly enjoyed what Fr. Charles Steen, O.F.M., did in his parish in the Diocese of Pretoria. He gathered the leaders of his small groups weekly to review the readings and the questions that would follow. He joined a small group, and that made all the difference in the world for him.

Upon his arrival at the parish, Charles found that only one family actually attended Mass. With the help of RENEW, his parish increased Mass attendance to sixty families. You can understand why Charles was a RENEW enthusiast.

Oudtshoorn

I could recount wonderful RENEW progress I heard about in large dioceses. These dioceses had excellent resources to help them achieve their goals.

Perhaps an overall picture of RENEW's impact can best be caught by recounting the experience of a very small diocese, for example, Oudsthoorn. Upon completion of the five seasons of RENEW, Oudsthoorn reported the following:

- RENEW had the greatest response of any program or process in the history of the diocese. People were now much more eager to work together in unity.
- Parishes were much more concerned about the less privileged. Street children were being cared for.
- Liturgies were more carefully prepared and more appreciated and enjoyed.
- The laity was far more involved than before.
- Sharing faith through Scripture had become a way of life.
- Many lapsed Catholics returned, and new members were received into the Church.

An example of RENEW's influence on attitudes in Oudsthoorn can be seen in the action of three racially separated churches: one for whites, one for black Africans, and one for the Coloured. On their own initiative through RENEW, the parishioners asked to form one single parish council and, thereafter, worked together in close harmony.

Port Elizabeth

Two parishioners captured how the RENEW experience in the Diocese of Port Elizabeth touched them personally and helped to change their lives. One parishioner said, "RENEW has transformed our parish from a skeptical, sometimes pessimistic, outlook to the realities of a modern, church-going, and God-fearing community. Wow, it has opened our eyes. We have had witnesses speak about their addictions and secular lifestyles, about being transfigured by the presence of God, and about his works being seen by the way he touches us and our neighbors through RENEW."

Another parishioner stated, "On a personal note, I have been spiritually strengthened. I can feel it culminating into an immanent intervention. God is real, his people are real, their real life situations display the power of an eternal force in action. It is awesome; it is breathtaking.

RENEW has been beneficial to us in so many ways and on so many levels. The true value of these past few months cannot be quantified. But the freedom that it has brought is something that will never depart from us!"

My particular interest in Port Elizabeth is related to the fact that my great-nephew, Jim McKeown, whom I mentioned earlier, is currently working for the diocese. He is there at an interesting time when Port Elizabeth is once again doing a RENEW process. Jim gave up his job in New York and the woman everyone thought he would marry. He decided he wanted to give his life to the poorest people in the world. He is involved with RENEW and is also tutoring and working with young students in black townships, helping them to gain entrance into the university—the one way for these young adults to escape the terrible poverty of their lives and to experience a more humane lifestyle in the larger community.

In this area, students have no chance to succeed unless they have a college background. Without a degree, they would be consigned to utter poverty. After starting with a small group of students, Jim now has three hundred come each day from 2:30 to 8 p.m. to be tutored and to learn social skills. He has a staff of twenty people, including one superstar who gave up a lucrative job to join Jim's team. Others are looking at this experience and, hopefully, will try to replicate it throughout the country. It makes us all remember how one person can make a difference. I pray daily for him and his efforts, and I ask you to join me in my prayers.

Anglican Dioceses

Another unique and interesting RENEW experience in South Africa was working with at least thirteen Anglican dioceses, including Johannesburg, George, and Cape Town. At the time, a number of their parishes were struggling with the problem of church attendance. An Anglican version of RENEW proved to be manna from heaven.

Ghana

Good news travels between continents

A married couple in the United States enjoyed RENEW very much and found it so helpful to their spiritual lives that they shared their RENEW story with their son, Fr. Mark Schramm, S.V.D. Mark, serving in Ghana at the time, was looking for help in the formation of his lay people. He also realized that the bishops of Ghana were looking for a way to respond to the African pastoral document *Ecclesia in Africa*. Could RENEW possibly be the answer?

Mark connected with Fr. Jack Farley, S.V.D., on our RENEW team, which led to a lengthy period of communication regarding planning and strategizing on how to bring RENEW to Ghana. Their efforts were well rewarded. On July 10, 1996, RENEW was presented with the finest opportunity we had ever had.

An hour and a half had been set aside at the annual meeting of the Ghanaian bishops to hear about RENEW. This was truly unique and set a tone supporting RENEW from the communion of bishops throughout the whole country. Jack and Cecilia gave that presentation, responded to questions, and were successful indeed.

The bishops agreed that the RENEW team could come and make a presentation to the entire presbyterates in all fifteen dioceses in Ghana. Amazingly, fourteen of those fifteen dioceses decided to move ahead in a united effort. This proved to be a very special and peak experience for RENEW. With such a massive effort blanketing the country, it was no surprise that there would be many opportunities for RENEW's model of connecting faith to life to become concrete reality.

Outreach Saves Family

One story helps to paint that picture. A family in a rural village had lost its father. Life was very difficult. The family was close to despair and decided to return to traditional religion because they had lost faith in Catholicism. They questioned, "If this is life, who can believe in God?" At that point, a RENEW small community entered the picture. The members reached out to help the family in all their basic needs and in their grieving process. The family not only remained in their Catholic faith but became stronger and more zealous than ever before. Multiply that type of outreach and action throughout all of Ghana.

A Cherished Bottle of Water

I was always touched by a story shared by Sr. Cheryl Erb, who worked closely with Jack throughout RENEW in Ghana. Always a cheerful and positive presence, she exuded great energy in her dynamic presentations. After a series of workshops, she was making a long car journey on an exceptionally hot and humid day. Throughout the trip she cherished the bottle of water that she clung to as her lifeline. During a break in the drive, a small impoverished boy caught Cheryl's eye. His eye was on the bottle she was carrying. What was she to do? She needed that water desperately, but obviously this frail boy needed it even more. Her heart could allow no other answer but to give her bottle to him. She was waiting to see him gobble that water down in record time. Then came a shock. The boy didn't even take a sip. Instead he brought it over to his mother and little sister sitting in the background. They needed that water even more than he did.

That little boy had every reason to be totally self-consumed with his own need, but stories like this remind us of how God's care and intimate love never cease to touch hearts and help us to be bigger persons. In so many ways, the people we meet evangelize us by their faith and caring.

Scripture: A Source of Life to Build Community

Bishop Thomas Mensah of Obuasi was so pleased with what RENEW had done for his newly formed young diocese that he commented,

> First and foremost, RENEW has blessed my diocese with a spirit-filled, competent, and committed Diocesan RENEW Team which has travelled the length and breadth of the diocese to form Parish RENEW Teams and small group leaders. I can now count on a team of dedicated priests and lay people for the building of vibrant faith communities in my young diocese.
>
> As a result of RENEW, faith-sharing has become an integral part of life in most parishes. Societies and groups gather around the Word of God in sacred Scripture not

merely as a book to be read but as a source of life for the building of community.

The same united leadership that launched RENEW in Ghana saw its way right through to the conclusion. RENEW had led so many people to discover and develop a deep love for the Scriptures that the bishops realized the momentum could not be lost. They formed an Apostolic Biblical Movement that would work through small Christian communities in a massive process to reach out to all Ghana and have people learn more about the Word of God that was so enlivening their spirits. The bishops had enthusiastically put their seal of approval on RENEW until the very end.

Fr. Jack Farley, prior to his ordination in 1960, had requested an assignment in Ghana. Some thirty years later, in the 1990s, RENEW helped him realize his dream. I was very moved when Jack shared with me that his time with RENEW had truly been the highlight of his priesthood.

Working with the faith-filled people of Ghana surely helped him come to that conviction. His time in Ghana had been spent with people who lived by the motto, "God is good, all the time."

Nigeria

Fr. Peter Otubusin, who brought RENEW to Nigeria and became its national leader, represents much of the spirit of the Church in Nigeria that we experienced in the 1990s. He is a tall man with flowing white robes, boundless energy, and rock-like faith. Peter symbolizes a young Church, less than one hundred fifty years old, with all the characteristics of youth: enthusiasm, vibrancy, dynamism, and hopefulness.

Where else in the world will you find huge lorries flying up and down the highways and byways with large signs proclaiming "Praise God," with pictures of the Blessed Mother along with every imaginable spiritual saying and symbol? Nigerian Catholics are not bashful about proclaiming their faith. Everything seems large. Where else will you find a parish with three thousand five hundred Catholics in RENEW small groups?

A most common saying in Nigeria is "We thank God." When good things happen, or even when fortune isn't kind, people say, "We thank God." God's will is their will.

A Country of Contrasts

In the 1990s, Nigeria was also a country of great contrasts. The easiest way for a priest to get a good laugh from his congregation in his Sunday homily was to mention government corruption. The large congregations would erupt in prolonged laughter.

Corruption began at the airport when you first landed. You would be cycled through several posts where bribes were subtly and not so subtly solicited. The wild scene at the airport in Lagos gained a world-wide reputation. The mother of one of our staff people did not want her daughter flying in and out of the Lagos airport. Why not? She had seen a sign in a small West Virginia airport warning people not to fly into Lagos. She assumed it must be dangerous, or at the least, very different.

Kano

Once, while disembarking at the airport in Kano in northern Nigeria, I was being put to the regular test. Finally, I said, "I've been here many times and know how the game is played." Immediately, with a wave of the hand, I was allowed to freely proceed. We enjoyed not giving in to that game.

At the same time, RENEW thrived in few places worldwide as it did in the Diocese of Kano. I remember visiting a parish one evening where one thousand people were engaged in RENEW small groups. I will never forget the scene: a large church with an extremely spacious court-yard surrounding it; small circles of people in their RENEW groups filled every inch of that area. The spirituality and zeal of these RENEW participants had been strengthened by substantial daily prayer commit-ments along with frequent fasting from 6 a.m. to 6 p.m.

One reason the parishes were so large was that Muslims controlling the north of Nigeria had made it illegal for Catholics to buy any new land. As a result, existing parishes expanded until they were bursting at the seams.

The tensions in the north between Muslims and Catholics were very real. Fr. Joe Bagobiri, a native Nigerian, was the diocesan director of RENEW for Kano. He had one thousand five hundred people involved in RENEW small groups in his parish. He was a leader and a man of courage. When a Christian, accused of proselytizing, was beheaded by the Muslims, it was Joe who led a protest throughout the city. He became our first true RENEW bishop when he was made the bishop of the newly created Diocese of Kafanchan. Naturally, one of his first moves was to initiate RENEW.

Considering the strong Muslim control in the north of Nigeria, it's amazing how RENEW flourished in that area. In contrast, the southeast area of Nigeria is populated by the Ibo people who are eighty-five percent Catholic. While they sit on top of incredible oil resources, the people are unfortunately poor. The money flows out, along with the oil. It is this part of the country, known as Biafra, that unsuccessfully fought for its independence from July 6, 1967 to January 15, 1970.

Southwest and the Yurizan Province

The main thrust of RENEW activity was in the heavily populated southwest area of the country and the Yurizan Province, under the leadership of Archbishop Felix Alaba Job and Fr. Peter Otubusin. It was Archbishop Job who had organized our tour of the province where we visited various bishops and spoke to their presbyterates. Once again, having strong leadership support was invaluable.

One day I asked Peter how he could explain the explosive growth of Christianity taking place in Nigeria. He said the gods of the past were very stern and punishing. "The Christian God," he said, "is loving and caring." Pope John Paul II emphasized this when he said that the message the people in our time need to hear was of the love and mercy of God—a powerful message for us to keep in mind.

Our timing was also fortuitous. Catholicism was blossoming as never before. A Dominican parish in the city of Lagos had six hundred people enter the Church at the Easter Vigil. Imagine an Easter Vigil with six hundred people being baptized as new Catholics. Americans might be happy with the idea but could hardly be pictured sitting through the baptisms along with all the other ceremonies. In Nigeria, that would be no problem. A festive Mass, lasting two or three hours, would be the norm. Everybody dressed in their finest and most colorful outfits. The people were joyous throughout the entire Mass.

Small Communities Follow RCIA

Another Easter Vigil example took place at Sacred Heart Parish in Benin City, which had two hundred ninety-six newly baptized. RENEW brought to this beautiful faith explosion an important pastoral approach. We encouraged all parishes to make as an ordinary part of their RCIA process the expectation that every newly baptized person automatically become part of a small faith-sharing community. What a difference this could make. How could one possibly track how well two hundred ninety-six or six hundred new converts were successfully incorporated into the parish community? As a member of a small community, the newly baptized would be well accounted for. Their spiritual growth would continue to flourish. People would not be lost when dropped into their larger parish communities.

How important that practice would be for our parishes in the United States. Studies show that all too many people, after their beautiful RCIA process, get lost to the Church within a few years. It's hard to continue to experience that same sense of community and nourishment that led them to their baptismal preparation. Perhaps it is easier for a new and youthful Church community in Africa to pick up on pastoral ideas such as this, but it is certainly critically important for us to be open to new approaches in our pastoral care of parishioners.

Consider the many ways in which RENEW was coming to Nigeria. Sr. Cecilia and Fr. Dominic Fucille of our international RENEW team met Archbishop Gabriel G. Ganaka of the Archdiocese of Jos in the Lagos airport. He showed them a prayer card that he had found in a church pew in Ireland. The prayer had fascinated him, and he kept it in his breviary and said the prayer daily. It was the RENEW Prayer.

Would you believe that the next day their paths crossed once again? This time Cecilia and Dominic lost no time in excitedly sharing the good news of RENEW. Right on the spot, Archbishop Ganaka invited them to initiate RENEW in his Archdiocese of Jos.

A Priest of Peace

I'll never forget an auto accident that tied up traffic for a large area. In the midst of it all Peter Otubusin jumped out of his van and ran up to the two cars at the center of the accident. The occupants were fighting mightily. Above the crowd Peter kept shouting, "Peace, peace to everyone. Everyone be peaceful and go back to your cars." Peter has the kind of presence that prompted everyone to do just as he asked, and peace was restored.

Peter was, indeed, a man of peace. One day he spoke about how well Christians and Muslims got along as neighbors in everyday life. However, he emphasized the strong influence of many Muslim leaders that was both antagonistic and hostile.

You can imagine how taken aback I was when Peter said he could not see how this volatile situation would not eventually lead to open hostility and even war between Muslims and Christians.

Along with Peter and people of good intention from all faiths, we pray that this will never come to be. Jesus, Prince of Peace, pray for us.

CHAPTER 28

Asia

Philippines and India

That our RENEW experience in the Philippines was as pleasurable as it was should come as no surprise. There have been such close ties between the Philippines and the United States over the years that it is natural to be very comfortable there, never feeling far from home. This is especially true because of the very welcoming, friendly, and gentle nature of the Filipino people, which we experienced in seven dioceses from 1991 to 1998.

Philippines

Success Depends upon Leadership

Our Philippine experience bore out two pastoral principles that we've emphasized over the years. Both are about the importance of leadership. The degree to which a bishop not only makes RENEW available to the people but actually believes deeply and takes strong leadership in promoting this spiritual process obviously makes all the difference. The same can be said for the clergy. When the pastor decides not to become involved in RENEW, the people, who had little to say about the matter, are frequently left discouraged and disappointed. For those given the opportunity to participate, great enthusiasm and edifying spiritual growth are inevitable.

Malolos and San Fernando Pampanga

As expected, the Diocese of Malolos had an extremely strong RENEW experience. After all, it was Bishop Cirilo Almario who had enthusiastically brought RENEW to the Philippines. He also had the insight to begin the RENEW process with an emphasis on the spiritual and, in particular, the formation of his priests. Donna and I had the pleasure of conducting reflection days for the priests of Malolos centered on the themes of conversion and community. This helped the priests more clearly understand the importance of their role in RENEW and undertake the process with greater zeal.

The extraordinary impact of RENEW in Malolos can be seen in four hundred ninety-nine small groups that were fully active in Season I and twice that number throughout Season II. As the small groups kept growing, RENEW truly became the focal point of spiritual activity for this wonderful diocese.

San Fernando Pampanga also had an excellent RENEW experience, albeit with a few bumps on the journey. People coming to initial RENEW trainings were stymied by the volcanic eruption of Mount Pinatubo, which caused many to turn back home. So powerful was the volcano that it resulted in zero visibility. Bishop Paciano Aniceto wondered whether RENEW should be put on hold because of the great amount of destruction. Mud had covered some places so completely that only a house number on a pole indicated a residence that lay beneath. The rice fields had been wiped out one week before harvest.

However, the priests of the diocese encouraged the bishop to proceed despite all their difficulties. And strongly move ahead they did. One of the most striking impacts of RENEW in San Fernando was the frequent reports of greatly improved homilies. Aside from the usual results of small communities, it was also reported that the number of marriages increased within the local Church.

A Fish Lover's Delight

RENEW next moved south to the islands in the central Philippines. But before we speak about this, I want to share one pleasant recollection from Malolos. We visited a seafood restaurant, the likes of which I had never seen before and have not seen since. You move about a huge fish market with every conceivable kind of fish, make your choice, then enter the dining area where the fish you selected is elegantly served.

Travel is a very helpful learning experience. If you believe that we Americans are ahead on almost everything, you come to find a delightful experience, like that restaurant, which widens your view of human imagination and enterprise.

Jaro and San Jose de Antique

Life in the Philippines begins bright and early in the morning. Our flight from Luzon to Iloilo in the central Philippines took off at 4 a.m. Any discomfort was more than made up for by Archbishop Alberto Piamonte in Jaro. He had a huge archdiocese involved in many activities, coupled with an overriding pastoral plan for the renewal of the diocese. Fortunately, the archbishop saw that RENEW small communities fit favorably into the existing plan. His vision turned out to be valid as the RENEW small communities achieved great popularity and were the highlight of an ensuing successful experience in Jaro.

From Jaro, Kathy Warren and I traveled to San Jose de Antique. It was a spectacular, three-hour ride along the coast. Even more spectacular was what we found in San Jose de Antique. Bishop Raul Martirez's dynamic leadership was immediately evident. He caught the spirit of RENEW hook, line, and sinker and took to it like a fish takes to water.

Once again our basic principle proved to be true. His strong leadership had a great effect upon the priests of the diocese and resulted in a very special RENEW experience. RENEW was made the primary focus there, and the leaders managed to bring RENEW to every nook and corner of the diocese, even to the most remote barrios. The poor and neglected were beautifully served in San Jose Antique through the instrumentality of RENEW.

RENEW's results in Antique were off the charts with regard to small-group involvement, numbers of confessions heard, and people returning to church. One of the most resistant pastors to RENEW became converted to the process: "This was even better than our fiesta! At our fiesta we were filled to capacity but two-thirds were out-of-towners.

Look! With RENEW, we have standing room only at our church, and they're all from our parish."

Bacolod and Gumaca

The island of Negros was our next stop. I had met Fr. Edgar Saguinsen at a conference at Notre Dame, and he had quickly taken to the notion of RENEW. It was not surprising that Edgar became the RENEW director of the Diocese of Bacolod. He did a good job of fine-tuning and adapting the RENEW small-community materials and bringing his own particular pastoral flavor to the RENEW experience.

But the task in Bacolod was far from easy. The diocese was horribly divided with half the priests in opposition to their new bishop, Bishop Camilo Gregorio. Unfortunately, it broke down to this fact: If you were for Bishop Gregorio you were for RENEW; if you were opposed to him you couldn't touch anything he was promoting. Despite RENEW being caught in the crossfire, there was great consolation in seeing how many people were able to participate in the RENEW small groups and have a rewarding small-group experience.

Fortunately, RENEW fared more favorably in Gumaca, under the pastoral guidance of Jack Farley and Kathy who oversaw RENEW servicing to the Philippines in the last half of the '90s. Gumaca had a spectacular launch at the cathedral. This involved parishes from all parts of the diocese including the plains, the islands, and the mountains. It's not to say that Gumaca didn't have its own difficulties, including the devastating typhoon Angela. Nevertheless, the overall RENEW experience was quite positive. The exceptional culmination ceremony involving three thousand people testified to this.

Much of Gumaca's success could be attributed to the leadership of Bishop Emilio Z. Marquez, which brings us back to a principle stated at the beginning.

Particularly frustrating was the number of parish priests who did not choose to become involved in the RENEW process in their dioceses. This, in effect, meant their parishioners were not going to be involved either. Certainly various pastoral reasons could be given for non-involvement, but the tremendous success of those who were involved had to raise serious questions for those who let a good opportunity go by. Pastoral zeal and leadership, like all renewal, is an ongoing issue calling for serious attention.

Feedback from our experience in the Philippines included a moving reflection. One man wrote, "Before RENEW I was a nobody. I was worth nothing—to anyone, to myself. Then I joined a RENEW small group. Through the scripture sharing I came to realize that I did matter—to God, even to others, and to myself. I *do* have worth and am important." If God's grace effected this conversion in even one person the entire Filipino effort was well worth it.

India

In 1992, RENEW struck gold in India with regard to leadership. The constant theme of our need for good pastoral leadership in the Church was more than satisfied with our work in the subcontinent.

Archbishop Marianus Arokiasamy of Madurai and Fr. Henrick Jose were an outstanding combination. Not only did Archbishop Arokiasamy give us the initial invitation to work in Tamil Nadu, but he also carried great influence with other bishops, providing strong pastoral guidance and support for RENEW in the entire province.

Henrick is a priest with rare pastoral qualities. I often felt that if I weren't director of the worldwide RENEW effort, Henrick could move in and carry on admirably.

Henrick recalls, "I could never imagine that within a short span of years our Church could witness such beautiful scenes: people longing to pray, thirsting for and being quenched by the word, celebrating lively liturgies, increasing their sense of belonging, and assuming responsibility for parish life and activities."

With the combination of this kind of leadership you know that RENEW prospered in India. RENEW helped small communities become the priority for all of southeast India. By the end of our RENEW work in the year 2000, Tamil Nadu was well prepared to join with all the dioceses of India in a common agreement to give small Christian communities the highest pastoral priority.

Rooftop Sharing

One of my fondest personal memories of India in the 1990s was an evening spent in a RENEW small-group meeting on a rooftop. The sharing throughout the meeting was very alive and vibrant. Naturally, the meeting was in the local language and dialect. My impressions were based on the amazing energy coming from the group. Walking home afterwards with the priest who had accompanied me, I asked him if the people were all from the same caste or if it was truly a mixed group. He assured me that it was a mixed group involving all different levels of society. The most wonderful feeling came over me as I realized and actually experienced the miracle of people from the poorest and richest castes all sharing faith in mutual respect and love. I thank God for the grace of that evening.

Flowers and Incense

Picture this scene. You are visiting a Catholic school where the students are engaged in the RENEW experience. A large auditorium is filled with many small circles of little children sitting on the floor with legs folded, encircling flowers and incense. With great enthusiasm the children are sharing their faith. It is truly a scene from another world and, believe me, you could not help but be emotionally moved.

Renewal in India

Another scene to remember: The pleasant night air of India is filled with the aroma of incense. A group of men and women are sitting in the living room of a small home. They face an open Bible in the center adorned with flower garlands.

A Hindu woman stands in the back doorway looking on with great curiosity and longing. The animation, friendship, and beautiful sense of belonging that she beholds make the gathering very appealing. With a wave of my hand, I welcome her to join us. She enters, smiling broadly. She has discovered the wonderful gift of a loving and caring community.

Reconciling Families, Sects, and Castes

Sr. Cecilia King vividly recalls another incident: "I was observing a series of RENEW small-group meetings because I wanted to find out if

RENEW could truly reach the poorest of people and if it could work in such a vastly different culture from our own. We were in a farming area. An aged woman, bowed down from working the fields, was sharing her experience:

"Sometimes, after many hours in the fields, my back hurts so badly that I feel like giving up on life. Then I think of God's love for me and of some of the wonderful thoughts and ideas shared at the RENEW meetings and, all of a sudden, I feel better and I go on with new hope and strength."

It was a beautiful moment for Cecilia, which showed her that the hearts of the people were being filled with new life.

Life Conversions

Priests, too, were affected. One priest, when he saw how the simple folk of his parish were so excited, decided to do something special himself. Now he spends one additional hour in prayer each day because he feels that, most of all, the people want a prayerful priest.

Jamil, a handsome twenty-eight-year-old man from Ooty, Tamil Nadu, gave public witness: "I was a villain, I was a drunkard, I did very bad things, and I didn't go to church. When RENEW came to our parish, I heard people talking about it, so I decided to go. I heard the Lord's call to me personally. Now, I have given up my bad ways and I want to share the Good News of Jesus Christ. I am a new person and a happy man, and I must do something special for Christ."

Fr. Matthew, a young priest in Ooty, Tamil Nadu, shared with his brother priests: "I strongly spoke against RENEW. I opposed it with full vigor. I considered it an 'import.' I felt we had sufficient programs of our own. I can't fully explain my conversion other than observing the excitement and interest of the laity. I now fully endorse RENEW and share faith with my people. It's the best thing I've ever done. My parish has become alive and I'm closer to my people."

Fr. G. Lourduraj, a priest of thirty-two years, told us how fifteen Hindu people in his parish converted to Catholicism because of RENEW. Many other Hindus were in the RENEW small groups and were thoroughly fascinated.

One man, who literally wanted to kill his son for marrying a woman of a lower caste, had a conversion of heart and embraced the young couple because of the prayers and efforts of his RENEW small group.

Favor Leads to Change of Lifestyle

Though untrained in public speaking, a courageous woman took the microphone at the cathedral parish in Madras. She said she spoke in the name of a few women who met regularly for faith-sharing in her poor hut.

Once, a group of young men, with nothing better to do, derided them with a steady stream of abusive language. The woman, as leader of the group, asked one of the young men for a favor. Would he come inside to read the Scriptures aloud for them because none of the women could read?

Caught off guard, he sheepishly entered her home. After reading he was too embarrassed to leave. Eventually his buddies peeked in to see what was keeping him. The following week, to everyone's surprise, the young man came on his own, bringing some friends with him.

The women were apprehensive. Were the young men on hand to cause more trouble? Their fears were put to rest. The young man said he had been unsettled a week earlier when he realized that the same tongue used to shout filthy language had also pronounced the words of Scripture.

He confronted his friends with this. Together they decided to clean up their language, read the Scriptures for the unlettered women, and join them in faith sharing.

Family Feud Ends with Forgiveness

Arokiaraj and his family were at enmity with his uncle and his uncle's family for over twenty-five years. They never spoke or associated in any way. Then RENEW came along and Arokiaraj showed interest in leadership training for faith-sharing groups. After a short experience of faith sharing, he realized he had to be authentic and give good example to others, so he took the giant leap of forgiveness. He and his family became reconciled with his uncle and the family. Now both families are promoting the RENEW process in their parishes.

Healing Prayer Leads to Sight

Alexander, forty-three, was paralyzed due to a brain tumor. He had lost his sight completely. All specialized medical treatments and hospitalizations proved futile. At this point Alexander's wife, Maria, implored the RENEW faith-sharing groups to pray for Alexander. The family did likewise. The parish RENEW team and the faith-sharing group visited Alexander each week and prayed with him and his family. To everyone's astonishment, Alexander began to improve gradually and after a few months he regained his sight. Now he moves around witnessing to this miracle while he and his family praise the Lord.

A Child Shall Lead Them

Arumi and his son, Arul, were estranged because the son had disgraced his father by a lack of responsibility that resulted in the loss of his job. In spite of repeated apologies, the father refused to forgive his son, and so they were separated for years. Arumi's grandson, Michael, ten, who participated in a faith-sharing group at school, was touched by the story of the Prodigal Son. He came home from school and confronted Grandpa Arumi. Arumi was converted by his grandchild. He met with his son, Arul, and publicly asked forgiveness. And now the father gives witness that if it were not for the angelic intervention of his grandchild, he wouldn't be now experiencing the peace and joy of unity in his family.

Personal Highlights

When I was a teenager I asked Dad which Thomas I was named after— Thomas Aquinas or Thomas the Apostle. My father was strong in his faith but had never had the benefits of Catholic education. I had hoped he would say the great theologian Thomas Aquinas, but he was not familiar with Aquinas. Dad quickly said, "You're named after Thomas the Apostle."

One of the highlights of my time in India was to be able to visit the cave outside of Madras where many believe the Apostle Thomas landed when he evangelized India. While the success of his mission is legendary, it also required time spent living in a cave where he could avoid persecution. To be in Thomas's cave, united with him in spirit, gave me the feeling that, by God's grace, RENEW was playing a significant part of Catholicism's brilliant history in India. RENEW was carrying on Thomas's work being God's instrument in bringing new life and vitality to the local faith community.

CHAPTER 29

Young Adults Searching

Airports and airplanes are interesting places in many ways. People who do not know one another find a certain ease at communicating, especially as a plane nears its destination. People feel some kind of bond and start opening up. It is amazing how many young people, recognizing me as a priest on a plane or in an airport, are willing to open up and share, have an interest in God, and want to talk about spiritual things. It is particularly interesting when I contrast this to the reaction from adults, but young people are more readily drawn into discussion. Maybe it is because they haven't been as close to the Church as some other age groups.

A Resolution

On a late Friday-night direct flight from San Francisco to Newark, I sat in an aisle seat. A young woman occupied the window seat, and there was an open seat between us. She was obviously enjoying the movie that was playing, laughing wholeheartedly. She seemed to be a wholesome young woman. We started to chat and I learned she was a Catholic and pregnant with her first child. However, she hadn't been to Mass since her first Communion. Her questions were, "What should I do with the baby? What religion would the baby be?" Her mother was a Buddhist, and wouldn't be encouraging her to return to the Catholic Church.

So we talked about the Catholic Church and how beautiful it is to raise a child within the Catholic community with all kinds of formation and a good and meaningful way of life. I shared with her the value of the sacraments and the richness the Church has to offer. She became very attentive. When we deplaned into a relatively empty Newark airport, she spotted her husband at a distance and shouted to him in a voice that resonated throughout the terminal, "We're going to church!"

Middle-Seat Advantages

On a flight into Atlanta, a national hub for connecting flights, I happened to sit in the dreaded middle seat. On one side was a young man, on the other a young woman. I began talking with the man, a Russian Jew, who was engrossed in a book about Jesus. "This Jesus is a very interesting fellow," he commented. So, we went on to talk about Jesus. It struck me: he's a searcher and is looking for more.

Then the young woman told me she was raised Catholic but was away from the Church. She used to be quite active in the parish, go to Mass, and pray the rosary regularly. Eventually she fell asleep, leaning against the window. As we were about to land she woke up, looked at her watch, realized we're going to be landing late, and said, "Oh my God, I'm going to miss my connecting flight." I replied, "Please, don't worry. We're landing in Atlanta. Your connecting flight will be late too."

After we deplaned I started heading down an escalator toward my connecting flight. Coming up the escalator right next to me was the same young woman. She admitted, "You're right, I'm going to make my connecting flight." Then she added, "And I'm going to start saying the rosary again."

Three Young Waitresses

The night before my RENEW presentation at a beautiful lake setting in the Diocese of Boise, Idaho, there was a festive dinner for all the priests of the diocese along with the deacons and their wives. Awards were to be given to priests ordained for forty and fifty years. At one point I stepped out to take a break. Three young waitresses caught me in the lobby and wanted to talk. We sat down and had a great chat. They had all kinds of questions about God, faith, and religion. At least one of the three wasn't

Catholic. Eventually, they invited the woman behind the desk to come over and join them. That conversation was the highlight of my trip.

The thought struck me how easy it would be for the local pastor to open his door every Sunday evening for young people to come and chat about God in an informal and relaxed way. The previous evening was so very real that I was convinced it could easily be replicated over and again. The interest and the curiosity are so very tangible.

The Missionary

I was in O'Hare International Airport in Chicago late at night, and my flight had been delayed. I also missed my connecting flight to Cedar Rapids, Iowa. I was sitting in an isolated area when I saw a young couple walking down the corridor. Even when they were at a distance I said to myself, "They are going to come over and talk to me." Within a few minutes they did come and started talking. The young man had received his theology degree from a non-denominational seminary and was preparing to go out and be a missionary for Christ. However, he had been raised Catholic and now was living in the diocese where I was to meet with the priests the next day. He was very curious about where the Catholic Church stood on numerous issues. Obviously he had been quite disconnected from the Church. When I boarded the somewhat empty plane this young couple also boarded. While our seats were far apart, that young man came up and sat next to me for the entire flight, because he wanted to hear more about the Catholic Church and what the Church was teaching.

The next day, when I was talking with the priests in Iowa, I wanted to share how young people are hungering for God. I recounted the conversation I had on the plane with a young man from their diocese who was heading out to be a missionary for another denomination. How badly we need to connect with the aspirations of our young people!

A Business Woman Decides

I was on a plane heading to make a presentation to a diocesan presbyterate, hoping the bishop would make a commitment to RENEW. On the plane a young business woman in her early thirties sat next to me. She learned that I was a priest, and we began to talk. She told me she and her husband were in a parish the Diocese of Trenton in New Jersey. I started telling her about *RENEW 2000*, which was soon coming to her diocese. I shared what happens in this process and how people meet in small groups, connecting faith with their daily lives. She started showing some interest but got up to go to the rest room. When she returned she had made her decision: "My husband and I are going to join one of the RENEW small groups."

A Drifter's Gratitude

In another instance, sitting next to me was a professional woman, in her late thirties, who was getting married in a few months. A former Catholic, she had drifted from the faith and wasn't really practicing anything. However, her mother was a daily communicant. This woman and I talked about the Church, its value, and the sacraments. I reminded her of some of the things that might have had meaning to her when she was practicing her faith.

I wrote down her address and later mailed her information about our work in RENEW and our ministry. Months later I received a beautiful thank you from this young woman. Who knows what happened to her? Nevertheless, it was an opportunity for someone who had drifted from the Church to easily engage in conversation and ask questions. She probably would never have knocked on a rectory door and asked to speak to a priest.

Attentive Irish Attendant

An airplane attendant in her mid-thirties sat on the armrest across the aisle from me, partially blocking the aisle for almost the entire trip. She was still searching and had been away from the Church. We talked about faith and religion and the values the Catholic Church has to offer. She figured that after our encounter perhaps she was on her way back to Catholicism. I left my business card with her. A few months later I was surprised by a Valentine card from her. Somehow that conversation had obviously affected her and stayed with her.

Thirst and Curiosity

One day, Michael Brough and I were flying on one of our RENEW missions. I told him about the number of young people who have seen my collar and have come to talk to me about religion. I may have been wrong about this, but he seemed a bit skeptical. Maybe the old man is having dreams about how many young people are coming to talk to him.

We were at a stopover sitting at a small round table in one of those large eating areas. Michael said he was going to get a soda. When he returned a couple of minutes later, his seat was taken. A young woman, twenty-five years old, was sitting there talking with me about God. Enough said.

Mixing with people on the road has convinced me that there's a tremendous spiritual hunger and a great curiosity in young people. It convinces me how every opportunity should be taken to make it easy for them to share and learn more about our Catholic faith. It's important to let God's grace work in that kind of sharing and conversation. This is also a good case for our efforts in promoting *Theology on Tap*. It also points out the value of wearing the collar. It makes it easy for people to connect, to share, and to search for God who gives meaning to our lives and meets the longings of our hearts.

The coming of the new millennium created a great amount of talk about new beginnings, new energy, and new and stronger spirituality. Our team took that call seriously. We wanted to enter this new century with a greater love than ever for the Lord, to be filled with a desire to help as many people as possible to experience God's incredible love and to become witnesses of his love to a needy world.

PART IV

CHAPTER 30

In God's Hands

The high hopes that many people brought into the new millennium began to fade quickly. Catastrophic events and disillusionment became the norm.

The dreams of three-quarters of a century ago that there would be no more war are unfulfilled. Nation after nation has entered into war in hopes of freeing previously enslaved people. In too many instances, however, new freedoms have been dashed by leadership that represented the "same old same old" and sometimes maybe even worse. Instability and confusion were hallmarks of this new chapter in history.

A good part of this instability was due to failures and even collapses in the field of economics. Even ancient nations like Greece were at the brink of bankruptcy. In our own country the number of jobless reached the highest levels in decades. No level of society was free from the fear of financial ruin.

Secularism became the new religion in much of the western world, leaving individuals to be their own ultimate judges. While at first attractive, in reality this has led to lives without direction or security. It is little wonder that atheism is growing so rapidly. In simple terms, the judgments of the individual ego take on primary importance. The results are a very disappointing nihilism that leads to despair.

While this picture may seem pessimistic, it is true. Fortunately, every age also brings new hope with its own inventions, medical breakthroughs, and great works in the field of art.

Many good and hopeful things also have been happening at RENEW International. God's providential care has been clearly seen in the people who have come into our lives, become part of our team and, in some instances, taken on important leadership positions.

RENEW Leadership

I realized that my usual high level of energy was ebbing. We needed new leadership to carry us into the future. God blessed us with younger creative talent.

Michael Brough

One such person was Michael Brough. The hiring of Michael in 1998 came like a bolt of light out of the blue. Sr. Alice pointed out one particularly interesting response to an Internet ad. I called Michael on a Thursday, and he came in for an interview on Friday. We discovered that Michael was a young Scotsman who had recently arrived in the United States with his young American bride and infant daughter.

Brilliant in his interview, Michael agreed to stay and participate in a brainstorming meeting, and he was an impressive contributor. Invited to join a number of us for dinner, he proved to be enjoyable company. Meanwhile, his poor wife must have wondered if Michael was lost in his new land.

Michael gave the name of Bishop Vincent Logan of Dunkeld, Scotland, as a reference. When I called Bishop Logan the next day, his immediate response was, "Don't let him get away." Without delay, I called Michael and asked him to please join us on Monday morning. Michael has it all: tremendous work ethic, great faith and zeal, high intelligence, and it showed in all his work—presentations, writing, and contacts with bishops and leaders.

Like cream that rises to the top, Michael quickly exhibited special skills and leadership ability. One of his greatest contributions was his work with the Archdiocese of Westminster. You can imagine what joy it brought to Michael that in just a few years he had returned to the

United Kingdom to play such an important role in the Church. Working with Cardinal Cormac Murphy-O'Connor and with the Church in the whole London area was an important undertaking for us. It was also one of our most successful efforts.

Michael worked carefully with the leadership in Westminster to assure this would not be a Yankee import but would have the stamp of being truly a part of the United Kingdom, including the name it took on, *At Your Word, Lord.* Despite the many hurdles presented by anything that was coming from overseas, Michael and the English director, Fr. Stuart Wilson, won over a good majority of the priests to enjoy a very fruitful and refreshing RENEW experience.

After another heart scare, I decided it was time to share more leadership responsibility and appointed Michael as assistant director. He was invaluable for both RENEW and me. By 2002, Michael was director. He introduced important and valuable approaches. More attention was given to the potential of the Internet and other electronic advances.

With his organized management style, Michael set up a new structure for the future. He brought on board valuable people from the business world. Mary Beth Oria, who was vice-president of finance and operations at Hanover Direct, became director of operations at RENEW. Deirdre Trabert Malacrea came directly from an important marketing position with PepsiCo and became our director of marketing. RENEW International was a larger ministerial community now and the combined insights and skills of these new leaders brought new dimensions to our services. Michael also hired Robert Kelly, a brilliant and gifted Scot, to coordinate the Resources and Publications team.

Best of all was Michael's bold and whole-hearted dedication to RENEW's mission. He quickly internalized RENEW International's history, spirituality, and philosophy and spoke about them as if he had been a part of RENEW forever.

As a young layman, Michael naturally had a great interest in the future of lay people's involvement in the Church. In the wake of the clergy sex-abuse scandal, a new and hopeful organization, the National Leadership Roundtable on Church Management, was initiated that was designed to help bishops and dioceses with their business expertise in areas of finance, management, and transparency. It provides a service many felt was long overdue. Because of Michael's great number of national contacts, he was invited to join the roundtable in May 2006. RENEW's journey had been greatly enriched by Michael's contributions and his close collaborative contact continues with RENEW to this day. In 2009, Michael led RENEW International through the Roundtable's Standards for Excellence program, which ensured that our organization, in all aspects, embraces the highest professional standards.

Sr. Terry Rickard, O.P.

In 2002, Mary Reddy, a valuable member of our staff, strongly suggested that we meet and interview Sr. Terry Rickard, O.P., whom she had known for some time. Terry had been director of vocations for the Dominican Sisters of Blauvelt and was looking for a new ministry. She quickly proved to be an extremely valuable addition.

Terry was hired as coordinator of new services and began restructuring our work on university campuses. She immediately hired some of the finest young ministerial people you would want to see working with young adults on campuses. Our young adult team inspired other students to become involved in *Campus RENEW* small communities. The RENEW team continued to enrich these small communities with excellent resources and workshops and kept consistent pastoral contact with young adults and their leaders.

Terry was also deeply involved in *Why Catholic?* to service Mobile, Alabama, the first diocese to undertake that process. Terry was soon meeting bishops and leaders who were inquiring into the value of introducing *Why Catholic?* in their dioceses. Terry's relational skills and outstanding ability to communicate with such a wide range of people, including everyone on our staff, is remarkable.

I believe an organization's strength is demonstrated when it is able to draw new leadership from within its own ranks. Terry soon became coordinator of our *Why Catholic?* effort and eventually assistant director of RENEW. After Michael's resignation, two or three people were given serious consideration for the role of director. Working with our Board of Trustees, we chose Sr. Terry as the most qualified person.

While I was well aware of her many abilities at the time of her appointment, I have been pleased with her wealth of talent as she has grown in the role of director, and now as president and executive director. Terry's main contribution has been to offer a wide variety of processes and publications that can be undertaken either by dioceses or by individual parishes or parish clusters.

Years before, a friend had cautioned me about what he envisioned as the inevitable demise of an organization once its founder was off the scene. By God's grace, however, we have been blessed with exceptional leadership that belies that fear. RENEW International is making an incredible spiritual impact that gives rise to the hope that the best is yet to come.

Responding to Today's Needs

RENEW International reads and responds to the signs of the times in a world that is evolving rapidly and to a large extent is also abandoning the richness of Christianity, a way of life that had given many of us stability and meaning.

RENEW International was quick to evaluate the needs of parishioners in our fast-paced and ever-changing society. The leadership showed great wisdom in beginning this new century with its successful *Why Catholic?* process. This was a beautiful response to peoples' need for identity, knowledge, and security.

The sexual abuse scandal in the United States was to occupy the Church and its critics for years to come. In fact, it stands as the greatest crisis in the Church since the Reformation. RENEW was the first to respond and to offer assistance to parishes and to individuals in the confusion and anger that accompanied the scandal. At the request of Archbishop Michael Sheehan and other bishops, RENEW developed *Healing the Body of Christ*, which has offered help to thousands of people who were left adrift in the middle of the scandal.

With the clergy themselves in a state of varied emotions, I give RENEW's staff credit for recognizing and responding to priests' need for support and affirmation. Creative efforts brought forth *Renewing the Priestly Heart*, RENEW's first major pastoral resource to help priests in their spiritual growth and priestly identity.

The wide range of processes and publications being introduced by RENEW and the number of dioceses being served are signs of the people we are. Despite much that has gone awry in society, we are people of hope. Our hope is based on a belief in God and in the new life that the Holy Spirit brings to spiritual renewal. With the Blessed Mother's loving care, that Spirit is strongly guiding and carrying RENEW International in this millennium.

CHAPTER 31

Why Catholic?

A s a young man I had a very inquiring mind. I wanted to believe with conviction, from the inside out, and not rely on what I was told. Particularly, my inquiry involved questions of greatest importance: Is there really a God? Is there a concrete basis for being Catholic?

Fortunately, in those days, there were apologetic books and many means to help people think through these issues and solidify their faith. Things are much different today. Many base their faith or lack of faith not necessarily on objective reasons but frequently on individual tastes and choices. In what church do I feel most comfortable?

This reality goes beyond judgments of doctrine; it also deeply affects moral choices. A study done during the summer of 2008 by sociologist Christian Smith was very revealing (as David Brooks wrote in "If It Feels Right," *NY Times*, 9/13/2011). This study of two hundred thirty 18-to-23-year-olds clearly showed that many decisions were made by personal choice or feeling. There was, for the most part, a lack of an objective sense of right or wrong. This did not necessarily mean that responders were living lives of immorality but rather showed how they faced life.

When asked to describe a moral dilemma they had faced, two-thirds of the young people either couldn't answer the question or described problems that are not moral at all. They gave examples such as whether they could afford to rent a certain apartment or whether they had enough quarters to feed the meter in a parking spot.

"When asked about wrong or evil they generally agreed that rape and murder are wrong," but didn't even consider morality with regard to "drunk driving, cheating in school, or cheating on a partner." Rather than choices based on any objective norms, choices were seen as very personal. As one respondent said, "I would do what I thought made me happy or how I felt. I have no other way of knowing what to do, but how I internally feel."

We can see from these examples the importance of knowing the realities of life, such as who are we, why we are here, where we came from. We also see the importance of having guidelines as to how to live in a way that gives glory to God, is healthy for ourselves, and creates a harmonious society.

The *Catechism of the Catholic Church*

In 1994 the Church, seeing these needs for guidance, published the *Catechism of the Catholic Church*. Before the *Catechism* was published many felt that this would be a very dry and dull presentation, an opinion based on their unfavorable recollections of having to memorize the *Baltimore Catechism*. The *Catechism of the Catholic Church* proved to be just the opposite. Its content is rich, interesting, and inspiring. If there is a problem connected with the *Catechism*, it is that it is voluminous.

RENEW addressed the challenge of making the contents more accessible to average people—and encouraged them to explore the *Catechism*—with a new resource, *Breaking Open the Catechism of the Catholic Church*. Our resource was published shortly after the *Catechism* itself. *Breaking Open the Catechism of the Catholic Church* was intended for small-community use, but it was also available for individual use. It proved to be very popular.

By the turn of the century, we realized the time had come for us to update our publication, based on feedback we had received. We also had published it before the creation of the U.S. Bishops Committee to Oversee Use of the Catechism.

Why Catholic? Attracts Many

We presented our four-volume series, now called *Why Catholic?*, to the bishops' committee and received strong approval. This helped *Why Catholic?* become attractive to bishops, pastors, and parishioners.

One bishop I visited told me that the title, *Why Catholic?*, was a stroke of genius because it immediately hit home and drew attention. In 2002, Sr. Terry made an important suggestion: Why not make this a full RENEW International program that could be used by parishes and entire dioceses? In this way, RENEW International would help a diocese establish a *Why Catholic?* diocesan team, provide training, consultation, all the resources needed for easy and efficient invitation and implementation. RENEW would also pastor the diocesan team over a four-year period and help in evaluating the process. Additionally, we would provide two annual total-parish events: adult enrichment workshops and retreats.

Through the RENEW International website, participants are also able to network across parishes and across the world via the *Why Catholic?* member bulletin board where they can share ideas and activities for implementing the process.

Why Catholic? has had the impact of a game-winning home run. At this writing we have worked with forty-nine dioceses involving hundreds of thousands of participants. This should not be surprising since early on it made such sense to bishops and pastors.

Bishop Paul Zipfel of Bismarck, North Dakota, remarked, "Shortly after beginning *Why Catholic?* one of the priests said to me, 'Bishop, this is precisely what we have needed for a long time. Thank you for introducing it.' He was not disappointed with the results, nor have I been. Since then, many of our people have chosen to continue meeting regularly to search for a greater growth in holiness and understanding of our faith. What greater results could we hope for?"

In presentations with diocesan leadership, I would always point out a reality all too familiar to them. Too many parents today are really unprepared for the work of forming their children in the Catholic faith because they themselves don't know their Catholic faith.

For pastors it made great sense. After all, the need for adult formation had been becoming more clear each year. Despite this need, the vast majority of parishes have no one assigned for the task of adult faith formation. By adopting *Why Catholic?* pastors are responding, without hiring an extra staff person, to an unfulfilled responsibility of offering formation for their people. *Why Catholic?* would provide outstanding materials, training, and all the other components that would strongly meet the need. Designed particularly for parents to use with children are *RENEWing Family Faith* bulletins for each week of the process and a mini-handbook, *How to Use the Family Faith Bulletins.*

The following feedback gives us a feel for the response to *Why Catholic?*

- Many parishioners made their first confessions in decades.
- In a particular neighborhood, one group was composed solely of fallen-away Catholics.
- A parishioner reported that reading the actual *Catechism* was the best sleeping pill going, but *Why Catholic?* was exciting and actually led her to be extremely interested in the *Catechism of the Catholic Church.*
- A leader decided to arrange a new group of her friends and neighbors who were inactive or marginally participating Catholics.
- Through *Why Catholic?* one person discovered the Bible: "It is unbelievably interesting all of a sudden."
- A pastor of a small rural parish was hoping to engage thirty to forty people for *Why Catholic?* and wound up having one hundred eighty-five participants.
- One group of twelve happened to be an entire family. The mother said the best gift she received was that her son stopped drinking.
- Another commented she always went to Mass but never had previously made friends there.
- One group did not realize that a gentleman participant had been away from Church since his young wife died of cancer ten years earlier. The group's faith encouraged the man to let go of his anger and return to the sacraments.

- Another said, "Being in a small community has given me the words to talk to my children about my faith."
- One fallen-away neighbor went to the communal penance service with the group and was moved to return to the sacraments after thirty-five years.

Parishes have implemented *Why Catholic?* groups in prisons and health-care facilities. It also has been welcomed on local college campuses. The main benefits that participants report are threefold:

- gaining a deeper appreciation for their faith
- developing a desire to delve more deeply into Scripture and the *Catechism*
- strengthening their commitment and confidence to reach out to others.

One tangible result has been that dioceses have seen small-group participants returning to the Church after years of absence. This is true of both the English- and Spanish-language experiences.

Marriages have also been strengthened as a result of spouses participating together. In Mecca, Diocese of San Bernardino, California, fifteen couples doing *¿Por qué ser católico?* who had been wed outside the Church have had their marriages blessed. This also occurred in Flemington, New Jersey, and a number of other places.

Miss Mary's Surprise

One of my favorite *Why Catholic?* stories comes from a parish in Arkansas. Two days before Thanksgiving, parishioner Martha Ullrich headed down Tanyard Mountain Road to bring a food basket to Miss Mary, a seventy-seven-year-old widow in the parish who was known for her warm smile and generous spirit. Martha found Miss Mary huddled by a small heater wearing a coat and gloves. Her small home was so cold and leaky that she had to cover everything she owned with plastic sheets. She had no running water, working plumbing, or adequate heat.

Martha Ullrich brought this story to her small *Why Catholic?* group. The group decided to live the Good News. They built a warm, dry, new house before Christmas arrived. Almost immediately, work began as people donated cash, building materials, labor, household items, and furniture. Members of the group also cooked for and fed the workers. A small house consisting of a kitchen, living area, bedroom, bathroom, and laundry was finished in three days. Miss Mary was naturally thrilled with her new home and proudly showed all visitors her new washer, dryer, shower with a built-in seat, her new stove, and new kitchen cabinets. Martha Ullrich said, "I think this was the best Christmas we've ever had."

Adapted for Many Cultures

In the RENEW tradition, an adaptation of *Why Catholic?* called *¿Por qué ser católico?* serves the Spanish-speaking community in the United States and worldwide by providing faith-sharing materials, workshops, and retreats created from within the Hispanic culture. Hispanic staff conduct all training, workshops, and retreats.

In 2008, *¿Por qué ser católico?* made its way into the Caribbean. With great enthusiasm, the Diocese of Ponce, Puerto Rico, began the process. *¿Por qué ser católico?* has had a dramatic impact on the lives of individual Catholics in Ponce. The same can be said for members of a parish in Chihuahua, Mexico.

Through the efforts of Fr. Alejandro Lopez-Cardinale, *¿Por qué ser católico?* was adapted for Venezuela, his homeland. *RENEW Venezuela,* a parish-based initiative, serves hundreds in the Archdiocese of Valencia. It has as one of its goals evangelizing students of the University of Carabobo. The initiative develops leaders by providing training in areas of faith—Scripture, prayer, discernment, morality, and the social teachings of the Church—while giving them tools to be Catholic leaders in business, education, and public service.

Parishes in the Archdiocese of Boston, including many that completed RENEW's *ARISE Together in Christ* process (see Chapter 33), began *Why Catholic?* in 2012. The process is available in English, Spanish, Portuguese, Vietnamese, Chinese, Lithuanian, and Haitian Creole.

At the request of the Diocese of Port Elizabeth, South Africa, in 2011 RENEW started rolling out an adapted experience of *Why Catholic?* to follow *RENEW Africa.* The materials are provided in English, Afrikaans, and Xhosa.

The Military Archdiocese

Since January 2006, Sr. Maureen Colleary has helped to bring *Why Catholic?* to the Catholic faithful living on military bases and installations around the world. She worked closely with the auxiliary bishops for the military services—Joseph Estabrook, F. Richard Spencer, and Neal J. Buckon—who supported the process and, when possible, helped Maureen give workshops during the training weekends. Timothy P. Broglio, archbishop for the military services, asked military chapels around the world to become involved.

To date RENEW International has touched over 40 different military communities in the Military Archdiocese, which encompasses all branches of the service in the continental United States and overseas. Besides the continental United States, Maureen has trained leaders in the United Kingdom, South Korea, Hawaii, and Germany.

Wiesbaden, Germany

"The small groups that form become electric," reports Jane Gottardi, coordinator of *Why Catholic?* in Weisbaden, Germany, "There is so much love in the sharing that it opens one's heart to fellow parishioners. It creates bonds and it strengthens our church community. Small groups offer respect, dignity, love, and trust in one another."

Jane, whose husband is an army general, emphasized the *Why Catholic?* approach of moving from faith to action. At the end of each session, group members promised one another to go out and in some way live the Good News until their next session. "Our faith tells us that in reaching outside the living of our faith and being instruments of good for others we are forever changed," Jane said.

Michele Puehler, also from Wiesbaden, shared how *Why Catholic?* eased her small community back into learning and sharing their faith. Through this process they expanded their own understanding of faith and gained a deeper awareness of their own faith stories. "We can relate our experiences to a real Jesus who is in our midst," said Michele.

From the same community, Jill Tidwell shared,

> *Why Catholic?* is not only a great review for those with a theological background but also a wonderful place for

RCIA candidates to continue their knowledge-seeking process, as well as those who just want to refresh their faith. Group members can share their deepest thoughts, fears, and experiences in a trusting faith environment that is all geared toward Jesus, His Word, and actions that he wants us to take. Putting faith into action in a group scenario is what it is all about.'

Honolulu, Hawaii

When Maureen introduced *Why Catholic?* to the Aliamanu Military Reservation Chapel and St. Damien Catholic Community in Honolulu, Hawaii, it gave people there the tools to grow even stronger in their faith as a community. Katie Hanna had this recollection:

> Our small military faith community in Hawaii was fertile ground for my family and for many others. We came together as a group many times throughout the week to share and grow in our faith. We knew that when we saw another person from our community, they had genuine care and concern for us and even prayed for us. One of the great treasures of being a Catholic is our sense of community and faith sharing, which allowed me to become a better sister in Christ and a better member of my faith community. I am truly thankful for that wonderful time of growth, and I hope that everyone can experience such a strong sense of community.

South Korea

In 2011, Bishop Richard Spencer sent his own message of gratitude to RENEW International:

> I write as a "witness" to the results of *Why Catholic?* programs conducted recently throughout the multiple United States Military Catholic communities located in the country of the Republic of South Korea. Beyond our expectations, we experienced and are experiencing growth in the numbers of our lay involvements. A truly renewed purpose of ministry has evolved that continues even after

three years have passed. Since we initiated *Why Catholic?*
our Catholic communities have been strengthened and
truly renewed. I thank you for your gift of ministry shared
with our military families.

One thing many people today are certain of is that their lives are filled
with confusion and doubt. Given that state, we can easily see that the
Catechism of the Catholic Church has been a wonderful gift for millions of
people. Yet, for reasons of available time and energy, it would be unrealistic to expect people to take on the full *Catechism* cold turkey.

Why Catholic? has been the bridge that has helped carry the riches
of the Church to hundreds of thousands of people. We have become
so accustomed to high numbers of people being involved in RENEW
International programs that we must avoid the presumption of success
and always give praise to God for how we have been blessed.

CHAPTER 32

Healing the Body of Christ

The most difficult period in my priesthood started in February 2002 as news of the sexual abuse scandal broke out on a daily basis with unrelenting and horrific reports. Actually, the boil had been building up for a long time and was now being lanced with all the ugliness the scandal involved. It's hard to explain the embarrassment and uneasiness I experienced every morning when I read the latest front-page report in *The New York Times*.

Victims and Families Suffer

The saddest and most crushing aspect was that, during their most impressionable years, innocent children and teens that had been entrusted to the care and guidance of abusive priests had had their lives torn apart in irreparable ways.

As we listened to and read the accounts of those who were abused, we learned much. So many adults who were abused as children or teens have still not recovered from the sexual abuse they experienced when they were young. Often the offending priest ingratiated himself to the parents. He was considered a trusted friend of the family and used his influence and authority to threaten the victims into submission and silence.

Whole families were affected. They were astounded to learn of the abuse of their child, their sibling, or their spouse and were sick over it. Victims often were depressed. They had difficulty relating to others or holding jobs. Some have taken their own lives. Some victims and their family members alike have left the Church.

An Unsettling Time

The priesthood, which had been revered by so many over my entire life, seemed to fall overnight into a state of disgrace and shame. The horrendous actions of some priests were spelled out in the media in extremely unsettling detail. It didn't take long to focus on how the scandal had been handled or, as reported, how it had been covered up by leadership in the Church. The magnitude of the situation soon became apparent, and some of the worst aspects were the reports surfacing of how abusive priests had been transferred from one parish to another or, with recommendations, from one diocese to another.

Some bishops relied on reports from psychiatrists who had assured them that abusive priests were cured and were ready to return to full pastoral activity. But lay people, priests, and the public in general were so angered as the massive number of priest abusers became evident, there was little patience for attempted explanations. Whether consciously or not, concern for the safety of children was being outweighed by a system caught up in the protection of priests. There is no excuse for what occurred. Children are God's gift to us and God's creation, and there should be total openness and honesty about the depth of damage done to these children.

Something I had railed against my whole priesthood was at the core of the problem. Clericalism had become such a strong part of priestly culture that it put the priest above and beyond question in a class of entitlement. Forgiveness was being too quickly dispensed. We were dealing with a sickness that was rarely, if ever, cured.

Easily overlooked was the overwhelming majority of priests who were living their daily lives prayerfully and making zealous efforts to serve the faithful entrusted to them. The image of priesthood had been badly damaged, and priests in general experienced strong negative feelings directed at them.

One priest in the Midwest told me he went about with a feeling of guilt, although he had never done anything wrong. Another priest in Massachusetts said he felt it extremely difficult to leave the rectory with his collar on. He was so fearful of the reactions and judgments people would make. My own reaction was not to crawl into a foxhole but to remain proud of my priesthood and do all I could to help the victims.

Counseling a woman who had been abused as an eleven-year-old helped me to gain great insight and compassion for victims. I had known her from childhood, and my heart was torn apart by this lasting damage inflicted by a respected brother priest. I had deep concern for victims and wanted everything possible to be done to help those who had suffered at the hands of priests. Yet I didn't want to lose the reality of the sacredness of priesthood itself. I was determined to wear my black suit and collar more often in the public square.

That's not to say it was always easy. Whereas my many trips through airports had frequently brought people to me for counsel and support, I now felt extremely uncomfortable in the airports my ministry brought me through.

On one occasion in Sarasota, Florida, a small group of young working professional women had sensed my uneasiness and asked if they could join me for a Danish. However, it wasn't always that way.

At an airport in Peoria, Illinois, all the passengers had gathered around the check-in desk inquiring about the news that our plane would be delayed due to mechanical problems. One woman took the opportunity of proclaiming to the gathering in loud, bitter tones, "This plane will never take off; there's a priest on it."

Catalyst for Healing

Given that background, it came as a great surprise to us to receive a call from Archbishop Michael Sheehan of Santa Fe, New Mexico, saying that when he attended the upcoming U.S. Catholic Conference of Bishops meeting in Dallas in June 2002, he intended to speak out and tell all the bishops how RENEW had helped him and his diocese in their time of greatest need.

That famous Dallas Conference spelled out the policy of zero tolerance that, as we now know, was implemented with mixed efficiency. The day that vote was televised nationally on two different channels, I watched and listened carefully, especially intrigued to hear what Archbishop Sheehan might say. As the day wore on I began to believe that he had either changed his mind or would not get the opportunity to speak.

I stopped watching the conference and went to my brother and sister-in-law's house for dinner where they were watching the proceedings. Lo and behold, I saw Archbishop Sheehan standing on a line of bishops who wished to make public statements.

The archbishop began by saying something every bishop knew—he had inherited the worst situation in the country. What he referred to was a great number of sexual abuse cases, along with many other problems of great magnitude. He went on to say, "I turned to RENEW and RENEW turned our diocese around to a very healthy and positive climate where we had thirty-five thousand people meeting on a weekly basis sharing their faith." Then came the shocker. He said, "RENEW International is ... in the process of putting together a program that will bring about great healing. We look forward to what RENEW will have ready for us in the very near future."

RENEW's Response: Total Team Effort

I was totally surprised since I didn't know that we were in the process of putting together such a program. It was a wild and difficult summer. We decided our process would be twofold: to help the healing of lay people and to address the need for healing among priests, with that sometimes involving their relationship with their bishop.

For our work with lay people we would use our forte of bringing people together in small communities. This involved first designing the appropriate themes for a six-week period that would help people to fully and strongly express their feelings—whatever they may be: betrayal, anger, frustration. There was a need for people to be able to look at the problem squarely and to vent without restriction in a small-community setting.

From there we looked at the Church's long history of being a Church of saints and sinners, dealing with the most difficult of all problems, forgiveness, and moved on to an appreciation of what strengths and spiritual richness the Church offered us. When my sister-in-law asked, "What will I say to my children and twenty-three grandchildren?" I replied, "Tell them not to let the actions of any sex offender separate them from the Eucharist."

Solid faith had not been built on the failures of individuals, no matter how exalted the individuals may be. Our faith should be built on our love for Jesus and the richness of the sacraments the Church provides, especially the Mass and the Eucharist that are so central to our Catholic faith. What could ever supplant the real Presence of Jesus in the Eucharist?

That summer involved the search for the best possible writers for our themes, evaluations of their material, constant communication and rewrites, and finally the piloting of materials—all within two months.

On a wider scale it involved our entire team in putting together a *Healing the Body of Christ* kit that offered guidelines for implementation, a facilitator's guide for small-community leader training, an invitational video synchronized with the facilitators' guide, the faith-sharing book, a guide for personal reflection, and a prayer card for healing.

It was a massive, intense effort on RENEW International's part to do all that we could to help people sort through the situation and, by the grace of God, come to healing.

Priests' Days of Reflection and Healing

While we were working assiduously on putting materials together for parishioners so they could be engaged in early fall, much was happening on still another track. This effort involved preparing for the Priests' Days of Reflection and Healing.

The format had to provide time for the priests to register their own reactions and feelings. In many cases, priests felt they had been "left out to dry" and were angry at their bishops. Anyone could raise a claim about a priest and he could be immediately removed, whereas no bishops were stepping down from their posts. In those instances there ensued an obvious disconnect between the bishop and the priests of a diocese.

Even in instances in which priests did not feel this disconnect, there was still the issue of the priests' need for healing themselves from the fallout from so many instances of abuse and people's expressions of anger, disbelief, frustration, etc.

Men who had fine reputations and were accepted by their brother priests were chosen to conduct these retreat days. Their sensitive approach did much to make these days successful. The priests were given the opportunity to share their feelings and hurts, and the bishops were given the opportunity to speak to the priests about the action taken by the U.S. Conference of Catholic Bishops. The facilitators themselves gave input that was very helpful for the priests to raise their spirits and move forward.

As in all RENEW experiences, we came to the conclusion that the Church is not some abstract notion outside ourselves. In the case of priests, we are men ordained for leadership positions. If the Church was to be healed, the healing had to begin with us. With faith and hope, we could provide the positive leadership that would help our people.

Restoring Some Hope

The success of all aspects of *Healing the Body of Christ* was very gratifying. More than one hundred dioceses as well as eight hundred individual parishes became involved. For many, the process not only involved a catharsis of their feelings but truly helped them to look at the nature of spirituality and the richness of our Catholic faith. Where else would they find a tradition of keen and astute insights from numerous saints over the ages providing us with such a rich treasure of wisdom? Where would they receive the strength and consolation the sacraments give us, and what could ever replace the Mass and the reception of the very Body and Blood of Christ?

The Spirit Alive

The response of parishioners at St. Mary of the Assumption Parish in the Archdiocese of Boston was typical. They used the process as a stepping-stone for regaining faith in the Church. Not surprisingly, according to Lisa Scarry, pastoral associate, the most common sentiment was, "I didn't realize I was so angry or felt so deeply about the subject."

Coming to terms with these issues had brought the parish community closer together and started the work needed to be done to restore broken confidence. "*Healing the Body of Christ* helped folks by offering an opportunity for deepening prayer and faith life, and allowing people to see their Church addressing the crisis in a positive way," said Fr. Bill Williams, pastor of St. Mary of the Assumption Parish.

Healing the Body of Christ helped people to affirm, once again, that our faith is not built on the actions of humans, be they in leadership or not. Usually our parents are the ones who introduce us to and form us in faith, which is built on the richness, truth, and spiritual guidance the Church provides. People not only felt healed of the confusion they may have been going through, but they came through the process with stronger faith than ever. They realized that the Holy Spirit is still very much guiding us, as has been the case through the centuries since the lifetime of Jesus.

Archbishop Michael Sheehan of Santa Fe, whose comments had initiated the whole process, was pleased with both the approach we had taken and the materials. As for the materials, he said, "They are both frank and sensitive to the challenge we face as a result of this scandal." Other comments were also gratifying.

Archbishop Timothy Dolan, then archbishop of Milwaukee, remarked, "If you're looking for a good Lenten resolution you can't go wrong in signing up for RENEW's *Healing the Body of Christ*. Everywhere I go people ask me, 'How can we learn from all these scandals? How can we get on and move ahead as a more purified, holier, more faithful Church?' Here's one way—RENEW."

Of the many positive reactions, the one that touched me the most came from a woman who reported that when she was eighteen years old she was sexually molested by a priest. She said, "Sitting in this group, feeling so cared for, gave me the confidence to express myself." This opportunity for thousands of people to open up and express their feelings, their hurts, and their confusion, was an opening that allowed the Holy Spirit once again to influence their spiritual journeys and restore positive feelings of hope.

I personally embrace that gift of hope. The scandals have been extremely humbling. In that stance of humility we are better able to see our faults and failures, both in what we have done and in what we have neglected to do. We may not immediately see some of the positive steps we would like to see in strengthening our Church, but I firmly believe the door has been opened to a path that will lead us more and more to be a truly renewed Church, a Church that is a light to the world.

I pray every day for the spiritual renewal of our Church, that we will respond to God's grace that is guiding us to bring light to the world and helping us become a magnet to draw people to live in that light.

If I want to see a renewed Church this naturally leads me to a difficult realization: such renewal must begin with me personally. It's easy to say what others and the Church as a whole should do, but the more I embrace the path of trying to grow spiritually and live a holier life, the more I will be an instrument in that Church renewal we all desire.

CHAPTER 33

Boston

ARISE Together in Christ

I n the early 1990s an inquiry came from, of all places, Boston, Massachusetts. I say "from all places" because, from the beginning, New England, more than any section of the country, had shown the least interest in RENEW. Fairly or not, I attributed this factor to a higher degree of clericalism than I had found throughout our travels in the United States. Lay involvement in Boston could not come anywhere near most areas in the Midwest.

Preliminary Steps

What made the call particularly interesting was that it came from the Chancery Office. Fr. John Sassani and Mary Ann McLaughlin, then assistant director of the Office of Spiritual Development, were curious about this RENEW experience they were hearing about. I was on the next plane to Boston. Thus began annual pilgrimages to that fair city.

Sharing mutual interests and updating each other on the latest developments made for interesting visits. On one occasion, John and Mary Ann arranged for us to speak to a gathering of all archdiocesan office and agency personnel. The people at that gathering showed real interest in RENEW, but, for whatever reasons, the result was the same. That interest never moved to the next level.

The appointment of Bishop Seán O'Malley, O.F.M.Cap., as archbishop of Boston was exciting for many in Boston and also for us at

RENEW. We had previously worked with Bishop Seán in the Diocese of Fall River and regarded him with the greatest respect and considered him a true friend. It is said that he arrived in Boston with the intention of initiating RENEW. Whether that be true or not, he certainly was faced with far more pressing problems. After all, he was sent to Boston to lead the archdiocese after the news of the sexual-abuse scandal broke, which was seen, in the common view, as centered in Boston. It's hard to imagine a more difficult challenge. Certainly much groundwork needed to be laid before RENEW, or any other positive move the archbishop may have been considering, could have been seriously adopted and implemented.

Our contacts with Boston took on new life and vitality. John and Mary Ann arranged for us to have direct contact with the people in positions of authority. Interest in RENEW was being kindled. Michael Brough and I made presentations to the Archdiocesan Council of Priests in the daytime and to the Archdiocesan Pastoral Council in the evening. The presentations went well with unanimous interest by the priests and with only two people on the pastoral council giving negative feedback. However, Archbishop O'Malley wisely realized the archdiocese was not yet prepared. Much more had to be done, especially in reviving the morale of the priests, many of whom felt betrayed and caught in the middle of the scandal and how it had been handled.

Sr. Terry Rickard: Ambassador to Boston

A critical meeting would be held on August 4, 2006 involving top decision makers of the archdiocese, along with a large number of good and insightful priests. My calendar became a little askew when my second open-heart surgery was scheduled for the end of July 2006. What to do?

In one of the best moves I ever made, I asked Sr. Terry Rickard to go to Boston and represent RENEW at that most important meeting.

Being holed up in the hospital was far from pleasant for me, but it turned out to be a great blessing for RENEW. From the beginning Terry could sense the tremendous amount of unrest and the preoccupation of the participants with many pressing matters. Wisely, she judged that taking the stance of listener was far more important than any presentation providing answers. The answers would have to come from the people of Boston, and the best approach RENEW could take would be one that was seen as directly meeting their unique and serious concerns.

Building Hope for the Future

The next step would involve a lot more listening; plans were made based on what was surfacing. A great amount of attention needed to be directed to the morale of the priests. A renewal of the priesthood was necessary if priests were expected to rally parishioners with new energy for their faith in the Church. The priests needed opportunities to more strongly support one another and to have more contact with their archbishop, who was faced with probably the most troubling circumstances ever faced by a U.S. bishop.

The Turning Point

Having gained the confidence of the priests and having the advantage of coming from the outside, Terry was able to play a helpful role in arranging the largest gathering of priests that was held in many years. The mutual sharing that occurred between the priests and their bishop that day was a very positive step in rebuilding trust and initiating a sense of hope for the future.

Later, there was another huge gathering of the clergy, which was a true turning point for recovery in Boston. The keynote speaker was Archbishop O'Malley who gave a strong leadership call for unity and mutual support. His own support for RENEW was laid out in the strongest terms. Outside speakers, Br. Loughlan Sofield, S.T., Fr. Bruce Neili, and Terry also added to this magnificently spirited day. In keeping with the strong spiritual tone to the day, the sacrament of reconciliation was made available and was celebrated by many. The priests left that assembly more united as a community.

As enthusiasm for a new collaborative process was growing, *ARISE Together in Christ / LEVÁNTATE. Unánomos en Cristo* was brought to life. It was obvious that an enormous effort would be required to actually get a commitment from parishes to sign up and participate in something so totally different from past experiences. The problems of the sexual abuse scandal, parish and school closings, and a cautious and conservative background still lingered.

Terry was joined by Sr. Honora Nolty, O.P., and Sr. Maureen Colleary who, in unison with the Boston office, deserve a world of credit for what they achieved. These three sisters represented the top tier at RENEW International and had records of success in everything they undertook. To see them in motion and imagine this kind of leadership throughout our country would be to envision an entirely different and vigorous Church in America. Their ability to reach lay people and their success in inviting and gaining the confidence of priests was remarkable. Once again, the work of the Spirit was mightily evident.

Comprehensive Coverage

The recruitment efforts had amazing success with over sixty percent of the two hundred ninety-two parishes in the archdiocese getting on board for *ARISE*. As late as Season V of *ARISE*, new parishes were still joining. With the massive preparation effort throughout the diocese, the mood had already changed by Season I. A survey of the archdiocese showed that seventy percent of the parishioners and priests were now willing to let go of the past and move ahead with hope and new life. Those positive numbers continued to increase over the course of *ARISE*.

ARISE in Boston was truly comprehensive, and the effects of *ARISE* were broad and lasting. Over thirty thousand people participated in small groups. Nursing homes and assisted living establishments became involved. Several campuses and prisons were engaged. The *ARISE* process also brought forth five parishes to initiate RENEW's *Theology on Tap* process.

The Boston Home Joins *ARISE*

The *ARISE* parish team at St. Gregory the Great Parish in Dorchester reached out to the Boston Home, a residence and care center for adults with advanced multiple sclerosis and other progressive neurological diseases, and suggested they form a small community at the home. Marilyn MacDonald, a resident, attended the leader workshop and completely organized and implemented the process there. Marilyn remarked, "All of us grew in embracing our faith. We learned to listen to God and to try to discern what he wants to do in us."

Testimonials Reveal Healing and New Life

Parishioners of St. Michael, St. Augustine, and St. Peter's Lithuanian —which had been amalgamated into a new parish in South Boston, reported, "Through *ARISE* we realized we had bonded—we had become friends. Not just social friends—we were friends made in the presence of Christ and his word. Healing is a painful process and takes time. It requires trust, humility, and daring. We see *ARISE* as not just another program but as essential and necessary if we are to keep our focus on being a real balanced and Christ-centered parish."

At St. Michael Parish, North Andover, participants summarized their convictions: "We are apostles by virtue of baptism into the Catholic Church and are called to continue the message of Christ: to touch the hearts of others, to spread the Gospel, and to love one another. This is Church. This is small Christian communities. This is *ARISE*!" The Milton Catholic Collaborative, an online community where people in need can connect with caring people who can help, also came out of *ARISE*. The feedback received from St. Eulalia's Parish in Winchester was typical: "Participants have reported that their hearts and lives were touched by the Scriptures, family bonds were strengthened, involvement in their parishes increased, and there was a heightened awareness of God's presence in their lives. Many were saddened when the experience ended and expressed a desire to continue their faith sharing in small Christian communities." In Brockton, the parishes of St. Edward and St. Nicholas combined into a newly-formed St. Edith Stein Parish. As with most parish mergers and closures, feelings of anger, resentment, frustration, and, especially, abandonment ensued. Many parishioners were left in a state of bewilderment: "In what direction is this parish going?" Given this background, evaluations of *ARISE* were very positive and brought forth the frequent comment that a program like this was needed. Other comments included the following:

- "Parishioners look forward to their faith-sharing sessions; it was an experience never had before."
- "Each season brought forth new members."

- "The parish consensus is that without *ARISE* we could not have been able to survive the storm of change. There is indeed a new sense of calm."
- "Through faith-sharing we have supported, nurtured, and sustained one another on the journey. Not only have we shared our faith, but we also shared our cultures and are ardent believers that we are all one."

Faith-sharing materials are available in English, Spanish, Portuguese, Haitian-Creole, Vietnamese, and Lithuanian. *ARISE* is available to all in a manner that truly represents the word "catholic."

A Blessing for RENEW Staff

God's action through *ARISE* certainly did great things for the people of Boston, but it has also been a great blessing for our entire team at RENEW International. *ARISE* took off like a fire set to dry leaves. For Terry it has further enriched her leadership qualities and has been a great asset in her role as president and executive director. With Honora, who nurtured and shepherded the process throughout the five seasons, *ARISE* has brought to full light the achievements of her very illustrious ministerial career. And for Maureen, *ARISE* has been still another chapter in her tenure as the longest serving member now on staff at RENEW International.

We are grateful to the people of Boston who responded to God's call to participate in *ARISE*. Their positive experience has helped the *ARISE* process to blossom in other dioceses and parishes throughout the country. The Diocese of Stockton, California, had ninety-seven percent of the parishes participating as well as two prisons and the University of the Pacific.

Other U.S. dioceses include San Angelo, Texas; Crookston, Minnesota; Fort Wayne-South Bend, Indiana, and Owensboro, Kentucky; Springfield-Cape Girardeau, Missouri.

In Quebec, Canada, the entire process has been translated and enculturated in French as *DEBOUT Ensemble dans le Christ*. The Archdiocese of St. Boniface in Manitoba and the Diocese of London in Ontario are also enjoying the process.

ARISE is in its early stages of growth but shows significant signs of making a major contribution to spirituality in our country.

We may have viewed Boston as least likely to be a dynamic hub of RENEW activity. How things have changed! We now see Boston as the energetic center of initiating one of RENEW International's greatest spiritual offerings. They have, in fact, occasioned a wave of interest in *ARISE* across the country.

CHAPTER 34

Longing
for the Holy

I t was a good idea, in fact a very good idea. Why, then, did it remain an idea for so long and not become a reality? The world is probably full of good ideas. It would be interesting to know the variety of reasons why these ideas never get off the ground. To me the challenge was fear and lack of confidence.

One afternoon in May 2003, a surge of energy and nerve overtook me; I picked up the phone and made the call. Did you ever make a phone call in which you hoped the person would be in while, at the same time, you would be greatly relieved if there was no answer? No such luck. He answered on the first ring.

"Hello, Fr. Ron Rolheiser speaking." A nervous stumbling voice returned with, "This is Fr. Tom Kleissler, Ron." What meaning would that have to him? I was calling one of the most popular spiritual writers in America. His schedule was beyond belief. It was incredible seeing the number of places he would be giving talks, teaching courses, and publishing articles and books. How could I ask him for something that was probably most precious of all to him—his time?

After a brief introduction, I came to the point—his time. "Fr. Ron, I know how busy you are and yet, for the benefit of the work I'm involved in, I think it would be extremely helpful if I could get to meet you. Is it possible you could give me an hour of your time? I'll be happy to fly to wherever you are if this could be worked into your schedule. Fr. Rolheiser replied, "Why don't you come up to Toronto where I'm currently living and we'll spend a day together rapping and exchanging ideas." And so it was that I met with one of the finest people of our time.

A Memorable Day with Ron Rolheiser

At the time, the SARS (severe acute respiratory syndrome) epidemic was taking place in Canada. People all over were wearing masks. But if Ron could live there, we could brave it for a day. Michael Brough, Deirdre Malacrea, Sr. Mary McGuinness, and I took off for Canada—a trip we will long remember.

A relaxed Ron Rolheiser was sitting on his porch awaiting our arrival. It was soon apparent that Ron was well versed and extremely comfortable on just about any topic we could bring up. Of great interest to us were some of Ron's ideas and plans for his future ministry and writings. His understanding of and insights into human nature in today's society, coupled with his own strong spirituality, was leading him to new ideas that he felt had to be written about and brought into public discourse.

During that day, the Holy Spirit was active, and our conversation moved to a possible connection between Ron Rolheiser's work and RENEW. Despite the fact that his work was by far the most popular of anything at the time, there were still many people who didn't take the time or effort to buy one of his books or participate in one of his conferences. Could RENEW introduce his work to a new circle of seekers?

We got up the nerve to propose that RENEW draw ideas from *The Holy Longing* or *The Shattered Lantern* and put them into the familiar format that we used for people to engage in faith-sharing. Once again, Ron more than surprised me. He certainly didn't cling to ownership of his ideas that were sweeping the country. Instead, he said he would be happy to see the content of his work made available in the formats RENEW made popular. His biggest difficulty was that he wouldn't have the time to personally undertake the writing of such material. He would, however, be more than happy to help us find the right author who could work with us and bring about the marriage of his work with the RENEW audience.

At this point, I was practically falling off my chair. So many petty issues that usually got in the way of cooperation were never even raised.

Ron was in favor of whatever would be good for the people and the spiritual health of the Church. It was as simple as that. He left no room for his ego to get in the way.

The day ended on a happy and down-to-earth note with Ron recalling his youthful days growing up on a farm in western Canada and catching every Saturday afternoon baseball game on the radio. He had amazing recall of who made the final out in different World Series and all sorts of other baseball trivia. It was a fun day with an amazing man. We were experiencing a bit of Church—just as it should be.

Metamorphosis: From Idea to Reality

One of our first follow-throughs was for Michael Brough and I to visit Michael Downey, as Ron had suggested. Downey is the cardinal's theologian in the Archdiocese of Los Angeles. It turned out that he would not be free for such an undertaking, but he did brainstorm with us a number of other possibilities.

In the meantime, Mary and I undertook the project of writing twelve sample sessions ourselves. This might be helpful for our eventual writer in getting a general sense of the direction we saw for the project.

Eventually we hired Wendy Wright from Creighton University to be the ghost writer for our project. She would write a session that we would critique, and she would subsequently edit. After that process was complete, we engaged her to take on the whole book. For RENEW, the project was now in the hands of Mary McGuinness. This assured two things: The project would definitely be brought to conclusion, and the project would be of the highest quality.

My accounts of various RENEW projects should make it clear that my largest involvement was always at the earliest stages: brainstorming the project itself, moving from idea to reality, searching for appropriate authors, piloting, and being very involved in what could be called marketing our project far and wide.

It would take another book to explain the interaction between Wendy Wright and Mary as they critiqued, edited, critiqued again, and rewrote each chapter of *Longing for the Holy*. Settling on the best questions for faith-sharing and coming up with good suggestions for action steps claimed the greatest amount of time.

Our piloting included sending drafts to readers across the country: present and former directors of RENEW, priests, directors of religious education, small Christian community participants, staff personnel, with special consideration in getting feedback from young adults. Small communities were chosen from across the country for piloting. Approval for the work had to be received from our theologians and finally from Archbishop John J. Myers of the Archdiocese of Newark.

While all the above was happening we hired Adele Gonzalez to write a counterpart to *Longing for the Holy*. She did a magnificent job incorporating Latino traditions into the twelve sessions of an original Hispanic work: *Sedientos de Dios*. Our Hispanic team of Sr. Veronica Mendez, R.C.D., Alma Garcia, Fr. Alejandro Lopez-Cardinale, and Manuel Hernandez worked hard on reviewing, editing, piloting the manuscript, and securing readers to review the work.

Sr. Barbara Ann Sgro, O.P., wrote the leadership manual, and she and Mary chose songs for *Longing for the Holy* as did the Hispanic team for the Spanish version. Chris Burns negotiated with various music publishers so we could provide a CD for each small-community leader. A great number of people were involved in brainstorming and selecting the title. Sr. Marion Honors, C.S.J., created a logo; Bob Kelly designed the covers and secured Jim Brisson to provide the format and interior design. Mary Beth Oria oversaw the entire production and distribution.

Meanwhile, Mary adapted *Longing for the Holy* for an audio book and worked with Don McGee who recorded the book and inserted the songs in appropriate sessions. Margarita Morales adapted *Sedientos de Dios* and Don secured Antonio Chiroldes, a New York-based actor, to record the manuscript. When we were ready to launch *Longing for the Holy*, Terry asked Sr. Maureen Colleary to be program manager. Once again, Maureen proved to be an innovator in presenting webinars from all over the country to multiple locations at once.

Green Bay, Wisconsin

The Diocese of Green Bay took on *Longing for the Holy* with great enthusiasm during Lent 2011 as a follow-up to Fr. Rolheiser's appearance in the diocese. More than fifty parishes committed to the process and almost two hundred group leaders were trained at workshops across the diocese. Testimony from participants reveals that they benefited from the process on a variety of levels.

When evaluations came in from St. Joseph/Sts. Peter and Paul Parish in Sturgeon Bay, one participant remarked, "The sharing was great, and it sure made me think spiritually on how to get closer to Jesus. I liked the references to modern-day saints putting the words and ideas into real life."

The deep sharing of thoughts, feelings, and emotions, and ways in which participants had strived to overcome problems in their lives touched many. One small-community leader remarked, "The leaders' book containing the listening instructions were an absolute joy to refresh my memory. I enjoyed it and hope to resume in fall."

Another commented on how the members' willingness and desire to know, share, and understand spirituality in their lives benefited all in the group. They were also amazed at how accepting participants were as they listened to different views of spirituality.

Many Long for Deeper Spirituality

In addition to Green Bay, *Longing for the Holy* and *Sedientos de Dios* took hold in one hundred seventy-two of the one hundred seventy-eight dioceses in the United States as well as several in Canada. Small-community leaders have been trained—either on site or through webinars—to facilitate the *Longing for the Holy* and *Sedientos de Dios* processes.

Claire C. from Baltimore, Maryland, exclaimed, "Our group loves *Longing for the Holy*. It has really touched our lives in special ways."

Longing for the Holy found fertile ground in small communities that had been meeting for five years at Immaculate Conception Parish in Somerville, New Jersey. "When we started doing *Longing for the Holy*," Margie Ellis said, "so many others heard about it and wanted to join because of the enthusiasm and seriousness of the people in the groups.... It's contagious."

"*Longing for the Holy* stretched through all generations," she continued. "So many people, especially senior citizens, said they are trying to enrich and deepen their prayer and spiritual life and *Longing for the Holy* was the answer. The young adults said they had to get started doing something to deepen their connection to God and this was the answer."

The session on the Eucharist had the most personal impact on participants. It gave them a greater understanding of the Eucharist and the people they were to become having participated in the Eucharist.

Being called to connect with Ron Rolheiser and to share ministry with him is more than I had hoped for. Of far greater importance is the exciting fact of how many more people are now reflecting on his great spiritual insights.

CHAPTER 35

RENEW Africa

R ENEW *Africa* began with a young man named Jeremiah Browne.

Jerry is a handsome young Irishman who didn't know what direction his life should take. Where did God fit in the picture? Jerry toured the world looking for answers. Part of that tour involved working as a laborer in New York, which he thoroughly enjoyed. His travels eventually led him to Australia where he also engaged in manual labor. There didn't seem to be a time or period in his life that he didn't enjoy.

Finally, a path that was laid out by the Lord led him to Port Elizabeth, South Africa, where he realized he was called to be a priest. Upon ordination Jerry took stock and realized that the most exciting and interesting thing he had encountered in his travels was small communities and, in particular, RENEW in the United States. Jerry, who serves as director of the Pastoral Development Office for the Diocese of Port Elizabeth, got in touch with Sr. Terry, and she agreed to fly to Port Elizabeth in January 2007 to visit this interesting young priest.

A Totally Collaborative Effort

These two very outgoing people hit it off immediately. It didn't take long before they were talking about a collaborative effort. So popular had RENEW been in South Africa that twenty years later they were talking about bringing our RENEW staff back.

Jerry set up visits and presentations in four dioceses including a meeting with the bishops' committee on evangelization in Pretoria. Terry and he listened to the needs of the Church in Africa today, dialogued with grassroots people in order to respond effectively, and took lots of notes.

Terry and Jerry started to work on basic concepts. *RENEW Africa*, as the process would be called, would have six main distinguishing points:

1. The themes would come from South Africa and the traditional RENEW experience.
2. The authors would be South African.
3. The logo and graphics would be designed in South Africa.
4. Material would be published in several South Africa languages.
5. Publishing and warehousing of resources would take place in Port Elizabeth.
6. The process would be sustainable. Seed money would be deposited in a separate account that would be available to fund other RENEW efforts.

These basic agreements have been adhered to and have resulted in a very successful RENEW effort in Port Elizabeth, where a local office was set up.

RENEW Africa represents some new emphases in our RENEW approach in the huge continent of Africa. More than ever, there is a thoroughness that reflects a concern for long-term results in effectiveness. For the first time, we are offering a RENEW process that is rooted in African culture with Fr. Jerry Browne as national director.

Sr. Marie Cooper Directs New Project

When *RENEW Africa* was in its infancy, Sr. Marie Cooper, S.J.C., a natural-born missionary, was appointed project director and went full steam ahead in our work in South Africa with all the zeal and energy one can muster. Working closely with Jerry, Marie collaborated in the production of resources to launch *RENEW Africa*.

Marie has been one of God's greatest gifts to RENEW International. Since joining the RENEW team in 2000, she has been involved in many aspects of RENEW's ministry. Marie grew up in a French-American atmosphere in New York City and entered the Sisters of St. Joseph of Cluny, whose motherhouse is in France. Fluent in French and a self-starter, Marie is comfortable in any situation, and her resourcefulness enables her to engage in multiple tasks at once.

Port Elizabeth

The Diocese of Port Elizabeth completed *RENEW Africa* in November 2010 and is committed to continuing to encourage and support small Christian communities. Resources were written with and for the people and published in English, Xhosa, and Afrikaans in order to reach the widest possible audience.

Parishes reported very positive responses in all areas: recognizing gifts among the members, expanding ministries to meet the needs, fostering vocations to ministry in the home, placing one's gifts at the service of the community, and improving financial support and fundraising. Young people, who accepted the invitation to join in outreach to the poor and the homebound, enthusiastically reported on their experiences and future plans. Parishes reported that new lectors, extraordinary ministers of the Eucharist, greeters, and ushers are coming forth from small Christian communities.

One woman told us, "It used to be so difficult to convince people that they could minister. Now, people are recognizing their gifts." Another said, "It was in my small Christian community that I realized God was calling me to be more involved in the Church." Still another proudly told the story of her small Christian community leading a fundraising effort to pay off the parish debt.

Testimonials

Testimonials from participants have been very positive. Many have found the *RENEW Africa* small communities as a pathway to revitalized faith. "I hadn't gone to church for years," wrote one participant, "but my neighbor invited me. It was so much easier to cross the threshold into his living room than to climb the stairs of the church. Eventually, I discovered it wasn't that hard to go back to church, and now I'm filled with joy."

For others, the *RENEW Africa* process made a clear connection between faith and life. "We can't ignore the call of the Gospel," a participant commented. "I knew I needed to take the first step to be reconciled with my brother, but couldn't. The faith of my community in me, and their prayers, gave me the courage to take the risk. We have been reconciled, and our whole family rejoices in our coming together again."

A participant in a small community in Port Elizabeth reported, "It was my small Christian community that got me through the tragic killing of my son. I was angry with everyone—even God. Members of my community would stop by and visit and pray with us. They helped start the healing process and supported our family. Eventually I was able to forgive the killer."

"Alleluia! We have already seen how *RENEW Africa* is beginning to renew every community in our diocese," said Bishop Michael Coleman of Port Elizabeth. "Alleluia! Alleluia!"

Small Christian Communities Forever

In a very short time, RENEW International has successfully listened to the needs of the Church in South Africa and responded by coordinating with the local people a strong effort to form and support small Christian communities. As a result, lay men and women have developed their gifts for ministry, young people have become more involved in their faith, and inactive Catholics have returned to their parishes.

At the request of the Diocese of Port Elizabeth, we started rolling out *Why Catholic?* adapted for Africa. Workshops began during July 2011, and faith sharing in the small Christian communities began in August. The materials are provided in English, Afrikaans, and Xhosa as they were for *RENEW Africa.*

The ongoing effort in the Diocese of Port Elizabeth demonstrates that "while *RENEW Africa* comes and *RENEW Africa* goes, small Christian communities go on forever." This is the slogan popularized throughout the process.

With the help of national advertising, small Christian communities welcomed the African editions of *Lenten Longings* for Cycle A (in English, Xhosa, and Afrikaans) not only in the Diocese of Port Elizabeth but also in a scattering of small communities in other dioceses. We foresee continued expansion to other small communities as publicity is renewed.

RENEW Africa Expands

In addition to Port Elizabeth, *RENEW Africa* has expanded into other dioceses. The Diocese of Queenstown, the Archdiocese of Johannesburg, and the Anglican Diocese of Saldanha Bay in Cape Town have launched the *RENEW Africa* process. The bishop of the Anglican Diocese of Table Bay, in the Cape Town area, has recently requested a presentation to its priests. We look forward to continued expansion of *RENEW Africa* and the many ways that continued training of local presenters will contribute to creating a sustainable effort and self-reliant Church in South Africa.

The *RENEW Africa* website pages provide a colorful, engaging, and informative experience for viewers and a link to further resources for member dioceses.

The extremely quick growth of the Church in Africa has, in every way, made Africa the hope of the Church for the future. What a gift it is for RENEW International to play a significant role at this historic time!

CHAPTER 36

Renewing the Priestly Heart

For many years it was a dream of mine to create a process to gather priests in small groups for faith sharing and collegial support. If anything, I believe the need for such a process has grown even greater as the number of priests has declined. Not only is it rare today for a rectory to have more than one priest, but more and more priests are ministering to two or more communities as parishes are clustered or merged. Opportunities for priests to share insights, experiences, and problems are hard to come by.

We know the true renewal of the Church depends largely on the renewal of priests. A parish priest has the power to nix a tremendous idea or project while, on the other hand, a whole parish can be lifted up by his own interest and excitement in what the parishioners are engaged in. Not only that, but this topic goes back to our original hopes for a renewed style of parish life and church in which anybody, pastors or parishioners, all bring their God-given talents together to be activated in a way that really brings about a vibrant Church. Everybody's ideas are valuable and listened to with interest. What a powerful and life-giving influence we would be for our world if we allowed our faith to impact all areas for the common good.

Priests won't lose the importance of their own role; in fact it would be enhanced. Our importance is not based on positions of power, systems of entitlement, and approaches that, in effect, position us as higher than others. We are in fact called to be servants to the people of God. It is only in this manner that we gain the very real and substantive support and love of our people. Our needs are met not by acting superior but by being to the people what the humble Jesus was when he washed the feet of the Apostles. This kind of approach to priesthood and the response it brings from the people of God truly meet all our priestly needs more than we could hope for.

Renewing the Priestly Heart has been a project close to my heart.

Renewing the Priestly Heart helps priests to open up to and share their thoughts on matters of importance to their lives in the priesthood. Each chapter centers on one of the important topics highlighted in Cardinal Timothy M. Dolan's book, *Priest for the Third Millennium*. These topics include subjects like homilies, relationship with parishioners, and celibacy.

I can't express sufficient gratitude to Sr. Terry Rickard who initiated and provided leadership in every aspect of this project. To begin with, she was involved in gathering a group of outstanding priests from throughout the country and listening to their ideas. Since it coincided so well with the themes in Cardinal Dolan's book, she had the courage to ask if we could base our work on the ideas that he expressed. He was more than willing. Terry then obtained the services of Fr. John Sassani, a pastor and a priest of more than thirty years in the Archdiocese of Boston, who carefully wove reflections and questions into twelve sessions, each covering one of these vital topics on living and serving as a priest today.

An important step was taken when Sr. Terry involved the priests of the Diocese of Davenport, Iowa, in a pilot effort. The responses were extremely positive, and *Renewing the Priestly Heart* is now working with dioceses and groups of priests throughout the country. Sr. Terry, who was named executive director of RENEW International in May 2006 and president in December 2009, is certainly fulfilling all hopes. The future of RENEW International will be extremely bright under her wise and dynamic leadership.

Early on, in one of the first gatherings of RENEW priests in Boston, one of the participants made a strong point: "If RENEW didn't do something special for the priests it would never have a lasting effect."

It was an interesting comment that repeatedly came to the mind of Sr. Terry and others in leadership. Throughout the years of RENEW, we realized that we had to do more for the spiritual development of our priests. A number of circumstances at this particular time were going to bring about the realization of this long cherished dream.

Over the years in the history of the Church, memorable opportunities have arisen for priests to share faith. Today is a new opportunity at a time when our good and faithful priests need all the support they can receive.

We are all very aware how social media have changed the way individuals and groups communicate. In contrast to social media, RENEW International has tried to bring people together in direct, face-to-face communication. From its inception, RENEW International has always encouraged parish priests to become part of a small community within their own parishes or ministries and to visit each small community in their parish or campus, etc., not as teachers but as listeners. Priests who have done so get a feel for the pulse of their parish/ministry and experience the rich spirituality of their people.

Gathering Priests in Small Communities

Today we have come full circle with *Renewing the Priestly Heart,* a process in which priests can practice what they preach and have good communication with other priests. It might seem strange to say but many priests are shy or reluctant to open up on personal and spiritual matters. Yet all need friendship and the support of other priests. *Renewing the Priestly Heart* helps priests break the social barrier in a small community setting where they have the opportunity to deepen prayer life, strengthen fraternal bonds, and enrich their daily pastoral ministry.

Those already meeting in groups, such as Fr. Tom Devery, director of the Office of Priest Personnel, Archdiocese of New York, recognize *Renewing the Priestly Heart* as a refreshing resource "for priests who want to bring new zeal to their lives and their priesthood." Fr. Devery continued,

> The last concern we priests seem to have is ourselves as individuals. We can easily get lost in the mix of issues and

responsibilities facing priests in this 21st century Church. One way I find my own bearings is by gathering with my peers to pray together and grapple with the really important aspects of life as a priest. *Renewing the Priestly Heart* is a fine resource for that kind of exchange.

For participating priests the rewards are great. *Renewing the Priestly Heart* small communities offer a place for priests to know, be, and become their true selves. Small groups provide a setting where humor and honesty are welcome, where the barrenness of life melts away, where friendship and support are offered—often for a lifetime.

EPILOGUE

Coming Full Circle

Thinking back to the beginning of my journey, you will recall the important role small communities played for me and other young priests I associated with. Our day-off gatherings on Tuesdays were more than just getting in a good game of basketball. We spoke about our parishes, our latest pastoral ideas and initiatives, our prayer lives, and all that was essential to our priesthood. It gives me joy and satisfaction to see that, decades later, RENEW International is providing the same opportunity for today's priests. Looking back to the past can be good for the soul, but looking forward to the future with enthusiasm can be truly exciting.

Many of the earlier topics are still very relevant to our priests. As I look at where RENEW International is today, I find particular gratification in the fact that we are helping priests in their own priestly lives and, at the same time, opening them up to the potential value of small communities in their parishes.

I may be nearing the end of my story but, by God's grace, I pray, in particular, that this emphasis on small Christian communities will help many priests in the various stages of their journey. If that be true, then all the effort that has gone into *Beyond My Wildest Dreams* has been well worth it.

The work of RENEW International continues strongly under the direction and leadership of Sr. Terry Rickard, O.P. Although I am now retired, I reflect in this book on my journey with RENEW when I was more directly involved.

There is so much more to the RENEW story than what is recorded here. I have simply written some personal memories that have stayed with me through the years.

It is too bad each reader couldn't get to know Sr. Terry personally. She is tremendously talented and has a personality that immediately engages people and establishes instant relationships. She was involved in, and was the driving force in, a number of the projects you have been reading about. Her dynamism and creativity enable RENEW International to continue to grow beyond my greatest hopes. As the Nigerians always say, "We thank God."

As for myself, at age eighty-two I work out daily, trying to recuperate from five fractured vertebrae and scoliosis. My quality of life is fine. Jesus endured very real suffering at the end of his life, even to his crucifixion. To be true Christians, we should expect to share to some degree in the path he took. I'm so fortunate to be given this special time to reflect and grow spiritually. We know that the Christian story leads to the resurrection. What a great life! Again and again, "We thank God—all the time."

ACKNOWLEDGEMENTS

I wish to thank Sr. Mary McGuinness, O.P., editor and advisor, without whose assistance this memoir would not have been written; Lynn Hull, who spent many hours in typing the manuscript from dictation; Sr. Terry Rickard, O.P., for her encouragement throughout and the valuable assistance of her staff; Mary Ann Jeselson, strong advocate for small Christian communities, for her suggestions and proofreading; Bob Heyer for urging us to publish RENEW even before its inception and for his professional advice; Charles Paolino for his outstanding editing, and Kathleen Ogle for organizing and overseeing final preparations for publishing.

The latter parts of this memoir were hindered by physical setbacks. During this time I am grateful for the extraordinary strong support of my brothers and sisters-in-law, Ed and Gert, Dick and Mary Jean, and Bob; Pat and George Erdman; Kathy and Jack Norris; Bob Ulesky; Jack Kreismer; Fr. Jim Burke; Sr. Jean Marie Darling, O.P.; Joe Duggan; Pat Foley; Monica Garofalo; Pat Kent; Jack and Carol McDermott; Tom Burns; Marilyn McVeigh; Sr. Thomas Marie Morris, O.P.; Dolly and Floyd Donahue, and many other relatives and friends, along with the Sisters of St. Dominic, Dr. Jim Morgan, and the nurses, staff, and nursing assistants at St. Catherine Health Care Center.

Finally, I thank God for everything and for everyone who influenced and blessed me during my life and, especially, on this journey of RENEW.

AFTERWORD

I feel uniquely privileged to be part of RENEW International at this moment in time. One of my nieces once asked me, "Aunt Terry, is RENEW your dream job?" Her question caused me to pause. As I reflected, I realized that it is more that I am living God's dream for the Church today through my work at RENEW. I am grateful for the legacy that Fr. Tom has passed on to me and my co-ministers at RENEW. We stand on the shoulders of RENEW's spiritual giants—many of whom are mentioned in this memoir—and the biggest giant of all, who happens to be a huge New York Giants fan, affectionately known as Fr. Tom. His memoir is a testament to the power of the Holy Spirit working in and through the gifts and strengths of myriad ordinary, faith-filled, and zealous women and men.

RENEW International has grown from its original single RENEW process by adapting that same process to different pastoral needs and services. RENEW enthusiastically uses all forms of technology and media, including social media, in order to preach the Gospel in new ways. However, the very core of all our programs and resources remains the same: to help people become better hearers and doers of the word of God. We continue to encourage and support the formation of small communities who gather prayerfully to reflect on and share the word of God and to live their faith more concretely in family, work, and community life. Over thirty years ago when RENEW began there were critical issues facing the Church and the world at large that demanded a new way to enliven the faith of Catholics and revitalize parish life. In light of the scandals that continue to rock the church, diminishing Mass attendance, and growing secularity, the need to renew the Church, reawaken faith. and reinvigorate parish life is even more urgent.

As RENEW moves into the future, we continue to imbibe the passionate missionary spirit of Fr. Tom. His love of the Lord and the Church and his commitment to helping the poor and building a more just society continue to form us into a prayerful community devoted to meeting the pastoral needs of the people of God. His apostolic energy and tremendous work ethic challenge us to use our gifts to further the mission of Christ. When I find myself unsure, I hear Tom's voice saying,

"Terry, it is God's work." When I worry about RENEW's finances, I hear him say, "Terry, forget about the money; the Holy Spirit will provide." When I feel satisfied with the completion of a new program or resource, I feel his prodding and probing: "So what is the next big thing that RENEW will develop to fulfill an unmet pastoral need in the Church?"

Tom's legacy is not about a program or an organization but about a way of renewing faith, building communities of hope and gospel action, and transforming the Church and the world. It is largely because of his inspiration and his work that diocesan spiritual renewal, parish small groups, faith-sharing, and faith-based action are now part of the fabric of Catholic life in the United States. We thank you, Tom, and, as you often remind us, we thank God.

Sr. Terry Rickard, O.P.
President and Executive Director
RENEW International

INDEX OF NAMES

Renewing the Priestly Heart

Based on the Insights of Archbishop Timothy M. Dolan

When priests feel overburdened and isolated, living their call to holiness and service becomes a challenge. By renewing their own hearts and spirits, priests can be joy-filled witnesses who bring Christ's message to others with zeal and authenticity. Rekindle this zeal by encouraging bonds of communion and fraternity. Candid, prayerful conversation on faith and priestly vocation in supportive small groups is an effective means to enrich priests' daily life, spirituality, and ministry.

Renewing the Priestly Heart contains 12 sessions of reflections and questions on topics of vital importance to living and serving as a priest today. A Special Audio Edition that contains 13 audio reflections on living the priestly life today by nationally known priests, a bishop, and religious, as well as all 12 sessions of the resource book in narrated form on CD is also available.

PRAYERTIME Cycle A, B, C: Faith-Sharing Reflections on the Sunday Gospels

This faith-sharing resource responds to the U.S. Bishops' suggestion that "every parish meeting can begin with the reading of the upcoming Sunday's Gospel, followed by a time of reflection and faith sharing."

With each Sunday's Gospel as a focus, *PRAYERTIME* proposes meaningful reflections, focused faith-sharing questions, related questions for consideration, and prayers as a source of spiritual nourishment and inspiration.

Use *PRAYERTIME* any time of year. It is an ideal resource for homily preparation, group faith sharing, and personal reflection.

This invaluable resource is also available in Spanish: *OREMOS Ciclo A, B, C Reflexiones sobre los Evangelios Dominicales para Compartir la Fe*

WHY CATHOLIC?
Journey through the Catechism

is a parish-based process of evangelization and adult faith formation from
RENEW International. This process, designed for sharing in small Christian
communities, is structured around exploring the important truths of our faith
as they are presented in the *Catechism of the Catholic Church* and in the *United
States Catholic Catechism for Adults*.

WHY CATHOLIC? helps nourish faith and enhance our sense of Catholic
identity. The process and materials encourage us to understand and live the
reasons why we are Catholic, and so lead us to a faith that is experienced more
authentically, connecting us more deeply and meaningfully to God, and to
others.

There are four books in the **WHY CATHOLIC?** series, each offering twelve
sessions:

PRAY: Christian Prayer

BELIEVE: Profession of Faith

CELEBRATE: Sacraments

LIVE: Christian Morality

WHY CATHOLIC? is far more than printed resources for faith-sharing in small communities. It is a complete integrated process providing materials and support both in print and on the web, together with opportunities for faith enrichment events and retreats for the whole parish, as well as a series of training workshops for small community leaders.

For each of the four ***WHY CATHOLIC?*** books, there is a Song CD. Each CD is a 12-song compilation of the songs suggested for the moments of prayer during the faith-sharing sessions. The CDs are available singly, or as a set.

Families can extend the fruits of the sharing on the same themes presented in the books by using *RENEWing Family Faith*: attractive four-color companion bulletins with activities and reflections for sharing among different age groups.

This process of faith-building through faith-sharing is also available in Spanish: *¿POR QUÉ SER CATÓLICO?*

ARISE Together in Christ

is a three-year, parish-centered process of spiritual renewal and evangelization that enables people to deepen their faith, develop a closer relationship with Christ, grow in community, and reach out in service to others. It emphasizes people living in good relationship with one another, as they make concrete applications of the gospel to their life situations.

ARISE Together in Christ is a total renewal experience for the parish, spiritually transforming people through small Christian communities, special parish activities, reflections for families with teens and children, and Christian social action. There are five six-week seasons:

Season One: **Encountering Christ Today**

Season Two: **Change Our Hearts**

Season Three: **In the Footsteps of Christ**

Season Four: **New Heart, New Spirit**

Season Five: **We Are the Good News!**

For each Season, RENEW International offers a faith-sharing book and a music CD with the songs suggested in the faith-sharing book.

For a complete, integrated experience of ARISE Together in Christ, RENEW International recommends using the resources as part of a comprehensive diocesan-wide, parish-based process that includes training for leaders, pastoral support and online tools and materials.

The faith-sharing books are designed principally for use by adults; however, they are complemented by materials for children and for youth. Both are designed around the same themes and the same Scripture passages as in the adult books.

ARISE for youth

Faith-sharing materials for each session of all five Seasons, written especially for youth. Also includes a separate *ARISE for youth Leader Guide*.

ARISE Family Sharing Pages

A friendly easy way to explore the same faith themes at home and in class. Four-page, full color worksheet for each session of each Season. Available for Grades 1-3, and Grades 4-6.

ARISE Together in Christ small communities materials appear in English, Spanish, French, Portuguese, Haitian Creole, and Vietnamese.

Scenes from a Parish

Special Edition DVD and Film Faith-Sharing Guides

In English and Spanish

Get a rare glimpse into one parish's real-world experience as it struggles to reconcile ideals of faith with the realities of today's changing and diverse culture.

View, reflect upon, and share faith with this special edition film and *Faith-Sharing Guide* and its important themes of welcoming the stranger, offering compassion, and feeding the hungry.

Ideal for parish-wide, small group, and personal viewing and reflection.

At Prayer with Mary

At Prayer with Mary offers seven sessions on the life and mystery of Mary that will deepen your appreciation of and devotion to our Blessed Mother Mary and enrich your prayer experiences. Over the centuries, Mary's example has inspired Christians to imitate her by saying "yes" to God's call in their own lives. Her faithfulness, as it is portrayed in the Gospel narratives, is a model of the prayerful kind of life Jesus calls us to. Scripture, Catholic teaching, personal testimonies, and Marian prayer—including the rosary—provide a renewed appreciation of Mary's place in today's world, where she, as always, points the way to Christ.

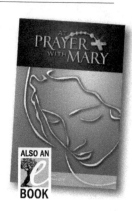

Also available as an eBook!

This 14-song CD is also available and contains the songs suggested for use during the moments of prayer.

Also available in Spanish: **No temas, María**

Absolute Amazement / Absoluto Asombro

This bilingual volume of mystical poems and reflections is a love story that has emerged from the poet's deep and passionate relationship with God. Readers are invited to take a break from their busy lives and to enter into a genuine religious experience that will remind them of their own closeness to God. Written by Irma Chávez, also known as Irma Lanzas.

LONGING FOR THE HOLY:
Spirituality for Everyday Life
Based on selected insights of Ronald Rolheiser, OMI

Experience how the gentle spiritual guidance and practical wisdom of best-selling Catholic author Fr. Ronald Rolheiser, OMI can enliven everyday life. Suitable for small community faith sharing or individual reflection, *Longing for the Holy* covers different dimensions of contemporary spiritual life for those who want to enrich their sense of the presence of God and develop a deeper spirituality.

The Participant's Book contains twelve sessions with prayers, reflections, sharing questions, and stories from saints and contemporary people of faith.

This resource is also available as a four CD-set audio edition, which has both narrated text and songs for all twelve sessions.

The songs suggested for the moments of prayer in the faith-sharing sessions are offered on the 13-song music CD.

The kit includes the essential ingredients to bring this engaging spiritual experience to your parish or small Christian community. Purchase of the kit provides membership benefits including the opportunity for web-based workshops as well as a web library of support materials.

Advent Awakenings

Advent is a time of spiritual
anticipation amidst the often distracting
preparations for Christmas. Stay
focused on the significance of this season
with **Advent Awakenings**, a four-session
faith-sharing experience grounded in the
Sunday gospel readings.

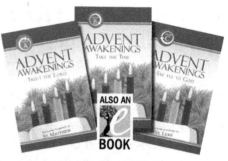

The **Advent Awakenings** series is based on the three-year cycle of the Lectionary.
Each book contains four sessions corresponding with the four Sundays of
Advent and presents themes drawn from the Sunday gospel readings, plus
enriching devotions for family use.

Appropriate for seasonal groups, small Christian communities, and individual
reflection and prayer.

Also available as an eBook!

A 15-song CD is also available and contains the songs
suggested for use during the prayerful reflections of each faith-
sharing session for years A, B, and C.

Also available in Spanish: **Reflexiones en Adviento**

Lenten Longings, Year A, B, C

Make a six-week retreat by exploring the Sunday readings of Lent. Based on the
three-year cycle of the Lectionary, each book contains six sessions corresponding
to the six weeks of Lent and presents themes drawn
from the year's Lenten readings. Simple language
and everyday metaphors steep you in the season's
promptings to surrender self, work for justice, and
deepen prayer life.

Lenten Longings is well suited for seasonal
groups, small Christian communities,
and individual reflection.

Also available as an eBook!

An 18-song CD is also available and contains the songs
suggested for use during the prayerful reflections of each faith-
sharing session for years A, B, and C.

Also available in Spanish: **Reflexiones en Cuaresma**